Python Architecture Pa

Master API design, event-driven structures, and package management in Python

Jaime Buelta

BIRMINGHAM—MUMBAI

Python Architecture Patterns

Producer: Tushar Gupta

Acquisition Editor - Peer Reviews: Saby D'silva

Project Editor: Parvathy Nair

Content Development Editor: Alex Patterson

Copy Editor: Safis Editor

Technical Editor: Tejas Mhasvekar

Proofreader: Safis Editor

Indexer: Pratik Shirodkar

Presentation Designer: Pranit Padwal

First published: January 2022

Production reference: 2020222

Published by Packt Publishing Ltd.
Livery Place
35 Livery Street
Birmingham
B3 2PB, UK.

ISBN 978-1-80181-999-2

www.packt.com

Contributors

About the author

Jaime Buelta has been a professional programmer for 20 years and a full-time Python developer for over 10. During that time, he has been exposed to a lot of different technologies while working for different industries and helping them achieve their goals; these industries include aerospace, industrial systems, video game online services, finance services and educational tools. He has been writing technical books since 2018, reflecting on lessons learned over his career, including *Python Automation Cookbook* and *Hands On Docker for Microservices in Python*. He is currently living in Dublin, Ireland.

Writing a book is always more than a single person's work. There're not only the people involved directly in polishing and improving the drafts, but also a lot of conversations and talks with exceptional people in the Python and tech community that shape the ideas in it. It also wouldn't be possible without the love and support from Dana, my amazing wife.

About the reviewer

Pradeep Pant is a computer programmer, software architect, AI researcher and open source advocate. Pradeep has been writing computer programs for more than 2 decades in various programming languages and platforms, such as microprocessor/Assembly, C, C++, Perl, Python, R, JavaScript, AI/ML, Linux, the cloud and many more. Pradeep holds a master's degree in physics and another master's in computer science. In his free time, Pradeep likes to write about his tech journey and learnings at `https://pradeeppant.com`.

Pradeep works with Ockham BV, a Belgium-based software development company. The company develops software in the quality and document management systems space.

Pradeep can be contacted through email or through professional networks:

- Email: `pp@pradeeppant.com`
- LinkedIn: `https://www.linkedin.com/in/ppant/`
- GitHub: `https://github.com/ppant`

Join our book's Discord space

Join the book's Discord workspace for a monthly *Ask me Anything* session with the author:
`https://packt.link/PythonArchitechture`

Table of Contents

Preface

The evolution of software means that, over time, systems grow to be more and more complex, and require more and more developers working on them in a coordinated fashion. As the size increases, a general structure arises from there. This structure, if not well planned, can become really chaotic and difficult to work with.

The challenge of software architecture is to plan and design this structure. A well-designed architecture makes different teams able to interact with each other while at the same time having a clear understanding of their own responsibilities and their goals.

The architecture of a system should be designed in a way that day-to-day software development is possible with minimal resistance, allowing for adding features and expanding the system. The architecture in a live system is also always in flux, and can be adjusted and expanded as well, reshaping the different software elements in a deliberate and smooth fashion.

In this book we will see the different aspects of software architecture, from the top level to some of the lower-level details that support the higher view. The book is structured in four sections, covering all the different aspects in the life cycle:

- Design before writing any code
- Architectural patterns to use proven approaches
- Implementation of the design in actual code
- Ongoing operation to cover changes, and verification that it's all working as expected

During the book we will cover different techniques across all these aspects.

Who this book is for

This book is for software developers that want to expand their knowledge of software architecture, whether experienced developers that want to expand and solidify their intuitions about complex systems, or less experienced developers who want to learn and grow their abilities, facing bigger systems with a broader view.

We will use code written in Python for the examples. Though you're not required to be an expert, some basic knowledge of Python is advisable.

What this book covers

Chapter 1, Introduction to Software Architecture, presents the topic of what software architecture is and why it is useful, as well as presenting a design example.

The first section of the book covers the *Design* phase, before the software is written:

Chapter 2, API Design, shows the basics of designing useful APIs that abstract the operations conveniently.

Chapter 3, Data Modeling, talks about the particularities of storage systems and how to design the proper data representation for the application.

Chapter 4, The Data Layer, goes over the code handling of the stored data, and how to make it fit for purpose.

Next, we will present a section that covers the different *Architectural patterns* available, which reuse proven structures:

Chapter 5, The Twelve-Factor App Methodology, shows how this methodology includes good practices that can be useful when operating with web services and can be applied in a variety of situations.

Chapter 6, Web Server Structures, explains web services and the different elements to take into consideration when settling on both the operative and the software design.

Chapter 7, Event-Driven Structures, describes another kind of system that works asynchronously, receiving information without returning an immediate response.

Chapter 8, Advanced Event-Driven Structures, explains more advanced usages for asynchronous systems, and some different patterns that can be created.

Chapter 9, Microservices vs Monolith, presents these two architectures for complex systems, and goes over their differences.

The *Implementation* section of the book covers how the code is written:

Chapter 10, Testing and TDD, talks about the fundaments of testing and how Test Driven Development can be used in the coding process.

Chapter 11, Package Management, follows the process of creating reusable parts of code and how to distribute them.

Finally, the last section deals about *Ongoing operations*, where the system is in operation and requires monitoring at the same time that is adjusted and changed:

Chapter 12, Logging, describes how to record what working systems are doing.

Chapter 13, Metrics, discusses aggregating different values to see how the whole system is behaving.

Chapter 14, Profiling, explains how to understand how code is executed to improve its performance.

Chapter 15, Debugging, covers the process of digging deep into the execution of code to find and fix errors.

Chapter 16, Ongoing Architecture, describes how to successfully operate architectural changes on running systems.

To get the most out of this book

- The book uses Python language for code examples, and assumes that the reader is comfortable reading it, though an expert level is not needed.
- Previous exposure to complex systems with multiple services will be advantageous to understand the different challenges software architecture presents. This should be simple for developers with a couple of years of experience or more.
- Familiarity with web services and REST interfaces is useful to better understand some elements.

Download the example code files

The code bundle for the book is hosted on GitHub at `https://github.com/PacktPublishing/Python-Architecture-Patterns`. We also have other code bundles from our rich catalog of books and videos available at `https://github.com/PacktPublishing/`. Check them out!

Download the color images

We also provide a PDF file that has color images of the screenshots/diagrams used in this book. You can download it here: `https://static.packt-cdn.com/downloads/9781801819992_ColorImages.pdf`

Conventions used

There are a number of text conventions used throughout this book.

`CodeInText`: Indicates code words in text, object names, module names, folder names, filenames, file extensions, pathnames, dummy URLs and user input. Here is an example: "For this recipe, we need to import the `requests` module."

A block of code is set as follows:

```
def leonardo(number):

    if number in (0, 1):
        return 1

    # EXAMPLE COMMENT
    return leonardo(number - 1) + leonardo(number - 2) + 1
```

Note that code may be edited for concision and clarity. Refer to the full code when necessary, which is available on GitHub.

Any command-line input or output is written as follows (notice the `$` symbol):

```
$ python example_script.py parameters
```

Any input in the Python interpreter is written as follows (notice the `>>>` symbol). Expected output will be reflected without the `>>>` symbol:

```
>>> import logging
>>> logging.warning('This is a warning')
WARNING:root:This is a warning
```

To enter the Python interpreter, call the `python3` command with no parameters:

```
$ python3
Python 3.9.7 (default, Oct 13 2021, 06:45:31)
[Clang 13.0.0 (clang-1300.0.29.3)] on darwin
```

```
Type "help", "copyright", "credits" or "license" for more information.
>>>
```

Any command-line input or output is written as follows:

```
$ cp example.txt copy_of_example.txt
```

Bold: Indicates a new term, an important word, or words that you see on the screen, for example, in menus or dialog boxes, also appear in the text like this. For example: "Select **System info** from the **Administration** panel."

Warnings or important notes appear like this.

Tips and tricks appear like this.

Get in touch

Feedback from our readers is always welcome.

General feedback: Email `feedback@packtpub.com`, and mention the book's title in the subject of your message. If you have questions about any aspect of this book, please email us at `questions@packtpub.com`.

Errata: Although we have taken every care to ensure the accuracy of our content, mistakes do happen. If you have found a mistake in this book we would be grateful if you would report this to us. Please visit, `http://www.packtpub.com/submit-errata`, selecting your book, clicking on the Errata Submission Form link, and entering the details.

Piracy: If you come across any illegal copies of our works in any form on the Internet, we would be grateful if you would provide us with the location address or website name. Please contact us at `copyright@packtpub.com` with a link to the material.

If you are interested in becoming an author: If there is a topic that you have expertise in and you are interested in either writing or contributing to a book, please visit `http://authors.packtpub.com`.

Share your thoughts

Once you've read *Python Architecture Patterns*, we'd love to hear your thoughts! Scan the QR code below to go straight to the Amazon review page for this book and share your feedback.

https://packt.link/r/1801819998

Your review is important to us and the tech community and will help us make sure we're delivering excellent quality content.

1
Introduction to Software Architecture

The objective of this chapter is to present an introduction to what software architecture is and where it's useful. We will look at some of the basic techniques used when defining the architecture of a system and a baseline example of the web services architecture.

This chapter includes a discussion of the implications that software structure has for team structure and communication. As the successful building of any non-tiny piece of software depends heavily on successful communication and collaboration between one or more teams of multiple developers, this factor should be taken into consideration. Also, the structure of the software can have a profound effect on how different elements are accessed, so how software is structured has ramifications for security.

Also, in this chapter, there will be a brief introduction to the architecture of an example system that we will be using to present the different patterns and discussions throughout the rest of the book.

In this chapter, we'll cover the following topics:

- Defining the structure of a system
- Dividing into smaller units
- Conway's Law in software architecture
- General overview of the example
- Security aspects of software architecture

Let's dive in.

Defining the structure of a system

At its core, software development is about creating and managing complex systems.

In the early days of computing, programs were relatively simple. At most, they perhaps could calculate a parabolic trajectory or factorize numbers. The very first computer program, designed in 1843 by Ada Lovelace, calculated a sequence of Bernoulli numbers. A hundred years after that, during the Second World War, electronic computers were invented to break encryption codes. As the possibilities of the new invention started to be explored, more and more complex operations and systems were designed. Tools like compilers and high-level languages multiplied the number of possibilities and the rapid advancement of hardware allowed more and more operations to be performed. This quickly created a need to manage the growing complexity and apply consistent engineering principles to the creation of software.

More than 50 years after the birth of the computing industry, the software tools at our disposal are incredibly varied and powerful. We stand on the shoulders of giants to build our own software. We can quickly add a lot of functionalities with relatively little effort, either leveraging high-level languages and APIs or using out-of-the-box modules and packages. With this great power comes the great responsibility of managing the explosion of complexity that it produces.

In the most simple terms, software architecture defines the structure of a software system. This architecture can develop organically, usually in the early stages of a project, but after system growth and a few change requests, the need to think carefully about the architecture becomes more and more important. As the system becomes bigger, the structure becomes more difficult to change, which affects future efforts. It's easier to make changes following the structure rather than against the structure.

Making it so that certain changes are difficult to do is not necessarily always a bad thing. Changes that *should* be made difficult could involve elements that need to be overseen by different teams or perhaps elements that can affect external customers. While the main focus is to create a system that's easy and efficient to change in the future, a smart architectural design will have a proper balance of ease and difficulty based on the requirements. Later in the chapter, we will study security as a clear example of when to keep certain operations difficult to implement.

At the core of software architecture, then, is taking a look at the big picture: to focus on where the system is going to be in the future, to be able to materialize this view, but also to help the present situation. The usual choice between short-term wins and long-term operation is very important in development, and its most common outcome is the creation of technical debt. Software architecture deals mostly with long-term implications.

The considerations for software architecture can be quite numerous and there needs to be a balance between them. Some examples may include:

- **Business vision**, if the system is going to be commercially exploited. This may include requirements coming from stakeholders like marketing, sales, or management. Business vision is typically driven by customers.
- **Technical requirements**, like being sure that the system is scalable and can handle a certain number of users, or that the system is fast enough for its use case. A news website requires different update times than a real-time trading system.
- **Security and reliability concerns**, the seriousness of which depends on how risky or critical the application and the data stored are.
- **Division of tasks**, to allow multiple teams, perhaps specialized in different areas, to work in a flexible way at the same time on the same system. As systems grow, the need to divide them into semi-autonomous, smaller components becomes more pressing. Small projects may live longer with a "single-block" or monolithic approach.
- **Use specific technologies**, for example, to allow integration with other systems or leverage the existing knowledge in the team.

These considerations will influence the structure and design of a system. In a sense, the software architect is responsible for implementing the application vision and matching it with the specific technologies and teams that will develop it. That makes the software architect an important intermediary between the business teams and the technology teams, as well as between the different technology teams. Communication is a critical aspect of the job.

To enable successful communication, a good architecture should define boundaries between the different aspects and assign clear responsibilities. The software architect should, in addition to defining clear boundaries, facilitate the creation of interface channels between the system components and follow up on the implementation details.

Ideally, the architectural design should happen at the beginning of system design, with a well thought-out design based on the requirements for the project. This is the general approach in this book because it's the best way to explain the different options and techniques. But it's not the most common use case in real life.

One of the main challenges for a software architect is working with existing systems that need to be adapted, making incremental approaches toward a better system, all while not interrupting the normal daily operation that keeps the business running.

Division into smaller units

The main technique for software architecture is to divide the whole system into smaller elements and describe how they interact with each other. Each smaller element, or unit, should have a clear function and interface.

For example, a common architecture for a typical system could be a web service architecture composed of:

- A database that stores all the data in MySQL
- A web worker that serves dynamic HTML content written in PHP
- An Apache web server that handles all the web requests, returns any static files, like CSS and images, and forwards the dynamic requests to the web worker

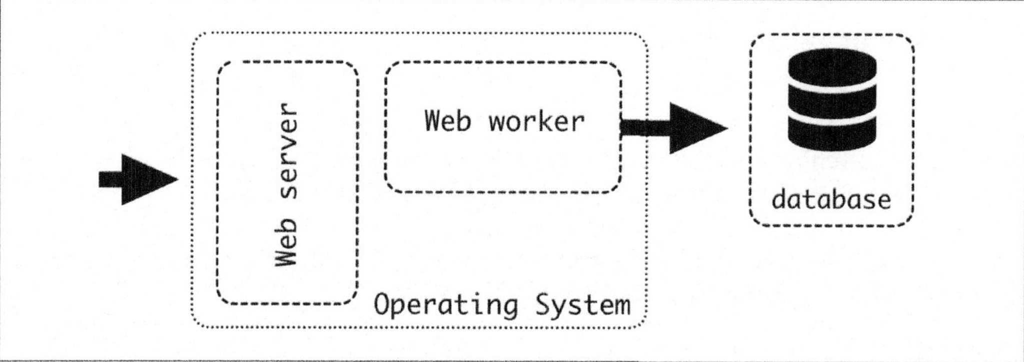

Figure 1.1: Typical web architecture

This architecture and tech stack has been extremely popular since the early 2000s and was called LAMP, an acronym made from the different open source projects involved: (L)inux as an operating system, (A)pache, (M)ySQL, and (P)HP. Nowadays, the technologies can be swapped for equivalent ones, like using PostgreSQL instead of MySQL or Nginx instead of Apache, but still using the LAMP name. The LAMP architecture can be considered the default starting point when designing web-based client/server systems using HTTP, creating a solid and proven foundation to start building a more complex system.

As you can see, every different element has a distinct function in the system. They interact with each other in clearly defined ways. This is known as the **Single-Responsibility principle**. When presented with new features, most use cases will fall clearly within one of the elements of the system. Any style changes will be handled by the web server and dynamic changes by the web worker. There are dependencies between the elements, as the data stored in the database may need to be changed to support dynamic requests, but they can be detected early in the process.

We will describe this architecture in greater detail in *Chapter 9*.

Each element has different requirements and characteristics:

- The database needs to be reliable, as it stores all the data. Maintenance work like backup- and recovery-related work will be important. The database won't be updated very frequently, as databases are very stable. Changes to the table schemas will be made through restarts in the web worker.
- The web worker needs to be scalable and not store any state. Instead, any data will be sent and received from the database. This element will be updated often. Multiple copies can be run, either in the same machine or in multiple ones to allow horizontal scalability.
- The web server will require some changes for new styling, but that won't happen very often. Once the configuration is properly set up, this element will remain quite stable. Only one web server per machine is required, as it's capable of load-balancing between multiple web workers.

As we can see, the work balance between elements is very different, as the web worker will be the focus for most new work, while the other two elements will be much more stable. The database will require specific work for us to be sure that it's in good shape, as it's arguably the most critical element of the three. The other two can recover quickly if there's a problem, but any corruption in the database will generate a lot of problems.

The most critical and valuable element of a system is almost always the stored data.

The communication protocols are also unique. The web worker talks to the database using SQL statements. The web server talks to the web worker using a dedicated interface, normally FastCGI or a similar protocol. The web server communicates with the external clients via HTTP requests. The web server and the database don't talk to each other.

These three protocols are different. This doesn't have to be the case for all systems; different components can share the same protocol. For example, there can be multiple RESTful interfaces, which is common in microservices.

In-process communication

The typical way of looking at different units is as different processes running independently, but that's not the only option. Two different modules inside the same process can still follow the Single-Responsibility principle.

The Single-Responsibility principle can be applied at different levels and is used to define the divisions between functions or other blocks. So, it can be applied in smaller and smaller scopes. It's turtles all the way down! But, from the point of view of architecture, the higher-level elements are the most important, as it's the higher level that defines the structure. Knowing how far to go in terms of detail is clearly important, but when taking an architectural approach, it is better to err on the "big picture" side rather than the "too much detail" one.

A clear example of this would be a library that's maintained independently, but it could also be certain modules within a code base. For example, you could create a module that performs all the external HTTP calls and handles all the complexity of keeping connections, retries, handling errors, and so on, or you could create a module to produce reports in multiple formats, based on some parameters.

The important characteristic is that in order to create an independent element, the API needs to be clearly defined and the responsibility needs to be well defined. It should be possible for the module to be extracted into a different repo and installed as a third-party element for it to be considered truly independent.

Creating a big component with internal divisions only is a well-known pattern called a monolithic architecture. The LAMP architecture described above is an example of that, as most of the code is defined inside the web worker. Monoliths are the usual de facto starts of projects, as normally at the start there's no big plan and dividing things strictly into multiple components doesn't have a big advantage when the code base is small. As the code base and system grow more and more complex, the division of elements inside the monolith starts to make sense, and later it may start to make sense to split it into several components. We will discuss monoliths further in *Chapter 9, Microservices vs Monolith*.

Inside the same component, communication is typically straightforward, as internal APIs will be used. In the vast majority of cases, the same programming language will be used.

Conway's Law – Effects on software architecture

A critical concept to always keep in mind while dealing with architectural designs is Conway's Law. Conway's Law is a well-known adage that postulates that the systems introduced in organizations mirror the communication pattern of the organization structure (`https://www.thoughtworks.com/insights/articles/demystifying-conways-law`):

> *Any organization that designs a system (defined broadly) will produce a design whose structure is a copy of the organization's communication structure.*
>
> *– Melvin E. Conway*

This means that the structure of the organization's people is replicated, either explicitly or otherwise, to form the software structure created by an organization. In a very simple example, a company that has two big departments - say, purchases and sales - will tend to create two big systems, one focused on buying and another on selling, that talk to each other, instead of other possible structures, like a system with divisions by product.

This can feel natural; after all, communication between teams is more difficult than communication within teams. Communication between teams would need to be more structured and require more active work. Communication inside a single group would be more fluid and less rigid. These elements are key for the design of a good software architecture.

The main thing for the successful application of any software architecture is that the team structure needs to follow the designed architecture quite closely. Trying to deviate too much will result in difficulties, as the tendency will be to structure, de facto, everything following group divisions. In the same way, changing the architecture of a system would likely necessitate restructuring the organization. This is a difficult and painful process, as anyone who has experienced a company reorganization will attest.

Division of responsibilities is also a key aspect. A single software element should have a clear owner, and this shouldn't be distributed across multiple teams. Different teams have different goals and focuses, which will complicate the long-term vision and create tensions.

The reverse, a single team taking ownership of multiple elements, is definitely possible but also requires careful consideration to ensure that this doesn't overstress the team.

If there's a big imbalance in the mapping of work units to teams (for example, too many work units for one team and too few for another team), it is likely that there's a problem with the architecture of the system.

As remote work becomes more common and teams increasingly become located in different parts of the world, communication is also impacted. That's why it has become very common to set up different branches to take care of different elements of the system and to use detailed APIs to overcome the physical barriers of geographical distance. Communication improvements also have an effect on the capacity for collaboration, making remote work more effective and allowing fully remote teams to work closely together on the same code base.

The recent COVID-19 crisis has greatly increased the trend of remote working, especially in software. This is resulting in more people working remotely and in better tools that are adapted to work in this way. While time zone differences are still a big barrier to communication, more and more companies and teams are learning to work effectively in full-remote mode. Remember that Conway's Law is very much dependent on the communication dependencies of organizations, but communication itself can change and improve.

Conway's Law should not be considered an impediment to overcome but a reflection of the fact that organizational structure has an impact on the structure of the software. Software architecture is tightly related to how different teams are coordinated and responsibilities are divided. It has an important human communication component.

Keeping this in mind will help you design a successful software architecture so that the communication flow is fluid at all times and you can identify problems in advance. Software architecture is, of course, closely tied to the human factor, as the architecture will ultimately be implemented and maintained by engineers.

Application example – Overview

In this book, we will be using an application as an example to demonstrate the different elements and patterns presented. This application will be simple but divided into different elements for demonstration purposes. The full code for the example is available on GitHub, and different parts of it will be presented in the different chapters. The example is written in Python, using well-known frameworks and modules.

The example application is a web application for microblogging, very similar to Twitter. In essence, users will write short text messages that will be available for other users to read.

The architecture of the example system is described in this diagram:

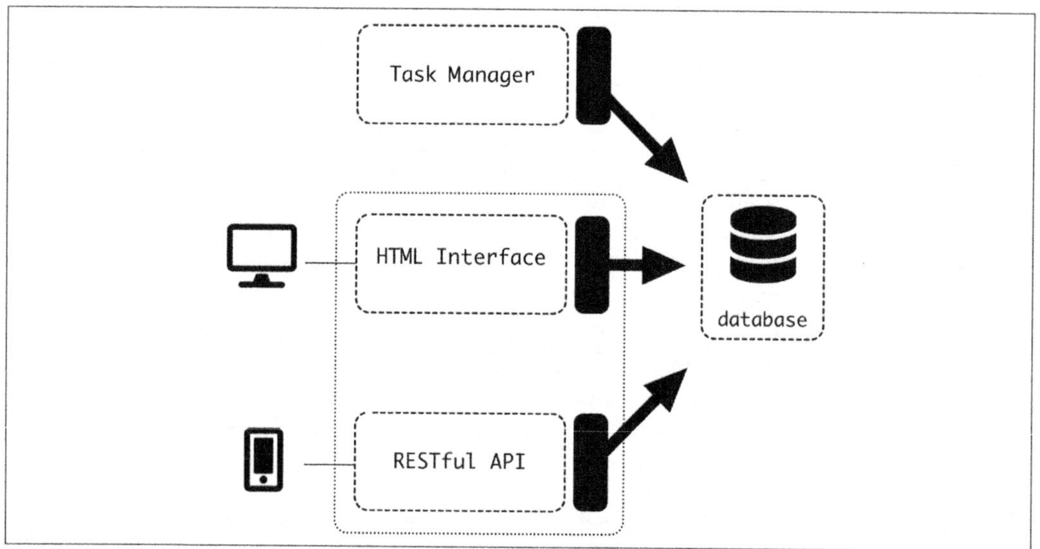

Figure 1.2: Example architecture

It has the following high-level functional elements:

- A public website in HTML that can be accessed. This includes functionality for login, logout, writing new micro-posts, and reading other users' micro-posts (no need to be logged in for this).
- A public RESTful API, to allow the usage of other clients (mobile, JavaScript, and so on) instead of the HTML site. This will authenticate the users using OAuth and perform actions similar to the website.

These two elements, while distinct, will be made into a single application, as shown in the diagram. The front-facing part of the application will include a web server, as we saw in the LAMP architecture description, which has not been displayed here for simplicity.

- A task manager that will execute event-driven tasks. We will add periodic tasks that will calculate daily statistics and send email notifications to users when they are named in a micro-post.
- A database that stores all the information. Note that access to it is shared between the different elements.
- Internally, a common package to ensure that the database is accessed correctly for all the services. This package works as a different element.

Security aspects of software architecture

An important element to take into consideration when creating an architecture is the security requirements. Not every application is the same, so some can be more relaxed in this aspect than others. For example, a banking application needs to be 100 times more secure than, say, an internet forum for discussing cats. The most common example of this is the storage of passwords. The most naive approach to passwords is to store them, in plain text, associated with a username or email address - say, in a file or a database table. When the user tries to log in, we receive the input password, compare it with the one stored previously, and, if they are the same, we allow the user to log in. Right?

Well, this is a very bad idea, because it can produce serious problems:

- If an attacker has access to the storage for the application, they'll be able to read the passwords of all the users. Users tend to reuse passwords (even if it's a bad idea), so, paired with their emails, they'll be exposed to attacks on multiple applications, not only the breached one.

This may seem unlikely, but keep in mind that any copy of the data stored is susceptible to attack, including backups.

- Another real issue is insider threats, workers who may have legitimate access to the system but copy data for nefarious purposes or by mistake. For very sensitive data, this can be a very important consideration.
- Mistakes like displaying the password of a user in status logs.

To make things secure, data needs to be structured in a way that's as protected as possible from access or even copying, without exposing the real passwords of users. The usual solution to this is to have the following schema:

1. The password itself is not stored. Instead, a *cryptographical hash* of the password is stored. This applies a mathematical function to the password and generates a replicable sequence of bits, but the reverse operation is computationally very difficult.
2. As the hash is deterministic based on the input, a malicious actor could detect duplicated passwords, as their hashes are the same. To avoid this problem, a random sequence of characters, called a *salt*, is added for each account. This will be added to each password before hashing, meaning two users with the same password but different salts will have different hashes.

3. Both the resulting hash and the salt are stored.
4. When a user tries to log in, their input password is added to the salt, and the result is compared with the stored hash. If it's correct, the user is logged in.

Note that in this design, the actual password is unknown to the system. It's not stored anywhere and is only accepted temporarily to compare it with the expected hash, after being processed.

This example is presented in a simplified way. There are multiple ways of using this schema and different ways of comparing a hash. For example, the `bcrypt` function can be applied multiple times, increasing encryption each time, which can increase the time required to produce a valid hash, making it more resistant to brute-force attacks.

This kind of system is more secure than one that stores the password directly, as the password is not known by the people operating the system, nor is it stored anywhere.

The problem of mistakenly displaying the password of a user in status logs may still happen! Extra care should be taken to make sure that sensitive information is not being logged by mistake.

In certain cases, the same approach as for passwords can be taken to encrypt other stored data, so that only customers can access their own data. For example, you can enable end-to-end encryption for a communication channel.

Security has a very close relationship with the architecture of a system. As we saw before, the architecture defines which aspects are easy and difficult to change and can make some unsafe things impossible to do, like knowing the password of a user, as we described in the previous example. Other options include not storing data from the user to keep privacy or reducing the data exposed in internal APIs, for example. Software security is a very difficult problem and is often a double-edged sword, and trying to make a system more secure can have the side effect of making operations long-winded and inconvenient.

Summary

In this chapter, we looked at what software architecture is and when it is required, as well as its focus on the long-term approach, which is characteristic of the discipline. We learned that the underlying structure of software is difficult to change and that that aspect should be taken into consideration when designing and changing a software system.

We described how the most important thing is to divide a complex system into smaller parts and assign clear goals and objectives to each of them, keeping in mind that these smaller parts can use multiple programming languages and refer to different scopes. We also described the LAMP architecture and how it's a widely successful starting point when creating simple web service systems.

We talked about how Conway's Law affects the architecture of a system, as underlying team structures have a direct impact on the implementation and structure of software. After all, software is operated and developed by humans, and human communication needs to be accounted for to implement it successfully.

We described the example that we will use throughout the book to describe the different elements and patterns we will present. Finally, we commented on the security aspects of software architecture and how creating barriers to accessing data as part of the structural design of a system can mitigate security issues.

In the next section of the book, we will talk about the different aspects of designing a system.

Join our book's Discord space

Join the book's Discord workspace for a monthly *Ask me Anything* session with the author: `https://packt.link/PythonArchitechture`

Part I

Design

We will first spend some time explaining the basic steps to designing a system. My suggestion is as follows: "Design is the first stage of any successful system, and encompasses everything that you work on before you begin implementation." In this section, we will focus on the general principles and core aspects of each element of the system.

Two main core elements should be at the forefront when designing each part of the system: The *interface*, or how an element of the system connects to the rest, and *data storage*, how this element stores information that can be retrieved later.

Both are critical. The interface defines what the system is and its functionality from the point of view of any user. A well-designed interface hides the implementation details and provides some abstractions that allow for a consistent and comprehensive way of performing actions.

The heart of virtually every successful working system is the data. This is where the value of the system lies. Any seasoned engineer will tell you that an organization can reconstruct a system when the data is available, even if the code that produced it is lost, rather than recover from a total loss of the data, even if the application code is available.

The storage of data is, then, the core of the system. There are many options we can choose from when it comes to storing our data. What kind of database? Store the data in one data storage facility, or several? The traditional way of using raw access to the database, typically in plain SQL statements, is not the most efficient option, and it's prone to problems when complex systems are involved. Other kinds of databases exist that don't even use SQL. We will look at multiple options along with their pros and cons.

Changing how the data is stored in the system is hard once the system is in operation. It isn't impossible but will require a lot of work. The storage option is arguably the founding stone when designing a new system, so be sure that the chosen option fits your requirements. It can be difficult to design something that isn't overly complex but also allows the allocated space to grow as the application starts to store more and more data as it's used.

This section of the book comprises the following chapters:

1. **API Design**, describing how to create useful, yet flexible, interfaces
2. **Data Modeling**, with different ways of handling and representing data to ensure that this critical aspect is well thought through from the outset

2

API Design

In this chapter, we will talk about the basic **application programming interface** (**API**) design principles. We will see how to start our design by defining useful abstractions that will create the foundation for the design.

We will then present the principles for RESTful interfaces, covering both the strict, academic definition and a more practical definition to help when making designs. We will look at design approaches and techniques to help create a useful API based on standard practices. We will also spend some time talking about authentication, as this is a critical element for most APIs.

We will focus in this book on RESTful interfaces, as they are the most common right now. Before that, there were other alternatives, including **Remote Procedure Call** (**RPC**) in the 80s, a way to make a remote function call, or **Single Object Access Protocol** (**SOAP**) in the early 2000s, which standardized the format of the remote call. Current RESTful interfaces are easier to read and take advantage of the already established usage of HTTP more strongly, although, in essence, they could potentially be integrated via these older specifications.

They are still available nowadays, although predominantly in older systems.

We will cover how to create a versioning system for the API, attending to the different use cases that can be affected.

We will see the difference between the frontend and the backend, and its interaction. Although the main objective of the chapter is to talk about API interfaces, we will also talk about HTML interfaces to see the differences and how they interact with other APIs.

Finally, we will describe the design for the example that we will use later in the book.

In this chapter, we'll cover the following topics:

- Abstractions
- RESTful interfaces
- Authentication
- Versioning the API
- Frontend and backend
- HTML interfaces
- Designing the API for the example

Let's take a look at abstractions first.

Abstractions

An API allows us to use a piece of software without totally understanding all the different steps that are involved. It presents a clear menu of actions that can be performed, enabling an external user, who doesn't necessarily understand the complexities of the operation, to perform them efficiently. It presents a simplification of the process.

These actions can be purely functional, where the output is only related to the input; for example, a mathematical function that calculates the barycenter of a planet and a star, given their orbits and masses.

Alternatively, they can deal with state, as the same action repeated twice may have different effects; for example, retrieving the time in the system. Perhaps even a call allows the time zone of the computer to be set, and two subsequent calls to retrieve the time may return very different results.

In both cases, the APIs are defining **abstractions**. Retrieving the time of the system in a single operation is simple enough, but perhaps the details of doing so are not so easy. It may involve reading in a certain way some piece of hardware that keeps track of time.

Different hardware may report the time differently, but the result should always be translated in a standard format. Time zones and time savings need to be applied. All this complexity is handled by the developers of the module that exposes the API and provides a clear and understandable contract with any user. "Call this function, and the time in ISO format will be returned."

While we are mainly talking about APIs, and throughout the book we will describe mostly ones related to online services, the concept of abstractions really can be applied to anything. A web page to manage a user is an abstraction, as it defines the concept of "user account" and the associated parameters. Another omnipresent example is the "Shopping cart" for e-commerce. It's good to create a clear mental image, as it helps to create a clearer and more consistent interface for the user.

This is, of course, a simple example, but APIs can hide a tremendous amount of complexity under their interfaces. A good example to think about is a program like `curl`. Even when *just* sending an HTTP request to a URL and printing the returned headers, there is a huge amount of complexity associated with this:

```
$ curl -IL http://google.com
HTTP/1.1 301 Moved Permanently
Location: http://www.google.com/
Content-Type: text/html; charset=UTF-8
Date: Tue, 09 Mar 2021 20:39:09 GMT
Expires: Thu, 08 Apr 2021 20:39:09 GMT
Cache-Control: public, max-age=2592000
Server: gws
Content-Length: 219
X-XSS-Protection: 0
X-Frame-Options: SAMEORIGIN

HTTP/1.1 200 OK
Content-Type: text/html; charset=ISO-8859-1
P3P: CP="This is not a P3P policy! See g.co/p3phelp for more info."
Date: Tue, 09 Mar 2021 20:39:09 GMT
Server: gws
X-XSS-Protection: 0
X-Frame-Options: SAMEORIGIN
Transfer-Encoding: chunked
Expires: Tue, 09 Mar 2021 20:39:09 GMT
```

```
Cache-Control: private
Set-Cookie: NID=211=V-jsXV6z9PIpszplstSzABT9mOSk7wyucnPzeCz-TUSfOH9_F-07V6-fJ5t9L2eeS1WI-p2G_1_zKa2Tl6nztNH-ur0xF4yIk7iT5CxCTSDsjAaasn4c6mfp3fyYXMp7q1wA2qgmT_hlYScdeAMFkgXt1KaMFKIYmp0RGvpJ-jc; expires=Wed, 08-Sep-2021 20:39:09 GMT; path=/; domain=.google.com; HttpOnly
```

This makes a call to `www.google.com` and displays the headers of the response using the `-I` flag. The `-L` flag is added to automatically redirect any request which is what is happening here.

Making a remote connection to a server requires a lot of different moving parts:

- DNS access to translate the server address `www.google.com` to an actual IP address.
- The communication between both servers, which involves using the TCP protocol to generate a persistent connection and guarantee the reception of the data.
- Redirection based on the result from the first request, as the server returns a code pointing to another URL. This was done owing to the usage of the `-L` flag.
- The redirection points to an HTTPS URL, which requires adding a verification and encryption layer on top of that.

Each of these steps also makes use of other APIs to perform smaller actions, which could involve the functionality of the operating system or even calling remote servers such as the DNS one to obtain data from there.

Here, the `curl` interface is used from the command line. While the strict definition of an API discard stipulates that the end user is a human, there's not really a big change. Good APIs should be easily testable by human users. Command-line interfaces can also be easily automated by bash scripts or other languages.

But, from the point of view of the user of `curl`, this is not very relevant. It is simplified to the point where a single command line with a few flags can perform a well-defined operation without worrying about the format to get data from the DNS or how to encrypt a request using SSL.

Using the right abstractions

For a successful interface, the root is to create a series of abstractions and present them to the user so that they can perform actions. The most important question when designing a new API is, therefore, to decide which are the best abstractions.

When the process happens organically, the abstractions are decided mostly on the go. There is an initial idea, acknowledged as an understanding of the problem, that then gets tweaked.

For example, it's very common to start a user management system by adding different flags to the users. So, a user has permission to perform action A, and then a parameter to perform action B, and so on. By adding one flag at a time, come the tenth flag, the process becomes very confusing.

Then, a new abstraction can be used; roles and permissions. Certain kinds of users can perform different actions, such as admin roles. A user can have a role, and the role is the one that describes the related permissions.

Note that this simplifies the problem, as it's easy to understand and manage. However, moving from "an individual collection of flags" to "several roles" can be a complicated process. There is a reduction in the number of possible options. Perhaps some existing users have a peculiar combination of flags. All this needs to be handled carefully.

While designing a new API, it is good to try to explicitly describe the inherent abstractions that the API uses to clarify them, at least at a high level. This also has the advantage of being able to think about that as a user of the API and see if things add up.

One of the most useful viewpoints in the work of software developers is to detach yourself from your "internal view" and take the position of the actual user of the software. This is more difficult than it sounds, but it's certainly a skill worth developing. This will make you a better designer. Don't be afraid to ask a friend or coworker to detect blind spots in your design.

However, every abstraction has its limits.

Leaking abstractions

When an abstraction is leaking details from the implementation, and not presenting a perfectly opaque image, it's called a leaky abstraction.

While a good API should try to avoid this, sometimes it happens. This can be caused by underlying bugs in the code serving the API, or sometimes directly from the way the code operates in certain operations.

A common case for this is relational databases. SQL abstracts the process of searching data from how it is actually stored in the database. You can search with complex queries and get the result, and you don't need to know how the data is structured. But sometimes, you'll find out that a particular query is slow, and reorganizing the parameters of the query has a big impact on how this happens. This is a leaky abstraction.

This is very common, and the reason why there are significant tools to help ascertain what is going on when running a SQL query, which is very detached from the implementation. The main one is the `EXPLAIN` command.

Operating systems are good examples of a system that generates good abstractions that don't leak the majority of the time. There are lots of examples. Not being able to read or write a file due to a lack of space (a less common problem now than three decades ago); breaking a connection with a remote server due to a network problem; or not being able to create a new connection due to reaching a limit in terms of the number of open file descriptors.

Leaky abstractions are, to a certain degree, unavoidable. They are the result of not living in a perfect world. Software is fallible. Understanding and preparing for that is critical.

> "*All non-trivial abstractions, to some degree, are leaky.*"
>
> – *Joel Spolsky's Law of Leaky Abstractions*

When designing an API, it is important to take this fact into account for several reasons:

- **To present clear errors and hints externally**. A good design will always include cases for things going wrong and try to present them clearly with proper error codes or error handling.

- **To deal with errors that could come from dependent services internally**. Dependent services can fail or have other kinds of problems. The API should abstract this to a certain degree, recovering from the problem if possible, failing gracefully if not, and returning a proper result if recovery is impossible.

The best design is the one that not only designs things when they work as expected, but also prepares for unexpected problems and is sure that they can be analyzed and corrected.

Resources and action abstractions

A very useful pattern to consider when designing an API is to produce a set of resources that can perform actions. This pattern uses two kinds of elements: **resources** and **actions**.

Resources are passive elements that are referenced, while actions are performed on resources.

For example, let's define a very simple interface to play a simple game guessing coin tosses. This is a game consisting of three guesses for three coin tosses, and the user wins if at least two of these guesses are correct.

The resource and actions may be as follows:

Resource	**Actions**	**Details**
HEADS	None	A coin toss result.
TAILS	None	A coin toss result.
GAME	START	Start a new GAME.
	READ	Returns the current round (1 to 3) and the current correct guesses.
COIN_TOSS	TOSS	Toss the coin. If the GUESS hasn't been produced, it returns an error.
	GUESS	Accepts HEADS or TAILS as the guess.
	RESULT	It returns HEADS or TAILS and whether the GUESS was correct.

A possible sequence for a single game could be:

```
GAME START
> (GAME 1)
GAME 1 COIN_TOSS GUESS HEAD
GAME 1 COIN_TOSS TOSS
GAME 1 COIN_TOSS RESULT
> (TAILS, INCORRECT)
GAME 1 COIN_TOSS GUESS HEAD
GAME 1 COIN_TOSS TOSS
GAME 1 COIN_TOSS RESULT
> (HEAD, CORRECT)
GAME 1 READ
> (ROUND 2, 1 CORRECT, IN PROCESS)
GAME 1 COIN_TOSS GUESS HEAD
GAME 1 COIN_TOSS TOSS
GAME 1 COIN_TOSS RESULT
> (HEAD, CORRECT)
GAME 1 READ
> (ROUND 3, 2 CORRECT, YOU WIN)
```

Note how each resource has its own set of actions that can be performed. Actions can be repeated if that's convenient, but it's not required. Resources can be combined into a hierarchical representation (like here, where `COIN_TOSS` depends on a higher `GAME` resource). Actions can require parameters that can be other resources.

However, the abstractions are organized around having a consistent set of resources and actions. This way of explicitly organizing an API is useful as it clarifies what is passive and what's active in the system.

Object-oriented programming (**OOP**) uses these abstractions, as everything is an object that can receive messages to perform some actions. Functional programming, on the other hand, doesn't fit neatly into this structure, as "actions" can work like resources.

This is a common pattern, and it's used in RESTful interfaces, as we will see next.

RESTful interfaces

RESTful interfaces are incredibly common these days, and for good reason. They've become the de facto standard in web services that serve other applications.

Representational State Transfer (**REST**) was defined in 2000 in a Ph.D. dissertation by Roy Fielding, and it uses HTTP standards as a basis to create a definition of a software architecture style.

For a system to be considered RESTful, it should follow certain rules:

- **Client-server architecture**. It works through remote calling.
- **Stateless**. All the information related to a particular request should be contained in the request itself, making it independent from the specific server serving the request.
- **Cacheability**. The cacheability of the responses should be clear, either to say they are cacheable or not.
- **Layered system**. The client cannot tell if they are connected to a final server or if there's an intermediate server.
- **Uniform interface**, with four prerequisites:
    - **Resource identification in requests**, meaning a resource is unequivocally represented, and its representation is independent
    - **Resource manipulation through representations**, allowing clients to have all the required information to make changes when they have the representation
    - **Self-descriptive messages**, meaning messages are complete in themselves
    - **Hypermedia as the Engine of Application State**, meaning the client can walk through the system using referenced hyperlinks
- **Code on demand**. This is an optional requirement, and it's normally not used. Servers can submit code in response to help perform operations or improve the client; for example, submitting JavaScript to be executed in the browser.

This is the most formal definition. As you can see, it's not necessarily based on HTTP requests. For more convenient usage, we need to limit the possibilities somewhat and set a common framework.

A more practical definition

When people talk colloquially about RESTful interfaces, normally they are understood as interfaces based on HTTP resources using JSON formatted requests. This is wholly compatible with the definition that we've seen before, but taking some key elements into consideration.

These key elements are sometimes ignored, leading to pseudo-RESTful interfaces, which don't have the same properties.

The main one is that **URIs (Uniform Resource Identifiers)** should describe clear resources, as well as HTTP methods and actions to perform on them, using the **CRUD (Create Retrieve Update Delete)** approach.

CRUD interfaces facilitate the performance of those actions: Create (save a new entry), Retrieve (read), Update (overwrite), and Delete entries. These are the basic operations for any persistent storage system.

There are two kinds of URIs, whether they describe a single resource or a collection of resources, as can be seen in the following table:

Resource	Example	Method	Description
Collection	`/books`	`GET`	List operation. Returns all the available elements of the collection, for example, all books.
		`POST`	Create operation. Creates a new element of the collection. Returns the newly created resource.
Single	`/books/1`	`GET`	Retrieve operation. Returns the data from the resource, for example, the book with an ID of 1.
		`PUT`	Set (Update) operation. Sends the new data for the resource. If it doesn't exist, it will be created. If it does, it will be overwritten.
		`PATCH`	Partial update operation. Overwrites only the partial values for the resource, for example, sends and writes only the email for the user object.
		`DELETE`	Delete operation. It deletes the resource.

The key element of this design is the definition of everything as a resource, as we saw before. Resources are defined by their URIs, which contain a hierarchical view of the resources, for example:

`/books/1/cover` defines the resource of the cover image from the book with an ID of 1.

For simplicity, we will use integer IDs to identify the resources in this chapter. In real-world operations, this is not recommended. They have no meaning at all, and, even worse, they can sometimes leak information about the number of elements in the system or their internal order. For example, a competitor could estimate how many new entries are being added each week. To detach from whatever internal representation, try to always use a natural key externally, if available, such as the ISBN number for books, or create a random **Universally Unique Identifier** (**UUID**).

Another problem with sequential integers is that, at high rates, the system may struggle to create them correctly, as it won't be possible to create two at the same time. This can limit the growth of a system.

Most of the input and output of the resources will be represented in JSON format. For example, this could be an example of a request and response to retrieve a user:

```
GET /books/1

HTTP/1.1 200 OK
Content-Type: application/json
{"name": "Frankenstein", "author": "Mary Shelley", "cover": "http://
library.lbr/books/1/cover"}
```

The response is formatted in JSON, as specified in `Content-Type`. This makes it easy to parse and analyze automatically. Note that the `avatar` field returns a hyperlink to another resource. This makes the interface walkable and reduces the amount of information that the client requires beforehand.

This is one of the most forgotten properties when designing RESTful interfaces. It is preferable to return full URIs to resources instead of indirect references, such as no-context IDs.

For example, when creating a new resource, include the new URI in the response, in the `Location` header.

To send new values to overwrite, the same format should be used. Note that some elements may be read-only, such as `cover`, and aren't required:

```
PUT /books/1
Content-Type: application/json
{"name": "Frankenstein or The Modern Prometheus", "author": "Mary
Shelley"}
HTTP/1.1 200 OK
Content-Type: application/json
{"name": "Frankenstein or The Modern Prometheus", "author": "Mary
Shelley", "cover": "http://library.com/books/1/cover"}
```

The **same representation should be used for input and output**, making it easy for the client to retrieve a resource, modify it, and then resubmit it.

This is really handy and creates a level of consistency that's very much appreciated when implementing a client. While testing, try to ensure that retrieving a value and resubmitting it is valid and doesn't create a problem.

When the resource will be directly represented by binary content, it can return the proper format, specified in the `Content-Type` header. For example, retrieving the avatar resource may return an image file:

```
GET /books/1/cover

HTTP/1.1 200 OK
Content-Type: image/png
...
```

In the same way, when creating or updating a new avatar, it should be sent in the proper format.

While the original intention of RESTful interfaces was to make use of multiple formats, for example, accepting XML and JSON, this is not very common in practice. JSON is, by and large, the most standard format these days. Some systems may benefit from using multiple formats, though.

Another important property is ensuring that some actions are **idempotent**, and others are not. Idempotent actions can be repeated multiple times, producing the same result, while repeating not-idempotent actions will generate different results. Evidently, the action should be identical.

A clear case of this is the creation of a new element. If we submit two identical `POST` creations of a new element of a resource list, it will create two new elements. For example, submitting two books with the same name and author will create two identical books.

This is assuming that there's no limitation to the content of the resource. If they are, the second request will fail, which will produce a different result to the first in any case.

On the other hand, two `GET` requests will produce the same result. The same is true for `PUT` or `DELETE`, as they'll overwrite or "delete again" the resource.

The fact that the only non-idempotent requests are `POST` actions simplifies significantly the design of measures to deal with problems when there's the question of whether it should be retried. Idempotent requests are safe to retry at any time, thereby simplifying the handling of errors such as network problems.

Headers and statuses

An important detail of the HTTP protocol that can sometimes be overlooked is the different headers and status codes.

Headers include metadata information about the request or response. Some of it is added automatically, like the size of the body of the request or response. Some interesting headers to consider are the following:

Header	Type	Details
`Authorization`	Standard	Credentials to authenticate the request.
`Content-Type`	Standard	The type of the body of the request, like `application/json` or `text/html`.
`Date`	Standard	When the message was created.
`If-Modified-Since`	Standard	The sender has a copy of the resource at this time. If it hasn't changed since then, a `304 Not Modified` response (with an empty body) can be returned. This allows the caching of data and saves time and bandwidth by not returning duplicated info. This can be used in `GET` requests.

X-Forwarded-From	De facto standard	Stores the IP where the message was originated, and the different proxies it went through.
Forwarded	Standard	Same as X-Forwarded-From. This is a newer header and less common still than X-Forwarded-From.

A well-designed API will make use of headers to communicate proper information, for example, setting Content-Type correctly or accepting cache parameters if possible.

A comprehensive list of headers can be found at https://developer.mozilla.org/en-US/docs/Web/HTTP/Headers.

Another important detail is to make good use of available status codes. Status codes provide significant information about what happened, and using the most detailed information possible for each situation will provide a better interface.

Some common status codes are as follows:

Status code	Description
200 OK	A successful resource access or modification. It should return a body; if it doesn't, use 204 No Content.
201 Created	A successful POST request that creates a new resource.
204 No Content	A successful request that doesn't return a body, for example, a successful DELETE request.
301 Moved Permanently	The accessed resource is now permanently located in a different URI. It should return a Location header with the new URI. Most libraries will follow up automatically for GET accesses. For example, the API is only accessible in HTTPS, but it was accessed in HTTP.
302 Found	The accessed resource is temporarily located in a different URI. A typical example is being redirected to a login page if authenticated.
304 Not Modified	A cached resource is still valid. The body should be empty. This status code is only returned if the client requested cached information, for example, using the If-Modified-Since header.

`400 Bad Request`	A generic error in the request. This is the server saying, "something went wrong on your end." A more descriptive message should be added to the body. If a more descriptive status code is possible, it should be preferred.
`401 Unauthorized`	The request is not allowed, as the request is not properly authenticated. The request may lack valid headers for authentication.
`403 Forbidden`	The request is authenticated, but it can't access this resource. This is different from the `401 Unauthorized` status in that the request is already correctly authenticated but doesn't have access.
`404 Not Found`	Probably the most famous status code! The resource described by the URI cannot be found.
`405 Method Not Allowed`	The requested method cannot be used; for example, the resource cannot be deleted.
`429 Too Many Requests`	The server should return this status code if there's a limit to the number of requests the client can do. It should return a description or more info in the body, and ideally, a `Retry-After` header indicating the time in seconds to the next retry.
`500 Server Error`	A generic error in the server. This status should only be used if an unexpected error happened in the server.
`502 Bad Gateway`	The server is redirecting the request to a different server, and the communication was incorrect. This error normally appears when some backend service is unavailable or incorrectly configured.
`503 Service Unavailable`	The server is currently unable to handle requests. Normally, this is a temporary situation, such as a load problem. It could be used to mark maintenance downtime, but this is generally rare.
`504 Gateway Timeout`	Similar to `502 Bad Gateway`, but in this case, the backend service didn't respond, provoking a timeout.

In general, non-descriptive error codes such as `400 Bad Request` and `500 Server Error` should be left for general situations. However, if there is a better, more descriptive status code, this should be used instead.

For example, a `PATCH` request to overwrite a parameter should return `400 Bad Request` if the parameter is incorrect for any reason, but `404 Not Found` if the resource URI is not found.

There are other status codes. You can check a comprehensive list, including details on each one, here: `https://httpstatuses.com/`.

In any error, please include some extra feedback to the user with a reason. A general descriptor can help the handling of unexpected cases and simplify debugging issues.

This is especially useful for `4XX` errors as they will help users of the API to fix their own bugs and iteratively improve their integration.

For example, the mentioned `PATCH` may return this body:

```
{
    "message": "Field 'address' is unknown"
}
```

This will give specific details about the problem. Other options include returning error codes, multiple messages in case there are multiple possible errors, and also duplicating the status code in the body.

Designing resources

The available actions in a RESTful API are limited to CRUD operations. Therefore, resources are the basic construction blocks for the API.

Making everything a resource helps to create very explicit APIs and helps with the stateless requirement for RESTful interfaces.

A stateless service means that all the information required to fulfill a request is either provided by the caller or retrieved externally, normally from a database. This excludes other ways of keeping information, such as storing information locally in the same server's hard drive. This makes any server capable of handling every single request, and it's critical in achieving scalability.

Elements that could be activated by creating different actions could be separated into different resources. For example, an interface simulating a pen could require the following elements:

- Opening and closing the pen.
- Writing something. Only an open pen can write.

In some APIs, like an object-oriented one, this could involve creating a pen object and changing its state:

```
pen = Pen()
pen.open()
pen.write("Something")
pen.close()
```

In a RESTful API, we need to create different resources for both the pen and its status:

```
# Create a new pen with id 1
POST /pens
# Create a new open pen for pen 1
POST /pens/1/open
# Update the new open text for the open pen 1
PUT /pens/1/open/1/text
# Delete the open pen, closing the pen
DELETE /pens/1/open/1
```

This may look a bit cumbersome, but RESTful APIs should aim to be higher level than the typical object-oriented one. Either create the text directly, or create a pen and then the text, without having to perform the open/close operation.

Keep in mind that RESTful APIs are used in the context of remote calls. This means that they can't be low level, as each call is a big investment compared with a local API, as the time per call will be a sensible part of the operation.

Note also that every single aspect and step gets registered and has its own set of identifiers and is addressable. This is more explicit than the internal state that can be found in OOP. As we've seen, we want it to be stateless, while objects are very much stateful.

Keep in mind that a resource doesn't need to be translated directly into a database object. That's thinking backward, from the storage to the API. Remember that you are not limited to that, and can compose resources that obtain information from multiple sources or that don't fit into a direct translation. We will see examples in the next chapter.

Dealing only with resources can require certain adaptations if coming from a more traditional OOP environment, but they are a pretty flexible tool and can allocate multiple ways of performing actions.

Resources and parameters

While everything is a resource, some elements make more sense as a parameter that interacts with the resource. This is very natural when modifying the resource. Any change needs to be submitted to update the resource. But, in other cases, some resources could be modified for other causes. The most common case is searches.

A typical search endpoint will define a `search` resource and retrieve its results. However, a search without parameters to filter is not really useful, so extra parameters will be required to define the search, for example:

```
# Return every pen in the system
GET /pens/search

# Return only red pens
GET /pens/search?color=red

# Return only red pens, sorted by creation date
GET /pens/search?color=red&sort=creation_date
```

These parameters are stored in query parameters, which are natural extensions to retrieve them.

As a general rule, only `GET` requests should have query parameters. Other kinds of request methods should provide any parameters as part of the body.

GET requests are also easy to cache if including the query parameters. If the search is returning the same values for each request, given that that's an idempotent request, the full URI, including the query parameters, can be cached even externally from the service.

By convention, all logs that store GET requests will also store the query params, while any parameter sent as a header or in the body of the request won't be logged. This has security implications, as any sensible parameter, such as a password, shouldn't be sent as a query parameter.

Sometimes, that's the reason to create POST operations that typically would be a GET request, but prefer to set parameters in the body of the request instead of query parameters. While it is possible in the HTTP protocol to set the body in a GET request, it's definitely very unusual.

An example of this could be searching by phone number, email, or other personal information, so a middle-man agent could intercept and learn about them.

Another reason to use POST requests is to allow a bigger space for parameters, as the full URL, including query parameters, is normally limited to 2K in size, while bodies are much less restricted in size.

Pagination

In a RESTful interface, any LIST request that returns a sensible number of elements should be paginated.

This means that the number of elements and pages can be tweaked from the request, returning only a specific page of elements. This limits the scope of the request and avoids very slow response times and waste transmission bytes.

An example could involve using the parameters page and size, for example:

```
# Return only first 10 elements
GET /pens/search?page=1&size=10
```

A well-constructed response will have a similar format to this:

```
{
    "next": "http://pens.pns/pens/search?page=2&size=10",
    "previous": null,
```

```
    "result": [
        # elements
    ]
}
```

It contains a `result` field with the resulting list and `next` and `previous` fields that are hyperlinks to the next and previous page, with a value of `null` if it is not available. This makes it easy to walk through all the results.

A `sort` parameter could also be useful to ensure consistency in pages.

This technique also allows multiple pages to be retrieved in parallel, which can speed up the downloading of information, doing several small requests instead of one big one. The objective, though, is to provide sufficient filter parameters for generally returning not too much information, being able to retrieve only the relevant information.

Pagination has a problem, which is that the data in the collection may change between multiple requests, especially if retrieving many pages. The problem is as follows:

```
# Obtain first page
GET /pens/search?page=1&size=10&sort=name

# Create a new resource that is added to the first page
POST /pens

# Obtain second page
GET /pens/search?page=2&size=10&sort=name
```

The second page now has a repeated element that used to be on the first page but has now moved to the second, and then there's one element that's not returned. Normally, the non-return of the new resource is not that much of a problem, as, after all, the retrieval of information started before its creation. However, the return of the same resource twice can be.

To avoid this kind of problem, there's the possibility of sorting by default the values by creation date or something analogous. This way, any new resource will be added at the end of pagination and will be consistently retrieved.

For resources that return inherently "new" elements, like notifications or similar, add an `updated_since` parameter to retrieve only the new resources since the most recent access. This speeds up access in a practical way and retrieves only the relevant information.

Creating a flexible pagination system increases the usefulness of any API. Be sure that your pagination definition is consistent across any different resources.

Designing a RESTful API process

The best way to start designing a RESTful API is to clearly state the resources and then describe them, including the following details:

- *Description*: Description of the action
- *Resource URI*: Note that this may be shared for several actions, differentiated by the method (for example, GET to retrieve and DELETE to delete)
- *Methods applicable*: The HTTP method to use for the action defined in this endpoint
- *(Only if relevant) Input body*: The input body of the request
- *Expected result in the body*: Result
- *Possible expected errors*: Returning status codes depending on specific errors
- *Description*: Description of the action
- *(Only if relevant) Input query parameters*: Query parameters to add to the URI for extra functionality
- *(Only if relevant) Relevant headers*: Any supported header
- *(Only if relevant) Returning status codes out of the ordinary (200 and 201)*: Different from errors, in case there's a status code that's considered a success but it's not the usual case; for example, a success returns a redirection

This will be enough to create a design document that can be understood by other engineers and allow them to work on the interface.

It is good practice, though, to start with a quick draft of the different URIs and methods, and to have a quick look at all the different resources that the system has without getting into too much detail, such as a body description or errors. This helps to detect missing resource gaps or other kinds of inconsistencies in the API.

For example, the API described in this chapter has the following actions:

```
GET    /pens
POST   /pens
POST   /pens/<pen_id>/open
PUT    /pens/<pen_id>/open/<open_pen_id>/text
DELETE /pens/<pen_id>/open/<open_pen_id>
GET    /pens/search
```

There are a couple of details that can be tweaked and improved here:

- It looks like we forgot to add the action to remove a pen, once created
- There are a couple of `GET` actions for retrieving information about the created resource that should be added
- In the `PUT` action, it feels a bit redundant to have to add `/text`

With this feedback, we can again describe the API as follows (modifications have an arrow):

```
GET    /pens
POST   /pens
GET    /pens/<pen_id>
DELETE /pens/<pen_id> ←
POST   /pens/<pen_id>/open
GET    /pens/<pen_id>/open/<open_pen_id> ←
PUT    /pens/<pen_id>/open/<open_pen_id> ←
DELETE /pens/<pen_id>/open/<open_pen_id>
GET    /pens/search
```

Note how the organization in the hierarchical structure helps to take a good look at all the elements and find either gaps or relations that may not be obvious at first glance.

After that, we can get into details. We can use the template described at the start of the section, or any other one that works for you. For example, we can define the endpoints to create a new pen and read a pen in the system:

Creating a new pen:

- *Description*: Creates a new pen, specifying the color.
- *Resource URI*: `/pens`
- *Method*: `POST`

- *Input body*:

```
{
    "name": <pen name>,
    "color": (black|blue|red)
}
```

- *Errors*:

```
400 Bad Request
```

Error in the body, such as an unrecognized color, a duplicated name, or a bad format.

Retrieving an existing pen:

- *Description*: Retrieves an existing pen.
- *Resource URI*: `/pens/<pen id>`
- *Method*: `GET`
- *Return body*:

```
{
    "name": <pen name>,
    "color": (black|blue|red)
    }
```

- *Errors*:

```
404 Not Found
The pen ID is not found.
```

The main objective is that these small templates are useful and to the point. Feel free to tweak them as expected, and don't worry about being too completist with the errors or details. The most important part is that they are **useful**; for example, adding a `405 Method Not Allowed` message could be redundant.

The API can also be designed using tools such as Postman (`www.postman.com`), which is an API platform that can be used to either design or test/debug existing APIs. While useful, it is good to be able to design an API without external tools, in case that's required, and because it forces you to think about the design and not necessarily the tool itself. We will also see how to use Open API, which is based more on the definition, and not so much on providing a test environment.

Designing and defining an API can also enable it to be structured in a standard manner afterward to take advantage of tools.

Using the Open API specification

A more structured alternative is to use a tool such as Open API (`https://www.openapis.org/`). Open API is a specification for defining a RESTful API through a YAML or JSON document. This allows this definition to interact with other tools to generate automatic documentation for the API.

It allows the definition of different components that can be repeated, both as input and output. This makes it easy to build consistent reusable objects. There are also ways of inheriting or composing from one another, thereby creating a rich interface.

Describing the whole Open API specification in detail is beyond the scope of this book. Most common web frameworks allow integration with it, generating the YAML file automatically or the web documentation that we'll see later. It was previously called Swagger and its web page (`https://swagger.io/`) has a very useful editor and other resources.

For example, this is a YAML file that describes the two endpoints described above. The file is available on GitHub: `https://github.com/PacktPublishing/Python-Architecture-Patterns/blob/main/pen_example.yaml`:

```
openapi: 3.0.0
info:
  version: "1.0.0"
  title: "Swagger Pens"
paths:
  /pens:
    post:
      tags:
      - "pens"
      summary: "Add a new pen"
      requestBody:
        description: "Pen object that needs to be added to the store"
        required: true
        content:
          application/json:
            schema:
              $ref: "#/components/schemas/Pen"
```

```
      responses:
        "201":
          description: "Created"
        "400":
          description: "Invalid input"
  /pens/{pen_id}:
    get:
      tags:
      - "pens"
      summary: "Retrieve an existing pen"
      parameters:
      - name: "pen_id"
        in: path
        description: "Pen ID"
        required: true
        schema:
          type: integer
          format: int64
      responses:
        "200":
          description: "OK"
          content:
            application/json:
              schema:
                $ref: "#/components/schemas/Pen"
        "404":
          description: "Not Found"

components:
  schemas:
    Pen:
      type: "object"
      properties:
        name:
          type: "string"
        color:
          type: "string"
          enum:
            - black
            - blue
            - red
```

In the `components` part, the `Pen` object gets defined, and then is used in both endpoints. You can see how both endpoints, `POST /pens` and `GET /pens/{pen_id}`, are defined and describe the expected input and output, taking into account the different errors that can be produced.

One of the most interesting aspects of Open API is the ability to automatically generate a documentation page with all the information to help any possible implementation. The generated documentation looks like this:

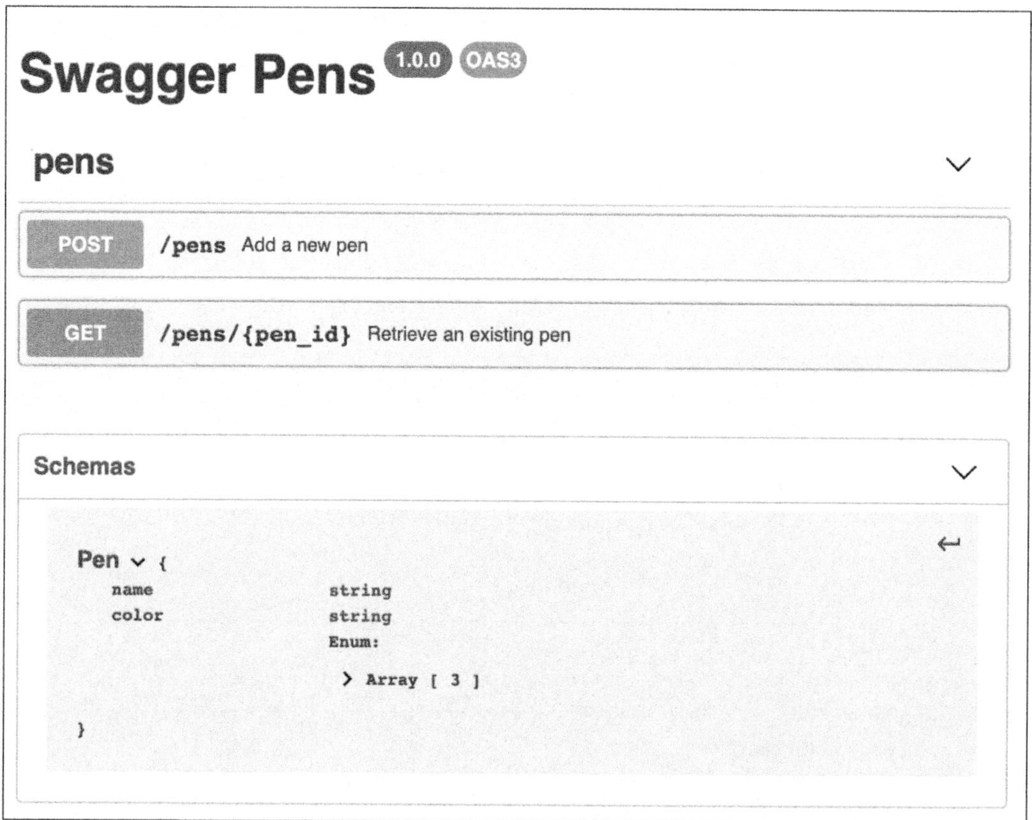

Figure 2.1: Swagger Pens documentation

If the YAML file describes your interface correctly and fully, this can be really useful. In some cases, it could be advantageous to work from the YAML to the API. This first generates the YAML file and allows work in both directions from there, both in the frontend direction and the backend direction. For an API-first approach, it may make sense. It's even possible to automatically create skeletons of clients and servers in multiple languages, for example, servers in Python Flask or Spring, and clients in Java or Angular.

Keep in mind that it's up to you to make the implementation match the definition closely. These skeletons will still require enough work to make them work correctly. Open API will simplify the process, but it won't magically solve all integration problems.

Each of the endpoints contains further information and can even be tested in the same documentation, thereby significantly helping an external developer who wants to use the API, as we can see in the next graphic:

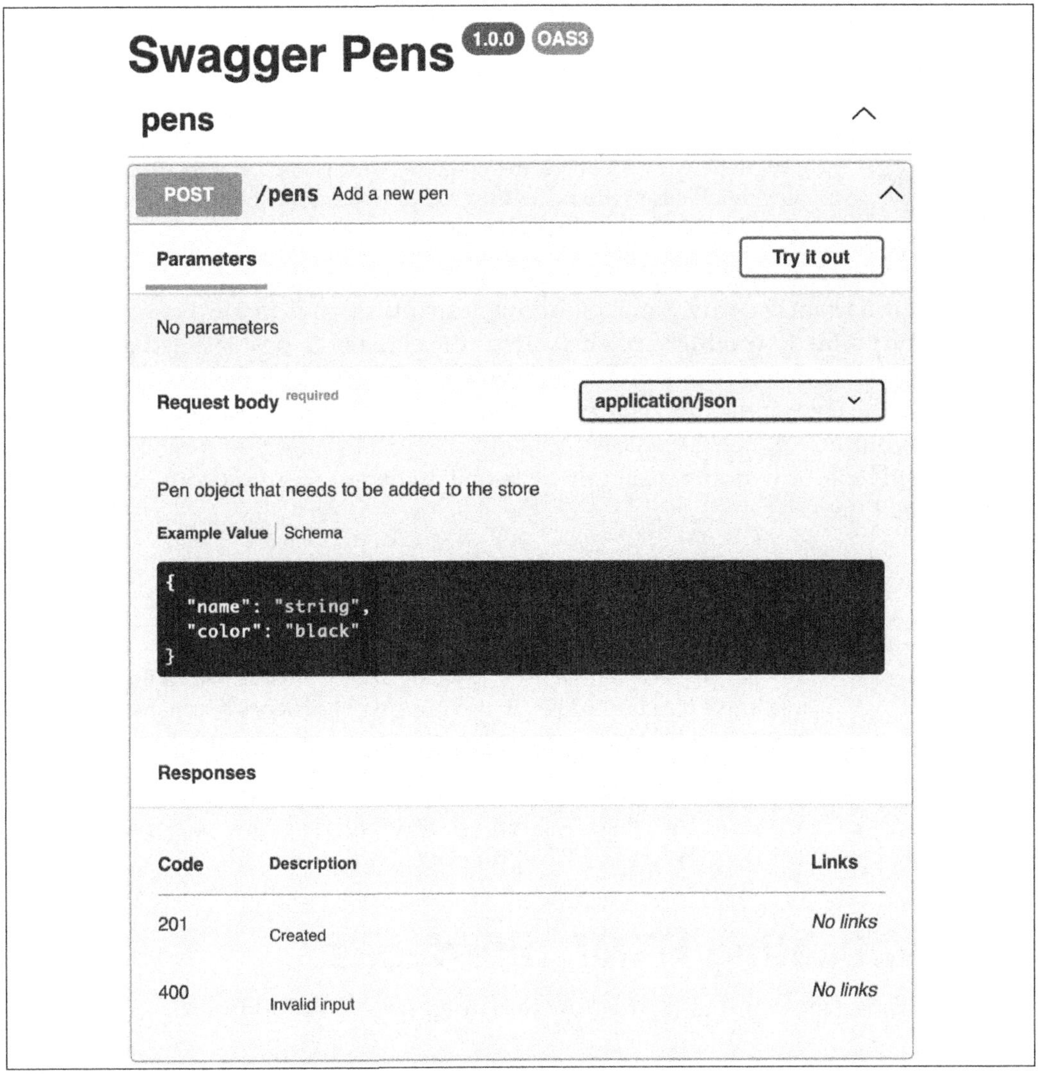

Swagger Pens 1.0.0 OAS3

pens

POST **/pens** Add a new pen

Parameters Try it out

No parameters

Request body required application/json

Pen object that needs to be added to the store

Example Value | Schema

```
{
  "name": "string",
  "color": "black"
}
```

Responses

Code	Description	Links
201	Created	*No links*
400	Invalid input	*No links*

Figure 2.2: Swagger Pens expanded documentation

Given that it's very easy to ensure that the server can generate this automatic documentation, even if the design is not started from an Open API YAML file, it's a good idea to generate it so as to create self-generating documentation.

Authentication

A critical part of virtually any API is the ability to distinguish between authorized and unauthorized access. Being able to log the user properly is critical, and a headache from the point of view of security.

Security is hard, so it's better to rely on standards to simplify the operation.

As we said before, these are just general tips, but in no way a comprehensive set of secure practices. This book is not focused on security. Please keep up with security issues and solutions, as this is a field that is always evolving.

The most important security issue regarding authentication is **to always use HTTPS endpoints in production**. This allows the channel to be protected against eavesdropping and makes communication private. Note that an HTTP website just means that the communication is private; you could be talking with the devil. But it's the bare minimum required to allow users of your API to send you passwords and other sensitive information without the fear that an external user is going to receive this information.

Normally, most architectures use HTTPS until the request reaches the data center or secure network, and then use HTTP internally. This permits a check on the data flowing internally but also protects data that is traveling across the internet. While less important these days, it also improves efficiency, as encoding requests in HTTPS require extra processing power.

HTTPS endpoints are valid for all access, but other details are specific depending on whether they are HTML interfaces or RESTful ones.

Authenticating HTML interfaces

In HTML web pages, normally, the flow to authenticate is as follows:

1. A login screen gets presented to the user.
2. The user enters their login and password and sends them to the server.

3. The server verifies the password. If correct, it returns a cookie with a session ID.
4. The browser receives the response and stores the cookie.
5. All new requests will send the cookie. The server will verify the cookie and properly identify the user.
6. The user can log out, removing the cookie. If this is done explicitly, a request will be sent to the server to delete the session ID. Typically, the session ID will have an expiry time for cleaning itself. This expiry can renew itself on each access or force the user to log in again from time to time.

It's important to set up the cookie as `Secure`, `HttpOnly`, and `SameSite`. `Secure` ensures that the cookie is only sent to HTTPS endpoints, and not to HTTP ones. `HttpOnly` renders the cookie inaccessible by JavaScript, which makes it more difficult to obtain the cookie via malicious code. The cookie will be sent automatically to the host that sets it. `SameSite` ensures that cookies are only sent when the origin of the source is a page from the same host. It can be set to `Strict`, `Lax`, and `None`. `Lax` allows you to navigate to the page from a different site, thereby sending the cookie, while `Strict` doesn't allow it.

You can obtain more information at the Mozilla SameSite Cookie page: `https://developer.mozilla.org/en-US/docs/Web/HTTP/Headers/Set-Cookie/SameSite`.

Possible bad usage of the cookie is through XSS (cross-site scripting) attacks. A compromised script reads that cookie, and then forges bad requests authenticated as the user.

Another important kind of security problem is **cross-site request forgery** (**CSRF**). In this case, the fact that the user is logged in on an external service is exploited by presenting a URL that will be automatically executed in a different, compromised website.

For example, while accessing a forum, a URL from a common bank is called, presented as an image, for example. If the user is logged in to this bank, the operation will be executed.

The `SameSite` attribute greatly reduces the risk of CSRF, but in case the attribute is not understood by older browsers, operations presented to the user by the bank should present a random token, making the user send both the authenticated request with the cookie and a valid token. An external page won't know a valid random token, making this exploit much more difficult.

The session ID that the cookie contains can either be stored in the database, being just a random unique identifier, or a rich token.

A random identifier is just that, a random number that stores the related information in the database, mainly, who is accessing and when the session expires. With every access, this session ID is queried to the server and the related information is retrieved. On very big deployments, with many accesses, this can create problems as it's less scalable. The database where the session ID is stored needs to be accessed by all workers, which can create a bottleneck.

One possible solution is to create a rich data token. This works by adding all the required information directly to the cookie; for example, storing the user ID, expiry, and so on, directly. This avoids database access, but makes the cookie possible to forge, as all information is in the open. To fix it, the cookie is signed.

The signature proves that the data was originated by a trusted login server and can be verified independently by any other server. This is more scalable and avoids bottlenecks. Optionally, the content can also be encrypted to avoid being read.

Another advantage of this system is that the generation of the token can be independent of the general system. If the token can be validated independently, there's no need for the login server to be the same as the general server.

Even more so, a single token signer can issue tokens for multiple services. This is the basis for **SSO** (**Single Sign-On**): log in to an auth provider and then use the same account in several related services. This is very common in common services such as Google, Facebook or GitHub, to avoid having to create a specific login for some web pages.

That operation mode, having a token authority, is the basis of the OAuth authorization framework.

Authenticating RESTful interfaces

OAuth has become a common standard for authenticating access for APIs, and RESTful APIs in particular.

There's a difference between authenticating and authorizing, and in essence, OAuth is an authorization system. Authenticating is determining who the user is, while authorizing is what the user is capable of doing. OAuth uses the concept of `scope` to return what the capabilities of a user are.

Most implementations of OAuth, such as OpenID Connect, also include the user information in the returning token to also authenticate the user, returning who the user is.

It is based on the idea that there's an authorizer who can check the identity of the user and provide them with a token with information allowing the user to log in. The service will receive this token and will log the user:

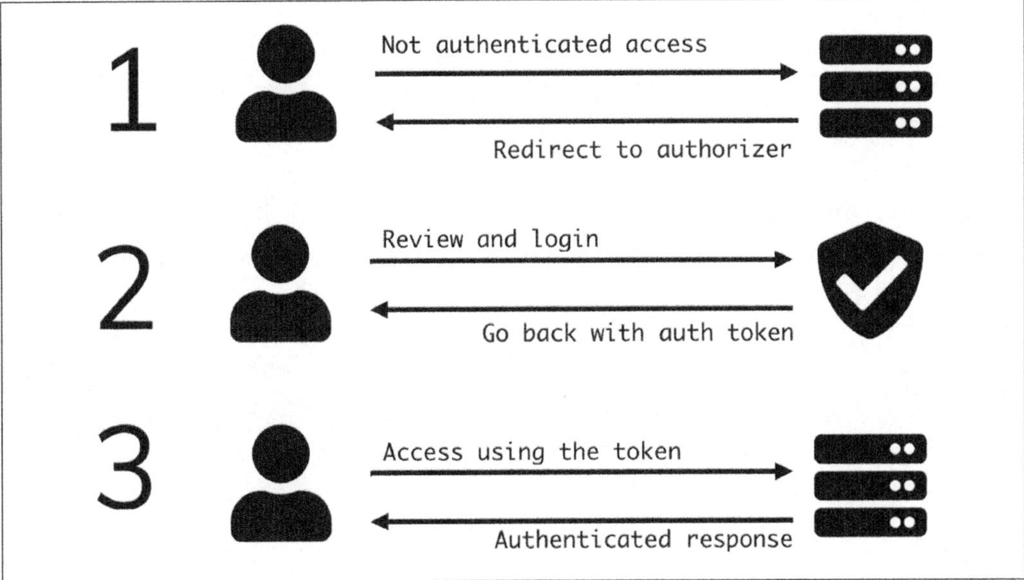

Figure 2.3: Authentication flow

The most common version at the moment is OAuth 2.0, which allows flexibility in terms of logging in and flow. Keep in mind that OAuth is not exactly a protocol, but provides certain ideas that can be tweaked to the specific use case.

This means that there are different ways in which you can implement OAuth, and, crucially, that different authorizers will implement it differently. Please verify their documentation with care when implementing the integration.

Generally, authorizers use the OpenID Connect protocol, which is based on OAuth.

There's an important difference in terms of whether the system accessing the API is the final user directly, or whether it accesses it on behalf of a user. An example of the latter could be a smartphone app to access a service like Twitter, or a service that needs to access the data stored for the user in GitHub, such as a code analysis tool. The app itself is not the one that performs the actions but transfers the actions of a user.

This flow is called the Authorization Code grant. The main characteristic is that the auth provider will present a login page to the user and redirect them with the authentication token.

For example, this could be the sequence of calls for the Authorization Code grant:

```
GET https://myservice.com/login
    Return a page with a form to initiate the login with authorizer.com

Follow the flow in the external authorize until login, with something
like.

POST https://authorizer.com/authorize
  grant_type=authorization_code
  redirect_uri=https://myservice.com/redirect
  user=myuser
  password=mypassword
    Return 302 Found to https://myservice.com/redirect?code=XXXXX

GET https://myservice.com/redirect?code=XXXXX
-> Login into the system and set proper cookie,
   return 302 to https://myservice.com
```

If the system accessing the API is from the end user directly, the Client Credentials grant type flow can be used instead. In this case, the first call will send `client_id` (user ID) and `client_secret` (password) to retrieve the authentication token directly. This token will be set in new calls as a header, authenticating the request.

Note that this skips a step, and is easier to automate:

```
POST /token HTTP/1.1
  grant_type=authorization_code
  &client_id=XXXX
  &client_secret=YYYY
    Returns a JSON body with
    {
  "access_token":"ZZZZ",
  "token_type":"bearer",
  "expires_in":86400,
}

Make new requests setting the header
Authorization: "Bearer ZZZZ"
```

While OAuth allows you to use an external server to retrieve the access token, that's not strictly required. It can be the same server as the rest. This is useful for this last flow, where the ability to log in with an external provider such as Facebook or Google is not as useful. Our example system will use the Client Credentials flow.

Self-encoded tokens

The returned tokens from the authorization server can contain sufficient information such that no external check with the authorizer is required.

As we've seen, including the user information in the token is important to determine who the user is. If not, we will end with a request that is capable of doing the work, but without information on behalf of who.

To do so, the token is typically encoded in a **JSON Web Token** (**JWT**). A JWT is a standard that encodes a JSON object in a URL-safe sequence of characters.

A JWT has the following elements:

- A header. This contains information on how the token is encoded.
- A payload. The body of the token. Some of the fields in this object, called claims, are standard, but it can allocate custom claims as well. Standard claims are not required and can describe elements such as the issuer (`iss`), or the expiration time of the token as Unix Epoch (`exp`).

- A signature. This verifies that the token was generated by the proper source. This uses different algorithms, based on the information in the header.

In general, a JWT is encoded, but it's not encrypted. A standard JWT library will decode its parts and verify that the signature is correct.

You can test the different fields and systems in the interactive tool: `https://jwt.io/`.

For example, to generate a token using `pyjwt` (`https://pypi.org/project/PyJWT/`), you'll need to install PyJWT using pip if not previously installed:

```
$ pip install PyJWT
```

Then, while opening a Python interpreter, to create a token with a payload with a user ID and an HS256 algorithm to sign it with the `"secret"` secret, you use the following code:

```
>>> import jwt
>>> token = jwt.encode({"user_id": "1234"}, "secret",
algorithm="HS256")
>>> token
'eyJ0eXAiOiJKV1QiLCJhbGciOiJIUzI1NiJ9.eyJ1c2VyX2lkIjoiMTIzNCJ9.
vFn0prsLvRu00Kgy6M8s6S2Ddnuvz-FgtQ7nWz6NoC0'
```

The JWT token can then be decoded and the payload extracted. If the secret is incorrect, it will produce an error:

```
>>> jwt.decode(token,"secret", algorithms=['HS256'])
{'user_id': '1234'}
>>> jwt.decode(token,"badsecret", algorithms=['HS256'])
Traceback (most recent call last):
 …
  jwt.exceptions.InvalidSignatureError: Signature verification failed
```

The algorithm to be used is stored in the headers, but it's a good idea, for reasons of security, to only validate the token with the expected algorithm and not rely on the header. In the past, there have been some security problems with certain JWT implementations and forgery of the tokens, as you can read here: `https://www.chosenplaintext.ca/2015/03/31/jwt-algorithm-confusion.html`.

The most interesting algorithms, though, are not symmetrical ones like `HS256`, where the same value is added for encoding and decoding, but public-private keys like RSA-256 (`RS256`). This allows the token to be encoded with the private key and verified with the public key.

This schema is very common, as the public key can be distributed widely, but only the proper authorizer who has the private key can be the source of the tokens.

Including the payload information that can be used to identify the user allows authentication of the requests using just the information in the payload, once verified, as we discussed earlier.

Versioning the API

Interfaces are rarely created fully formed from scratch. They are constantly being tweaked, with new features added, and bugs or inconsistencies fixed. To better communicate these changes, it's useful to create some sort of versioning to transmit this information.

Why versioning?

The main advantage of versioning is to shape the conversation about what things are included when. This can be bug fixes, new features, or even newly introduced bugs.

If we know that the current interface released is version `v1.2.3`, and we are about to release version `v1.2.4`, which fixes bug X, we can talk about it more easily, as well as creating release notes informing users of that fact.

Internal versus external versioning

There are two kinds of versions that can get a bit confused. One is the internal version, which is something that makes sense for the developers of a project. This is normally related to the version of the software, usually with some help from version control, such as Git.

This version is very detailed and can cover very small changes, including small bug fixes. The aim of it is to be able to detect even minimal changes between software to allow the detection of bugs or the introduction of code.

The other is the external version. The external version is the version that people using the external service are going to be able to perceive. While this can be as detailed as the internal one, that is normally not that helpful to users and can provide a confusing message.

This largely depends on the kind of system and who their expected users are. A highly technical user will appreciate the extra details, but a more casual one will not.

For example, an internal version may distinguish between two different bug fixes, as this is useful to replicate. An externally communicated version can combine them both in "multiple bug fixes and improvements."

Another good example of when it's useful to make a difference is when the interface changes massively. For example, a brand-new revamp of the look and feel of a site could use "Version 2 interface," but this can happen over multiple internal new versions, to be tested internally or by a selected group (for example, beta testers). Finally, when the "Version 2 interface" is ready, it can be activated for all users.

One way of describing the external version could be to call it a "marketing version."

Note that here we are avoiding the term "release version" as it could be misleading. This version is only used to communicate information externally.

This version will be more dependent on marketing efforts than technical implementation.

Semantic versioning

A common pattern for defining versions is to use semantic versioning. Semantic versioning describes a method with three increasing integers that carry different meanings, in descending order of incompatibility:

```
vX.Y.Z
```

X is called the **major** version. Any change in the major version will mean backward-incompatible changes.

Y is the **minor** version. Minor changes may add new features, but any change will be backward compatible.

Z is the **patch** version. It will only make small changes such as bug fixes and security patches, but it doesn't change the interface itself.

The `v` at the start is optional but helps to indicate that it's a version number.

This means that software designed to work with `v1.2.15` will work with versions `v1.2.35` and `v1.3.5`, but it won't work with version `v2.1.3` or version `v1.1.4`. It may work with version `v1.2.14`, but it may have some bug that was corrected later.

Sometimes, extra details can be added to describe interfaces that are not ready, for example, `v1.2.3-rc1` (release candidate) or `v1.2.3-dev0` (development version).

Normally, before the software is ready for release, the major number is set to zero (for example, `v0.1.3`), making version `v1.0.0` the first one to be publicly available.

This semantic versioning is very easy to understand and gives good information about changes. It is widely used, but it has some problems in certain cases:

- Strictly adopting the major version for systems that don't have clear backward compatibility can be difficult. This was the reason why the Linux kernel stopped using proper semantic versioning, because they will never update the major version, as every single release needed to be backward compatible. In that case, a major version can be frozen for years and years and stops being a useful reference. In the Linux kernel, that happened with version 2.6.X, which remained for 8 years until version 3.0 was released in 2011 without any backward-incompatible change.
- Semantic versioning requires a pretty strict definition of the interface. If the interface changes often with new features, as happens typically with online services, the minor version increases quickly, and the patch version is of almost no use.

For online services, the combination of both will make only a single number useful, which is not a great use of it. Semantic versioning works better for cases that require multiple API versions working at the same time, for example:

- The API is very stable and changes very rarely, though there are regular security updates. Every couple of years, there's a major update. A good example is databases, such as MySQL. Operative systems are another example.

- The API belongs to a software library that can be used by multiple supported environments; for example, a Python library compatible with Python 2 for version v4 and Python 3 for v5. This can allow several versions to be kept alive if required.

If the system effectively has a single version running at the same time, it is better to not add the extra effort to keep proper semantic versioning in place as the effort is not worth the reward in terms of the kind of investment required.

Simple versioning

Instead of doing strict semantic versioning, a simplified version can be done instead. This won't carry the same kind of meaning, but it will be a constantly increasing counter. This will work to coordinate teams, although it won't require the same kind of commitment.

This is the same idea as the build number that can be created automatically by compilers, an increasing number to distinguish one version from another and work as a reference. However, a plain build number can be a bit dry to use.

It is better to use a similar structure to semantic versioning, as it will be understandable by everyone; but instead of using it with specific rules, it is looser than that:

- Normally, for a new version, increase the patch version.
- If either the patch version gets too high (in other words, 100, 10, or another arbitrary number), increase the minor version and set the patch version to zero.
- Alternatively, if there's any special milestone for the project, as defined by the people working on it, increase the minor number earlier.
- Do the same with the major version number.

This will allow the numbers to be increased in a consistent way without worrying too much about meaning.

This structure works very well for things like online cloud services, which, in essence, require an increasing counter, as they have a single version deployed at the same time. In this case, the most important use of the version is internal usage and won't require the maintenance that strict semantic versioning requires.

Frontend and backend

The usual way of dividing different services is by talking about the "frontend" and the "backend." They describe the layers of software, where the layer closer to the end user is the frontend, and the one behind is the backend.

Traditionally, the frontend is the layer that takes care of the presentation layer, next to the user, and the backend is the data access layer, which serves the business logic. In a client-server architecture, the client is the frontend and the server is the backend:

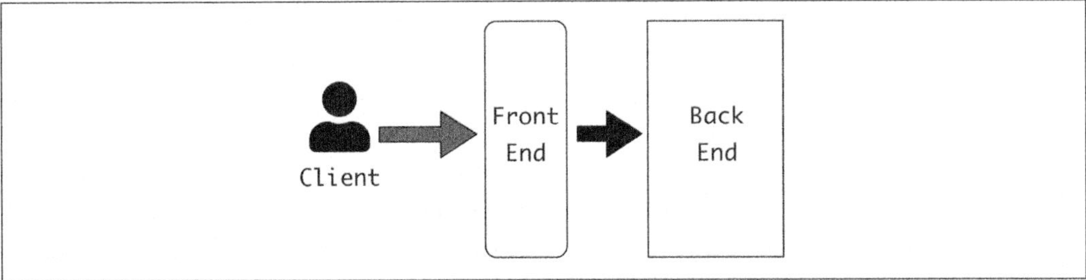

Figure 2.4: Client-Server architecture

As architectures grow more complex, these terms become somewhat polysemic, and they are usually understood depending on the context. While *frontend* is almost always understood as the user interface directly, *backend* can be applied to multiple layers, meaning the next layer that gives support to whatever system is being discussed. For example, in a cloud application, the web application may use a database such as MySQL as the storage backend, or in-memory storage such as Redis as the cache backend.

The general approach for the frontend and backend is quite different.

The frontend focuses on the user experience, so the most important elements are usability, pleasing design, responsiveness, and so on. A lot of that requires an eye for the "final look" and how to make things easy to use. Frontend code is executed in the final user, so compatibility between different types of hardware can be important. At the same time, it distributes the load, so performance is most important from the point of view of the user interface.

The backend focuses more on stability. Here, the hardware is under strict control, but the load is not distributed, making performance important in terms of controlling the total resources used. Modifying the backend is also easier, as changing it once changes it for all the users at the same time. But it's riskier, as a problem here may affect every single user. This environment primes more to focus on solid engineering practices and replicability.

The term full stack engineer is commonly used to describe someone who is comfortable doing both kinds of work. While this can work in certain aspects, it's actually quite difficult to find someone who is equally comfortable or who is inclined to work on both elements in the longer term.

Most engineers will naturally tend toward one of the sides, and most companies will have different teams working on both aspects. In a certain way, the personality traits for each work are different, with frontend work requiring more of an eye for design, and backend users being comfortable with stability and reliability practices.

In general, some common technologies used for the frontend are as follows:

- HTML and associated technologies such as CSS
- JavaScript and libraries or frameworks to add interactivity, such as jQuery or React
- Design tools

Backend technologies, as they are under more direct control, can be more varied, for example:

- Multiple programming languages, either scripting languages such as Python, PHP, Ruby, or even JavaScript using Node.js, or compiled languages such as Java or C#. They can even be mixed, making different elements in different languages.
- Databases, either relational databases such as MySQL or PostgreSQL, or non-relational ones such as MongoDB, Riak, or Cassandra.
- Web servers, such as Nginx or Apache.
- Scalability and high-availability tools, such as load balancers.
- Infrastructure and cloud technologies, such as AWS services.
- Container-related tech, like Docker or Kubernetes.

The frontend will make use of interfaces defined by the backend to present the actions in a user-friendly way. There can be several frontends for the same backend, a typical example being multiple smartphone interfaces for different platforms, but that use the same API to communicate with the backend.

Keep in mind that frontend and backend are conceptual divisions, but they don't necessarily need to be divided into different processes or repositories. A common case where the frontend and backend live together are web frameworks such as Ruby on Rails or Django, where you can define the frontend HTML interface at the same time as the backend controllers that handle the data access and business logic. In this case, the HTML code is served directly from the same process that performs access to the data. This process separates the concerns using the Model View Controller structure.

Model View Controller structure

The Model View Controller, or MVC, is a design that separates the logic of a program into three distinct components.

> The Model View Controller pattern started very early in the design of graphic user interfaces and has been used in that area since the first full graphic interactive interfaces in the 80s. In the 90s, it started being introduced as a way of handling web applications.

- This structure is really successful as it creates a clear separation of concepts:
- The Model manages the data
- The Controller accepts input from the user and transforms it into the manipulation of the model
- The View represents the information for the user to understand

In essence, the Model is the core of the system, as it deals with the manipulation of the data. The Controller represents the input, and the View represents the output of the operations.

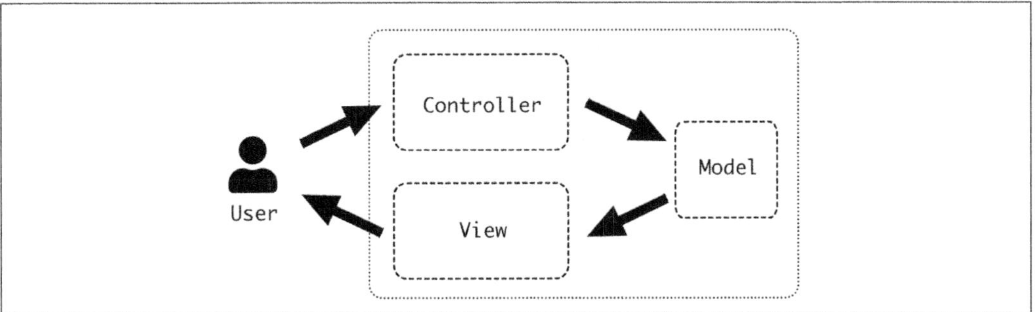

Figure 2.5: The Model View Controller pattern

The MVC structure can be considered at different levels, and it can be regarded as fractal. If several elements interact, they can have their own MVC structure, and the model part of a system can talk to a backend that provides information.

The MVC pattern can be implemented in different ways. For example, Django claims it is a Model View *Template*, as the controller is more the framework itself. However, these are minor details that don't contradict the general design.

The Model is arguably the most important element of the three as it's the core part of it. It contains the data access, but also the business logic. A rich Model component works as a way of abstracting the logic of the application from the input and output.

Commonly, some of the barriers between controllers get a bit blurry. Different inputs may be dealt with in the Controller, producing different calls to the Model. At the same time, the output can be tweaked in the Controller before being passed to the view. While it's always difficult to enforce clear, strict boundaries, it's good to keep in mind what the main objective of each component is so as to provide clarity.

HTML interfaces

While the strict definition of APIs works for interfaces that are designed to be accessed by other programs, it's good to spend a bit of time talking about the basics of how to create a successful human interface. For this purpose, we will talk mainly about HTML interfaces, aimed at being used by the end user in a browser.

Most of the concepts that we will deal with apply to other kinds of human interfaces, such as GUIs or mobile applications.

HTML technologies are highly related to RESTful ones because they were developed in parallel during the early days of the internet. Typically, they are presented intertwined in modern web applications.

Traditional HTML interfaces

The way traditional web interfaces work is through HTTP requests, only using the `GET` and `POST` methods. `GET` retrieves a page from the server, while `POST` is paired with some form that submits data to the server.

This was a prerequisite, as browsers only implemented these methods. While, nowadays, most modern browsers can use all HTTP methods in requests, it's still a common requirement to allow compatibility with older browsers.

While this is certainly more restrictive than all the available options, it can work well for simple website interfaces.

For example, a blog is read way more often than is written, so readers make use of a lot of `GET` requests to get the information, and perhaps some `POST` requests to send back some comments. The need to remove or change a comment was traditionally small, although it can be allocated with other URLs where `POST` is used.

Note that browsers will ask you before retrying a `POST` request as they are not idempotent.

An HTML interface doesn't work in the same way as a RESTful interface because of these limitations, but it can also improve with a design that takes the abstractions and resources approach in mind.

For example, some common abstractions for a blog are as follows:

- Each post, with associated comments
- A main page with the latest posts
- A search page that can return posts that contain a certain word or tag

This is very similar to the interface in resources, where only the two resources of "comment" and "post,", which will be separated in a RESTful way, will be joined in the same concept.

The main limitation of traditional HTML interfaces is that every change needs to refresh the whole page. For simple applications like a blog, this can work quite well, but more complex applications may require a more dynamic approach.

Dynamic pages

To add interactivity to the browser, we can add some JavaScript code that will perform actions to change the page directly on the browser representation; for example, selecting the color of the interface from a drop-down selector.

This is called manipulating the **Document Object Model** (**DOM**), which contains the representation of the document as defined by the HTML and possibly the CSS. JavaScript can access this representation and change it by editing any parameters or even adding or removing elements.

From JavaScript, independent HTTP requests can also be done, so we can use that to make specific calls to retrieve details that can be added to improve the experience of the user.

For example, for a form to input an address, a dropdown may select the country. Once selected, a call to the server will retrieve the proper regions to incorporate the input. If the user selects **United States**, the list of all states will be retrieved and be available in the next dropdown. If the user selects **Canada**, the list of territories and provinces will be used instead:

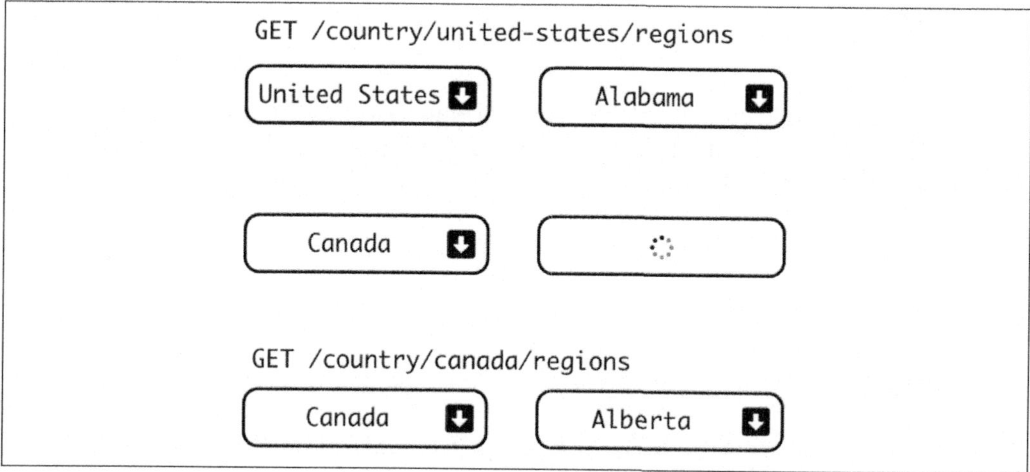

Figure 2.5: Improving user experience with appropriate dropdowns

Another example, that reverses the interface somewhat, could be to use the ZIP code to determine the state automatically.

There is actually a service to retrieve this information called `https://zippopotam.us/`. It can be called and returns not only the state but further information, in JSON format.

These kinds of calls are called **Asynchronous JavaScript And XML** (**AJAX**). Although the name mentions XML, it's not required, and any format can be retrieved. At the moment, it is very common to use JSON or even plain text. One possibility is to use HTML, so an area of the page can be replaced with snippets that come from the server:

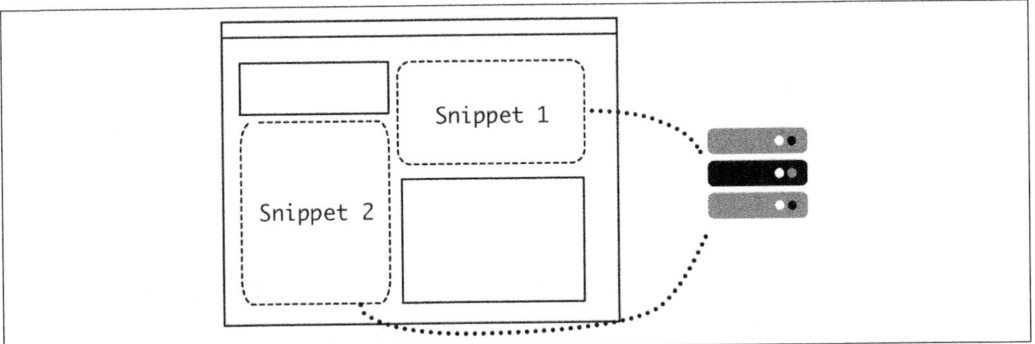

Figure 2.6: Using HTML to replace areas of the page

Raw HTML, although somewhat inelegant, can be effective, so it's very common to use a RESTful API returning JSON to retrieve the expected data for these small elements and then modify the DOM with it through JavaScript code. Given that the objective of this API is not to replace the HTML interface in its entirety, but complement it, this RESTful API will likely be incomplete. It won't be possible to create a full experience using only these RESTful calls.

Other applications go directly to the point of creating an API-first approach and create the browser experience from there.

Single-page apps

The idea behind a single-page app is easy. Let's open a single HTML page and change its content dynamically. If there's any new data to be required, it will be accessed through a specific (typically RESTful) API.

This completely detaches the human interface, understood as the elements that have the responsibility of displaying the information to a human, from the service. The service serves a RESTful API exclusively, without worrying about the representation of the data.

This kind of approach is sometimes called API-first as it designs a system from the API to the representation, instead of creating it the other way around, which is the natural way in which it is created in an organic service.

Although there are specific frameworks and tools designed with this objective in mind, such as React or AngularJS, there are two main challenges with this kind of approach:

- The technical skill required to create a successful human interface on a single page is quite high, even with the help of tools. Any non-trivial representation of a valid interface will require keeping a lot of state and dealing with multiple calls. This is prone to have errors that compromise the stability of the page. The traditional approach for browser pages works with independent pages that limit the scope of each step, which is easier to handle.

Keep in mind that there are interface expectations carried by the browser that can be difficult to avoid or replace, for example, hitting the back button.

- The need to design and prepare the API beforehand can result in a slow start for the project. It requires more planification and upfront commitment, even if both sides are developed in parallel, which also has its challenges.

These issues ensure that this approach is not usually done for new applications starting from scratch. However, if the application started with another kind of user interface, like a smartphone application, it could leverage the already existing REST API to generate an HTML interface that replicates the functionality.

The main advantage of this approach is detaching the application from the user interface. Where an application starts its development as a small project with a regular HTML interface, the risk is that any other user interface will tend to conform to the HTML interface. This can quickly add up to a lot of technical debt and compromise the design of the API, as the abstractions that are used will likely be derived from the existing interface, instead of the most adequate ones.

A whole API-first approach greatly separates the interface, so creating a new interface is as easy to use as the already existing API. For applications that require multiple interfaces, such as an HTML interface, but also different smartphones applications for iOS and Android, that could be a good solution.

A single-page application can also be quite innovative in terms of presenting a full interface. This can create rich and complex interfaces that deviate from what could be understood as a "web page," as in the case of a game or an interactive application.

Hybrid approach

Going all-in with a single-page application, as we've seen, can be quite challenging. To a certain degree, it is using a browser to overwrite its usage.

That's why normally the design doesn't go that far and creates a more traditional web interface. This interface is still recognizable as a web application but relies heavily on JavaScript to obtain information using a RESTful interface. This can happen as a natural step to migrating from a traditional HTML interface to a single-page app, but it may also be a conscious decision.

This approach combines the previous two. On the one hand, it still requires an HTML interface for the general approach of the interface, with clear pages to navigate. On the other, it creates a RESTful API that fills most of the information and uses JavaScript to make use of this API.

This approach is similar to the dynamic page one, but there is an important difference, which is the intention to create a coherent API that can be used without being totally tailored to the HTML interface. That changes the approach significantly.

In practice, this tends to create a less complete RESTful API, as some of the elements may be added directly to the HTML part of it. But, at the same time, it allows the iterative migration of elements into the API, starting with certain elements, but adding more as time goes by. This stage is very flexible.

Designing the API for the example

As we described in the first chapter, *General Overview of the Example*, we need to set the definition for the different interfaces that we will be working on in the example. Remember that the example is a microblogging application that will allow users to write their own text microposts so that they are available for others to read.

There are two main interfaces in the example:

- An HTML interface for allowing users to interact with the service using a browser
- A RESTful interface for allowing the creation of other clients like a smartphone app

In this chapter, we will describe the design of the second interface. We will start with a description of the different basic definitions and resources that we will use:

- **User**: A representation of the user of the application. It will be defined by a username and a password to be able to login.
- **Micropost**: A small text of up to 255 characters posted by a *User*. A *Micropost* can be optionally addressed to a *User*. It has also the time it was created.
- **Collection**: The display of *Microposts* from a *User*.
- **Follower**: A *User* can follow another *User*.
- **Timeline**: An ordered list of the *Microposts* by the followed *Users*.
- **Search**: Allow a search by *User* or by text contained in *Microposts*.

We can define these elements as resources in a RESTful way, in the way introduced earlier in the chapter, first as a quick description of the URIs:

```
POST   /api/token
DELETE /api/token
GET    /api/user/<username>
GET    /api/user/<username>/collection
POST   /api/user/<username>/collection
GET    /api/user/<username>/collection/<micropost_id>
PUT    /api/user/<username>/collection/<micropost_id>
PATCH  /api/user/<username>/collection/<micropost_id>
DELETE /api/user/<username>/collection/<micropost_id>
GET    /api/user/<username>/timeline
GET    /api/user/<username>/following
POST   /api/user/<username>/following
DELETE /api/user/<username>/following/<username>
GET    /api/user/<username>/followers
GET    /api/search
```

Note that we added `POST` and `DELETE` resources for `/token` to deal with login and logout.

Once this brief design is complete, we can flesh out the definition of each endpoint.

Endpoints

We will describe all the API endpoints in a bit more detail, following the template introduced previously in this chapter.

Login:

- *Description*: Using the proper authentication credentials, return a valid access token. The token needs to be included in the requests as the `Authorization` header.
- *Resource URI*: `/api/token`
- *Method*: `POST`
- *Request body*:

```
{
 "grant_type": "authorization_code"
    "client_id": <client id>,
    "client_secret": <client secret>
}
```

- *Return body*:

```
{
  "access_token": <access token>,
  "token_type":"bearer",
  "expires_in":86400,
}
```

- *Errors*:

```
400 Bad Request Incorrect body.
400 Bad Request Bad credentials.
```

Logout:

- *Description*: Invalidate the bearer token. If successful, it will return a `204 No Content` error.
- *Resource URI*: `/api/token`
- *Method*: `DELETE`
- *Headers*: `Authentication: Bearer: <token>`
- *Errors*:

```
401 Unauthorized Trying to access this URI without being
properly authenticated.
```

Retrieve user:

- *Description*: Returns the username resource.
- *Resource URI*: `/api/users/<username>`
- *Method*: `GET`
- *Headers*: `Authentication: Bearer: <token>`
- *Query Parameters*:

```
size Page size.
page Page number.
```

- *Return body*:

```
{
    "username": <username>,
    "collection": /users/<username>/collection,
}
```

- *Errors*:

```
401 Unauthorized Trying to access this URI without being
authenticated.
404 Not Found Username does not exist.
```

Retrieve user's collection:

- *Description*: Returns the collection of all microposts from a user, in paginated form.
- *Resource URI*: `/api/users/<username>/collection`
- *Method*: `GET`
- *Headers*: `Authentication: Bearer: <token>`
- *Return body*:

```
{
    "next": <next page or null>,
    "previous": <previous page or null>,
    "result": [
        {
            "id": <micropost id>,
            "href": <micropost url>,
            "user": <user url>,
            "text": <Micropost text>,
```

```
            "timestamp": <timestamp for micropost in ISO 8601>
        },
        ...
    ]
}
```

- *Errors*:

```
401 Unauthorized Trying to access this URI without being
authenticated.
404 Not Found Username does not exist.
```

Create new micropost:

- *Description*: Create a new micropost.
- *Resource URI*: `/api/users/<username>/collection`
- *Method*: `POST`
- *Headers*: `Authentication: Bearer: <token>`
- *Request body*:

```
{
    "text": <Micropost text>,
    "referenced": <optional username of referenced user>
}
```

- *Errors*:

```
400 Bad Request Incorrect body.
400 Bad Request Invalid text (for example, more than 255
characters).
400 Bad Request Referenced user not found.
401 Unauthorized Trying to access this URI without being
authenticated.
403 Forbidden Trying to create a micropost of a different user
to the one logged in.
```

Retrieve micropost:

- *Description*: Returns a single micropost.
- *Resource URI*: `/api/users/<username>/collection/<micropost_id>`
- *Method*: `GET`
- *Headers*: `Authentication: Bearer: <token>`

- *Return body*:

```
{
    "id": <micropost id>,
    "href": <micropost url>,
    "user": <user url>,
    "text": <Micropost text>,
    "timestamp": <timestamp for micropost in ISO 8601>,
    "referenced": <optional username of referenced user>
}
```

- *Errors*:

```
401 Unauthorized Trying to access this URI without being
authenticated.
404 Not Found Username does not exist.
404 Not Found Micropost ID does not exist.
```

Update micropost:

- *Description*: Update the text for a micropost.
- *Resource URI*: `/api/users/<username>/collection/<micropost_id>`
- *Method*: `PUT, PATCH`
- *Headers*: `Authentication: Bearer: <token>`
- *Request body*:

```
{
    "text": <Micropost text>,
    "referenced": <optional username of referenced user>
}
```

- *Errors*:

```
400 Bad Request Incorrect body.
400 Bad Request Invalid text (for example, more than 255
characters).
400 Bad Request Referenced user not found.
401 Unauthorized Trying to access this URI without being
authenticated.
403 Forbidden Trying to update a micropost of a different user
to the one logged in.
404 Not Found Username does not exist.
404 Not Found Micropost ID does not exist.
```

Delete micropost:

- *Description*: Delete a micropost. If successful, it will return a `204 No Content` error.
- *Resource URI*: `/api/users/<username>/collection/<micropost_id>`
- *Method*: `DELETE`
- *Headers*: `Authentication: Bearer: <token>`
- *Errors*:

```
401 Unauthorized Trying to access this URI without being
authenticated.
403 Forbidden Trying to delete a micropost of a different user
to the one logged in.
404 Not Found Username does not exist.
404 Not Found Micropost ID does not exist.
```

Retrieve user's timeline:

- *Description*: Returns the collection of all microposts from the timeline of a user, in paginated form. The microposts will be returned by timestamp order, with the oldest being returned first.
- *Resource URI*: `/api/users/<username>/timeline`
- *Method*: `GET`
- *Headers*: `Authentication: Bearer: <token>`
- *Return body*:

```
{
    "next": <next page or null>,
    "previous": <previous page or null>,
    "result": [
        {
            "id": <micropost id>,
            "href": <micropost url>,
            "user": <user url>,
            "text": <Micropost text>,
            "timestamp": <timestamp for micropost in ISO 8601>,
            "referenced": <optional username of referenced user>
        },
        ...
    ]
}
```

- *Errors*:

```
401 Unauthorized Trying to access this URI without being
authenticated.
404 Not Found Username does not exist.
```

Retrieve the users a user is following:

- *Description*: Returns a collection of all users that the selected user is following.
- *Resource URI*: `/api/users/<username>/following`
- *Method*: `GET`
- *Headers*: `Authentication: Bearer: <token>`
- *Return body*:

```
{
    "next": <next page or null>,
    "previous": <previous page or null>,
    "result": [
        {
            "username": <username>,
            "collection": /users/<username>/collection,
        },
        ...
    ]
}
```

- *Errors*:

```
401 Unauthorized Trying to access this URI without being
authenticated.
404 Not Found Username does not exist.
```

Follow a user:

- *Description*: Causes the selected user to follow a different user.
- *Resource URI*: `/api/users/<username>/following`
- *Method*: `POST`
- *Headers*: `Authentication: Bearer: <token>`
- *Request body*:

```
{
    "username": <username>
}
```

- *Errors*:

```
400 Bad Request The username to follow is incorrect or does not
exist.
400 Bad Request Bad body.
401 Unauthorized Trying to access this URI without being
authenticated.
404 Not Found Username does not exist.
```

Stop following a user:

- *Description*: Stops following a user. If successful, it will return a `204 No Content` error.
- *Resource URI*: `/api/users/<username>/following/<username>`
- *Method*: `DELETE`
- *Headers*: `Authentication: Bearer: <token>`
- *Errors*:

```
401 Unauthorized Trying to access this URI without being
authenticated.
403 Forbidden Trying to stop following a user who is not the
authenticated one.
404 Not Found Username to stop following does not exist.
```

Retrieve a user's followers:

- *Description*: Returns, in paginated form, all followers of this user.
- *Resource URI*: `/api/users/<username>/followers`
- *Method*: `GET`
- *Headers*:`Authentication: Bearer: <token>`
- *Return body*:

```
{
    "next": <next page or null>,
    "previous": <previous page or null>,
    "result": [
        {
            "username": <username>,
            "collection": /users/<username>/collection,
        },
        ...
    ]
}
```

- *Errors*:

```
401 Unauthorized Trying to access this URI without being
authenticated.
404 Not Found Username does not exist.
```

Search microposts:

- *Description*: Returns, in paginated form, microposts that fulfill the search query.
- *Resource URI*: `/api/search`
- *Method*: `GET`
- *Headers*: `Authentication: Bearer: <token>`
- *Query parameters*:

```
username: Optional username to search. Partial matches will be
returned.
text: Mandatory text to search, with a minimum of three
characters. Partial matches will be returned.
```

- *Return body*:

```
{
    "next": <next page or null>,
    "previous": <previous page or null>,
    "result": [
        {
            "id": <micropost id>,
            "href": <micropost url>,
            "user": <user url>,
            "text": <Micropost text>,
            "timestamp": <timestamp for micropost in ISO 8601>,
            "referenced": <optional username of referenced user>
        },
    ]
}
```

- *Errors*:

```
400 Bad Request No mandatory query parameters.
400 Bad Request Incorrect value in query parameters.
401 Unauthorized Trying to access this URI without being
authenticated.
```

Review of the design and implementation

This two-step approach of presenting and designing a new API enables you to quickly see whether something is out of place as regards the design. Then, it can be iterated over until fixed. The next step is to start with the implementation, as we will see in forthcoming chapters.

Summary

In this chapter, we described how the basics of API design are to create a set of useful abstractions that allow users to perform actions without having to care about the internal details. This led to describing how to define an API with resources and actions.

This definition of an API has evolved to cover RESTful interfaces that follow certain properties that make them very interesting for web server design. We described a bunch of useful standards and techniques when designing RESTful interfaces to create consistent and complete interfaces, including the OpenAPI tools. We went through authentication details as it's a very important element for APIs.

Remember that extra care should be advised when securing APIs that have external usage. We went through some general ideas and common strategies, but note that this book does not focus on security. This is a critical aspect of the design of any API and should be done carefully.

We covered the ideas behind versioning and how to create a proper versioning schema that's tailored to the specific use case for the API. We also covered the differences between the frontend and the backend and how this can be generalized. We also covered the MVC pattern, which is a very common way to structure software.

We described the different options for HTML interfaces to provide a complete overview of the different interfaces in web services. We covered different options in terms of how an HTML service can be constructed and interact with other APIs.

Finally, we presented the design for the RESTful interface for the example, while reviewing the general design and endpoints.

Another critical element of design is the data structure. We will cover this next.

Join our book's Discord space

Join the book's Discord workspace for a monthly *Ask me Anything* session with the author: `https://packt.link/PythonArchitechture`

3
Data Modeling

The core of any application is its data. At the very root of any computer application, it's a system designed to deal with information, receiving it, transforming it, and returning either the same information or insightful elements extracted from it. The stored data is a crucial part of this cycle, as it allows you to use information that has been communicated before.

In this chapter, we will talk about how we can model the stored data from our application and what the different options are to store and structure the data to be persisted.

We will start by describing the different database options that are available, which are critical to understanding their different applications, but we will mostly focus, during the chapter, on relational databases, as they are the most common type. We will describe the concept of a transaction to ensure that different changes are applied in one go.

We will describe different ways that we can increase the scope of a relational database by using multiple servers, and what the use cases for each option are.

After that, we will describe different alternatives when designing a schema to ensure that our data is structured in the best possible way. We will discuss how to enable fast access to data through the usage of indices.

In this chapter, we'll cover the following topics:

- Types of databases
- Database transactions

- Distributed relational databases
- Schema design
- Data indexing

Let's start with an introduction to the different databases out there.

Types of databases

All the persistent data from an application should live in a database. As we've discussed, data is the most critical aspect of any application, and proper handling of it is critical to ensure the viability of the project.

Technically, databases are collections of data themselves and are handled by the **database management system** (**DBMS**), the software that allows the input and output of data. Normally, the word "database" is used for both the collection and the management system, depending on the context. Most DBMSes will allow access to multiple databases of the same kind, without being able to cross data between them, to allow logical separation of the data.

Databases have been a critical tool for most of the time software systems have been available. They create an abstraction layer that allows accessing data without having to worry too much about how the data is structured by the hardware. Most databases allow the structure of the data to be defined without having to worry about how that's implemented behind the curtains.

As we saw in *Chapter 2*, *API Design*, this abstraction is not perfect and sometimes we will have to understand the internals of databases to improve the performance or do things in "the proper way."

DBMSes are among the most invested and mature projects in software. Each DBMS has its own quirks, to the point where there's a specific job role for a "database expert": the **Database Administrator (DBA)**.

The DBA role was quite popular for a long time and required highly specialized engineers, to the point of DBAs specializing in a single specific DBMS. The DBA will act as the expert in the database, both in knowing how to access it and ensuring that any changes done to it work adequately. They normally are the only ones allowed to perform changes or maintenance tasks in the database.

Performance improvements in hardware and software and external tools to handle database complexity have made this role less common, though it's still in use by some organizations. To a certain degree, the architect role overtakes parts of this role, though with more of a supervising role and less of a gatekeeping one.

There are multiple DBMSes available on the market, with a good selection of open source software that covers most use cases. Roughly speaking, we can divide the existing DBMS alternatives into this non-exhaustive classification:

- **Relational databases**: The default standard in databases. Use SQL query language and have a defined schema. Examples are open source projects like MySQL or PostgreSQL, or commercial ones like Oracle or MS SQL Server.
- **Non-relational databases**: New alternatives to the traditional databases. This is a diverse group with multiple alternatives, and includes very different options like MongoDB, Riak, or Cassandra.
- **Small databases**: These databases are aimed to be embedded into the system. The most famous example is SQLite.

Let's take a more in-depth look at them.

Relational databases

These are the most common databases and the first idea that comes to mind when talking about databases. The relational model for databases was developed in the 1970s, and it's based on creating a series of tables that can be related to each other. Since the 1980s, they have become incredibly popular.

Each defined table has a number of fields or columns that are fixed and data is described as records or rows. Tables are theoretically infinite, so more and more rows can be added. One of the columns is defined as the *primary key* and uniquely describes the row. Therefore, it needs to be unique.

If there is a value that's unique and descriptive enough, it can be used for the primary key; this is called a *natural key*. Natural keys can also be a combination of fields, though that limits their convenience. When a natural key is not available, an increasing counter can be handled directly by the database to ensure it is unique per row. This is called a *surrogate key*.

The primary key is used to reference that record, when necessary, in other tables. This creates the relation aspect of the database. When a column in a table makes reference to another table, this is called a *foreign key*.

These references can produce one-to-one relationships; one-to-many, when a single row can be referenced in multiple rows in another table; or even many-to-many, which requires an intermediary table to cross over the data.

All this information needs to be described in the schema. The schema describes each table, what the fields and types of each are, as well as the relations between them.

Relations in relational databases are really constraints. That means that a value can't be deleted if it's still referenced somewhere. Relational databases come from a strict mathematical background, though that background's implemented in different degrees of strictness.

It's important to note that defining the schema requires thinking ahead and being aware of the changes that can be made. Defining types before having data also requires keeping in mind possible improvements. While the schema can be changed, it's always a serious operation that, if not taken with proper care, can lead to the database not being available for some time, or, in the worst-case scenario, data can be changed or processed inconsistently.

A query can also be executed that searches for data fulfilling certain conditions. For that, tables can be joined based on their relationships.

Virtually all relational databases are interacted with using Structured Query Language, or SQL. This language has become the standard to work with relational databases and follow the same concepts that we've described here. It describes both how to query the database and how to add or change data contained there.

The most relevant characteristic of SQL is that it is a declarative language. This means that the statements describe the result instead of the procedure to obtain it, as is typical with imperative languages. This abstracts the internal details away from the *how* to focus on the *what*.

Imperative languages describe the control flow and are the most common languages. Examples of imperative languages are Python, JavaScript, C, and Java. Declarative languages are normally restricted to specific domains (Domain-Specific Languages, or DSLs) that allow you to describe the result in simpler terms, while imperative languages are more flexible.

This characteristic makes SQL portable between systems, as the internals of the *how* can be different in different databases. Using a specific relational database and adapting to another is relatively easy.

This is used sometimes to set up a local database for running tests that's different from the final database that will be in place once the system is in production. This is possible in some web frameworks, but it requires some caveats, as complex systems sometimes have to use specific characteristics for a particular database, making it impossible to perform an easy replacement of this kind.

While relational databases are very mature and flexible and are used in very different scenarios, there are two main problems that are difficult to deal with. One is requiring a predefined schema, as we said above. The other, and more serious after a certain size, is dealing with scale. Relational databases are thought to be a central access point that's accessed, and there need to be some techniques to scale once the limit of vertical scaling has been reached.

We will talk about specific techniques to deal with this issue and increase the scalability of relational databases later in this chapter.

Non-relational databases

Non-relational databases are a diverse group of DBMSes that do not fit into the relational paradigm.

Non-relational databases are also called NoSQL, emphasizing the relational nature of the SQL language, standing for either "not SQL" or "Not Only SQL," to be more reflective of adding possibilities and not removing them.

While there have been non-relational databases even before the introduction of relational databases and alongside them, since the 2000s, there has been an introduction or recovery of methods and designs that look to alternative options. Most of them aim to address the two main weak spots in relational databases, their strictness and scalability issues.

They are very varied and have very different structures, but the most common kinds of non-relational systems are the following groups:

- Key-value stores
- Document stores
- Wide-column databases
- Graph databases

Let's describe each of them.

Key-value stores

Key-value stores are arguably the simplest of all databases in terms of functionality. They define a single key that stores a value. The value is totally opaque to the system, not being able to be queried in any way. There's even, in some implementations, no way of querying keys in the system; instead, they need to be an input to any operation.

This is very similar to a hash table or dictionary but on a bigger scale. Cache systems are normally based on this kind of data store.

While the technology is similar, there's an important differentiation between a cache and a database. A cache is a system that stores data already calculated to speed up its retrieval, while a database stores raw data. If the data is not in the cache, it can be retrieved from a different system, but if it's not in the database, either the data is not stored or there has been a big problem.

That's why cache systems tend to store information only in memory and are more resilient to restarts or problems, making them easier to deal with. If a cache is missing, the system works, just slower.

It's very important that information is not ultimately stored in cache systems that are not backed up by proper storage. It's a mistake that sometimes happens inadvertently, for example, with temporal data, but the risk is to get a problem at the wrong time and lose the data, so be aware of it.

The main advantage of this system is, on the one hand, the simplicity of it, allowing the quick storage and retrieval of data. It also allows you to horizontally scale to a great extent. As each key is independent of the rest, they can even be stored in different servers. Redundancy can also be introduced in the system, making multiple copies for each key and value, though this makes the retrieval of information slower, as the multiple copies need to be compared to detect data corruption.

Some examples of key-value databases are **Riak** and **Redis** (if used with durability enabled).

Document stores

Document stores revolve around the concept of a "document," which is similar to a "record" in relational databases. Documents, though, are more flexible, as they don't need to follow a predefined format. They also typically allow embedding more data in subfields, something that relational databases normally don't do, relying instead on creating a relationship and storing that data in a different table.

For example, a document can look like this, here represented as JSON:

```
{
    "id": "ABCDEFG"
    "name": {
        "first": "Sherlock",
        "surname": "Holmes"
    }
    "address": {
        "country": "UK",
        "city": "London",
        "street": "Baker Street",
        "number": "221B",
        "postcode": "NW16XE"
    }
}
```

Documents are normally grouped in collections, which are similar to "tables." Normally documents are retrieved by a unique ID that acts as the primary key, but queries can also be constructed to search fields created in the document.

So, in our case, we could retrieve the key (ID) `ABCDEFG`, like in a key-value store; or make richer queries like "get me all entries in the `detectives` collection whose `address.country` equals `UK`," for example.

Keep in mind that, while it is technically possible to create a collection with documents totally independent and with different formats, in practice, all documents in a collection will follow a somewhat *similar* format, with optional fields or embedded data.

Documents in one collection can be related to documents in another collection by their ID, creating a reference, but normally these databases don't allow you to create join queries. Instead, the application layer should allow you to retrieve this linked information.

In general, documents favor embedding information over creating references. This could lead to denormalizing information, repeating the information in several places. We will talk more about denormalization later in the chapter.

Some examples of document stores are **MongoDB** (`https://www.mongodb.com/`) and **Elasticsearch** (`https://www.elastic.co/elasticsearch/`).

Wide-column databases

Wide-column databases are structured with their data separated by columns. They create tables with certain columns, but they are optional. They also can't natively relate a record in one table with another.

They are a bit more capable of being queried than pure key-value stores but require more upfront design work on what kinds of queries are possible in the system. This is more restrictive than in document-oriented stores where there is more flexibility in doing that after the design is done.

Normally, columns are related and can only be queried in a particular order, meaning that if columns A, B, and C exist, a row can query based on either A, A and B, or A, B, and C, but not just C or B and C, for example.

They are aimed at very big database deployments with high availability and replicated data. Some examples of wide-column databases are **Apache Cassandra** (`https://cassandra.apache.org/`) and Google's **Bigtable** (`https://cloud.google.com/bigtable`).

Graph databases

While the previous non-relational databases are based on giving up the ability to create relationships between elements to gain other features (like scalability or flexibility), graph databases go in the opposite direction. They greatly enhance the relationship aspect of the elements to create complex graphs.

They store objects that are nodes and edges, or relationships between the nodes. Both edges and nodes may have properties to better describe them.

The query capabilities of graph databases are aimed at retrieving information based on relationships. For example, given a list of companies and providers, is there any provider in a supply chain of a specific company that is in a specific country? Up to how many levels? These questions may be easy to answer for the first level in a relational database (obtain the suppliers of the company and their countries), but quite complex and consuming for the third-level relations.

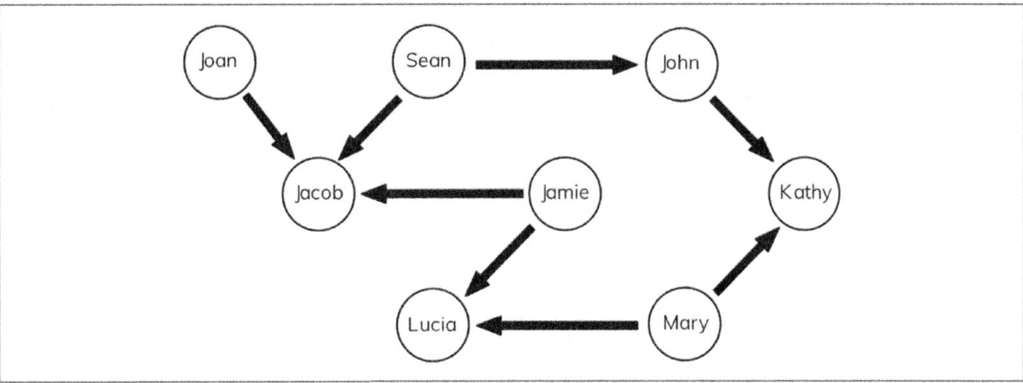

Figure 3.1: Example of data that is typical of graph databases

They are typically used for social graphs, where there are connections between people or organizations. Some examples are **Neo4j** (`https://neo4j.com/`) or **ArangoDB** (`https://www.arangodb.com/`).

Small databases

This group is a bit special compared with the rest. It's composed of database systems that are not differentiated as an independent process, working as an independent client-server structure. Instead, they are embedded into the code of the application, reading directly from the hard drive. They are normally used in simple applications that run as a single process and want to keep the information in a structured way.

A crude, yet effective, way of representing this method is to save information as a JSON object into a file and recover it when required, for example, client settings for a smartphone app. The settings file is loaded when the application starts from memory, then saved if there's any change.

For example, in Python code, this could be represented like this:

```
>>> import json
>>> with open('settings.json') as fp:
...     settings = json.load(fp)
...
>>> settings
{'custom_parameter': 5}
>>> settings['custom_parameter'] = 3
>>> with open('settings.json', 'w') as fp:
...     json.dump(settings, fp)
```

For small amounts of data, this structure may work, but it has the limitation that it's difficult to query. The most complete alternative is SQLite, which is a full-fledged SQL database, but it's embedded into the system, without requiring external calls. The database is stored in a binary file.

SQLite is so popular that it's even supported in a lot of standard libraries, without requiring an external module, for example, in the Python standard library.

```
>>> import sqlite3
>>> con = sqlite3.connect('database.db')
>>> cur = con.cursor()
>>> cur.execute('''CREATE TABLE pens (id INTEGER PRIMARY KEY DESC,
name, color)''')
<sqlite3.Cursor object at 0x10c484c70>
>>> con.commit()
>>> cur.execute('''INSERT INTO pens VALUES (1, 'Waldorf', 'blue')''')
<sqlite3.Cursor object at 0x10c484c70>
>>> con.commit()
>>> cur.execute('SELECT * FROM pens');
<sqlite3.Cursor object at 0x10c484c70>
>>> cur.fetchall()
[(1, 'Waldorf', 'blue')]
```

This module follows the DB-API 2.0 standard, which is the Python standard to connect to databases. It aims to standardize access to different database backends. This makes it easy to create a higher-level module that can access multiple SQL databases and swap them with minimal changes.

You can check the full DB-API 2.0 specification in PEP-249: `https://www.python.org/dev/peps/pep-0249/`.

SQLite implements most of the SQL standard.

Database transactions

Storing data can be a complex operation internally for a database. In some cases, it can include changing the data in a single place, but there are operations that can affect millions of records in a single operation, for example, "update all records created before this timestamp."

How broad and possible these operations are highly depends on the database, but they are very similar to relational databases. In that case, normally there's the concept of a *transaction*.

A transaction is an operation that happens in one go. It either happens or it doesn't, but the database is not left in an inconsistent state in the middle. For example, if the operation described before of "update all records created before this timestamp" can produce an effect where, through an error, only half of the records are changed, then it's not a transaction, but multiple independent operations.

It can happen that there's an error in the middle of a transaction. In that case, it will go back all the way to the start of it, so no record will change.

This characteristic can become a strong requirement for the database in some applications, and it's called *atomicity*. That means the transaction is atomic when it's applied. This characteristic is the main one of the so-called ACID properties.

The other properties are consistency, isolation, and durability. The four properties are, then:

- *Atomicity*, which means that the transaction is applied as one unit. It is either applied completely or not.
- *Consistency*, which means that the transaction is applied taking into account all restrictions that are defined in the database. For example, foreign key constraints are respected, or any stored triggers that modify the data applied.

- *Isolation*, which means that parallel transactions work in the same way that they were run one after the other, ensuring that one transaction is not affecting another. Obviously, the exception is the order in which they are run, which may have an impact.
- *Durability*, which means that, after a transaction is reported as completed, it won't be lost even in the event of a catastrophic failure, like the database process crashing.

These properties are the gold standard to take care of data. It means that the data is safe and consistent.

Most relational databases have the concept of starting a transaction, performing several operations, and then finally committing the transaction so all the changes are applied in one go. If there's a problem, the transaction will fail, reverting to the previous state. A transaction can also be aborted if, during the performance of operations, any problem, like a constraint issue, is detected.

This way of operating allows creating extra verification steps, as inside the transaction, data can still be queried and be validated before finally committing it.

ACID transactions have a cost in terms of performance, and especially in terms of scalability. The need for durability means that data needs to be stored on disk or other permanent support before being returned from the transaction. The requirement for isolation means that each open transaction requires operating in a way that it can't see new updates, which may require temporary data to be stored until the transaction is completed. Consistency also requires checks to ensure that all constraints are fulfilled, which may require complex checks.

Virtually all relational databases are fully ACID compliant, and that has become a defining characteristic of them. In the non-relational world, things are more flexible.

Scaling the database with multiple servers or nodes with these properties proves difficult, though. This system creates distributed transactions, running on multiple servers at the same time. Maintaining full ACID transactions in databases with more than one server is extremely difficult, and has a heavy penalty in terms of performance, because of the extra delay caused by understanding what the other nodes have done and rolling back the transaction if there's a failure in any of them. The problems also increase in a non-linear way, sort of working against the advantages of having multiple servers.

While this is possible, a lot of applications can work around these limitations. We will see some useful patterns.

Distributed relational databases

As we've discussed before, relational databases weren't designed with scalability in mind. They are great for enforcing strong data assurances, including ACID transactions, but their preferred way of operating is through a single server.

This can impose limitations in terms of how big an application can be using relational databases.

It is worth noting that a database server can grow vertically, which means using better hardware. Increasing the capacity of a server or replacing it with a bigger one is an easier solution for high demand than applying some of these techniques, but there's a limit. In any case, please double-check that the expected size is big enough. These days, there are servers in cloud providers that reach 1 terabyte of RAM or more. That's enough to cover a huge number of cases.

Note that these techniques are useful to grow a system after it is up and running, and can be added to most usages of relational databases.

The disadvantage of the ACID properties is *eventual consistency*. Instead of an atomic operation that gets processed in a single go, the system gradually translates to the desired system. Not every part of the system has the same state at the same time. Instead, there are certain delays while this change is propagating in the system. The other big advantage is that we can increase the availability, as it won't depend on a single node to make the change, and any non-available elements will catch up after recovering. Because of the distributed nature of the cluster, this may involve consulting different sources and trying to reach a quorum between them.

It depends greatly on the application you have in mind when considering if loosening some of the ACID properties is worth doing. Critical data, where a delay or data corruption has a higher impact and may not be acceptable, may not be a good fit for a distributed database.

In order to increase the capacity, the first thing is to understand what the data access of the application is.

Primary/replica

A very common case is that the number of reads is much higher than writes. Or, talking in SQL terms, the number of `SELECT` statements is much higher than the `UPDATE` or `DELETE` ones. This is very typical of applications where there's way more access to information than updates to information, for example, a newspaper, where there's a lot of access to read a news article, but not so many new articles comparatively.

A common pattern for this situation is to create a cluster adding one or more read-only copies of the database, and then spread the reads across them, a situation similar to this one:

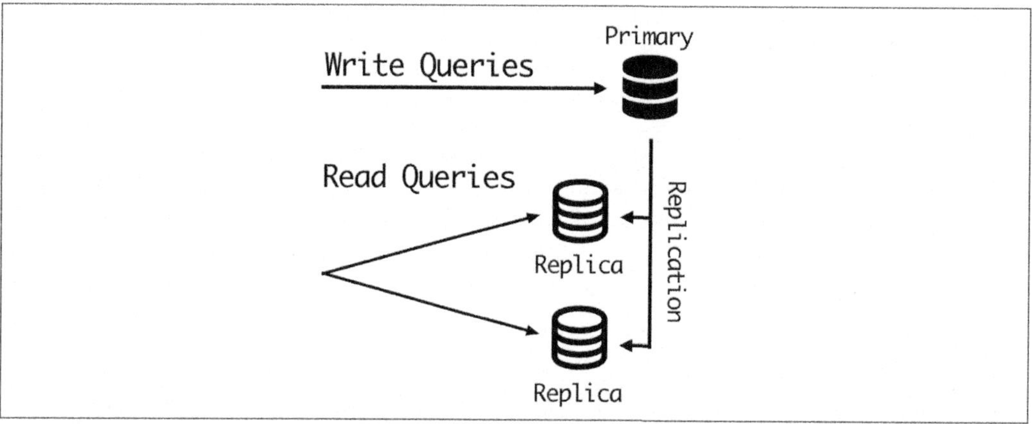

Figure 3.2: Dealing with multiple Read queries

All the writes go to the primary node, and then that gets disseminated to the replica nodes automatically. Because the replicas contain the whole database, and the only write activity comes from the primary, this increases the number of queries that can run at the same time in the system.

This system is natively supported by most relational databases, especially the most common ones, MySQL and PostgreSQL. The write nodes are configured as primary, and the replicas are pointed at the primary to start copying the data. After some time, they'll be up to date and in sync with the primary.

Every new change in the primary will be replicated automatically. This, though, has a delay, called a replication lag. This means that the data just written won't be available to read for some time, typically less than a second.

Replication lag is a good indicator of the wellbeing of the database. If the lag increases over time, it's an indication that the cluster is not capable of handling the level of traffic and requires adjustments. This time will be greatly influenced by the network and general performance of each of the nodes.

An operation to avoid, then, is to write and immediately read the same or related data in an external operation, as this can cause inconsistent results. This can be solved either by keeping the data temporarily, avoiding the need for the query, or by making it possible to address a specific read to the primary node, to ensure that the data is consistent.

These direct reads should be used only when necessary, as they go against the idea of reducing the number of queries to the primary server. That was the reason to set up multiple servers!

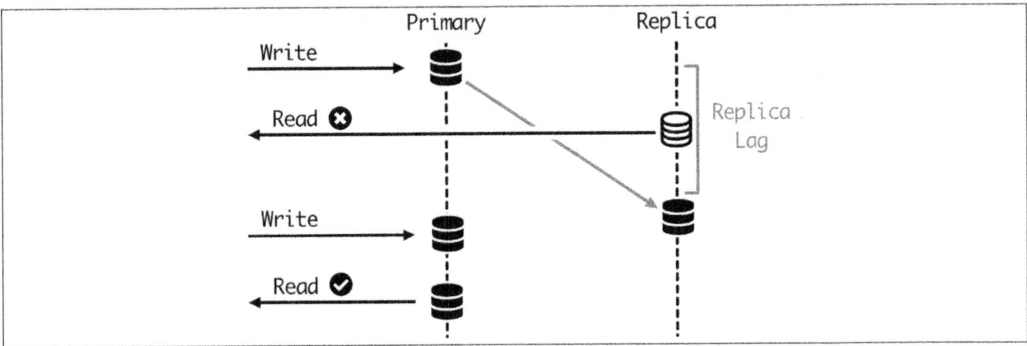

Figure 3.3: A specific Read query on the primary node

This system also allows there to be redundancy of data, as it's always being copied to the replicas. If there's a problem, a replica can be promoted to be the new primary.

A replica server doesn't fulfill exactly the same role as a backup, though it can be used with a similar intent. A replica is intended to perform a quick action and maintain the availability of the system. Backups are easier and cheaper to run and allow you to keep a historical record of the data. Backups can also be located in a very different location than the replica, while a replica requires a good network connection with the primary.

Do not skip doing backups, even if there are replicas available. Backups will add a security layer in case of catastrophic failure.

Note that this way of structuring the database may require adapting the application level to be aware of all the changes and access to different database servers. There are existing tools such as Pgpool (for PostgreSQL) or ProxySQL (for MySQL) that stay in the middle of the path and redirect the queries. The application addresses the queries to the proxies, and then the proxy redirects them based on the configuration. There are cases, like the write and read pattern that we've seen above, that are not covered easily and may require specific changes in the application code. Be sure to understand how these kinds of tools work and run some tests before running them in your application.

A simpler case of this structure is to create offline replicas. These can be created from a backup and not updated from the live system. These replicas can be useful to create queries that don't require up-to-date information, in cases where perhaps a daily snapshot is good enough. They are common in applications like statistical analysis or data warehousing.

Sharding

If the application has a higher number of writes, the primary-replica structure may not be good enough. Too many writes are directed to the same server, which creates a bottleneck. Or if the system traffic grows enough, there's a limit to the number of writes that a single server can accept.

A possible solution is to horizontally partition the data. This means dividing the data into different databases according to a specific key, so all related data can go to the same server. Each of the different partitions is called a shard.

Note that "partitioning" and "sharding" can be considered synonyms, though in reality sharding is only if the partition is horizontal, separating a single table into different servers. Partitioning can be more general, like dividing a table into two, or splitting into different columns, which is not typically called sharding.

The partition key is called the shard key, and based on its value, each row will be allocated a specific shard.

Col A	Col B	Col C	Shard Key
			🔑
			🔑
			...
			🔑

F(🔑) = Shard A → Shard A
F(🔑) = Shard B → Shard B
F(🔑) = Shard B → Shard B

Figure 3.4: Shard keys

The name *shard* comes from the videogame Ultima Online, which, in the late 90s, used this strategy to create a "multiverse" where different players could play the same game on different servers. They called them "shards," as they were aspects of the same reality, but contained different players in them. The name stuck and it's still used to describe the architecture.

Any query needs to be able to determine what the proper shard is to be applied to. Any query that affects two or more shards may be impossible to do or can only be performed in succession. Of course, this excludes the possibility of performing these queries in a single transaction. In any case, these operations will be very expensive, and should be avoided as much as possible. Sharding is a fantastic idea when the data is naturally partitioned, and very bad when queries affecting multiple shards are performed.

Some NoSQL databases allow native sharding that will take care of all these options automatically. A common example is MongoDB, which is even capable of running queries in multiple shards in a transparent manner. These queries will be slow, in any case.

The choosing of the sharding key is also crucial. A good key should follow natural partitions between data, so performing cross-shard queries is not required. For example, if the data of a user is independent of the rest, which may happen with a photo-sharing application, the user identifier could be a good shard key.

Another important quality is that the shard to address the query needs to be determined based on the shard key. That means that every query needs to have the shard key available. This means that the shard key should be an input of every operation.

Another property of the shard key is that the data should be ideally portioned in a way that shards have the same size, or at least they are similar enough. If one shard is much bigger than the rest, that could lead to problems of imbalanced data, not enough distributing of the queries, and having one shard being the bottleneck.

Pure sharding

On pure shards, the data is all partitioned in shards and the shard key is an input of every operation. The shard is determined based on the shard key.

To ensure that the shards are balanced, each key is hashed in a way that is equally distributed between the number of shards. A typical case is to use a modulo operation, for example. If we have 8 shards, we determine which shard the data is partitioned into based on a number that's equally distributed.

User ID	Operation	Shard
1234	1234 mod 8	2
2347	2347 mod 8	3
7645	7645 mod 8	5
1235	1235 mod 8	3
4356	4356 mod 8	4
2345	2345 mod 8	1
2344	2344 mod 8	0

If the shard key is not a number, or if it's not evenly distributed, a hash function can be applied. For example, in Python:

```
>>> import hashlib
>>> shard_key = 'ABCDEF'
>>> hashlib.md5(shard_key.encode()).hexdigest()[-6:]
'b9fcf6'
>>> int('b9fcf6', 16)  # Transform in number for base 16
12188918
>>> int('b9fcf6', 16) % 8
6
```

This strategy is only possible if the shard key is **always** available as input for every operation. When this is not an option, we need to look at other options.

Changing the number of shards is not an easy task, as the destination for each key is decided by a fixed formula. It is possible, though, to grow or reduce the number of shards with some preparation in advance.

We can create "virtual shards" that point to the same server. For example, to create 100 shards, and use two servers, initially the virtual shard distribution will be like this:

Virtual Shard	Server
0-49	Server A
50-99	Server B

If the number of servers needs to be increased, the virtual shard structure will change in this way.

Virtual Shard	Server
0-24	Server A
25-49	Server C
50-74	Server B
75-99	Server D

This change to the specific server that corresponds to each shard may require some code change, but it's easier to handle as the shard key calculation won't change. The same operation can be applied in reverse, though it may create imbalance, so it needs to be done with care.

Virtual Shard	Server
0-24	Server A
25-49	Server C
50-99	Server B

Each of the operations requires changing the location of data based on the shard key. This is a costly operation, especially if a lot of data needs to be exchanged.

Mixed sharding

Sometimes it is not possible to create pure shards and a translation from the input is required to determine the shard key. This is the case, for example, when a user is logging in if the shard key is the user ID. The user will log in using their email, but that needs to be translated to the user ID to be able to determine the shard to search the information.

In that case, an external table can be used purely to translate the input of a particular query to the shard key.

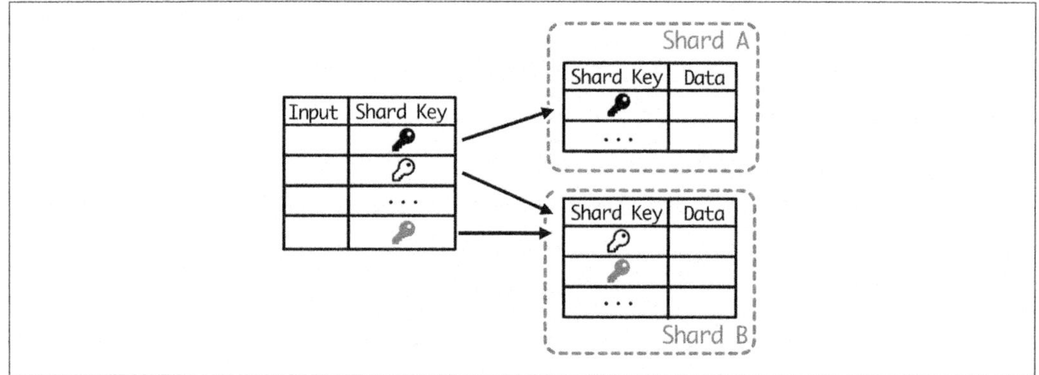

Figure 3.5: External tables to translate the input of shard keys

This creates a situation where a single shard is responsible for this translation layer. This shard can be used exclusively for this, or also act as any other shard.

Keep in mind that this requires a translation layer for each possible input parameter that's not directly the shard key, and that it requires keeping all the information of all shards in a single database. This needs to be kept under control and store as little information as possible, to avoid issues.

This strategy can be used as well to store, directly, what shard key goes to what shard, and perform a query instead of a direct operation, as we saw above.

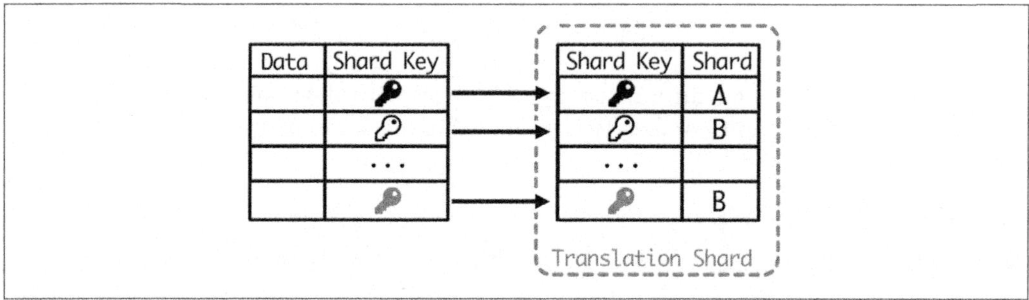

Figure 3.6: Storing shard keys to shards

This has the inconvenience that determining the shard based on the key requires a query in a database, especially with a big database. But it also allows changing the shard of the data in a consistent way, which can be used to adapt the number of shards, like growing or reducing the number. And it can be done without requiring downtime.

If the specific shard, not only the shard key, is stored in this translation table, the assignment of the shard to the key can be changed one by one, and in a continuous manner. The process will be approximately like this:

1. Shard key X is assigned to server A in the reference table. This is the start state.
2. Data from server A for shard key X is copied to server B. Note that no query involving shard key X is directed to server B yet.
3. Once all the data is copied, the entry for the reference table for shard key X is changed to server B.
4. All queries for shard key X are directed to server B.
5. Data from shard key X in server A can be cleaned.

Step 3 is the critical step, and needs to happen only after all the data is copied, and before any new write is performed. A way of ensuring this is to create a flag in the reference table that can stop or delay the writing of data while the operation is in place. This flag will be set up right before *step 2* and removed after *step 3* is completed.

This process will produce a smooth migration over time, but it requires enough space to work, and can take a significant amount of time.

Downscale operations are more complicated than upscale, as the increase in space allows for ample room. Fortunately, it is rare that a database cluster needs to downscale, as most applications will grow over time.

Please allow ample time to complete the migration. Depending on the size and complexity of the dataset, it can take a lot of time to migrate, up to hours or even days for extreme cases.

Table sharding

An alternative to sharding by shard key, for smaller clusters, is to separate tables or collections by server. This means that any query in table X is directed to a specific server, and the rest of the queries are directed to another. This strategy only works for unrelated tables, as it's not possible to perform joins between tables in different servers.

Note that this can be considered, being pedantic, as not properly sharding, though the structure is similar.

This works as a less complicated alternative, but it's way less flexible. It's only recommended for relatively small clusters where there's a big imbalance in size between one or two tables and the rest, for example, if one table stores logs that are much bigger than the rest of the database and are sparingly accessed.

Advantages and disadvantages of sharding

In summary, the main advantages of sharding are:

- Allows spreading writes over multiple servers, increasing the write throughput of the system
- The data gets stored in multiple servers, so massive amounts of data can be stored, without limiting the data that can be stored in a single server

In essence, sharding allows the creation of big, scalable systems. But it also has disadvantages:

- Sharded systems are more complicated to run and have some overhead in terms of configuring different servers, and so forth. While any big deployment will have its problems, sharding requires more work than a primary-replica setup, as the maintenance and operation need to be planned with more care and operations will take longer.
- Native support for sharding is available only in a small number of databases, like MongoDB, but relational databases don't have the feature implemented natively. This means that the complexity needs to be handled with ad hoc code, which will require an investment in developing it.
- Some queries will be impossible or almost impossible to do once the data is sharded. Aggregation and joins, depending on how the data is partitioned, won't be possible. The shard key needs to be selected carefully, as it will have a big implication on what queries are possible or not. We also lose the ACID properties, as some operations may need to involve more than one shard. A sharded database is less flexible.

As we've seen, designing, operating, and maintaining a sharded database only makes sense for very big systems, when the number of actions in the database requires such a complex system.

Schema design

For databases that need to define a schema, the specific design to use is something that needs to be considered.

This section will talk specifically about relational databases, as they are the ones that enforce a stricter schema. Other databases are more flexible in their changes, but they also benefit from spending some time thinking about their structure.

Changing the schema is an important action that will require planning and, certainly, a long-term view needs to be applied to the design.

We will talk later in the chapter about how to change the schema of a database. We only need to remark here that mutating the database schema is an unavoidable part of the process of building a system. Nonetheless, it's a process that needs to be taken with respect and understanding what the possible problems are. It's definitely a good idea to spend time thinking about and ensuring an adequate design for the schema.

The best way to start the design of a schema is to draw the different tables, fields, and their relationships, if there are foreign keys pointing to other tables.

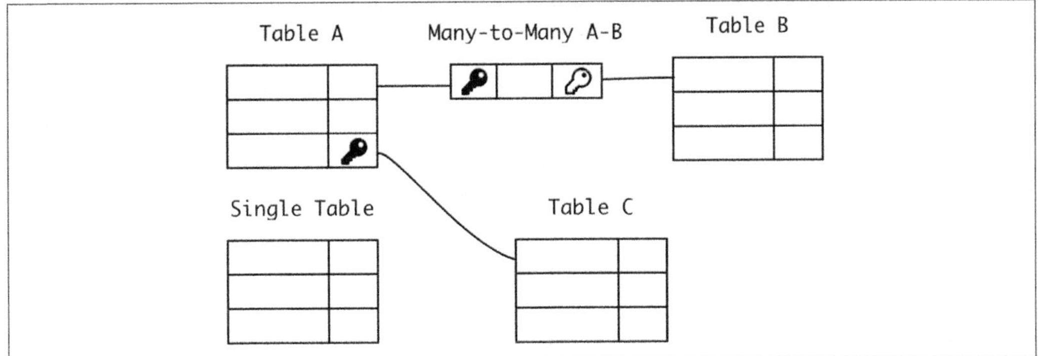

Figure 3.7: Drawing a schema

The presentation of this data should allow you to detect possible blind spots or the repetition of elements. If the number of tables is too big, it may be necessary to divide it into several groups.

Though there are tools that can help with this work, personally, it helps me to hand-draw these relationships, as it helps me think of the different relationships and construct a mental image of the design.

Each of the tables can have foreign key relationships with others of different kinds:

- **One-to-many**, where a single reference is added for multiple elements of another table. For example, a single author is referenced in all their books. A simple foreign key relationship works in this case, as the Books table will have a foreign key to the entry in Authors. Multiple book rows can have a reference to the same author.

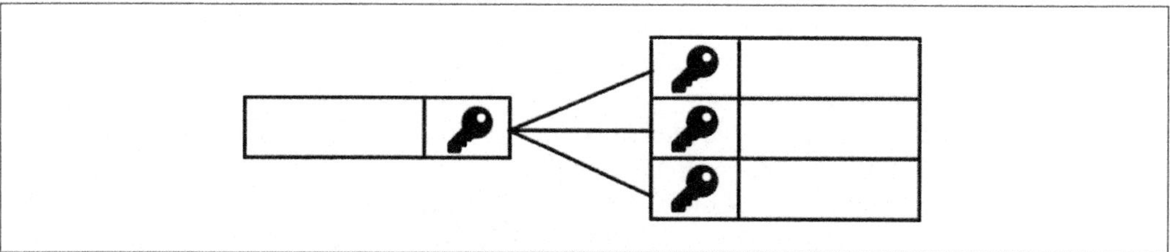

Figure 3.8: The key in the first table references multiple rows in the second

- **One-to-zero or -one** are specific cases where a row can be related to only another. For example, let's assume an editor can be working on a book (and only one book at a time). The reference for the editor in the Books table is a foreign key that can be set to `null` if there's no editing process. Another back reference from the editor to the book will ensure that the relationship is unique. Both references need to be changed in a transaction.

Strict one-to-one relationships, like a book and a title, where both are always related, are typically better modeled as adding all the information into a single table.

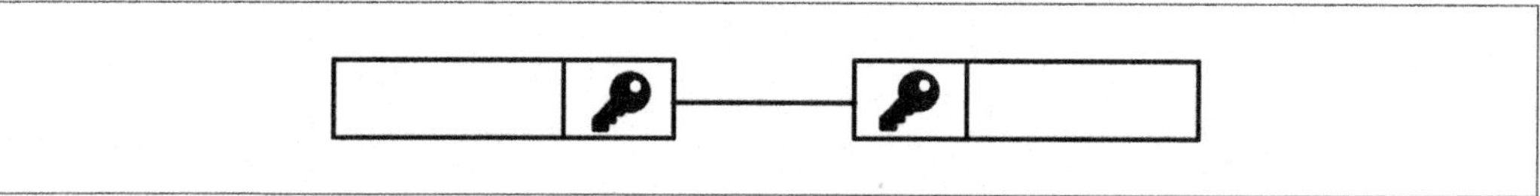

Figure 3.9: The relationship only makes it possible to match two rows

- **Many-to-many**, where there can be multiple assignments in both directions. For example, a book may be categorized under different genres. A single genre will be assigned to multiple books, and a single book can be assigned to more than one genre. Under a relational data structure, there's a need for an intermediary extra table that makes that relationship, which will point to both the book and the genre.

This extra table may include more information, for example, how accurate the genre is for the book. That way, it could describe books that are 50% horror and 90% adventure.

Outside of the relational data world, sometimes there's not such a pressing need for creating many-to-many relationships, and instead they can be directly added as a collection of tags. Some relational databases now allow more flexibility in allowing fields that are lists or JSON objects, which can be used in this way, simplifying the design.

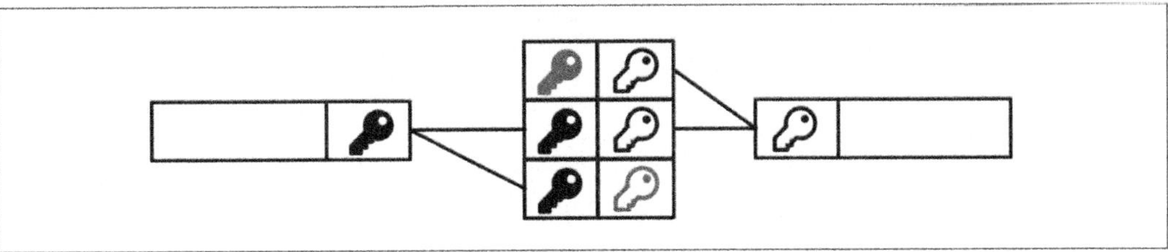

Figure 3.10: Note the intermediary table allows multiple combinations. The first table can reference multiple rows of the second, and the second multiple rows of the first

In most cases, the types of fields to store for each of the tables are straightforward, though certain details should be considered:

- **Allowing enough space to grow in the future**. Some fields, like strings, require defining a maximum size to store. For example, storing a string representing an email address will require a maximum of 254 characters. But sometimes the size is not obvious, like storing the name of a customer. In these cases, it's better to err on the safe size and increase the limit.
- The limits should be enforced not only for the database, but also above this level, to always allow any API or UI that deals with the field to handle it gracefully.

When dealing with numbers, in most cases regular integers will be enough to represent most used numbers. Though some databases accept categories like `smallint` for 2 bytes or `tinyint` for 1-byte values, it's not recommended to make use of them. The difference in space used will be minimal.

- **The internal database representation doesn't need to be the same as what's externally available**. For example, the time stored in the database should always be in UTC, and then translated to the user's time zone.

Storing the time always in UTC format allows using a consistent time in the server, in particular if there are users in different time zones. Storing the time by applying the time zone for the user produces non-comparable times in the database and using the default time zone of the server can produce different results based on the position of the server, or even worse, inconsistent data if more than one server in different time zones is involved. Ensure that all times are stored in the database in UTC.

Another example is if prices are stored, it's better to store them in cents, to avoid float numbers, and then present them as dollars and cents.

For example, this means that a price of $99.95 will be stored as the integer `9995`. Dealing with float arithmetic can create problems for prices, and prices can be translated into cents for easy handling.

The internal representation doesn't need to follow the same conventions if storing them in a different format is better for some reason.

- **At the same time, it's better to represent the data naturally**. A typical example of that is the overabundance of using numeric IDs to represent rows that have natural keys or using `Enums` (small integers assigned to represent a list of options) instead of using short strings instead. While these choices made sense some time ago, when space and processing power were more restrictive, now the performance improvement is negligible, and storing data in an understandable way helps greatly while developing.

For example, instead of using an integer field to store colors, where 1 means `RED`, 2 means `BLUE`, and 3 means `YELLOW`, use a short string field using the strings `RED`, `BLUE`, and `YELLOW`. The storing difference is negligible even if there are millions of records, and it's way easier to navigate the database.

We will see a bit later about normalization and denormalization, which are related to this concept.

- **No design will be perfect or complete**. In a system under development, the schema will always require changes. This is totally normal and expected and should be accepted as such. Perfect is the enemy of good. The design should try to be as simple as possible to adjust for the current needs of the system. Overdesign, trying to advance every possible future need and complicating the design, is a real problem that can waste efforts in laying the ground for needs that never materialize. Keep your design simple and flexible.

Schema normalization

As we've seen, in relational databases, a key concept is the foreign key one. Data can be stored in a table and linked to another. This split in data means that a set of limited data can, instead of being stored in a single table, be split in two.

For example, let's take a look at this table, initially with the field `House` as a string:

Characters

id	Name	House
1	Eddard Stark	Stark
2	Jon Snow	Stark
3	Daenerys Targaryen	Targaryen
4	Jaime Lannister	Lannister

To ensure that the data is consistent and there are no errors, the field `House` can be normalized. This means that it's stored in a different table, and a `FOREIGN KEY` constraint is enforced, in this way.

Characters

id	Name	HouseId (FK)
1	Eddard Stark	1
2	Jon Snow	1
3	Daenerys Targaryen	3
4	Jaime Lannister	2

Houses

id	Name	Words
1	Stark	Winter is coming
2	Lannister	Hear me roar
3	Targaryen	Fire and blood

This way of operating *normalizes* the data. No new entry with a new `House` can be added unless it is first introduced in the `Houses` table. In the same way, an entry in `Houses` cannot be deleted while a single entry in `Characters` contains a reference. This ensures that the data is very consistent and there are no problems, like introducing a typo like `House` *Lanister* (single n) for a new entry, which may complicate later queries.

It also has the advantage of being able to add extra information for each of the entries in `Houses`. In this case, we can add the `Words` of the `House`. The data is also more compact, as repeated information is stored in a single pace.

On the other hand, this has a couple of issues. First of all, any reference to a `Character` that needs to know the information of the `House` needs to perform a `JOIN` query. In the first `Characters` table, we could generate our query in this way:

```
SELECT Name, House FROM Characters;
```

While in the second schema, we will require this one:

```
SELECT Characters.Name, Houses.Name
FROM Characters JOIN Houses ON Characters.HouseId = Houses.id;
```

This query will take longer to execute, as information needs to be compounded from two tables. For big tables, this time can be extensive. This can also require a `JOIN` from different tables if we add, for example, a `PreferredWeapon` field and a `Weapons` normalized table for each `Character`. Or we can add even more tables as the `Characters` table grows in fields.

It will also take longer to insert and delete data, as more checks need to be performed. In general, operations will take longer.

Normalized data is also difficult to shard. The concept of normalization of keeping every element described in its own table and reference from there is inherently difficult to shard, as it makes partitioning very difficult.

Another problem is that the database is more difficult to read and operate. Deletes need to happen in an ordered fashion, which gets more difficult to follow as more fields are being added. Also, complex `JOIN` queries need to be performed for simple operations. The queries are longer and more complicated to generate.

While this normalization structure, creating foreign keys through numerical identifiers, is pretty typical, it's not the only option.

To improve the clarity of the database, natural keys can be used to simplify them, describing the data in this way. Instead of using an integer as the primary key, we use the `Name` field on the `Houses` table.

Characters

Id	Name	House (FK)
1	Eddard Stark	Stark
2	Jon Snow	Stark
3	Daenerys Targaryen	Targaryen
4	Jaime Lannister	Lannister

Houses

Name (PK)	Words
Stark	Winter is coming
Lannister	Hear me roar
Targaryen	Fire and blood

This not only removes the usage of an extra field, but it also allows you to make the reference with a descriptive value. We recover our original query, even if the data is normalized.

As we described before, the extra space of storing a string instead of a single integer is negligible. Some developers are very much against natural keys and prefer to use integer values, but nowadays there's not really a solid technical reason for limiting yourself.

Only when we want to obtain the information in the `Words` field will we need to perform a `JOIN` query:

```
SELECT Name, House FROM Characters;
```

This trick, anyway, may not avoid the usage of `JOIN` queries in normal operation. Perhaps there are a lot of references and the system is having problems with the amount of time that it's taking to perform queries. In that case, it may be necessary to reduce the need to `JOIN` tables.

Denormalization

Denormalization is the opposing action to normalization. Where normalizing data splits it into different tables to ensure that all the data is consistent, denormalizing regroups information into a single table to avoid the necessity to `JOIN` tables.

Following our example above, we want to replace a `JOIN` query like this:

```
SELECT Characters.Name, Houses.Name, House.Words
FROM Characters JOIN Houses ON Characters.House = Houses.Name;
```

Which follows this schema:

Characters

Id	Name	House (FK)
1	Eddard Stark	Stark
2	Jon Snow	Stark
3	Daenerys Targaryen	Targaryen
4	Jaime Lannister	Lannister

Houses

Name (PK)	Words
Stark	Winter is coming
Lannister	Hear me roar
Targaryen	Fire and blood

For a query similar to this, querying a single table, use something like this:

```
SELECT Name, House, Words FROM Characters
```

To do so, the data needs to be structured in a single table.

Characters

id	Name	House	Words
1	Eddard Stark	Stark	Winter is coming
2	Jon Snow	Stark	Winter is coming
3	Daenerys Targaryen	Targaryen	Fire and blood
4	Jaime Lannister	Lannister	Hear me roar

Note that information is duplicated. Every `Character` has a copy of the `Words` of the `House`, something that was not required before. This means denormalization uses more space; in a big table with many rows, way more space.

Denormalization also increases the risk of inconsistent data, as there's nothing ensuring that there's not a new value that's a typo of an old value, or that, by mistake, incorrect `Words` are added to a different `House`.

But, on the other hand, we are now free of having to `JOIN` tables. For big tables this can speed up processing, both read and writes, quite a lot. It also removes the concerns for sharding, as now the table can be partitioned on whatever shard key that's convenient and will contain all the information.

Denormalization is an extremely common option for the use cases that typically fall under NoSQL databases, which remove the capability to perform `JOIN` queries. For example, document databases embed data as subfields into a bigger entity. While it certainly has its cons, it's a trade-off that makes sense in some operations.

Data indexing

As data grows, the access to data starts getting slower. Retrieving exactly the proper data from a big table full of information requires performing more internal operations to locate it.

While we will describe data indexing in relation to relational databases, most of the fundamentals are applicable to other databases.

This process can be greatly speeded up by organizing the data smartly in a way that is easy to search. This leads to creating indexes that allow you to locate data very quickly by searching through them. The basics of an index is to create an external sorted data structure that points to one or more fields of each of the records of the database. This index structure is always kept sorted as data in the table changes.

For example, a short table may contain this information

id	Name	Height (cm)
1	Eddard	178
2	John	173
3	Daenerys	157
4	Jaime	188

In the absence of an index, to query what entry has the highest height, the database will need to individually check each of the rows and sort them. This is called a **full table scan**. A full table scan can be very costly if the table has millions of rows.

By creating an index for the `Height` field, a data structure that is always sorted is kept in sync with the data.

id	Name	Height (cm)
1	Eddard	178
2	John	173
3	Daenerys	157
4	Jaime	188

Height (cm)	id
188	4
178	1
173	5
157	3

Because it is always sorted, making any query related to the height is easy to fulfill. For example, obtaining what the top 3 heights are doesn't require any checking, just retrieving the first three records from the index, and determining heights between 180 and 170 is also easy, using search methods in sorted lists, like a binary search. Once again, if this index doesn't exist, the only way to find these queries is by checking each record in the table.

Note that the index doesn't cover all the fields. The `Name` field is not indexed, for example. Another index may be required to cover other fields. The same table accepts multiple indices.

The primary key of a table is always indexed, as it needs to be a unique value.

Indexes can be combined, creating an index for two or more fields. These composite indices sort the data based on the ordered combination of both fields, for example, a composite index that is `(Name, Height)` will quickly return the height for `Names` starting with `J`. A composite index of `(Height, Name)` will do the opposite, priming the height and then sorting the `Name` field.

Querying in composite indices for only the first part of the index is possible. In our example, an index of `(Height, Name)` will always work for querying `Height`.

The usage or not of indexes to retrieve the information is done automatically by the database; the SQL query doesn't change at all. Internally, the database will run the query analyzer before running a query. This part of the database software will determine how to retrieve the data, and what indexes to use, if any.

The query analyzer needs to run quickly, as determining what the best possible way to search for information is can take more time than running a naïve approach and returning the data. This means that, sometimes, it will make mistakes and not use the optimal combination. The SQL command `EXPLAIN`, used before another SQL statement, will display how the query will be interpreted and run, which allows you to understand and tweak it to improve its execution time.

Keep in mind that using different independent indices in the same query may not be possible. Sometimes the database won't be able to perform a faster query by combining two indices as the data needs to be correlated between them, and that may be a costly operation.

Indexes greatly speed up the queries that use them, especially for big tables with thousands or millions of rows. They are also used automatically, so they don't add extra complexity to the generation of queries. So, if they are so great, why not index absolutely everything? Well, indices also have some issues:

- Each index requires extra space. While this is optimized, adding a lot of indexes in a single table will use more space, both in the hard drive and in RAM.
- Each time the table changes, all indices in the table need to be adjusted to be sure that the index is properly sorted. This is more noticeable in new data being written, like records being added or indexed fields being updated. Indices are a trade-off between spending more time on writing to speed up the reading. For tables that are write heavy, this trade-off may not be adequate, and maintaining one or more indices can be counterproductive.
- Small tables don't really benefit from being indexed. The difference between a full table scan and an indexed search is small if the number of rows is below the thousands.

As a rule of thumb, it's better to try to create indices *after* the need is detected. Once a slow query is discovered, analyze if an index will improve the situation, and only then create it.

Cardinality

An important characteristic of the usefulness of each index is its **cardinality**. This is the number of different values that an index contains.

For example, the `Height` index in this table has a cardinality of 4. There are four different values.

id	Height (cm)
1	178
2	165
3	167
4	192

A table like this has only a cardinality of 2.

id	Height (cm)
1	178
2	165
3	178
4	165

An index with low cardinality has low quality, as it's not able to speed up the search as much as expected. An index can be understood as a filter that allows you to reduce the number of rows to search. If, after applying the filter, the table has not been greatly reduced, the index won't be useful. Let's use an extreme example to describe it.

Imagine a table with a million rows indexed by a field that's the same in all of them. Now imagine that we make a query to find a single row in a different field that's not indexed. If we use the index, we won't be able to speed up the process, as the index will return every single row in the database.

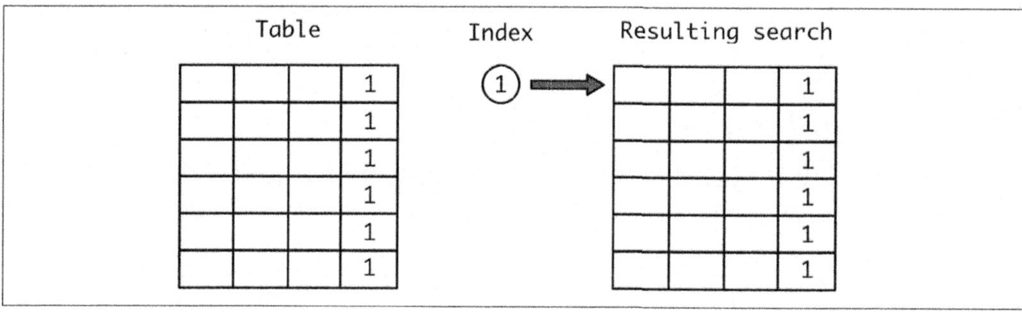

Figure 3.11: Returning every single row from a query using an unhelpful index

Now imagine it with two values. Half of the rows of the table are returned first, and then we need to query them. This is better, but using the index has some overhead compared with just performing a full table scan, so in practice, this is not very advantageous.

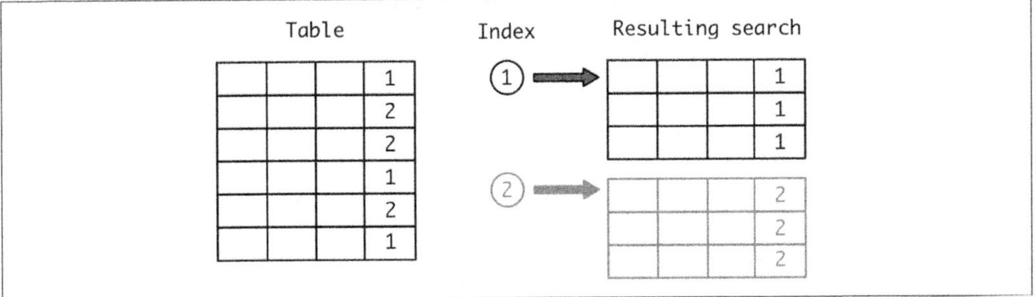

Figure 3.12: Returning rows using an index with two values

As we increase the cardinality of the index, adding more and more values, the index is more useful.

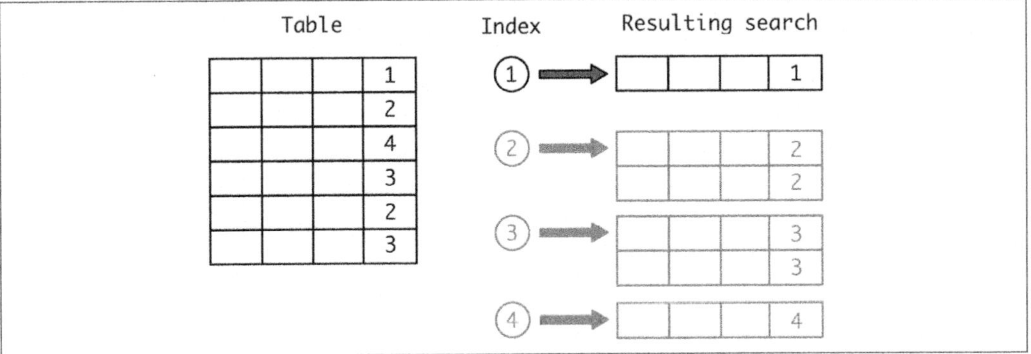

Figure 3.13: Returning rows using an index with four values

With a higher cardinality, the database is able to discriminate better and to point to a smaller subsection of values, which speeds up greatly access to the proper data.

As a rule of thumb, ensure that the cardinality of an index is always 10 or higher. Lower than that is probably not good enough to use as an index. The query analyzer will take the cardinality value into account to see whether to use the index or not.

Keep in mind that the cardinality of fields that only allow a small number of values, such as `Booleans` and `Enums`, is always limited and makes them bad candidates to be indexed, at least on their own. On the other hand, values that are unique will always have the highest possible cardinality and they are good candidates for indexing. Primary keys are always indexed automatically for this reason.

Summary

In this chapter, we described different methods and techniques to deal with the storage layer, both from the point of view of the different capacities and options available in the database itself, and how the code of our application can interact to store and retrieve information.

We described the different kinds of databases, both relational and non-relational, and what the differences and usages of each are, and how the concept of a transaction, one of the fundamental characteristics of relational databases, allows compliance with ACID properties. As some of the non-relational databases are aimed at dealing with data on a large scale and are distributed, we presented some of the techniques to scale up relational systems, as that kind of database was not initially designed to deal with multiple servers.

We continued by describing how we can design a schema and what the pros and cons are for normalizing and denormalizing the data. We also described why we index fields and when it's counterproductive.

In *Chapter 4, The Data Layer*, we will see how to design the data layer.

Join our book's Discord space

Join the book's Discord workspace for a monthly *Ask me Anything* session with the author:
`https://packt.link/PythonArchitechture`

4
The Data Layer

The modeling of data when interacting with the application code is as important as how that data is stored in storage. The data layer is the layer that developers will interact with most often, so creating a good interface is critical to create a productive environment.

In this chapter, we will describe how to create a software data layer that interacts with storage to abstract the specifics of storing data. We will see what Domain-Driven Design is, how to use an Object-Relational Mapping framework, and more advanced patterns, like Command Query Responsibility Segregation.

We will also talk about how to make changes to the database as the application evolves and, finally, techniques to deal with legacy databases when the structure has already been defined before our involvement.

In this chapter, we will look at the following topics:

- The Model layer
- Database migrations
- Dealing with legacy databases

Let's start by giving the context of the data design as part of the Model part of the **Model-View-Controller** (MVC) pattern.

The Model layer

As we saw when we presented the Model-View-Controller architecture in *Chapter 2, API Design*, the Model layer is the part that's intimately related with the data and storing and retrieving it.

The Model abstracts all the data handling. This not only includes database access but also the related business logic. This creates a two-layer structure:

- The internal data modeling layer, handling the storage and retrieval of data from the database. This layer needs to understand the way the data is stored in the database and handles it accordingly.
- The next layer creates business logic and uses the internal data modeling layer to support it. This layer is in charge of ensuring that the data to be stored is consistent and enforces any relationships or constraints.

It's very common to deal with the data layer as a pure extension of the database design, removing the business level or storing it as code in the Controller part. While this is doable, it's better to think about whether it's good to explicitly add the business layer on top and ensure there's separation between the entity models, which makes good business sense, and the database models, which contain the details on how to access the database.

Domain-Driven Design

This way of operating has become common as part of Domain-Driven Design. When DDD was first introduced, it was aimed mainly at bridging the gap between the specific application and the technology implementing it to try to use proper nomenclature and ensure that the code was in sync with the real operations that the users of the code would use. For example, banking software will use methods for *lodging* and *withdrawing* funds, instead of *adding* and *subtracting* from an account.

DDD is not only naming methods and attributes in a way that's consistent with the proper jargon of the domain, but also replicating the uses and flows.

When paired with **Object-Oriented Programming (OOP)**, DDD techniques will replicate the concepts required by the specific domain as objects. In our previous example, we would have an `Account` object that accepts the methods `lodge()` and `withdraw()`. These would probably accept a `Transfer` object that would keep the proper balance in the source of the funds.

These days, DDD is understood as the creation of this business-oriented interface in the Model layer, so we can abstract the internals on how that's being mapped into accesses to the database and present a consistent interface that replicates the business flows.

DDD requires an intimate knowledge of the specific domain at hand to create an interface that makes sense and properly models the business actions. It requires close communication and collaboration with business experts to be sure that all possible gaps are covered.

For a lot of different concepts, the Model works purely as a replication of the schema of the database. This way, if there's a table, it gets translated into a Model that accesses that table, replicates the fields, etc. An example of this is storing the user in a table with username, full name, subscription, and password fields.

But remember that it is not a hard requirement. A Model can use multiple tables or combine multiple fields in a way that makes more business sense, even not exposing some fields as they should remain internal.

We will use a relational database using SQL as our default example, as it is the most common kind of database. But everything that we are discussing is highly applicable to other kinds of databases, especially to document-based databases.

For example, the example of the user above has the following fields in the database as columns in a SQL table:

Field	**Type**	**Description**
`Username`	`String`	Unique username
`Password`	`String`	String describing the hashed password
`Full name`	`String`	Name of the user
`Subscription end`	`Datetime`	Time when the subscription ends
`Subscription type`	`Enum (Normal, Premium, NotSubscribed)`	Kind of subscription

But the Model may expose the following:

Attribute/Method	Type	Description
`username`	String attribute	Directly translates the username column
`full_name`	String attribute	Directly translates the full_name column
`subscription`	Read-only property	Returns the subscription type column. If the subscription has ended (as indicated in the subscription end column), it returns `NotSubscribed`
`check_password(password)`	Method	Internally checks whether the `password` input is valid by comparing it with the hash password column and returns whether it is correct or not

Note that this hides the password itself, as its internal details are not relevant outside the database. It also hides the internal subscription fields, presenting instead a single attribute that performs all the relevant checks.

This Model transforms the actions from the raw database access to a fully defined object that abstracts the access to the database. This way of operating, when mapping an object to a table or collection, is called **Object-Relational Mapping** (**ORM**).

Using ORM

As we've seen above, in essence, ORM is performing mapping between the collections or tables in a database, and generating objects in an OOP environment.

While ORM itself refers to the technique, the way it is usually understood is *as a tool*. There are multiple ORM tools available that do the conversion from SQL tables to Python objects. This means that, instead of composing SQL statements, we will set up properties defined in classes and objects that will then be translated automatically by the ORM tool and will connect to the database.

For example, a low-level access for a query in the "pens" table could look like this:

```
>>> cur = con.cursor()
>>> cur.execute('''CREATE TABLE pens (id INTEGER PRIMARY KEY DESC,
name, color)''')
<sqlite3.Cursor object at 0x10c484c70>
>>> con.commit()
```

```
>>> cur.execute('''INSERT INTO pens VALUES (1, 'Waldorf', 'blue')''')
<sqlite3.Cursor object at 0x10c484c70>
>>> con.commit()
>>> cur.execute('SELECT * FROM pens');
<sqlite3.Cursor object at 0x10c484c70>
>>> cur.fetchall()
[(1, 'Waldorf', 'blue')]
```

Note that we are using the DB-API 2.0 standard Python interface, which abstracts away the differences between different databases, and allows us to retrieve the information using the standard `fetchall()` method.

To connect Python and an SQL database, the most common ORMs are the ones included in the Django framework (`https://www.djangoproject.com/`) and SQLAlchemy (`https://www.sqlalchemy.org/`). There are other less-used options, such as Pony (`https://ponyorm.org/`) or Peewee (`https://github.com/coleifer/peewee`), that aim to have a simpler approach.

Using an ORM, like the one available in the Django framework, instead of creating a `CREATE TABLE` statement, we describe the table in code as a class:

```
from django.db import models

class Pens(models.Model):
     name = models.CharField(max_length=140)
     color = models.CharField(max_length=30)
```

This class allows us to retrieve and add elements using the class.

```
>>> new_pen = Pens(name='Waldorf', color='blue')
>>> new_pen.save()

>>> all_pens = Pens.objects.all()
>>> all_pens[0].name
'Waldorf'
```

The operation that in raw SQL is an `INSERT` is to create a new object and then use the `.save()` method to persist the data into the database. In the same way, instead of composing a `SELECT` query, the search API can be called. For example, this code:

```
>>> red_pens = Pens.objects.filter(color='red')
```

Is equivalent to this code:

```
SELECT * FROM Pens WHERE color = 'red;
```

Using an ORM, compared with composing SQL directly, has some advantages:

- Using an ORM detaches the database from the code
- It removes the need for using SQL (or learning it)
- It removes some problems with composing SQL queries, like security issues

Let's take a closer look at these advantages and see their limits.

Independence from the database

First of all, using an ORM detaches the database usage from the code. This means that a specific database can be changed, and the code will run unchanged. This can be useful sometimes to run code in different environments or to quickly change to use a different database.

A very common use case for this is to run tests in SQLite and use another database like MySQL or PostgreSQL once the code is deployed in production.

This approach is not problem-free, as some options may be available in one database and not in another. It may be a viable tactic for new projects, but the best approach is to run tests and production in the same technologies to avoid unexpected compatibility problems.

Independence from SQL and the Repository pattern

Another advantage is that you don't need to learn SQL (or whatever language is used in the database backend) to work with the data. Instead, the ORM uses its own API, which can be intuitive and closer to OOP. This can reduce the barrier to entry to work with the code, as developers that are not familiar with SQL can understand the ORM code faster.

Using classes to abstract the access to the persistent layer from the database usage is called the **Repository pattern**. Using an ORM will make use of this pattern automatically, as it will use programmatic actions without requiring any internal knowledge of the database.

This advantage also has the counterpart that the translation of some actions can be clunky and produce highly inefficient SQL statements. This is especially true for complicated queries that require you to `JOIN` multiple tables.

A typical example of this is the following example code. The `Books` objects have a reference to their author that's stored in a different table and stored as a foreign key reference.

```
for book in Books.objects.find(publisher='packt'):
    author = book.author
    do_something(author)
```

This code is interpreted in the following way:

```
Produce a query to retrieve all the books from publisher 'packt'
For each book, make a query to retrieve the author
Perform the action with the author
```

When the number of books is high, all those extra queries can be very costly. What we really want to do is

```
Produce a query to retrieve all the books from publisher 'packt',
joining with their authors
For each book, perform the action with the author
```

This way, only a single query is generated, which is much more efficient than the first case.

This join has to be manually indicated to the API, in the following way.

```
for book in Books.objects.find(publisher='packt').select_
related('author'):
    author = book.author
    do_something(author)
```

> The need to require the addition of extra information is actually a good example of leaking abstractions, as discussed in *Chapter 2*. You are still required to understand the details of the database to be able to create efficient code.

This balance for ORM frameworks, between being intuitive to work with and sometimes requiring an understanding of the underlying implementation details, is a balance that needs to be defined. The framework itself will take a more or less flexible approach depending on how the specific SQL statements used are abstracted over a convenient API.

No problems related to composing SQL

Even if the developer knows how to deal with SQL, there's a lot of gotchas when working with it. A pretty important advantage is that using an ORM avoids some of the problems of dealing with the direct manipulation of SQL statements. When directly composing SQL, it ends up becoming a pure string manipulation to generate the desired query. This can create a lot of problems.

The most obvious ones are the requirement to compose the proper SQL statement, and not to generate a syntactically invalid SQL statement. For example, consider the following code:

```
>>> color_list = ','.join(colors)
>>> query = 'SELECT * FROM Pens WHERE color IN (' + color_list + ')'
```

This code works for values of `colors` that contain values but will produce an error if `colors` is empty.

Even worse, if the query is composed using input parameters directly, it can produce security problems. There's a kind of attack called an **SQL injection attack** that is aimed at precisely this kind of behavior.

For example, let's say that the query presented above is produced when the user is calling a search that can be filtered by different colors. The user is directly asked for the colors. A malicious user may ask for the color `'red'; DROP TABLE users;`. This will take advantage of the fact that the query is composed as a pure string to generate a malicious string that contains a hidden, non-expected operation.

To avoid this problem, any input that may be used as part of a SQL query (or any other language) needs to be *sanitized*. This means removing or escaping characters that may affect the behavior of the expected query.

Escaping characters means that they are properly encoded to be understood as a regular string, and not part of the syntax. For example, in Python, to escape the character " to be included in a string instead of ending the string definition, it needs to be preceded by the \ character. Of course, the \ character needs to be escaped if it needs to be used in a string, in this case doubling it, using \\.

For example:

```
"This string contains the double quote character \"
and the backslash character \\."
```

While there are specific techniques to manually compose SQL statements and sanitize the inputs, any ORM will sanitize them automatically, greatly reducing the risk of SQL injection by default. This is a great win in terms of security and it's probably the biggest advantage for ORM frameworks. Manually composing SQL statements is generally understood as a bad idea, relying instead on an indirect way that guarantees that any input is safe.

The counterpart is that, even when having a good understanding of the ORM API, there are limits to the way elements are read for certain queries or results, which may lead to operations that are much more complicated or inefficient using an ORM framework than creating a bespoke SQL query.

This typically happens when creating complex joins. The queries created from the ORM are good for straightforward queries but can struggle to create queries when there are too many relationships, as it will overcomplicate them.

ORM frameworks will also have an impact in terms of performance, as they require time to compose the proper SQL query, encode and decode data, and do other checkups. While for most queries this time will be negligible, for specific ones perhaps this will greatly increase the time taken to retrieve the data. Unfortunately, there's a good chance that, at some point, a specific, tailored SQL query will need to be created for some action. When dealing with ORM frameworks, there's always a balance between convenience and being able to create exactly the right query for the task at hand.

Another limit of ORM frameworks is that SQL access may allow operations that are not possible in the ORM interface. This may be a product of specific plugins or capabilities that are unique to the database in use.

If using SQL is the way to go, a common approach is to use prepared statements, which are immutable queries with parameters, so they are replaced as part of the execution in the DB API. For example, the following code will work in a similar way to a `print` statement.

```
db.execute('SELECT * FROM Pens WHERE color={color}', color=color_input)
```

This code will safely replace the color with the proper input, encoded in a safe way. If there's a list of elements that need to be replaced, that could be done in two steps: first, preparing the proper template, with one parameter per input, and second, making the replacement. For example:

```
# Input list
>>> color_list = ['red', 'green', 'blue']
# Create a dictionary with a unique name per parameter (color_X) and
the value
>>> parameters = {f'color_{index}': value for index, value in
enumerate(color_list)}
>>> parameters
{'color_0': 'red', 'color_1': 'green', 'color_2': 'blue'}
# Create a clausule with the name of the parameters to be replaced
# by string substitution
# Note that {{ will be replaced by a single {
>>> query_params = ','.join(f'{{{param}}}' for param in  parameters.
keys())
>>> query_params
'{color_0},{color_1},{color_2}'
# Compose the full query, replacing the prepared string
>>> query = f'SELECT * FROM Pens WHERE color IN ({query_params})'
>>> query
'SELECT * FROM Pens WHERE color IN ({color_0},{color_1},{color_2})'
# To execute, using ** on front of a dictionary will put all its keys
as
# input parameters
>>> query.format(**parameters)
'SELECT * FROM Pens WHERE color IN (red,green,blue)'
# Execute the query in a similar way, it will handle all
# required encoding and escaping from the string input
   >>> db.execute(query, **query_params)
```

In our examples, we are using a `SELECT *` statement that will return all the columns in the table for simplicity, but this is not the correct way of addressing them and should be avoided. The problem is that returning all columns may not be stable.

New columns can be added to a table, so retrieving all columns may change the retrieved data, increasing the chance of producing a formatting error. For example:

```
>>> cur.execute('SELECT * FROM pens');
<sqlite3.Cursor object at 0x10e640810>
# This returns a row
```

```
>>> cur.fetchone()
(1, 'Waldorf', 'blue')
>>> cur.execute('ALTER TABLE pens ADD brand')
<sqlite3.Cursor object at 0x10e640810>
>>> cur.execute('SELECT * FROM pens');
<sqlite3.Cursor object at 0x10e640810>
# This is the same row as above, but now it returns an extra element
>>> cur.fetchone()
(1, 'Waldorf', 'blue', None)
```

An ORM will handle this case automatically, but using raw SQL requires you to take this effect into account and always include explicitly the columns to retrieve to avoid problems when making changes in the schema later on.

```
>>> cur.execute('SELECT name, color FROM pens');
<sqlite3.Cursor object at 0x10e640810>
>>> cur.fetchone()
('Waldorf', 'blue')
```

Backward compatibility is critical when dealing with stored data. We will talk more about that later in the chapter.

Queries generated programmatically by composing them are called **dynamic queries**. While the default strategy should be to avoid them, preferring prepared statements, in certain cases dynamic queries are still very useful. There's a level of customization that can be impossible to produce unless there's a dynamic query involved.

Exactly what is considered a dynamic query may depend on the environment. In some cases, any query that's not a stored query (a query stored in the database itself beforehand and called with some parameters) may be considered dynamic. From our point of view, we will consider dynamic queries any queries that require string manipulation to produce the query.

Even if the selected way to access the database is raw SQL statements, it's good to create an abstraction layer that deals with all the specific details of the access. This layer should be responsible for storing data, in the proper format in the database, without business logic on that.

ORM frameworks will typically work a bit against this, as they are capable of handling a lot of complexity and will invite you to overload each of the defined objects with business logic. When the translation between the business concept and the database table is direct, for example, a user object, this is fine. But it's definitely possible to create an extra intermediate layer between the storage and the meaningful business object.

The Unit of Work pattern and encapsulating the data

As we've seen before, ORM frameworks directly translate between tables in the database and objects. This creates a representation of the data itself, in the way it's stored in the database.

In most situations, the design of the database will be tightly related to the business entities that we've introduced in the DDD philosophy. But that design may require an extra step, as some entities may be detached from the internal representation of the data, as it's stored inside the database.

The creation of methods representing actions that are unique entities is called the **Unit of Work pattern**. This means that everything that happens in this high-level action is performed as a single unit, even if internally it is implemented with multiple database operations. The operation acts atomically for the caller.

If the database allows for it, all the operations in a unit of work should be produced inside a transaction to ensure that the whole operation is done in one go. The name Unit of Work is very tightly associated with transactions and relational databases and normally is not used in databases that are not capable of creating transactions, though the pattern can still be used conceptually.

For example, we saw earlier the example of an `Account` class that accepts `.lodge()` and `.withdraw()` methods. While it is possible to directly implement an `Account` table that contains an integer representing the funds, we can also automatically create with any change a double-entry accountability system that keeps track of the system.

`Account` can be called **a Domain Model** to indicate that it's independent of the database representation.

To do so, each `Account` should have `debit` and `credit` internal values that change accordingly. If we also add an extra `Log` entry, in a different table, for keeping track of movements, it may be implemented as three different classes. The `Account` class will be the one to be used to encapsulate the log, while `InternalAccount` and `Log` will correspond to tables in the database. Note that a single `.lodge()` or `.withdraw()` call will generate multiple accesses to the database, as we'll see later.

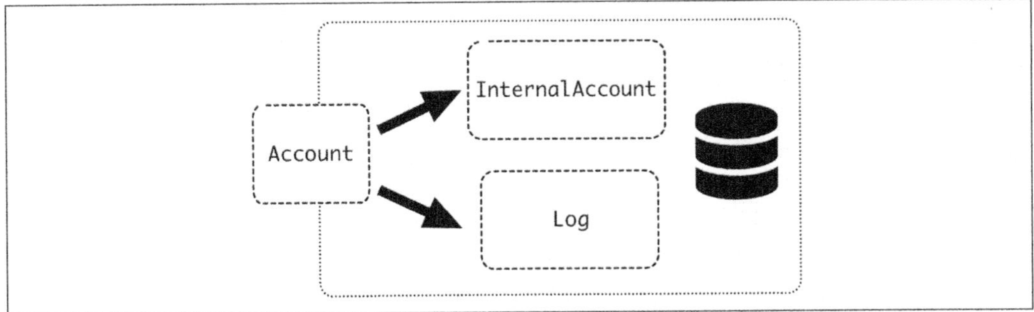

Figure 4.1: Design of the Account class

The code could be something like this:

```
class InternalAccount(models.Model):
    ''' This is the model related to a DB table '''
    account_number = models.IntegerField(unique=True)
    initial_amount = models.IntegerField(default=0)
     amount = models.IntegerField(default=0)


class Log(models.Model):
    ''' This models stores the operations '''
    source = models.ForeignKey('InternalAccount',
                               related_name='debit')
    destination = models.ForeignKey('InternalAccount',
                                    related_name='credit')
    amount = models.IntegerField()
    timestamp = models.DateTimeField(auto_now=True)


    def commit():
        ''' this produces the operation '''
        with transaction.atomic():
            # Update the amounts
                self.source.amount -= self.amount
```

```
        self.destination.amount += self.amount
            # save everything
            self.source.save()
            self.destination.save()
            self.save()


class Account(object):
    ''' This is the exposed object that handled the operations '''

    def __init__(self, account_number, amount=0):
        # Retrieve or create the account
        self.internal, _ = InternalAccount.objects.get_or_create(
            account_number=account_number,
            initial_amount=amount,
            amount=amount)

    @property
    def amount(self):
        return self.internal.amount

    def lodge(source_account, amount):
        '''
        This operation adds funds from the source
        '''
        log = Log(source=source_account, destination=self,
                  amount=amount)
        log.commit()

    def withdraw(dest_account, amount):
        '''
        This operation transfer funds to the destination
        '''
        log = Log(source=self, destination=dest_account,
                  amount=amount)
        log.commit()
```

The `Account` class is the expected interface. It is not related directly to anything in the database but keeps a relation to the `InternalAccount` using the unique reference of the `account_number`.

The logic to store the different elements is presented in a different class than the ORM models. This can be understood in the way that the ORM model classes are the **Repositories** classes and the `Account` model is the **Unit of Work** class.

In some manuals, they use Unit of Work classes, leaving them without much context, just as a container to perform the action to store the multiple elements. Nevertheless, it's more useful to assign a clear concept behind the `Account` class to give context and meaning. And there could be several actions that are appropriate for the business entity.

Whenever there's an operation, it requires another account, and then a new `Log` is created. The `Log` references the source, destination, and amount of the funds, and, in a single transaction, performs the operation. This is done in the `commit` method.

```
def commit():
    ''' this produces the operation '''
    with transaction.atomic():
        # Update the amounts
           self.source.amount -= self.amount
           self.destination.amount += self.amount
        # save everything
        self.source.save()
        self.destination.save()
        self.save()
```

In a single transaction, indicated by the usage of the `with transaction.atomic()` context manager, it adds and subtracts funds from the accounts, and then saves the three related rows, the source, the destination, and the log itself.

The Django ORM requires you to set this atomic decorator, but other ORMs can work differently. For example, SQLAlchemy tends to work more by adding operations to a queue and requiring you to explicitly apply all of them in a batch operation. Please check the documentation of the specific software you are using for each case.

A missing detail due to simplicity is the validation that there are enough funds to perform the operation. In cases where there aren't enough funds, an exception should be produced that will abort the transaction.

Note how this format allows for each `InternalAccount` to retrieve every `Log` associated to the transactions, both debits and credits. That means it can be checked that the current amount is correct. This code will calculate the amount in an account, based on the logs, and that can be used to check the amount is correct.

```
class InternalAccount(models.Model):
    ...

    def recalculate(self):
        '''
        Recalculate the amount, based on the logs
        '''
        total_credit = sum(log.amount for log in self.credit.all())
        total_debit = sum(log.amount for log in self.debit.all())
        return self.initial_amount + total_credit - total_debit
```

The initial amount is required. The `debit` and `credit` fields are back-references to the `Log`, as defined in the `Log` class.

From the point of view of a user only interested in operating with `Account` objects, all these details are irrelevant. This extra layer allows us to cleanly abstract from the database implementation and store any relevant business logic there. This can be the exposed business Model layer (of the Domain Model) that handles relevant business operations with the proper logic and nomenclature.

CQRS, using different models for read and write

Sometimes a simple CRUD model for the database is not descriptive of how the data flows in the system. In some complex settings, it may be necessary to use different ways to read the data and to write or interact with the data.

A possibility is that sending data and reading it happen at different ends of a pipeline. For example, this is something that happens in event-driven systems, where the data is recorded in a queue, and then later processed. In most cases, this data is processed or aggregated in a different database.

Let's see a more specific example. We store sales for different products. These sales contain the SKU (a unique identifier of the product sold) and the price. But we don't know, at the time of the sale, what the profit from the sale is, as the buying of the product depends on fluctuations of the market. The storing of a sale goes to a queue to start the process to reconcile it with the price paid. Finally, a relational database stores the final sale entry, which includes the purchase price and profit.

The flow of information goes from the Domain Model to the queue, then by some external process to the relational database, where it is then represented with a relational model in an ORM way, and then back to the Domain Model.

This structure is called **Command Query Responsibility Segregation** (**CQRS**), meaning that the Command (write operations) and Query (read operations) are separated. The pattern is not unique to event-driven structures; they are typically seen in these systems because their nature is to detach the input data from the output data.

The Domain Model may require different methods to deal with the information. The input and output data has a different internal representation, and sometimes it may be easier to clearly distinguish them. It's anyway a good idea to use an explicit Domain Model layer for CQRS to group the functionality and treat it as a whole. In certain cases, the models and data may be quite different for read and write. For example, if there's a step where aggregated results are generated, that may create extra data in the read part that's never written.

A description of the process of how the read and write parts connect is out of scope in our examples. In our example, that process would be how the data is stored in the database, including the amount paid.

The following diagram depicts the flow of information in a CQRS structure:

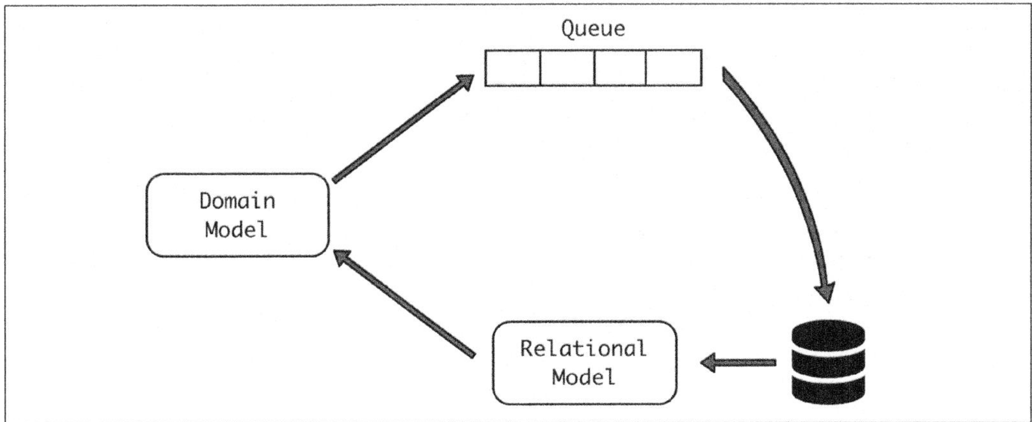

Figure 4.2: The flow of information in a CQRS structure

Our model's definition could be like this:

```
Class SaleModel(models.Model):
    ''' This is the usual ORM model '''
    Sale_id = models.IntegerField(unique=True)
```

```
    sku = models.IntegerField()
    amount = models.IntegerField()
    price = models.IntegerField()

class Sale(object):
    '''
        This is the exposed Domain Model that handled the operations
        In a domain meaningful way, without exposing internal info
    '''

    def __init__(self, sale_id, sku, amount):
        self.sale_id = sale_id
        self.sku = sku
        self.amount = amount
        # These elements are won't be filled when creating a new
element
        self._price = None
        self._profit = None

    @property
    def price(self):
        if self._price is None:
            raise Exception('No price yet for this sale')
        return self._price

    @property
    def profit(self):
        if self._profit is None:
            raise Exception('No price yet for this sale')
        return self._profit


       def save(self):
            # This sends the sale to the queue
            event = {
                'sale_id': self.sale_id,
                'sku': self.sku,
                'amount': self.amount,
            }
            # This sends the event to the external queue
            Queue.send(event)
```

```
    @classmethod
    def get(cls, sale_id):
        # if the sale is still not available it will raise an
        # Exception
        sale = SaleModel.objects.get(sale_id=sale_id)
        full_sale = Sale(sale_id=sale_id, sku=sale.sku,
                         amount=sale.amount)
        # fill the private attributes
        full_sale._price = sale.price
        full_sale._profit = sale.amount - full_sale._price
        return full_sale
```

Note how the flow is different for save and retrieve:

```
# Create a new sale
sale = Sale(sale_id=sale_id, sku=sale.sku, amount=sale.amount)
sale.save()

# Wait some time until totally processed
full_sale = Sale.get(sale_id=sale_id)
# retrieve the profit
full_sale.profit
```

CQRS systems are complex, as the data in and the data out is different. They also normally incur some delay in being able to retrieve the information back, which can be inconvenient.

Another important problem in CQRS systems is the fact that the different pieces need to be in sync. This includes both the read and write models, but also any transformation that happens within the pipeline. Over time, this creates a maintenance requirement, especially when backward compatibility needs to be maintained.

All these problems make CQRS systems complicated. They should be used with care only when strictly necessary.

Database migrations

An unavoidable fact of development is that software systems are always changing. While the pace of changes in the database is typically not as fast as other areas, there are still changes and they need to be treated carefully.

Data changes are roughly categorized into two different kinds:

- **Format or schema changes**: New elements, like fields or tables, to be added or removed; or changes in the format of some fields.
- **Data changes**: Requiring changing the data itself, without modifying the format. For example, normalizing an address field including the zip code, or making a string field uppercase.

Backward compatibility

The basic principle related to changes in the database is backward compatibility. This means that any single change in the database needs to work **without** any change in the code.

This allows you to make changes without interrupting the service. If the changes in the database require a change in the code to understand it, the service will have to be interrupted. This is because you can't apply both changes at the same time, and if there is more than one server executing the code, it can't be applied simultaneously.

Of course, there's another option, which is to stop the service, perform all the changes, and restart again. While this is not great, it could be an option for small services or if scheduled downtime is acceptable.

Depending on the database, there are different approaches to data changes.

For relational databases, given that they require a fixed structure to be defined, any change in the schema needs to be applied to the whole database as a single operation.

For other databases that don't force defining a schema, there are ways of updating the database in a more iterative way.

Let's take a look at the different approaches.

Relational schema changes

In relational databases, each individual schema change is applied as a SQL statement that operates like a transaction. The schema change, called a **migration**, can happen at the same time that some transformation of the data (for example, transforming integers to strings) takes place.

Migrations are SQL commands that perform changes in an atomic way. They can involve changing the format of tables in the database, but also more operations like changing the data or multiple changes in one go. This can be achieved by creating a single transaction that groups these changes. Most ORM frameworks include support to create migrations and perform these operations natively.

For example, Django will automatically create a migration file by running the command `makemigrations`. This command needs to be run manually, but it will detect any change in the models and make the proper changes.

For example, if we add an extra value `branch_id` in the class introduced before

```
class InternalAccount(models.Model):
    ''' This is the model related to a DB table '''
    account_number = models.IntegerField(unique=True)
    initial_amount = models.IntegerField(default=0)
    amount = models.IntegerField(default=0)
    branch_id = models.IntegerField()
```

Running the command `makemigrations` will generate the proper file that describes the migration.

```
$ python3 manage.py makemigrations
Migrations for 'example':
  example/migrations/0002_auto_20210501_1843.py
    - Add field branch_id to internalaccount
```

Note that Django keeps track of the state in the models and automatically adjusts the changes creating the proper migration files. The pending migrations can be applied automatically with the command `migrate`.

```
$ python3 manage.py migrate
Operations to perform:
  Apply all migrations: admin, auth, contenttypes, example, sessions
Running migrations:
  Applying example.0002_auto_20210501_1843... OK
```

Django will store in the database the status of the applied migrations, to be sure that each one is applied exactly once.

Keep in mind that, to properly use migrations through Django no alterations outside of this method should be made, as this can confuse and create conflicts. If you need to apply changes that can't be replicated automatically with a change in the model, like a data migration, you can create an empty migration and fill it with your custom SQL statements. This can create complex, custom migrations, but that will be applied and kept in track with the rest of the automatically created Django migrations. Models can also be explicitly marked as not-handled by Django to manage them manually.

For more details about Django migrations, check the documentation at `https://docs.djangoproject.com/en/3.2/topics/migrations/`.

Changing the database without interruption

The process to migrate the data, then, needs to happen in the following order:

1. The old code and the old database schema are in place. This is the starting point.
2. The database applies a migration that's backward compatible with the old code. As the database can apply this change while in operation, the service is not interrupted.
3. The new code taking advantage of the new schema is deployed. This deployment won't require any special downtime and can be performed without interrupting the process.

The critical element of this process is step 2, to ensure that the migration is backward compatible with the previous code.

Most of the usual changes are relatively simple, like adding a new table or column to a table, and you'll have no problem with that. The old code won't make use of the column or table, and that will be totally fine. But other migrations can be more complex.

For example, let's imagine that a field `Field1` that has so far been an integer needs to be translated into a string. There'll be numbers stored, but also some special values like `NaN` or `Inf` that are not supported by the database. The new code will decode them and deal with them correctly.

But obviously, a change that migrates the code from an integer to a string is going to produce an error if this is not taken into account in the old code.

To solve this problem, it needs to be approached as a series of steps instead:

1. The old code and the old database schema are in place. This is the starting point.
2. The database applies a migration adding a new column, `Field2`. In this migration, the value from `Field1` is translated into a string and copied.
3. A new version of the code, intermediate code, is deployed. This version understands there may be one (`Field2`) or two columns (`Field1` and `Field2`). It uses the value in `Field2`, not the one in `Field1`, but if there's a write, it should overwrite both.

To avoid having a problem with possible updates between the application of the migration and the new code, the code will need to check if the column `Field1` exists, and if it does and has a different value than `Field2`, update the latter before performing any operation.

4. A new migration removing `Field1`, now unused, can be applied.

In the same migration, the same caveat as above should be applied – if the value in `Field1` is different from the one in `Field2`, overwrite it with `Field1`. Note how the only case where this may happen is if it has been updated with the old code.

5. The new code that is only aware of `Field2` can now be deployed safely.

Depending on whether `Field2` is an acceptable name or not, it may be possible that a further migration is deployed changing the name from `Field2` to `Field1`. In that case, the new code needs to be prepared in advance to use `Field2` or, if not present, `Field1`.

A new deployment could be done after that to use only `Field1` again:

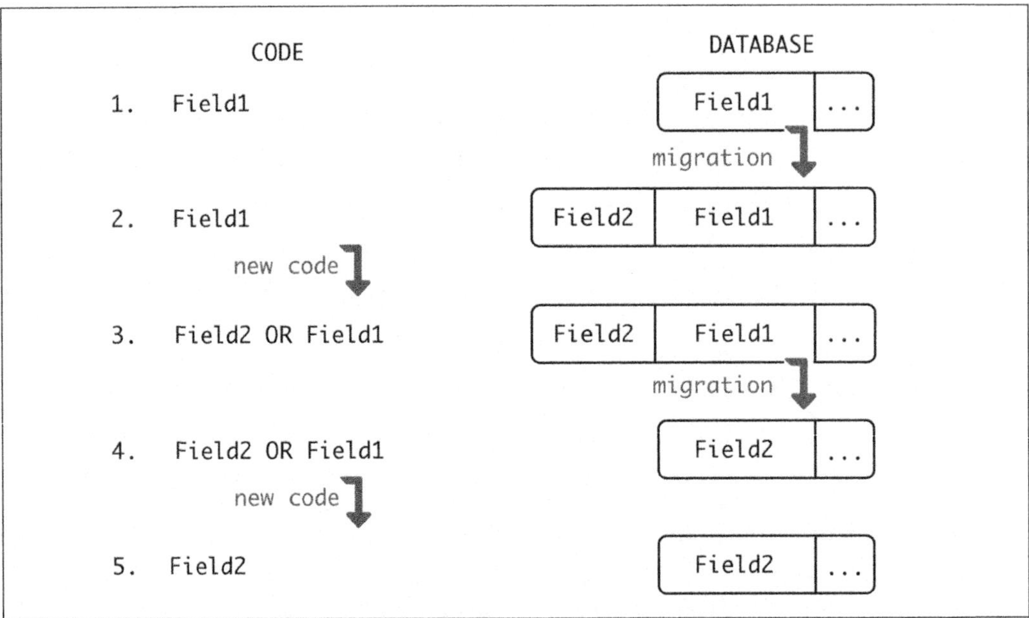

Figure 4.3: Migrating from Field1 to Field2

If this seems like a lot of work, well, it is. All these steps are required to enforce smooth operation and achieve no downtime. The alternative is to stop the old code, perform the migration with the format change in `Field1`, and then start the new code. But this can cause several problems.

The most obvious is the downtime. While the impact can be minimized by trying to set up a proper maintenance window, most modern applications are expected to work 24x7 and any downtime is considered a problem. If the application has a global audience, it may be difficult to justify a stop just for avoidable maintenance.

The downtime also may last a while, depending on the migration side. A common problem is testing the migration in a database much smaller than the production one. This can create an unexpected problem when running in production, taking much longer than anticipated. Depending on the size of the data, a complex migration may take hours to complete. And, given that it will run as part of a transaction, it needs to be totally completed before proceeding or it will be rolled back.

If possible, try to test the migrations of the system with a big enough test database that's representative. Some operations can be quite costly. It's possible that some migrations may need to be tweaked to run faster or even divided into smaller steps so each one can run in its own transaction to run in a reasonable time. It's even possible in some cases that the database will require more memory to allow the migration to run in a reasonable amount of time.

But another problem is the risk of introducing a step, at the start of the new code, that can have problems and bugs, either related to the migration, or unrelated. With this process, after the migration is applied, there's no possibility of using the old code. If there's a bug in the new code, it needs to be fixed and a newer version deployed. This can create big trouble.

While it's true that, as migrations are not reversible, applying a migration is always a risk, the fact that the code stays stable helps mitigate problems. Changing a single piece of code is less risky than changing two without being able to revert either of them.

Migrations may be reversible, as there could be steps that perform the reverse operation. While this is theoretically true, it is extremely difficult to enforce in real operations. It's possible that a migration like removing a column is effectively not reversible, as data gets lost.

This way migrations need to be applied very carefully and by ensuring that each step is small and deliberate.

Keep in mind how migrations inter-operate with the techniques that we talked about related to distributed databases. For example, a sharded database will need to apply each migration independently to each of the shards, which may be a time-consuming operation.

Data migrations

Data migrations are changes in the database that don't change the format but change the values of some fields.

These migrations are produced normally either to correct some error in the data, like a bug that stores a value with some encoding error, or to move old records to a more up-to-date format. For example, including zip codes in all addresses, if not already present, or to change the scale of a measurement from inches to centimeters.

In either case, these actions may need to be performed for all rows or only for a selection of them. Applying them only to the relevant subset, if possible, can greatly speed up the process, especially for big databases.

In cases like the scale change described above, the process may require more steps to ensure that the code can handle both scales and differentiate between them. For example, with an extra field describing the scale. In this case, the process will be as follows:

1. Create a migration to set a new column, `scale`, to all rows, with a default value of `inches`. Any new row introduced by the old code will automatically set up the values correctly, by using a default value.
2. Deploy a new version of the code able to work with both inches and centimeters reading the value in `scale`.
3. Set up another migration to change the value of measurement. Each row will change both the `scale` and the `measurement` accordingly. Set the default value for `scale` to `centimeters`.
4. Now all the values in the database are in centimeters.
5. Optionally, clean up by deploying a new version of the code that doesn't access the `scale` field and understands only centimeters, as both scales are not used. After that, a new migration removing the column can also be run.

Step 5 is optional and normally there's not a great appetite for this kind of cleanup, as it's not strictly necessary and the versatility of having the extra column may be worth keeping for future usage.

As we discussed before, the key element is to deploy code that's able to work with both database values, the old and the new, and understand them. This allows for a smooth transition between the values.

Changes without enforcing a schema

One of the flexible aspects of non-relational databases is the fact that there's typically not an enforced schema. Instead, the stored documents accept different formats.

This means that, instead of an all-or-nothing change as for relational databases, a more continuous change and dealing with multiple formats is preferred.

Instead of the application of migrations, which is a concept not really applicable here, the code will have to perform the changes over time. In this case, the steps are like this:

1. The old code and the old database schema are in place. This is the starting point.
2. Each of the documents in the database has a `version` field.
3. The new code contains a Model layer with the migration instructions from the previous version to the new one – in our example above, to translate `Field1` from integer to string.
4. Every time that a particular document is accessed, the `version` is checked. If it's not the latest, `Field1` is transformed into a string, and the version is updated. This action happens before performing any operation. After the update, the operation is performed normally.

   This operation runs alongside the normal operation of the system. Given enough time, it will migrate, document by document, the whole database.

> The `version` field may not be strictly necessary, as the type of `Field1` may be easy to infer and change. But it presents the advantage that it makes the process explicit, and can be concatenated, migrating an old document from different versions in a single access.
>
> If the `version` field is not present, it may be understood as `version 0` and be migrated to `version 1`, now including the field.

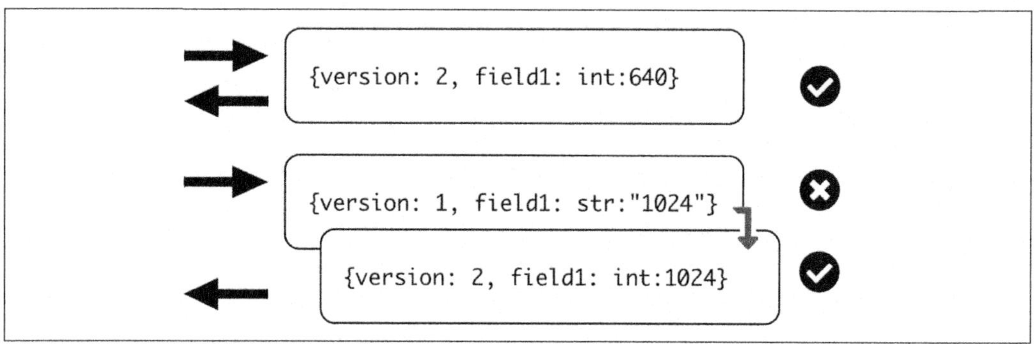

Figure 4.4: Changes over time

This process is very clean, but sometimes leaving data in the old format for a long time, even if it's not accessed, may not be advisable. It may cause that code to migrate from `version` 1 to 2, `version` 2 to 3, etc, if still present in the code. If this is the case, an extra process running alongside may be covering every document, updating and saving it until the whole database is migrated.

This process is similar to the one described for data migration, though databases enforcing schemas need to perform migrations to change the format. In a schema-less database, the format can be changed at the same time as the value.

In the same way, a pure data change, like the example seen before where it was changing the scale, can be performed without the need for a migration, slowly changing the database as we described here. Doing it with a migration ensures a cleaner change, though, and may allow a simultaneous change in format.

Also note that, if this functionality is encapsulated in the internal database access layer, the logic above this one may use the newer functionality without caring about old formats, as they'll be translated on the fly.

While there's still data in the database with the old `version`, the code needs to be able to interpret it. This can cause some accumulation of old tech, so it's also possible to migrate all the data in the background, as it can be done document to document, filtering by the old version, while everything is in operation. Once this background migration is done, the code can be refactored and cleaned to remove the handling of obsolete versions.

Dealing with legacy databases

ORM frameworks can generate the proper SQL commands to create the database schema. When designing and implementing a database from scratch, that means that we can create the ORM Model in code and the ORM framework will make the proper adjustments.

This way of describing the schema in code is called **declarative**.

But sometimes, we need to work with an existing database that was created previously by manually running SQL commands. There are two possible use cases:

- **The schema will never be under the control of the ORM framework**. In this case, we need a way to detect the existing schema and use it.
- **We want to use the ORM framework from this situation to control the fields and any new changes**. In this scenario, we need to create a Model that reflects the current situation and move from there to a *declarative* situation.

Let's take a look at how to approach these situations.

Detecting a schema from a database

For certain applications, if the database is stable or it's simple enough, it can be used as-is, and you can try to minimize the code to deal with it. SQLAlchemy allows you to automatically detect the schema of the database and work with it.

SQLAlchemy is a very powerful ORM-capable library and arguably the best solution to perform complex and tailored accesses to a relational database. It allows complex definitions on how exactly tables relate to each other and allows you to tweak queries and create precise mappings. It's also more complex and potentially more difficult to use than other ORM frameworks such as the Django ORM.

To automatically detect a database, you can automatically detect the tables and columns:

```
>>> from sqlalchemy.ext.automap import automap_base
>>> from sqlalchemy.sql import select
>>> from sqlalchemy import create_engine

# Read the database and detect it
>>> engine = create_engine("sqlite:///database.db")
>>> Base = automap_base()
>>> Base.prepare(engine, reflect=True)

# The Pens class maps the table called "pens" in the DB
>>> Pens = Base.classes.pens

# Create a session to query
>>> session = Session(engine)

# Create a select query
>>> query = select(Pens).where(Pens.color=='blue')
# Execute the query
>>> result = session.execute(query)
>>> for row, in result:
...     print(row.id, row.name, row.color)
...
1 Waldorf blue
```

Note how the described names for the table `pens` and columns `id`, `name`, and `color` are detected automatically. The format of the query is also very similar to what a SQL construction will be.

SQLAlchemy allows more complex usages and the creation of classes. For more information, refer to its documentation: `https://docs.sqlalchemy.org/`.

The Django ORM also has a command that allows you to dump a definition of the defined tables and relationships, using `inspectdb`.

```
$ python3 manage.py inspectdb > models.py
```

This creates a `models.py` file that contains the interpretation of the database based on the discovery that Django can do. This file may require adjustments.

These methods of operation work perfectly for simple situations, where the most important part is to not spend too much effort having to replicate a schema in code. Other situations, where the schema gets mutated and requires better handling and control over the code, require a different approach.

Check the Django documentation for more information: `https://docs.djangoproject.com/en/3.2/howto/legacy-databases/`.

Syncing the existing schema to the ORM definition

In other situations, there's a legacy database that was created by a method that cannot be replicated. Perhaps it was done through manual commands. The current code may use the database, but we want to migrate the code so we are up-to-date with it so we can, on one hand, understand exactly what the different relations and formats are, and on another, allow the ORM to make controlled changes to the schema in a compatible way. We will see the latter as migrations.

The challenge in this case is to create a bunch of Models in the ORM framework that are up-to-date with the definition of the database. This is easier said than done, for several reasons:

- There can be database features that are not exactly translated by the ORM. For example, ORM frameworks don't deal with stored procedures natively. If the database has stored procedures, they need to be either removed or replicated as part of the software operation.

> Stored procedures are code functions inside the database that modify it. They can be manually called by using a SQL query, but normally they are triggered by certain operations, like inserting a new row or changing a column. Stored procedures are not very common these days, as they can be confusing to operate, and instead, in most cases, system designs tend to see databases as storage-only facilities, without the capacity to change the data that is stored. Managing stored procedures is complicated, as they can be difficult to debug and keep in sync with external code.
>
> Stored procedures can be replicated by code that handles that complexity as part of a single Unit of Work action when the action will be triggered. This is the most common approach these days. But, of course, migrating already-existing stored procedures into external code is a process that may not be easy and requires care and planning.

- ORM frameworks can have their quirks in how to set up certain elements, which may not be compatible with the already-existing database. For example, how certain elements are named. The Django ORM doesn't allow you to set custom names for the indices and constraints. For a while, the constraint can remain only in the database, but "hidden" in the ORM, but in the long run that can create problems. This means that at some point, the index name needs to be changed externally to the compatible name.
- Another example of this is the lack of support for composite primary keys in the Django ORM, which may require you to create a new numeric column to create a surrogate key.

These limitations require that the creation of Models is done carefully and there are checks needed to ensure that they work as expected with the current schema. The created schema based on the code Models in the ORM framework can be produced and compared with the actual schema until there's parity or they are close enough.

For example, for Django, the following general procedure can be used:

1. Create a dump of the database schema. This will be used as a reference.
2. Create the proper Model files. The starting point could be the output from the `inspectdb` command described above.

Note that the `inspectdb` creates the Models with their metadata set to not track changes in the database. That means that Django labels the Models as not tracked for changes as migrations. Once verified, this will need to be changed.

3. Create a single migration with all the required changes for the database. This migration is created normally, with `makemigrations`.
4. Use the command `sqlmigrate` to produce a SQL dump of the SQL statements that will be applied by the migration. This generates a database schema that can be compared with the reference.
5. Adjust the differences and repeat from step 2 onward. Remember to delete the migration file each time to generate it from scratch.

   Once the migration is tweaked to produce exactly the results that are currently applied, this migration can be applied using the parameter `--fake` or `-fake-initial`, meaning that it will be registered as applied, but the SQL won't run.

This is a very simplified method. As we discussed above, there are some elements that can be difficult to replicate. Changes to the external database to solve incompatibility problems may be required.

On the other hand, sometimes it can be okay to live with small differences that are not creating any problems. For example, a different name in the primary key index may be something that can be acceptable and fixed later. Normally, these kinds of operations require a long time to be totally completed from a complex schema. Plan accordingly and do it in small increments.

After that, changes can be applied normally by changing the Models and then autogenerating migrations.

Summary

In this chapter, we described what the principles behind Domain-Driven Design are, to orient the abstraction of storing data and use rich objects that follow business principles. We also described ORM frameworks and how they can be useful to remove the need to deal with low-level interaction with specific libraries to work with the storage layer. We described different useful techniques for the code to interact with the database, like the Unit of Work pattern, which is related to the concept of a transaction, and CQRS for advanced cases where the write and read are addressed to different backends.

We also discussed how to deal with database changes, both with explicit migrations that change the schema and with more soft changes that migrate the data as the application is running.

Finally, we described different methods to deal with legacy databases, and how to create models to create a proper software abstraction when there's no control over the current schema of the data.

Join our book's Discord space

Join the book's Discord workspace for a monthly *Ask me Anything* session with the author: `https://packt.link/PythonArchitechture`

Part II

Architectural Patterns

To be able to produce successful designs, it's not necessary to start from scratch. Instead, your efforts are better put into understanding which common architectural patterns have already been proven successful.

In this section of the book, we will see different ideas that are common across a lot of successful systems. All these elements are useful in specific contexts, and we will see what their strengths and limitations are over the following chapters:

1. **The Twelve-Factor App Methodology**, explaining this methodology
2. **Web Server Structures**, describing how to deal effectively with response-request services
3. **Event-Driven Structure Basics**, introducing how to work with events and communicate different services with them
4. **Advanced Event-Driven Structures**, for creating complex flows of information, priorities, and CQRS
5. **Microservices vs Monolith**, explaining the differences between them and the tools for dealing with them

We will introduce you to the Twelve-Factor App methodology, as it contains a list of useful suggestions for dealing with the specifics of services. We will also get into the specifics of web server request-response structures, which are normally the foundation of servers.

We will also cover event-driven systems, taking two chapters to be sure to cover the basic and more advanced uses. Event-driven systems are asynchronous by nature, meaning that the calling system won't wait until the processing is done, and in a lot of cases, there won't even be something similar to a response. These systems are very useful for dealing either with triggering multiple services with the same input or for generating results that take a long time to process.

We'll also discuss monolithic systems compared with microservices, and the different tools and techniques to use in both cases, including migrating from one to the other.

5
The Twelve-Factor App Methodology

When designing a software system, it's not a good idea to reinvent the wheel each time for each new project. Certain parts of software are common to most web service projects. Learning some of the known practices that have proven successful over time is important to avoid making easily fixed mistakes.

In this chapter, we will focus on the Twelve-Factor App methodology. This methodology is a series of recommendations that are well proven for web services that are deployed on the web.

The Twelve-Factor App has its origins in Heroku, a company that provides easy access to deployments. Some of the factors are more general than others, and everything should be considered general advice and not necessarily an imposition. The methodology is less applicable outside of web cloud services, but it's still a good idea to review it and try to extract useful information.

We will present the base details for this methodology during the chapter and will spend some time describing in more detail some of the most important factors that this methodology covers.

In this chapter, we'll cover the following topics:

- Intro to the Twelve-Factor App
- Continuous Integration
- Scalability
- Configuration
- The Twelve factors
- Containerized Twelve-Factor Apps

Let's start by introducing the basic concepts of the Twelve-Factor App.

Intro to the Twelve-Factor App

The Twelve-Factor App is a methodology with 12 different aspects or factors that cover good practices to follow while designing a web system. They aim to provide clarity and simplify some of the possibilities, detailing patterns that are known to work.

The factors are generic enough to not be prescriptive in how to implement them or force the use of specific tools, and at the same time, give clear direction. The Twelve-Factor App Methodology is opinionated in the sense that it aims to cover cloud services in a scalable way, and also promotes the idea of **Continuous Integration** (**CI**) as a critical aspect of these kinds of operations. This also leads to a reduction in the differences between a local, development environment and a production environment.

These two aspects, consistency between local and production deployments, and CI, interact, as it allows the system to be tested in a consistent way, both in a development environment and while running the tests in a CI system.

Scalability is another key element. As cloud services require working with a variable workload, we need to allow our service to be capable of growing and be able to process more requests coming into the system without any issues.

A third general problem that we will cover, and which is also central to the Twelve-Factor App, is the challenge of configuration. Configuration allows the same code to be set up in different environments, while also tweaking some features to adjust them in certain situations.

Continuous Integration

Continuous Integration, or CI, is the practice of automating the running of tests when new code is submitted to a central repository. Whereas, when originally introduced back in 1991, it could be understood as running a "nightly build", as running the tests took time and was expensive, these days, it is commonly understood as running a set of tests with each new code submission.

The objective is to produce code that always works. After all, if it's not, it is detected quickly by the failing tests. This fast feedback loop helps developers to increase their speed and create a safety net that allows them to focus on whatever feature they are implementing and leave it to the CI system to run the totality of tests. The discipline of running the tests automatically and on every single test greatly helps to ensure high-quality code, as any error is detected quickly.

This is also dependent on the quality of the tests that are run, so in order to have a good CI system, it is important to understand the importance of good tests and to refine the testing procedure regularly, both to ensure that it gives us an adequate level of confidence and that it runs fast enough not to cause a problem.

Fast enough, when dealing with a CI system can vary. Keep in mind that the tests will run in the background, automatically, without the involvement of a developer, so they may take a while to return a result, compared with the quick feedback that a developer will expect when debugging a problem. As a very general approximation, aim to have your test pipeline finished in around 20 minutes or less, if that is possible.

CI is based on the capacity of automating whatever system is used as a central repository for code, so tests are launched as soon as new changes are forthcoming from a developer. It is very common to use a source control system like `git`, and add a hook that automatically runs the tests.

In a more practical approach, `git` is normally used under a cloud system like GitHub (`https://github.com/`) or GitLab (`https://about.gitlab.com/`). Both of them have other services that integrate with them and allow operations to be run automatically through some configuration. Examples include TravisCI (`https://www.travis-ci.com/`) and CircleCI (`https://circleci.com/`). In the case of GitHub, they have their own native system called GitHub Actions. All of these are based on the idea of adding a special file to configure the service, thereby simplifying the setup and run of a pipeline.

A CI pipeline is a succession of steps that are run in order. If there's an error, it will stop the execution of the pipeline and report whatever problem has been detected, allowing for early detection and feedback for developers. Typically, we build the software into a testable state and then run the tests. If there are different kinds of tests, such as unit and integration tests, run them both, either one after the other or in parallel.

A typical pipeline to run tests could do the following:

1. As it starts in a new, empty environment, install the required dependency tools to run the tests; for example, a particular version of Python and a compiler, or a static analysis tool that will be used in *step 3*.
2. Perform any build command to prepare the code, such as compiling or packetizing.
3. Run static analysis tools like `flake8` to detect style problems. If the results reveal problems, stop here and report.
4. Run the unit tests. If the results are incorrect, stop here and show the errors.
5. Prepare and run other tests, such as integration or system tests.

These stages may be run, in certain cases, in parallel. For example, *steps 3* and *4* may run at the same time as there is no dependency between the cases, whereas *step 2* needs to be completed before moving on to *step 3*. These steps can be described in some CI systems to allow for faster execution.

The keyword in a CI pipeline is **automation**. To allow the pipeline to be executed, all the steps need to be able to be run automatically, without any manual intervention. This requires that any dependency is also able to be set up automatically. For example, elements like databases or other dependencies, if required for tests, need to be allocated.

A common pattern is that CI tools allocate a virtual machine that allows a database to start up so that it's available in the environment, including the usual suspects such as MySQL, PostgreSQL, and MongoDB. Keep in mind that the database will start empty, and if test data needs to be seeded, it will need to be done during the setting up of the environment. Check the documentation for your specific tool for more details.

One possibility is to use Docker to build one or more containers that will standardize the process and make all dependencies explicit in the building process. This is becoming an increasingly common option.

We will talk more about Docker in *Chapter 8, Advanced Event-Driven Structures*.

Some of the factors of the Twelve-Factor App play a part in the setup of a CI pipeline, as they aim to have code that is easy to build, to be deployed either for testing or operating and configuration.

Scalability

Cloud systems are expected to behave correctly under high loads, or at least to adjust between different loads. This requires the software to be **scalable**. Scalability is the ability of the software to be allowed to grow and accept more requests, mostly by increasing resources.

There are two types of scalability:

- Vertical scalability: Increasing resources to each node, making them more powerful. This is the equivalent of buying a more powerful computer; adding more RAM, more hard drive space, a faster CPU...
- Horizontal scalability: Adding more nodes to the system, without them being necessarily more powerful. For example, instead of having two web servers, increase them to five.

In general, horizontal scalability is considered more desirable. In a cloud system, the capacity of adding and removing nodes can be automated, allowing for deployments to adjust automatically based on the number of current requests flowing into the system. Compared with the traditional way of operating, where the system had to be dimensioned for the moment of maximum system load, this can greatly reduce costs since, most of the time, the system will be underutilized.

For example, let's compare a situation where, at noon, the system requires 11 servers, when most customers are connected. At midnight, the system is at its lowest utilization point, and only 2 servers are required.

The following diagram shows a typical situation when the number of servers grows based on the load:

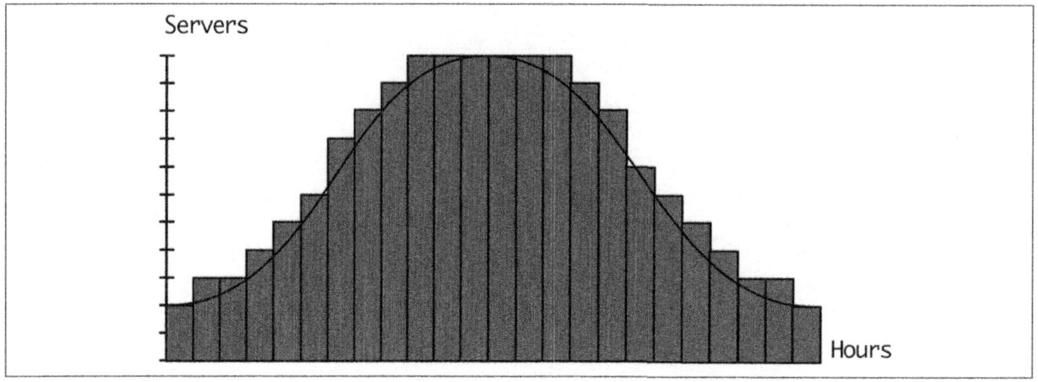

Figure 5.1: Service scaling up and down over time

The traditional situation will make use of 264 cost units (11 servers * 24 hours), while automatically scaling uses approximately 166 cost units, saving a considerable number of resources.

Even more so, a traditional system requires extra headroom to allow for unexpected spikes that could occur. Normally, a system will be set up to allow at least a 30% extra load, maybe even more. In that case, the cost is permanently added.

To allow a system to be horizontally scalable, it needs to be stateless. This means that each node is indistinguishable. Each request will be allocated to a node in some sort of rotation, distributing the load across all nodes. All state from each request needs to come either from the request itself (input parameters) or from an external storage source. From the point of view of the application, each request comes in an empty space and cannot be carried over in any event. That means not storing anything in the local hard drive or local memory between requests.

Storing information intra-request, for example, composing a file with information from the database to return it in the request is OK, although keeping it in memory, if possible, will likely be faster than using the hard drive.

The external storage source will typically be a database, but it's also common to use storage services more oriented to store files or other big blobs of binary data, for example, AWS S3.

AWS S3 is a web service that allows a file to be stored and retrieved from a URL. It allows the creation of a *bucket*, which will contain a number of *keys* or paths; for example, accessing a URL similar to `https://s3.amazonaws.com/mybucket/path/to/file` so it can upload and download file-like objects. There are also plenty of libraries to help deal with the service, such as `boto3` for Python.

This service is very useful for working with files in a scalable way, and it allows configuration in such a way that access for reading can be done publicly, enabling the pattern of storing the data through your system, and then allowing the user to read it from the public URL, thereby simplifying the system.

Refer to the AWS documentation for more information: `https://aws.amazon.com/s3/`

A cache should also be kept outside of each individual node, using tools such as Riak or memcached. Internal caches, using local memory, have the problem that they likely won't be used, as the next relevant request will likely be served by another node in the system. Using an external service allows all nodes to access the cache and improves the general performance of the system.

Keep in mind that the whole system cannot be stateless. In particular, the storage elements, such as databases and caches, require a different way of operating, as they are the ones storing the data. We discussed how to scale storage systems in *Chapter 3, Data Modeling*.

Configuration

One of the basic ideas of the Twelve-Factor App is that the code is unique, but it can be adjusted through configuration. This enables the same code to be used and deployed in different environments.

The use of different environments allows testing environments to be set up, where tests can be run without affecting production data. They are a more controlled place for experimenting or trying to replicate real problems in a sandbox. There's also another environment that is not typically thought of as such, which is the local development environment, where developers are able to check that the system works.

Creating a comprehensive and easy-to-use local environment is a critical aspect of developer productivity. When working with a single service or process, such as a web server, it is relatively easy to set up, as most projects will allow starting in a dev mode, but once there are more elements, it becomes more difficult to set up.

Complex settings have been quite common for years. There has been a relatively recent push to use virtual machines that could be set up from scratch, and more recently, containerization to ensure that it's easy to start it from a known point.

Configuring the system is more difficult than it appears at first sight. There's always a growing number of parameters to take care of. In complex systems, it is important to structure parameters in certain ways to allow them to be divided into more manageable parts.

Configuration parameters can be divided into two main categories:

- **Operational configuration**: These are parameters that connect different parts of the system or that are related to monitoring; for example, the address and credentials for the database, the URL to use to access an external API, or setting the level of logging to `INFO`. These config parameters are only changed when there's a change in the cluster, but the external behavior of the application doesn't change; for example, a change to log only `WARNING` logs or higher, or the credentials are replaced to rotate them.
- These parameters are under the control of operations and are normally changed transparently or during maintenance. A misconfiguration in these parameters is normally a serious problem as it can affect the functionality of the system.
- **Feature configuration**: These parameters change external behavior, enabling or disabling features or changing aspects of the software; for example, theming parameters to set the color and header images; or enabling the premium feature to allow a charge for premium access, or updating the parameters of a mathematical model that changes how the internal calculation of orbits are performed.

  These parameters are irrelevant as regards the operation of the software. A misconfiguration here will likely not cause problems, as it will continue to operate normally. Changes here are more under the control of developers or even business managers to enable a feature at a particular point in time.

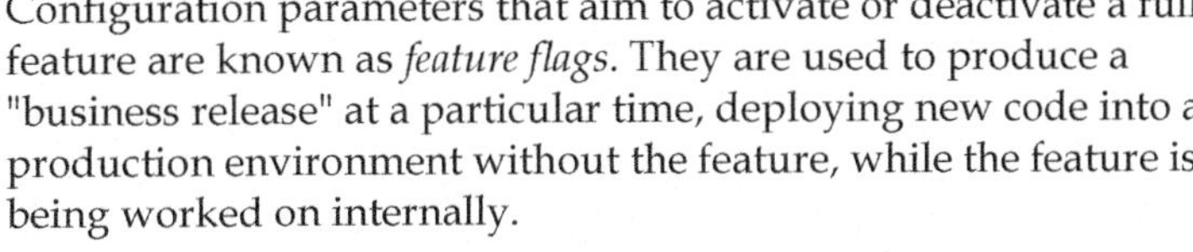

> Configuration parameters that aim to activate or deactivate a full feature are known as *feature flags*. They are used to produce a "business release" at a particular time, deploying new code into a production environment without the feature, while the feature is being worked on internally.
>
> Once the feature is ready for release, after thoroughly testing it, the code can be deployed beforehand in production, and the full feature can be activated just by changing the proper config parameter.
>
> This allows us to keep working in small increases toward a big feature, such as a revamp of the user interface, while at the same time building and releasing small increments frequently. Once the feature is released, the code can be refactored to remove the parameter.

These two categories have different aims and, normally, are maintained by different people. While the operational configuration parameters are tightly related to a single environment and require parameters that are correct for the environment, the feature configuration normally moves between the local development to test it until it is changed in the production one with the same value.

Traditionally, the configuration has been stored in one or more files, typically grouped by environment. This creates a file called `production.cnf` and another one called `staging.cnf` that are attached to the code base, and depending on the environment, one or the other is used. This entails certain problems:

- Making a configuration change is, de facto, a code change. This limits the speed of changes that can be performed and cause problems with scope.
- When the number of environments grows, the number of files grows at the same time. This can cause errors as a result of duplication; for example, a mistake that changes the wrong file is not reverted and is unexpectedly deployed later. Old files may also not be removed.
- Centralizing control among developers. As we've seen, some of these parameters are not necessarily under the control of developers, but ops teams. Storing all the data in the code base makes it more difficult to create a division between jobs, requiring both teams to access the same files. While this is fine for small teams, over time, it makes sense to try to reduce the need to have big groups of people accessing the same file to only care about half of it.

- Storing sensitive parameters such as passwords in files and storing them in the code repo is an obvious security risk, as anyone with access to the repo can use these credentials to access all environments, including production.

These problems render it unadvisable to store the configuration directly as files inside the code base. We will see how the Twelve-Factor App deals with it specifically in the *Configuration* factor.

The Twelve Factors

The factors for Twelve-Factor Apps are as follows:

1. **Code base**. Store the code in a single repo and differentiate only by configuration.
2. **Dependencies**. Declare them explicitly and clearly.
3. **Config**. Config through the environment.
4. **Backing services**. Any backing service should be treated as an attached resource.
5. **Build, release, run**. Differentiate between build and run states.
6. **Processes**. Execute the app as a stateless process.
7. **Port binding**. Expose services through ports.
8. **Concurrency**. Set up the services as processes.
9. **Disposability**. Fast start and graceful shutdown.
10. **Dev/prod parity**. All environments should be as similar as possible.
11. **Logs**. Send logs to event streams.
12. **Admin processes**. Run one-off admin processes independently.

The factors can be grouped around different concepts:

- *Code base*, *Build, release, run*, and *Dev/prod parity* work around the idea of generating a single application that runs in different environments, differentiating only through configuration
- *Config*, *Dependencies*, *Port binding*, and *Backing services* work around the configuration and connectivity of different services
- *Processes*, *Disposability*, and *Concurrency* are related to the scalability concept
- *Logs* and *Admin processes* are practical ideas involved with monitoring and one-off processes

Let's take a look at all four of these groups.

Build once, run multiple times

One of the key concepts around the Twelve-Factor App is that it's easy to build and manage, but at the same time, it's a unified system. This means that there's no ad hoc code that's changed from one version to another, just configurable options.

The aim of the *Code base* factor is that all the software for an app is a single repo, with a single state, without special branches for each customer, or a special functionality that's only available in a particular environment.

Very specific environments are typically called *snowflake environments*. Anyone that has dealt with them knows how painfully difficult they are to maintain, and that's why the objective for the Twelve-Factor App is to remove them, or at least make them change based just on the configuration.

This means that the code to deploy is always the same, and only the configuration changes. This allows easy testing of all the configuration changes and does not introduce blind spots.

Note that a single system may have multiple projects, living in multiple repos, that individually fulfill the Twelve-Factor App and work together. Other factors talk about interoperation on applications.

Keeping multiple applications working together, through coordinated APIs, is always a challenge and requires good coordination across teams. Some companies adopt the monorepo approach, where there's a single repository with all the company projects living in multiple subdirectories, to be sure that there's a complete view of the whole system and a single state across the whole organization.

This also has its own challenges, and requires greater coordination across teams and can present big challenges for big repos.

A single code base allows a strict differentiation of the stages in the *Build, release, run* factor. This factor ensures that there are three distinct stages:

- The build stage transforms the content of the code repo into a package or executable that will be run later

- The release stage uses this built package, combines it with the proper configuration for the selected environment, and sets it ready for execution
- The run stage finally executes the package in the selected environment

As we discussed previously, the configuration lives in a different place to the code base. This separation makes sense, and it could be also under source control. It may be stored as files, but the access can then be separated by environment, something that makes sense, as some environments, like production, are more critical than others. Storing the configuration as part of the code base makes it difficult to perform that separation.

Keep in mind that more than one file can be combined, allowing the parameters to be separated into feature and operational configurations.

Because stages are strictly divided, it's not possible to change the configuration or the code after the code is deployed. This requires a new release in any case. This makes the releases very explicit, and each one should be executed independently. Note that the run stage may need to be executed again in case there's a new server or the server crashes, so the aim should be for this to be as easy to do as possible. As we are seeing, a common thread through the Twelve-Factor App is strict separation, so that each element is easy to recognize and to operate. We will check how to define the configuration in other factors.

Performing tests after the build stage also ensures that the code remains without changes between the tests and the release and operation.

Because of this strict separation, in particular, in the build stage, it's easy to follow the *Dev/prod parity*. In essence, a development environment is the same as a production one, as they use the same building stage, but with proper configuration to run locally. This factor also makes it possible to use the same (or as close as possible) backing services, like databases or queues, to ensure that local development is as representative as a production environment. Container tools such as Docker, or provisioning tools such as Chef or Puppet, can also help in automatically setting up environments that contain all the required dependencies.

Obtaining a fast and easy process to develop, build, and deploy is critical for speeding up the cycle and adjusting quickly.

Dependencies and configurations

The Twelve-Factor App advocates the explicit definition of dependencies and configuration and, at the same time, is opinionated in terms of how to do them and provides solid standards that are proven.

That is why, in the *Config* factor, it talks about storing all the configuration for the system in **environment variables**. Environment variables are independent from code, which allows retention of the strict differentiation that we talked about in the *Build, release, run factor* and avoidance of the problems that we described previously in storing them in files inside the code base. They are also language- and OS-independent, and easy to work with. Injecting environment variables into a new environment is also easy.

This is preferred to other alternatives, such as setting different files into the code base describing environments like `staging` or `production`, because they allow more granularity, and because this kind of handling ends up creating too many files and changing the code for environments that are not affected; for example, having to update the code base for a `demo` environment that is short-lived.

Although the Twelve-Factor App encourages dealing with configurations in a variable-independent way, the reality of the work means that there are a limited number of environments and their configuration should be stored somewhere. The key element is storing it in a different place to the code base, managed only on the *release* stage. This allows plenty of flexibility.

Keep in mind that for local development, these environment variables may need to be changed independently to test or debug different features.

Configuration can be obtained in configuration files directly from the environment using standard libraries; for example, in Python:

```
import os
PARAMETER = os.environ['PATH']
```

This code will store in the constant `PARAMETER` the value of the `PATH` environment variable. Be careful as the lack of a `PATH` environment variable will generate a `KeyError` as it won't be present in the `environ` dictionary.

For the following examples, keep in mind that the defined environment variables need to be defined in your environment. These definitions are not included, to simplify the explanation. You can run Python, adding a local environment, by running `$ MYENVVAR=VALUE python3`.

To allow for optional environment variables, and protect against them going missing, use `.get` to set up a default value:

```
PARAMETER = os.environ.get('MYENVVAR', 'DEFAULT VALUE')
```

As a general recommendation, it's better to raise an exception because there's a missing configuration variable than to continue with a default parameter. This makes configuration problems easier to spot, as it will stop when the process starts, failing loudly. Remember, following the Twelve-Factor App ideas, you want to describe things explicitly and any problem should fail as early as possible in order to be able to fix it correctly instead of passing without detection.

Note that environment variables are always defined as text. If the value needs to be in a different format, it needs to be converted, for example:

```
NUMBER_PARAMETER = int(os.environ['ENVINTEGERPARAMETER'])
```

This presents a common problem when defining a `Boolean` value. Defining this translation code as follows is incorrect:

```
BOOL_PARAMETER = bool(os.environ['ENVBOOLPARAMETER'])
```

If the value of `ENVPARAMETER` is `"TRUE"`, the value of `BOOL_PARAMETER` is `True` (Boolean). But if the value of `ENVPARAMETER` is `"FALSE"`, the value of `BOOL_PARAMETER` is also `True`. This is because the string `"FALSE"` is a non-empty string and gets converted into `True`. Instead, the standard library package, `distutils`, can be used:

```
import os
from distutils.util import strtobool
BOOL_PARAMETER = strtobool(os.environ['ENVBOOLPARAMETER'])
```

`strtobool` returns not `True` or `False` as `Booleans`, but `0` or `1` as integers. This normally works correctly, but if you need strict `Boolean` values, add `bool` like this: `bool(strtobool(os.environ['ENVPARAMETER']))`

Environment variables also allow the injection of sensitive values such as secrets without storing them in the code base. Keep in mind that the secret will be available to inspect in the environment of the execution, but typically that's protected so only authorized team members can access it through `ssh` or similar in the environment.

As part of this configuration, any *backing services* should be defined as well as environment variables. Backing services are external services that the app uses over the network. They could be databases, queues, caching systems, or suchlike. They can be local to the same network or external services, such as APIs handled by an external company or AWS services.

From the point of view of the app, this differentiation should be irrelevant. The resources should be accessed by a URI and credentials, and, as part of the configuration, can be changed based on the environment. This makes the resources loosely coupled, and means they can be replaced easily. If there is a migration and the database needs to be moved between two networks, we can start the new database, perform a new release with a configuration change, and the app will point to the new database. This can be done with no code changes.

To allow the concatenation of multiple applications, the *Port binding* factor ensures that any service exposed is a port, which may be different depending on the service. This makes it easy to consider each app a backing service. Preferably, it should be exposed in HTTP as this makes it very standard to connect to.

For applications, use HTTP over port `80` when possible. This makes all connections easy with URLs such as `http://service-a.local/`.

Some applications require the combination of several processes working in conjunction. For example, it is typical for a web server for a Python application, such as Django, to use an application server like uWSGI to run it, and then a web server like nginx or Apache to serve it and the static files.

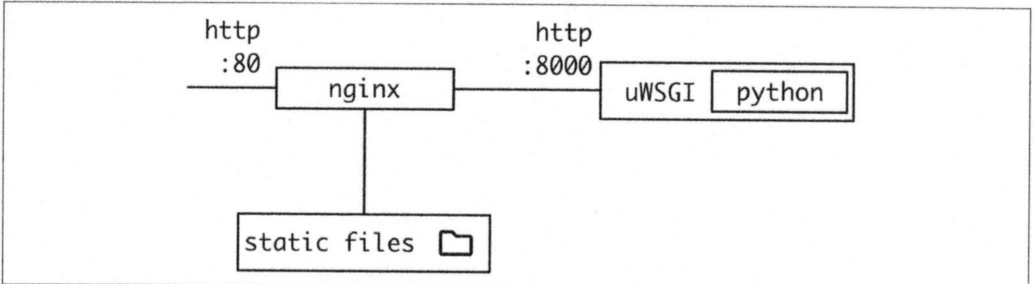

Figure 5.2: Connecting a web server and application server

They all connect by exposing a known port and protocol, which makes the setup easy.

On the same note, for clarity, all library *dependencies* should be explicitly set up and not rely on the pre-installation of certain packages in the existing operating system. The dependencies should be described through a dependency declaration, like a `requisites.txt` pip file for Python.

Dependencies should then be installed as part of the build stage, with commands such as `pip install -r requirements.txt`.

Keep in mind that the specific Python version is also a dependency that should be controlled tightly. The same is true of other required OS dependencies. Ideally, the OS environment should be created from scratch with the dependencies specified.

Even more so, dependencies should be isolated to ensure that there are no implicit dependencies that are not tightly controlled. Dependencies should also be defined as tightly as possible, to avoid the problem of different versions of dependencies being installed if new versions are released upstream.

For example, in a pip file, a dependency can be described in different ways:

```
requests
requests>=v2.22.0
requests==v2.25.1
```

The first way accepts any version, so it will typically use the latest. The second describes a minimum (and optionally maximum) version. The third version pins a specific version.

This is equivalent to other package management systems in operative systems, like `apt` in Ubuntu. You can install a specific version with `apt-get install dependency=version`.

Using very explicit dependencies makes the builds repeatable and deterministic. It ensures a lack of unknown changes during the build stage because a new version has been released. While most new packages will be compatible, it may also *sometimes* introduce changes that affect the behavior of the system. Even worse, those changes will be introduced **inadvertently**, causing severe problems.

Scalability

We talked earlier in the chapter about the why's of scalability. The Twelve-Factor App also talks about how to successfully grow or reduce the system.

The *Processes* factor talks about making sure that the run stage consists of starting one or more processes. These processes should be stateless and share nothing, meaning that all the data needs to be retrieved from an external backing service like a database. A temporal local disk can be used for temporal data within the same request, although their use should be kept to a minimum.

For example, a file upload may use the local hard drive to store a temporal copy and then process the data. After the data is processed, the file should be deleted from the disk.

If possible, try to use memory for this temporal storage as it will make this distinction more strict.

The next property that processes need to fulfill is their *disposability*. The processes need to be able to be started and stopped quickly, and at any time.

Starting quickly allows the system to react quickly to releases or restarts. The aim should be to take not more than a few seconds to have the process up and running. Quick turnaround is also important to allow rapid growth of the system in case more processes are being added for scale purposes.

The opposite is to allow the graceful shutdown of the process. This can be required for scale-down situations, to be sure that any request is not interrupted in this case. By convention, processes should be stopped by sending the `SIGTERM` signal.

Working with Docker containers automatically uses this convection by sending a `SIGTERM` signal to the main process whenever the container needs to be stopped. If the process doesn't stop itself after a grace period, it will be killed instead. The grace period can be configured if necessary.

Be sure that the main process for the container can receive `SIGTERM` and deal with it properly to ensure a graceful stopping of the container.

For example, for a web request, a graceful shutdown first will curtail the acceptance of any new requests, will finish any requests in the queue, and finally, will shut down the process. Web requests are typically quick to answer, but for other processes, such as long asynchronous tasks, it may take a long time to stop if they need to finish the current task.

Instead, long task workers should return the job to the queue and cancel the execution. This way, the task will be performed again, and to ensure that this doesn't duplicate actions, we need to ensure that all tasks can be canceled by waiting until the end of it to save its results and wrapping them into a transaction or similar.

In some cases, it may be necessary to distinguish between the bulk of the preparation job and the saving of results part. We either want to wait, if the job is saving the results at the time of shut down, or stop execution and return the task to the queue. Some save operations may require calling systems that don't accept transactions. The acceptable time for shutting down long-running processes may be longer than for web servers.

Processes should also be robust against unexpected stoppages. These stoppages could be caused by bugs, hardware errors, or, in general, unexpected surprises that always appear in software. Creating a resilient queue system that can retry in case a task is interrupted will help greatly in these instances.

Because the system is created through processes, based on that, we can scale out by creating more of them. Processes are independent and can be run at the same time on the same server or others. This is the basis of the *Concurrency* factor.

Keep in mind that the same application can use multiple processes that coordinate among them to handle different tasks and each process may have a different number of copies. In our previous example above, with an nginx server and uWSGI one, the optimal number may be to have a single nginx process for many more times the number of uWSGI workers.

The traditional deployment process was to set up a physical server (or virtual machine) for a node and fit a number of elements, which normally included tailoring the number of workers until finding the optimal figure to make proper use of the hardware.

With containers, this process is somehow reversed. Containers tend to be more lightweight and more can be created. While the optimization process is still required, with containers, it's more about creating a unit and then checking how many of them a single node can fit, as containers can be moved around nodes more easily, and the resulting apps tend to be smaller. Instead of finding out what is the proper size of the application for a given server, we figure out how many copies of a small application fit in a server, knowing that we can use different server sizes or add more servers with ease.

Adding more nodes, as they are independent and stateless, becomes an easy operation under a Twelve-Factor App. That allows the size of the entire operation to be adjusted to the load of the system. This can be a manual operation, to slowly add new nodes as the system grows in load and requests, or it can be done automatically, as we described earlier in the chapter.

The Twelve-Factor App doesn't demand that this scale is done automatically, but definitively enables it. Automating the adjustment should be treated with care, as it requires careful metrics on the load of the system. Allow time to perform tests to make the proper adjustments.

The Twelve-factor App processes should also be run by some sort of operating system process manager, like `upstart` or `systemd`. These systems ensure that the processes remain running, even in the event of a crash, handle graceful manual restarts, and also manage output streams gracefully. We will talk more about output streams as part of logs.

When working with containers, this changes a bit, as the equivalent is mostly handling containers more than processes. Instead of an operating system process manager, the work is performed by a container orchestrator that ensures that the containers are running properly and capturing any output stream. Inside the container, the processes can start without being under the control of a manager. The container will stop if the process is stopped.

Restarting the processes automatically, combined with a quick start up time and resilience in shutdown situations, makes the app dynamic and capable of self-repairing in case there is an unexpected problem that causes a process to crash. It also allows controlled shutdowns to be used as part of a general operation to avoid long-running processes and act as a contingency plan for memory leaks or other kinds of long-running problems.

This is equivalent to the old trick of turning it off and then turning it back on! If it can be done very quickly, it can save a lot of situations!

Monitoring and admin

A comprehensive monitoring system is important for detecting problems and analyzing the operation of the system. While it's not the only monitoring tool, logs are a critical part of any monitoring system.

Logs are text strings that provide visibility of the behavior of a running app. They should always include a timestamp on when they were generated. They are generated as the code is being executed, giving information on the different actions as they happen. The specifics about what to log can vary significantly by application, but typically frameworks will automatically create logs based on common practices.

For example, any web-related software will log requests received, something like this, for example:

```
[16/May/2021 13:32:16] "GET /path HTTP/1.1" 200 10697
```

Note that it includes:

- A timestamp for when it was generated `[16/May/2021 13:32:16]`
- The HTTP `GET` method and the `HTTP/1.1` protocol

- The accessed path - `/path`
- The returned status code - `200`
- The size of the request - `10697`

This kind of log is called an access log and will be generated in different formats. At the very least, it should always include the timestamp, HTTP method, path, and status code, but it can be configured to return extra information, such as the IP of the client making the request, or the time that it took to process the request.

Access logs are also generated by web servers including nginx and Apache. Configuring them properly to adjust the information produced is important for operational purposes.

Access logs are not the only useful ones. Application logs are also very useful. Application logs are generated inside the code and can be used to communicate significant milestones or errors. Web frameworks prepare the logs, so it's easy to generate new ones. For example, in Django, you can create logs this way:

```
import logging
logger = logging.getLogger(__name__)
...

def view(request, arg):

    logger.info('Testing condition')
    if something_bad:
        logger.warning('Something bad happened')
```

This will generate logs like these:

```
2021-05-16 14:01:37,269 INFO Testing condition
2021-05-16 14:01:37,269 WARNING Something bad happened
```

We will get into more details about logs in *Chapter 11, Package Management*.

The *Logs* factor suggests that logs shouldn't be managed by the process itself. Instead, logs should be printed in their own standard output without any intermediate step. The environment surrounding the process, like the operating system process manager described in the *Concurrency* factor, should be charged with receiving the logs, combining them, and routing them properly to a long-term archival and monitoring system. Note that this configuration is totally out of the application's control.

For local development, just showing the logs in a terminal may be enough for development purposes.

This is in contrast to storing the logs as log files in the hard drive. This has the problem of requiring the logs to be rotated and ensure that there's enough space. This also requires the different processes to coordinate in terms of having a similar policy for log rotation and storage. Instead, standard outputs can be combined and aggregated together for a whole image of the system, and not a single process.

The logs can also be directed toward an external log indexing system, such as the ELK Stack (Elasticsearch, Kibana, and Logstash: `https://www.elastic.co/products/`), which will capture logs and provide analytic tools to search through them. External tools are also available, including Loggly (`https://www.loggly.com/`) or Splunk (`https://www.splunk.com/`) to avoid maintenance. All these tools allow standard output logs to be captured and redirected to their solutions.

In the container world, this recommendation makes even more sense. Docker orchestration tools can easily capture the standard output from the containers and then redirect them to somewhere else.

These other tools can provide capabilities like searching and finding specific events in a particular time window, observing trends such as changes in the number of requests per hour, and even creating automatic alerts based on certain rules, such as an increase in the number of `ERROR` logs over a period of time over and above a certain value.

The *Admin processes* factor covers some processes that sometimes need to be run for specific operations, but are not part of the app's normal operation. Examples include the following:

- Database migrations

- The production of ad hoc reports, such as generating a one-off report for certain sales or detecting how many records are affected by a bug
- Running a console for debugging purposes

Executing commands in a console in a production environment should be used only when no other alternative is available, and not as a way of removing the need to create specific scripts for recurring operations. Extreme caution should apply. Keep in mind that an error in a production environment can create a serious problem. Treat your production environment with the proper respect.

These operations are not part of the day-to-day operation, but may need to be run. The interface is clearly different. To execute them, they should run in the same environment as the regular processes, using the same code base and configuration. These admin operations should be included as part of the code base to avoid problems with mismatched code.

In traditional environments, it may be necessary to log in to a server through `ssh` to allow the execution of this process. In container environments, a full container can be started exclusively to execute the process.

This is very common in cases of migrations, for example. A preparation command may consist of running the build to execute migrations.

This should be done before the actual release, to ensure that the database is migrated. Refer to *Chapter 4* for more details on migrations.

To run these admin commands in containers, the container image should be the same one that runs the application, but called with a different command, so the code and environment are the same as in the running application.

Containerized Twelve-Factor Apps

Although the Twelve-Factor App methodology is older than the current trend toward containerization using Docker and related tools, it's very aligned. Both tools are oriented toward scalable services in the cloud, and containers help to create patterns that match the ones described in the Twelve-Factor methodology.

We will talk more about Docker containers in *Chapter 8, Advanced Event-Driven Structures.*

The most important, arguably, is the fact that the creation of an invariant container image that then gets run works very well with the *Build, release, run* factor and with being very explicit with *Dependencies*, as the whole image will include details such as the specific OS to use and any library. Including the build process as part of the repository also helps in the implementation of the *Code base* factor.

Each container also works as a *Process*, which allows scaling by creating multiple copies of the same container, using the *Concurrency* model.

While containers are usually thought of conceptually as lightweight virtual machines, it's better to think of them as a process wrapped in its own filesystem. This is closer to the way they operate.

The concept of containers makes them easy to start and stop, leaning into the *Disposability* factor, and connecting one to another through an orchestration tool such as Kubernetes makes it easy to also set up the *Backing services* factor, and it's also easy to share services between specific ports in containers following the *Port binding* factor. In most cases, however, they'll be shared as web interfaces on the standard port `80`.

In Docker and orchestrator tools like Kubernetes, it is very easy to set up different environments injecting environment variables, thereby fulfilling the *Configuration* factor. This environment configuration, as well as a description of the cluster, can be stored in files, which allow multiple environments to be created easily. It also includes tools for handling properly secrets, so they are properly encrypted and are not stored in the configuration files to avoid leaking secrets.

Another critical advantage of containers is the fact that a cluster can be replicated easily locally, as the same image that runs in production can run in a local environment, with only small changes in its configuration. This helps greatly in ensuring that the different environments are kept up to date, as demanded by the *Dev/Prod parity* factor.

In general, the container approach works toward defining a cluster and instigating a clear separation between different services and containers in a consistent manner. This brings together different environments, as the development environment can replicate the production setup on a small scale.

Sending information to standard output as per the *Logs* factor is also a great way to store logs as container tools will receive and deal with or redirect those logs adequately.

Finally, the *Admin processes* can be handled by launching the same container image with a different command that runs the specific admin command. This can be handled by the orchestrator if it needs to happen regularly, such as running the migrations prior to a deployment, or if it's a periodic task.

As we can see, working with containers is a great way of following the recommendations for the Twelve-Factor App, as the tools work in the same direction. This doesn't mean that they are done for free, but that there's a significant degree of alignment between the methodology and the ideas behind containers.

This is not surprising as both come from a similar background, dealing with web services that need to be run in the cloud.

Summary

In this chapter, we saw that it's good to have solid and reliable patterns to build software to be sure that we stand over the shoulder of tested decisions that we can use to shape new designs. For web services living in the cloud, we can use the Twelve-Factor App methodology as a guideline for a lot of useful advice.

We discussed how the Twelve-Factor App is aligned with two main ideas – CI and scalability.

CI is the practice of constantly validating any new code by running tests automatically after the code is shared. This creates a safety net that enables developers to move quickly, although it requires discipline to properly add automated tests as new features are being developed.

We also discussed the concept of scalability, or the capacity for software to allow more load by adding more resources. We talked about why it is important to allow the software to grow and reduce based on the load, even to the point to be able to adjust dynamically. We also saw how making the system stateless is key to achieving scalable software.

We saw the challenges for configuration, something that the Twelve-Factor App also deals with, and how not every configuration parameter is equal. We described how configuration can be divided into Operational configuration and Feature configuration, which can help divide and give the proper context to each parameter.

We went through each of the factors for the Twelve-Factor App, and divided them into four different groups, relating them, and explaining how the different factors support each other. We divided the factors into groups:

- Build once, run multiple times, based on the idea of generating a single package that runs in a different environment
- Dependencies and configuration, around the configuration and software and service dependencies of the application
- Scalability, to achieve the scalability that we talked about before
- Monitoring and admin with other elements to deal with the operation of the software while in operation

Finally, we spent some time talking about how the Twelve-Factor App ideas are very much in line with what containerization is about, and how different Docker features and concepts allow us to easily create Twelve-Factor Apps.

Join our book's Discord space

Join the book's Discord workspace for a monthly *Ask me Anything* session with the author: `https://packt.link/PythonArchitechture`

6

Web Server Structures

Web servers are the most common servers for remote access at the moment. Web services based on HTTP are flexible and powerful.

In this chapter, we will see how web servers are structured, starting by describing how the basic request-response architecture works, and then diving into a LAMP-style architecture in three layers: the web server itself, the workers executing the code, and an intermediate layer that controls those workers and presents a standardized connection to the web server.

We will describe each layer in detail, presenting a specific tool, such as nginx for the web server, uWSGI for the intermediate layer, and the Python Django framework for the specific code inside the worker. We will describe each of them in detail.

We will also include the Django REST framework, as it's a tool that builds on top of Django to generate RESTful API interfaces.

Finally, we will describe how extra layers can be added on top for greater flexibility, scalability, and performance.

In this chapter, we'll cover the following topics:

- Request-response
- Web architecture
- Web servers

- uWSGI
- Python workers
- External layers

Let's start by describing the basis of the request-response architecture.

Request-response

The classical server architecture is heavily based on request-response to communicate. A client sends a request to a remote server and the server processes it and returns a response.

This communication pattern has been prevalent since the era of mainframes and works in an analog manner as software communicates internally with a library, but over a network. The software calls a library and receives a response from it.

An important element is the time delay between the sending of the request and the reception of the response. Internally, it is rare that a call takes more than a couple of milliseconds, but for a network, it may be measured in hundreds of milliseconds and seconds, very commonly.

Network calls are very dependent on where the server is located. A call within the same data center will be fast, perhaps taking less than 100 milliseconds, while a connection to an external API will likely take close to a second or more.

Times will also be highly variable, as the network conditions may affect them greatly. This time difference makes it important to handle it properly.

The usual strategy when making requests is to make them synchronously. That means that the code stops and waits until the response is ready. This is convenient, as the code will be simple, but it's also inefficient, as the computer will be not doing anything while the server is calculating the response and it's being transferred through the network.

The client can be improved to perform multiple requests at the same time. This can be done when the requests are independent of each other, allowing it to make them in parallel. An easy way to achieve this is to use a multithreaded system to perform them, so they can speed up the process.

Typically, a flow will be required, with some requests that can be performed in parallel and others that require waiting until information is received. For example, a common request to retrieve a web page will make one request to retrieve the page and later will download multiple files referenced (e.g. header files, images) in parallel.

We will see later in the chapter how this effect can be designed to increase the responsiveness of web pages.

The fact that the network is more unreliable than a local call, requires better error handling that understands this fact. Any request-response system should take extra care about capturing different errors, and retry, as network problems typically are transient, and can be recovered if retried after waiting.

As we saw in *Chapter 2, API Design* the multiple status codes from HTTP can give detailed information.

Another characteristic of the request-response pattern is that a server cannot call the client proactively, only return information. This simplifies the communication, as it's not entirely bidirectional. The client is required to initiate the request, and the server only needs to listen for new requests coming. This also makes both roles asymmetrical and requires the client to know where the server is, usually by its DNS address and the port to access (by default, port 80 for HTTP and 443 for HTTPS).

This characteristic makes some communication patterns difficult to achieve. For example, full bidirectional communication, where two parts want to initiate the sending of messages, is difficult to achieve with request-response.

A crude example of this is a message server implemented only in request-response. Two clients require the usage of an intermediate server.

This basic structure is common in applications like forums or social networks that allow the users to have some sort of direct messaging between users.

Each user can perform two actions:

- Request any new message addressed to them
- Send a new message to another user

A user needs to check periodically whether there are new messages available through polling. This is inefficient, as it's likely that for any new message there'll be a significant number of checks that return "no new messages available." Even worse, there could be a significant delay before noticing that a new message is available if the checks are not performed often enough.

In real applications, normally this polling is avoided by sending a notification in a way that's proactive towards the client. For example, mobile OSes have a system to deliver notifications, enabling the server to send a notification through an external API provided by the OS to notify the user of a new message. An older alternative is to send an email with the same goal.

There are other alternatives, of course. There are P2P alternatives, where two clients can connect to each other, and there are connections with a server through websockets that can remain open, allowing the server to notify the user of new information. They both deviate from the request-response architecture.

Even with these limitations, request-response architecture is the basis of web services and has been proven to be very reliable over the decades. The possibility of having a central server that controls communication and can take a passive role in accepting new requests makes the architecture simple to implement and quick to evolve, and simplifies the client's work. The centralized aspect allows a lot of control.

Web architecture

We introduced in the introduction of the chapter the LAMP architecture, which is the base for the web server architecture:

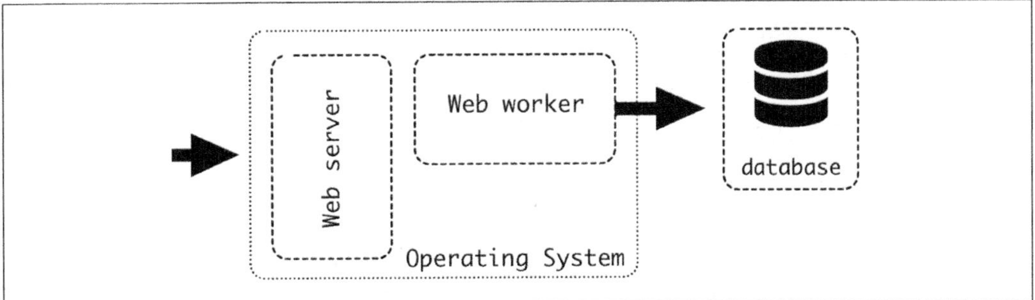

Figure 6.1: The LAMP architecture

The LAMP architecture is more general, but we will take a closer look at the web server and web worker. We will use specific tools, based on the Python ecosystem, but we will discuss possible alternatives.

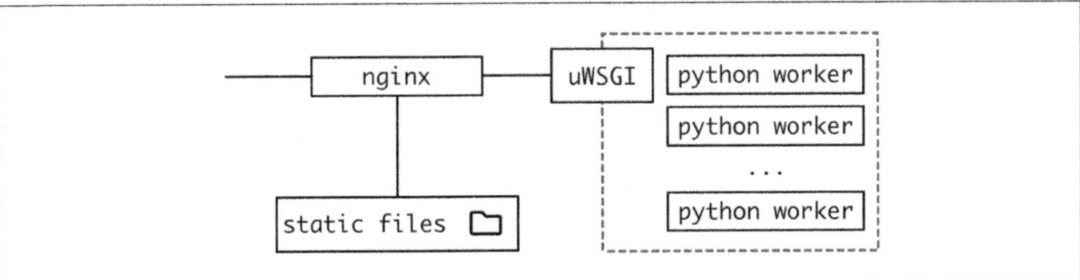

Figure 6.2: More detailed architecture in a Python environment

From the point of view of an incoming request, a web request accesses the different elements.

Web servers

The **web server** exposes the HTTP port, accepts incoming connections, and redirects them towards the backend. One common option is nginx (`https://www.nginx.com/`). Another common option is Apache (`https://httpd.apache.org/`). The web server can directly serve a request, for example, by directly returning static files, permanent redirects, or similar simple requests. If the request requires more computation, it will be directed towards the backend, acting as a reverse proxy.

The primary objective of the web server in the presented architecture is to work as a reverse proxy, accepting HTTP requests, stabilizing the input of data, and queuing the incoming requests.

A basic configuration for nginx could look like this. The code is available on GitHub at `https://github.com/PacktPublishing/Python-Architecture-Patterns/blob/main/chapter_06_web_server/nginx_example.conf`.

```
server {
    listen 80 default_server;
    listen [::]:80 default_server;

    error_log /dev/stdout;
    access_log /dev/stdout;

       root /opt/;

    location /static/ {
        autoindex on;
        try_files $uri $uri/ =404;
    }

    location / {
        proxy_set_header Host $host;
        proxy_set_header X-Real-IP $remote_addr;
         uwsgi_pass unix:///tmp/uwsgi.sock;
         include uwsgi_params;
    }

}
```

The directive `server` opens and closes the basic block to define how to serve the data. Note each line ends with a semicolon.

In nginx parlance, each server directive defines a virtual server. Normally there will be only one, but multiple can be configured, for example, to define different behaviors based on the DNS addressed.

Inside, we have a basic configuration on what port to serve – in our case, port 80 and both IPv4 and IPv6 addresses. The `default_server` clause means this is the server to be used by default:

```
listen 80 default_server;
listen [::]:80 default_server;
```

IPv4 is the common address with four numbers, like **`127.0.0.1`**. IPv6 is longer, and it's intended as a replacement for IPv4. For example, an IPv6 address can be expressed as **`2001:0db8:0000:0000:0000:ff00:0042:7879`**. IPv4 addresses have already been exhausted, meaning that there are no new addresses available. IPv6 will in the long run provide enough to avoid this problem, though IPv4 is still widely used, and probably will remain in use for a long time yet.

Next, we define where the static files are, both in terms of the external URL, and what is the mapping with some section of the hard drive.

Note the static location needs to be defined before the reverse proxy:

```
root /opt/;

location /static/ {
    autoindex on;
    try_files $uri $uri/ =404;
}
```

`root` defines the starting point, while `location` starts a section that will serve the URL `/static/file1.txt` from the file located in the hard drive at `/opt/static/file1.txt`.

`try_files` will scan for files in the URI and raise a 404 error if it's not there.

`autoindex` automatically generates an index page to check the contents of a directory.

This option is typically disabled in production servers, but it's very handy to detect problems with static files while running in test mode.

It's important in production environments to serve static files directly from the web server, instead of doing them further along the line with the Python worker. While this is possible, and a common case when working in a development environment, it's very inefficient. The speed and memory usage will be much bigger, while a web server is optimized to serve static files. Please always remember to serve static files in production through a web server.

Serving static content externally

An alternative is to use an external service to handle files, like AWS S3, that allows you to serve static files. The files then will be under a different URL than the service, for example:

- The service URL is `https://example.com/index`
- The static files are in `https://mybucket.external-service/static/`

All the references inside the service web pages, then, should point to the external service endpoint.

This way of operating requires you to push the code to the external service as part of the deployment. To allow for uninterrupted deployments, remember that the static content needs to be available before. Another important detail is to upload them with a different path, so static files between deployments are not confused.

This is easy to do using different root paths. For example:

1. Version `v1` of the service is deployed. This is the starting point. The static content is served from `https://mybucket.external-service/static/v1/`.

   The calls to the service, like `https://example.com/index`, return all their static content pointing at version `v1`.
2. Once `v2` of the service is ready, the first thing to do is to push it to the external service, so it's available in `https://mybucket.external-service/static/v2/`. Note that, at this point, no user is accessing `/static/v2`; the service is still returning `/static/v1`.

   Deploy the new service. Once it is deployed, the users will start accessing `/static/v2` when they call `https://example.com/index`.

As we've seen in previous chapters, the key for a seamless deployment is to perform actions in small increments, and each step must perform actions that are reversible and prepare the terrain so there's no moment when something that's required is not ready.

This approach can be used for big operations. In a JavaScript-heavy interface, like a single-page application, changing the static files effectively can be a new deployment. The underlying service API can remain the same but changing the downloaded version for all JavaScript code and other static content, which in effect will deploy a new version.

We talked about single-page apps in *Chapter 2*.

This structure makes both versions of the static content available at the same time. This can also be used to make tests or release beta versions. As the service is returning whether to use version A or B, this can be set dynamically.

For example, adding an optional parameter in any call to overwrite the returned version:

- Calling `https://example.com/index` returns the default version, for example, `v2`.
- Calling `https://example.com/index?overwrite_static=v3` returns the specified version instead, like `v3`.

Other options are returning `v3` for specific users, like beta testers or internal staff. Once `v3` is deemed correct, it can be changed to be the new default with a small change in the service.

This approach can be taken to the extreme to push any single commit to the source control to the public S3 bucket, and then test in any environment, including production. This can help to generate a very fast feedback loop where QA or product owners can quickly see changes in their own browser, without requiring any deployment or special environment.

Don't feel limited to a unique integer as the version number; it can work as well with a random UUID or SHA of the content generated automatically. Web storage is quite cheap, so it would require a lot of versions with very big files to really start to worry about cost. And old versions can be deleted periodically.

While this approach can be very aggressive and not viable for all applications, for an application that requires many changes in a rich JavaScript interface or to make drastic changes to the look and feel, it can be highly productive.

This external serving can be combined with **CDN (content delivery network)** support for a multiregional proxy. This will distribute the files around the world to provide a copy of it closer to the user.

Think of a CDN as an internal cache by the company providing the service. For example, we have a service where their servers are located in Europe, but a user is accessing it from Japan. This company has servers in Japan that store a copy of the static content. That means that the user can access the files with much lower latency than if the request had to reach a server in Europe, more than 8,000 kilometers away.

Using a CDN is very powerful for truly global audiences. They are especially useful for serving data that requires low latency around the world. For example, broadcasting near real-time video.

Video broadcast online is typically transferred as small video chunks of a few seconds in duration. An index file keeps track of what is the latest chunk generated, so clients can be kept up to date. This is the basis of the format **HTTP Live Streaming**, or **HLS**, very common as the transfer of data is done directly through HTTP.

The data can be distributed internally between the different servers from the company providing the CDN service quite quickly, as they'll use dedicated networks between them instead of using an external network.

In any case, using an external service to store the static files will, obviously, remove the need to configure the web server for them.

Reverse proxy

Let's continue describing the web server configuration. After describing the static files, we need to define a connection to the backend, acting as a reverse proxy.

A reverse proxy is a proxy server that can redirect a received request towards one or more defined backends. In our example, the backend is the uWSGI process.

A reverse proxy works in a similar way as a load balancer, though load balancers can work with more protocols, while a reverse proxy is only capable of working with web requests. On top of distributing requests across different servers, it can also add some features like caching, security, SSL termination (receiving a request in HTTPS and connecting to other servers using HTTP), or, in this particular case, receive a web request and transfer it to through a WSGI connection.

The web server will be able to communicate with the backend in multiple ways, allowing flexibility. This can use different protocols, like FastCGI, SCGI, straight HTTP for pure proxying, or, in our case, connecting directly to the uWSGI protocol. We need to define it to connect through either a TCP socket or a UNIX socket. We will use a UNIX socket.

TCP sockets are designed to allow communication between different servers, while UNIX sockets are designed to communicate processes locally. UNIX sockets are a little bit lighter for communication inside the same host and they work like a file, allowing you to assign them permissions to control what process can access what socket.

The socket needs to be coordinated with the way uWSGI is configured. As we will see later, the uWSGI process will create it:

```
location / {
   proxy_set_header Host $host;
   proxy_set_header X-Real-IP $remote_addr;
   include uwsgi_params;
    uwsgi_pass unix:///tmp/uwsgi.sock;
}
```

First of all, the root of the server is at the `/` URL. It's important to make the static content before the reverse proxy, as the locations are checked in order. So any request for a `/static` request gets detected before checking for `/` and it's properly treated.

The core of the reverse proxy configuration is the `uwsgi_pass` clause. This specified where to redirect the requests. `include uwgi_params` will add a bunch of standard configurations to be passed to the next stage.

`uwsgi_params` is actually a defined file included by default in nginx config that adds a lot of `uwsgi_param` statements with elements like `SERVER_NAME`, `REMOTE_ADDRESS`, etc.

More `uwsgi_param` can be added if necessary, in a similar way to the headers.

Extra elements can be added as HTTP headers. They'll be added to the request, so they are available further down the request.

```
        proxy_set_header Host $host;
        proxy_set_header X-Real-IP $remote_addr;
```

In this case, we are adding the `Host` header, with information about the requested host. Note that the `$host` is an indication to nginx to fill the value with the host the request is addressed to. In the same way, the header `X-Real-IP` is added with the IP address from the remote address.

Setting headers correctly to pass on is unappreciated work, but can be critical to properly monitor problems. Setting headers may require doing so at different stages. As we will discuss later, a single request can pass through multiple proxies, and each of them needs to adequately forward the headers.

In our configuration, we only use a single backend, as uWSGI will balance between different workers. But, if necessary, multiple backends can be defined, even mixing UNIX and TCP sockets, defining a cluster.

```
upstream uwsgibackends {
  server unix:///tmp/uwsgi.sock;
  server 192.168.1.117:8080;
  server 10.0.0.6:8000;
}
```

Later, define the `uwsgi_pass` to use the cluster. The requests will be equally spread over the different backends.

```
uwsgi_pass uwsgibackends;
```

Logging

We also need to track any possible error or access. There are two different logs that `nginx` (and other web servers) produces:

- **Error log**: The error log tracks possible problems from the web server itself, like not being able to start, configuration problems, etc.
- **Access log**: The access log reports any request accessing the system. This is the basic information about the system flowing. It can be used to find specific problems like 502 errors when the backend cannot be connected, or, when treated as aggregated, it can detect problems like an abnormal number of error status codes (`4xx` or `5xx`).

We will talk in further detail about logs in *Chapter 11*.

Both logs are critical information that needs to be adequately detected. Following the Twelve-Factor App, we should treat them as streams of data. The easiest is to redirect them both to standard output.

```
access_log /dev/stdout;
error_log /dev/stdout;
```

This requires nginx to not start as a daemon process, or if it is, capture the standard output properly.

Another option is to redirect the log into a centralized log facility, using the proper protocol. This directs all the logs into a centralized server that captures the information. In this example, we send it to a syslog host in `syslog_host`.

```
error_log syslog:server=syslog_host:514;
access_log syslog:server=syslog_host:514,tag=nginx;
```

This protocol allows you to include tags and extra information that can help separate the origin of each log later.

Being able to distinguish the source of each log is critical and always requires a bit of tweaking. Be sure to spend some time making the logs easy to search. It will greatly simplify the work when an error in production requires gathering information.

Advanced usages

A web server is very powerful, and shouldn't be underestimated. Other than acting purely as a proxy, there are a lot of other features that can be enabled like returning custom redirects, overwriting the proxy with a static page for maintenance windows, rewriting URLs to adjust changes, providing SSL termination (decrypt receiving HTTPS requests to pass them decrypted through regular HTTP, and encrypt the result back), caching requests, splitting the requests based on percentages for A/B testing, choosing a backend server based on geolocalization of the requester, etc.

Be sure to read the documentation of `nginx` at `http://nginx.org/en/docs/` to read all the possibilities.

uWSGI

The next element of the chain is the uWSGI application. This application receives the requests from `nginx` and redirects them into independent Python workers, in WSGI format.

Web Server Gateway Interface (WSGI) is a Python standard to deal with web requests. It's very popular and supported by a lot of software, both from the sending end (like `nginx`, but also other web servers like Apache and GUnicorn) and from the receiving end (virtually every Python web framework, like Django, Flask, or Pyramid).

uWSGI will also start and coordinate the different processes, handling the lifecycle for each of them. The application works as an intermediary, starting a group of workers receiving the requests.

uWSGI is configured through a `uwsgi.ini` file. Let's see an example, available on GitHub at `https://github.com/PacktPublishing/Python-Architecture-Patterns/blob/main/chapter_06_web_server/uwsgi_example.uni`.

```
[uwsgi]
chdir=/root/directory
wsgi-file = webapplication/wsgi.py
master=True
socket=/tmp/uwsgi.sock
vacuum=True
processes=1
```

```
max-requests=5000
# Used to send commands to uWSGI
master-fifo=/tmp/uwsgi-fifo
```

The first element defines what the working directory is. The application will be launched here, and other file references will work from here:

```
chdir=/root/directory
```

Then, we describe where the `wsgi.py` file is, which describes our application.

The WSGI application

Inside this file is the definition of the `application` function, which uWSGI can use to address the internal Python code, in a controlled way.

For example:

```
def application(environ, start_response):
    start_response('200 OK', [('Content-Type', 'text/plain')])
    return [b'Body of the response\n']
```

The first parameter is a dictionary with predefined variables that detail the request (like `METHOD`, `PATH_INFO`, `CONTENT_TYPE`, and so on) and parameters related to the protocol or environment (for example, `wsgi.version`).

The second parameter, `start_response`, is a callable that allows you to set up the return status and any headers.

The function should return the body. Note how it's returned in byte stream format.

> The difference between text streams (or strings) and byte streams was one of the big differences introduced in Python 3. To summarize it, byte streams are raw binary data, while text streams contain meaning by interpreting that data through a particular encoding.
>
> The differentiation between both can be a bit baffling sometimes, in particular since Python 3 makes the difference explicit, and that clashes with some previous lax practices, especially when dealing with ASCII content that can be represented in the same way.

Keep in mind that text streams need to be encoded to be transformed into byte streams, and byte streams need to be decoded into text streams. Encoding is moving from the abstract representation of text to the precise representation of binary.

For example, the Spanish word "cañón" contains two characters not present in ASCII, ñ and ó. You can see how encoding them through UTF8 replaces them with specific binary elements described in UTF8:

```
>>> 'cañón'.encode('utf-8')
b'ca\xc3\xb1\xc3\xb3n'
>>> b'ca\xc3\xb1\xc3\xb3n'.decode('utf-8')
'cañón'
```

The function can also work as a generator and use the keyword `yield` instead of `return` when the returning body needs to be streamed.

Any function that uses `yield` is a generator in Python. This means that when called, it returns an iterator object that returns elements one by one, normally to be used in loops.

This is very useful for situations where each element of the loop takes some time to process but can be returned without being required to calculate every single item, reducing latency and memory usage, as not all elements need to be maintained in memory.

```
>>> def mygenerator():
...     yield 1
...     yield 2
...     yield 3
>>> for i in mygenerator():
...     print(i)
...
1
2
3
```

In any case, the WSGI file is normally created by default by whatever framework is used. For example, a `wsgi.py` file created by Django will look like this.

```
import os

from django.core.wsgi import get_wsgi_application

os.environ.setdefault("DJANGO_SETTINGS_MODULE", "webapplication.
settings")

application = get_wsgi_application()
```

Note how the function `get_wsgi_application` will automatically set up the proper application function, and connect it with the rest of the defined code - a great advantage of using an existing framework!

Interacting with the web server

Let's continue with the `uwsgi.ini` configuration with the socket configuration:

```
socket=/tmp/uwsgi.sock
vacuum=True
```

The `socket` parameter creates the UNIX socket for the web server to connect to. It was discussed before in this chapter, when talking about the web server. This needs to be coordinated on both sides, to ensure they connect properly.

uWSGI also allows you to use a native HTTP socket, using the option `http-socket`. For example, `http-socket = 0.0.0.0:8000` to serve all addresses on port 8000. You may use this option if the web server is not on the same server and needs to communicate through the network.

When possible, avoid exposing uWSGI directly publicly over the internet. A web server will be safer and more efficient. It will also serve static content much more efficiently. If you really must skip the web server, use the option `http` instead of `http-socket`, which includes a certain level of protection.

The `vacuum` option cleans up the socket when the server is closed.

Processes

The next parameters control the number of processes and how to control them:

```
master=True
processes=1
```

The `master` parameter creates a master process that ensures that the number of workers is correct, restarting if not, and deals with the process lifecycle, among other tasks. It should always be enabled in production for smooth operation.

The `processes` parameter is very straightforward and describes how many Python workers should be started. Received requests will be load balanced across them.

The way uWSGI generates new processes is through pre-forking. This means that a single process gets started, and after the application is loaded (which may take a while), it's cloned through a fork process. This sensibly speeds up the startup time for new processes, but at the same time, relays that the setup of the application can be duplicated.

This assumption, on rare occasions, may cause problems with certain libraries that, for example, open file descriptors during initializations that cannot be shared safely. If that's the case, the parameter `lazy-apps` will make each worker start from scratch, independently. This is slower, but it creates more consistent results.

Choosing the right number of processes is highly dependent on the application itself and the hardware that supports it. The hardware is important as a CPU with multiple cores will be able to run more processes efficiently. The amount of IO vs CPU usage in the application will determine how many processes can be run by the CPU core.

Theoretically, a process not using IO and purely crunching numbers will use the whole core without wait periods, not allowing the core to switch to another process meanwhile. A process with high IO, with the core idle while waiting for results from the database and external services, will increase its efficiency by performing more context switches. This number should be tested to ensure the best results. A common starting point will be two times the number of cores, but remember to monitor the system to tweak it and obtain the best results.

An important detail about the created processes is that they deactivate the creation of new threads by default. This is an optimization choice. In the majority of web applications, there's no need to create independent threads inside each of the workers, and that allows you to deactivate the Python GIL, speeding up the code.

The **Global Interpreter Lock** or **GIL** is a mutex lock that only allows a single thread to have control of the Python process. This means that, inside a single process, no two threads can run at the same time, something that multi-core CPU architecture makes possible. Note that multiple threads may be waiting for IO results while another runs, which is a usual situation in real-life applications. The GIL is typically held and released constantly, as each operation first holds the GIL and then releases it at the end.

The GIL is commonly blamed for inefficiencies in Python, though the effect is only perceived in high-CPU multi-threaded operations in native Python (as opposed to using optimized libraries like NumPy), which are not as usual and are already slow to start with.

These interactions with the GIL are only wasteful if no threads will be run, so that's why uWSGI deactivates it by default.

If threads need to be used, the option `enable-threads` will enable them.

Process lifecycle

During the time of operation, processes won't stay static. Any working web application will need to reload with new code changes regularly. The next parameters are related to how processes are created and destroyed.

```
max-requests=5000
# Used to send commands to uWSGI
master-fifo=/tmp/uwsgi-fifo
```

`max-requests` specifies the number of requests to be processed by a single worker before being restarted. Once the worker gets to this number, uWSGI will destroy it and create another worker from scratch, following the usual process (fork by default, or using `lazy-apps` if configured).

This is useful to avoid problems with memory leaks or other sorts of stale problems, where the performance of a worker gets degraded over time. Recycling the workers is a protective measure that can be taken pre-emptively, so even if a problem is present, it will be corrected before it causes any issues.

Remember that, based on the Twelve-Factor App, web workers need to be able to be stopped and started at any time, so this recycling is painless.

uWSGI will also recycle the worker when it's idle, after serving its 5,000th request, so it will be a controlled operation.

Keep in mind this recycling may interfere with other operations. Depending on the startup time, it may take a few seconds or worse (especially if `lazy-apps` is used) to start the worker, potentially creating a backlog of requests. uWSGI will queue the incoming requests. In our example configuration, there's only a single worker defined in `processes`. With multiple workers this can be mitigated, as the rest of the workers will be able to handle the extra load.

When multiple workers are involved, if each of them will restart after their 5,000th request, a stampede problem can be created where one after another all the workers are recycled. Keep in mind that the load is distributed through the workers equally, so this count will be in sync across the multiple workers. While the expectation is that, for example, with 16 workers, at least 15 of them will be available, in practice we might find that all are being recycled at the same time.

To avoid this problem, use the `max-requests-delta` parameter. This parameter adds a variable number for each worker. It will multiply the delta for the worker ID (a unique consecutive number for each worker starting from 1). So, configuring a delta of 200, each worker will have the following:

Worker	Base max-request	Delta	Total requests to recycle
Worker 1	5,000	1 * 200	5,200
Worker 2	5,000	2 * 200	5,400
Worker 3	5,000	3 * 200	5,600
...			
Worker 16	5,000	16 * 200	8,200

This makes the recycling happen at different times, increasing the number of workers available at the same time, as they won't restart simultaneously.

This problem is of the same kind as what's called a cache stampede. This is produced where multiple cache values are invalidated at the same time, producing the regeneration of values at the same time. Because the system expects to be running under some cache acceleration, suddenly having to recreate a significant portion section of the cache may produce a serious performance problem, to the point of the complete collapse of the system.

To avoid this, avoid setting fixed times for the cache to expire, such as a certain hour of the clock. This can happen, for example, if a backend gets updated with news for the day at midnight, making it tempting to expire the cache at this time. Instead, add an element to make the different keys expire at slightly different times to avoid this problem. This can be achieved by adding a small random amount of time to the expiry time for each of the keys, so they can reliably be refreshed at different times.

The `master-fifo` parameter creates a way to communicate with uWSGI and send commands:

```
# Used to send commands to uWSGI
master-fifo=/tmp/uwsgi-fifo
```

This creates a UNIX socket in `/tmp/uwsgi-fifo` that can receive commands in the form of characters redirected to it. For example:

```
# Generate a graceful reload
echo r >> /tmp/uwsgi-fifo

# Graceful stop of the server
echo q >> /tmp/uwsgi-fifo
```

This method allows for better handling of situations than sending signals, as there are more commands available and it allows for quite granular control of the processes and the whole uWSGI.

For example, sending `Q` will produce a direct shutdown of uWSGI, while `q` will produce a graceful one. A graceful shutdown will start by stopping accepting new requests in uWSGI, then waiting until any request in the internal uWSGI queue is being processed, and when a worker has finished its request, stopping it in an orderly fashion. Finally, when all workers are done, stop the uWSGI master process.

The graceful reload with `r` takes a similar approach, keeping the requests in the internal queue and waiting until the workers are done to stop them and restart them. It will also load any new configuration related to uWSGI itself. Note that, during the time of the operation, the internal uWSGI listen queue may be filled up, causing problems.

The size of the listen queue can be tweaked with the `listen` parameter, but keep in mind that there's a limit set up by Linux that you may need to change as well. Defaults are 100 for listen and 128 for the Linux configuration.

Do tests before changing those to big values, as churning through a big backlog of tasks has its own problems.

If the loading of processes is done through the fork process, after starting up the first one, the rest will be copies, so they will be loaded quite quickly. By comparison, using `lazy-apps` may delay achieving full capacity as each individual worker will need to be individually started from scratch. This can produce an extra load on the server, depending on the number of workers and the startup procedure.

A possible alternative for `lazy-apps` is to use the `c` option, reloading the workers with chain reloading. This reloads each worker independently, waiting until a single worker is totally reloaded before moving to the next one. This procedure doesn't reload the uWSGI configuration but will do with code changes in the workers. It will take longer, but it will work at a controller pace.

Reloading a single server under load may be complicated. Using multiple uWSGI servers simplifies the process. In this situation, reloads should happen at different times to allow you to distribute the load.

A cluster-style approach can be taken in using multiple servers to perform this dance, creating copies of the uWSGI configuration in multiple servers and then recycling them one at a time. While one is reloading, the others will be able to handle the extra load. In extreme situations, an extra server can be used to produce extra capacity during the reload.

This is common in cloud environments where an extra server can be used and then destroyed. In Docker situations, new containers can be added to provide this extra capacity.

For more information about the `master-fifo` and accepted commands, including how to pause and resume the instance, and other exotic operations, check the uWSGI documentation at `https://uwsgi-docs.readthedocs.io/en/latest/MasterFIFO.html`.

uWSGI is a very powerful application that has almost endless possibilities for configuration. Its documentation is overwhelming in the amount of detail it contains, but it's incredibly comprehensive and insightful. You can learn a lot, not only about uWSGI but also about how the whole web stack works. I highly recommend going through slowly, but surely, to learn a lot. You can access the documentation at `https://uwsgi-docs.readthedocs.io/`.

Python worker

The core of the system is the Python WSGI worker. This worker receives the HTTP requests from uWSGI after they're routed by the external web server, etc.

This is where the magic happens, and it is specific to the application. This is the element that will see faster iteration than the rest of the links of the chain.

Each framework will interact in a slightly different way with the requests, but in general, they will follow similar patterns. We will use Django as an example.

We won't discuss all aspects of Django or go into a deep dive of its features but will use a selection to look at some lessons that are useful for other frameworks.

The Django project is really well documented. Seriously, it has always been distinguished by its world-class documentation, since the project started. You can read it here: `http://www.djangoproject.com`.

Django MVT architecture

Django borrows heavily from the MVC structure but tweaks it a bit into what's called **MVT (Model-View-Template)**:

- The Model remains the same, the representation of the data and interacting with the storage.

- The View receives the HTTP request and processes it, interacting with the different Models that may be required.
- The Template is a system to generate HTML files, from values passed on.

This changes Model-View-Controller a bit, though the result is similar.

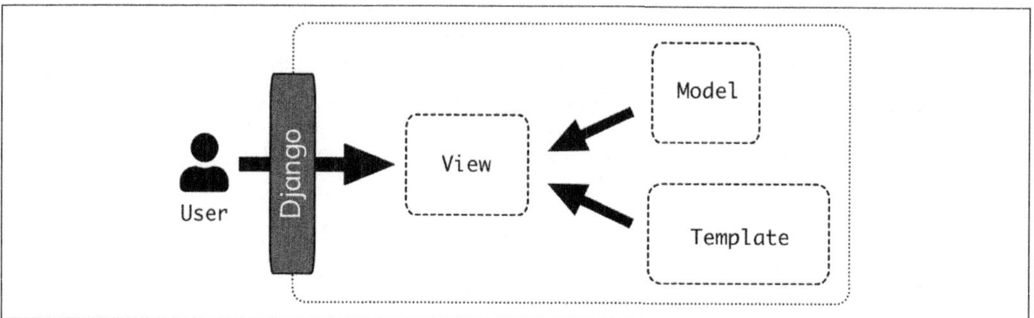

Figure 6.3: The Model-View-Controller

The Model works the same in both systems. The Django View acts as a combination of the View and the Controller, and the Template is a helping system for the View component of the Django View.

The templating system is not strictly required to be used, as not every Django interface requires an HTML page as a result.

While Django was designed to create HTML interfaces, there are ways of creating other types of interfaces. In particular, for RESTful interfaces, the Django REST framework (`https://www.django-rest-framework.org`) allows you to expand the functionality and generate self-documented RESTful interfaces easily.

We will look at the Django REST framework later in the chapter.

Django is a powerful and comprehensive framework and has some assumptions on how things are supposed to run, such as using the Django ORM or using its templating system. While doing so is "swimming with the current," it's definitely possible to take other approaches and tailor any part of the system. This can involve elements like not using templates, using a different templating system, using a different ORM library like SQLAlchemy, and adding extra libraries to connect to different databases, including ones not supported natively by Django (like NoSQL databases). Do not let the constraints of the system limit you from achieving your goals.

Django is opinionated in the way that it presents a lot of elements working together with certain assumptions. They are tightly related to each other. If that's an impediment, for example, because you need to use wildly different tools, a good alternative can be Pyramid (`https://trypyramid.com`), a Python web framework designed to build your own combination of tools to ensure flexibility.

Routing a request towards a View

Django provides the tools to perform the proper routing from a particular URL to a specific View.

This is done in the `urls.py` file. Let's see an example.

```
from django.urls import path
from views import first_view, second_view

urlpatterns = [
    path('example/', first_view)
    path('example/<int:parameter>/<slug:other_parameter>', second_view)
]
```

The required Views (that are typically declared as functions) are imported from whatever module they are currently in into the file.

The `urlpatterns` list defines an ordered list of URL patterns that will be tested against an input URL.

The first `path` definition is very straightforward. If the URL is `example/`, it will call the View `first_view`.

The second `path` definition contains definitions to capture parameters. It will transform the defined parameters properly and pass them over to the view. For example, the URL `example/15/example-slug` will create these parameters:

- `parameter=int(15)`
- `other_parameter=str("example-slug")`

There are different types of parameters that can be configured. `int` is self-explanatory, but `slug` is a limited string that will include only alphanumeric, _ (underscore), and - (dash) symbols, excluding characters like `.` or other symbols.

There are more types available. There's also a `str` type that can be too broad. The character `/` is understood as special in URLs and it's always excluded. This allows for easy separation of parameters. The type `slug` should cover more typical use cases for parameters inside a URL.

Another option is to generate the paths directly as regex. If you are familiar with the regex format, this can be very powerful and allow a great deal of control. At the same time, regexes can grow really complex and difficult to read and use.

```
from django.urls import re_path

urlpatterns = [
    re_path('example/(?P<parameter>\d+)/', view)
]
```

This was the only option available previously in Django. As you can see for the example, equivalent to `example/<int:parameter>/`, the new path-defined URL patterns are easier to read and to deal with.

An intermediate option is to define types to be sure that they match specific values, for example, creating a type to match only months like `Apr` or `Jun`. If the type is defined in this way, an incorrect pattern like `Jen` will return a 404 automatically. Internally, this will require writing a regex to match the proper string anyway, but afterwards, it can transform the value. For example, to transform the month `Jun` to either the number 1, normalize it as `JUNE`, or any other value that makes sense later. The complexity of the regex will be abstracted by the type.

Keep in mind that the patterns are checked in order. That means that, if a pattern may fulfil two paths, it will select the first one. This may have unintended effects when a previous path "hides" the next one, so the least restrictive patterns should be positioned later.

For example:

```
from django.urls import path

urlpatterns = [
    path('example/<str:parameter>/', first_view)
    path('example/<int:parameter>/', second_view)
]
```

No URL will ever get passed to `second_view`, as any parameter that is an integer will be captured first.

This kind of error is usually possible in most URL routers in web frameworks, as most of them are pattern-based. Keep an eye in case it affects your code.

The interesting stuff happens inside of the View.

The View

The View is the central element of Django. It receives the request information, plus any parameters from the URL, and processes it. The View normally will use the different Models to compose the information, and finally returns a response.

The View is in charge of deciding if there's any change in behavior based on the request. Note that the routing towards the View only distinguishes between different paths, but other distinctions like HTTP method or parameters will need to be differentiated here.

This makes it a very common pattern to differentiate between POST and GET requests to the same URL. A common usage in web pages is to make a form page to display the empty form, and then POST to the same URL. For example, in a form with a single parameter, the structure will be similar to the following example:

This is intended as pseudocode to not complicate it.

```
def example_view(request):
    # create an empty form
    form_content = Form()

    if request.method == 'POST':
        # Obtain the value
            value = request.POST['my-value']
            if validate(value):
                # Perform actions based on the value
             do_stuff()
```

```
            content = 'Thanks for your answer'
        else:
            content = 'Sorry, this is incorrect' + form_content

    elif request.method == 'GET':
        content = form_content

    return render(content)
```

While it's true that Django includes a form system that simplifies the validation and reporting of forms, this structure can grow legs and become tiresome. In particular, the multiple nested `if` blocks are confusing.

We won't go into details with the form system in Django. It is quite complete and allows you to render rich HTML forms that will validate and show possible errors to the user. Read the Django documentation to know more.

Instead of that, dividing the View with two different subfunctions may be clearer.

```
def display_form(form_content, message=''):
    content = message + form_content
    return content


def process_data(parameters, form_content):
    # Obtain the value
        if validate(parameters):
            # Perform actions based on the value
         do_stuff()
         content = 'Thanks for your answer'
    else:
         message = 'Sorry, this is incorrect'
         content = display_form(form_content , message)

    return content


def example_view(request):
    # create an empty form
```

```
    form_content = Form()

    if request.method == 'POST':
        content = process_data(request.POST, form_content)
    elif request.method == 'GET':
        content = display_form(form_content)

    return render(content)
```

The challenge here is to preserve the fact that, when the parameters are incorrect, the form needs to be rendered again. By the principle of **DRY** (**Don't Repeat Yourself**), we should try to locate that code in a single place. Here, in the `display_form` function. We allow some customization of the message to add some extra content, in case the data is incorrect.

In a more complete example, the form will be tweaked to show the specific errors. Django forms are able to do this automatically. The process will be to create a form with the parameters from the request, validate it, and print it. It automatically will produce the proper error messages, based on the type of each of the fields, including custom types. Again, refer to Django's documentation for more information.

Note that the `display_form` function gets called both from `example_view` and also inside `process_data`.

HttpRequest

The key element for passing information is the `request` parameter. This object's type is `HttpRequest`, and contains all the information that the user is sending in the request.

Its most important attributes are:

- `method`, which contains the used HTTP method.
- If the method is `GET`, it will contain a `GET` attribute with a `QueryDict` (a dictionary subclass) containing all the query parameters in the request. For example, a request such as:

  ```
  /example?param1=1&param2=text&param1=2
  ```

Will produce a `request.GET` value like this:

```
<QueryDict: {'param1': ['1', '2'], 'param2': ['text']}>
```

Note that the parameters are stored internally as a list of values, because query parameters accept multiple parameters with the same key, though that's not usually the case. They'll return a unique value when queried anyway:

```
>>> request.GET['param1']
2
>>> request.GET['param2']
text
```

They'll be all reported in order, with the latest value being returned. If you need to access all values, use the method `getlist`:

```
>>> request.GET.getlist('param1')
['1', '2']
```

All the parameters are defined as strings, needing to be converted to other types if necessary.

- If the method is `POST`, an analogous `POST` attribute will be created. In this case, it will be filled first by the body of the request, to allow encoding form posts. If the body is empty, it will fill the values with query parameters like the `GET` case.

POST multiple values will commonly be used in multiple selection forms.

- `content_type` with the MIME type of the request.
- `FILES`, including data for any uploaded files in the request, for certain `POST` requests.
- `headers`, a dictionary containing all the HTTP headers of the request and headers. Another dictionary, `META`, contains extra information from headers that may be introduced and are not necessarily HTTP-based, like `SERVER_NAME`. In general, it is better to obtain information from the `headers` attribute.

There are also some useful methods to retrieve information from the request, for example:

- `.get_host()` to obtain the name of the host. It will interpret the different headers to determine the proper host, so it's more reliable than directly reading the `HTTP_HOST` header.
- `.build_absolute_uri(location)` to generate a full URI, including the host, port, etc. This method is useful to create full references to return them.

These attributes and methods, combined with the parameters described in the request, allow you to retrieve all the relevant information necessary for processing the request and call the required Models.

HttpResponse

The `HttpResponse` class handles the information being returned by the View to the web server. The return from a View function needs to be an `HttpResponse` object.

```
from django.http import HttpResponse
def my_view(request):
    return HttpResponse(content="example text", status_code=200)
```

The response has a default `status_code` of 200 if it's not specified.

If the response needs to be written in several steps, it can be added through the `.write()` method.

```
response = HttpResponse()
response.write('First part of the body')
response.write('Second part of the body')
```

The body can also be composed as an iterable.

```
body= ['Multiple ', 'data ', 'that ', 'will ', 'be ', 'composed']
response = HttpResponse(content=body)
```

All responses from `HttpResponse` will be composed completely before being returned. It is possible to return responses in a streaming way, meaning that the status code will be returned first and chunks of the body will be sent over time. To do that, there's another class called `StreamingHttpResponse` that will work in that way, and can be useful for sending big responses over time.

Instead of using integers to define the status code, it's better to use the defined constants available in Python, for example:

```
from django.http import HttpResponse
from http import HTTPStatus

def my_view(request):
    return HttpResponse(content="example text", status_code=HTTPStatus.
OK)
```

This makes the usage of each status code more explicit and helps increase the readability of the code, making them explicitly `HTTPStatus` objects.

You can see all the status codes defined in Python here: `https://docs.python.org/3/library/http.html`. Note the name is their standard HTTP status code name, as defined in several RFC documents, for example, `201 CREATED`, `404 NOT FOUND`, `502 BAD GATEWAY`, etc.

The `content` parameter defines the body of the request. It can be described as a Python string, but it also accepts binary data, if the response is not plain text. If that's the case, a `content_type` parameter should be added to adequately label the data with the proper MIME type.

```
HttpResponse(content=img_data, content_type="image/png")
```

It is very important that the returned `Content-Type` matches the format of the body. This will make any other tool, like a browser, properly interpret the content adequately.

Headers can also be added to the response using the `headers` parameter.

```
headers = {
    'Content-Type': 'application/pdf',
    'Content-Disposition': 'attachment; filename="report.pdf"',
}
response = HttpResponse(content=img_data, headers=header)
```

> `Content-Disposition` can be used to label the response as an attachment that should be downloaded to the hard drive.
>
> Also, we can set up the `Content-Type` header either manually through the `headers` parameter or through the `content_type` parameter directly.

Headers are also stored in the response when it is accessed as a dictionary:

```
response['Content-Disposition'] = 'attachment; filename="myreport.pdf"'
del response['Content-Disposition']
```

There are specialized subclasses for common cases. Instead of using a generic `HttpResponse`, for JSON encoded requests, it's better to use `JsonResponse`, which will correctly fill the Content-Type and encode it:

```
from django.http import JsonResponse
response = JsonResponse({'example': 1, 'key': 'body'})
```

In the same style, the `FileResponse` allows you to download a file directly, providing a file-like object and directly filling the headers and content type, including if it needs to be an attachment

```
from django.http import FileResponse
file_object = open('report.pdf', 'rb')
response = FileResponse(file_object, is_attachment=True)
```

The response can also be created by rendering a template. This is the usual way of doing so for HTML interfaces, which was what Django was originally designed for. The `render` function will automatically return an `HttpResponse` object.

```
from django.shortcuts import render

def my_view(request):
    ...
    return render(request, 'mytemplate.html')
```

Middleware

A key concept in WSGI requests is that they can be chained. This means that a request can go through different stages, wrapping a new request around the orinal at each stage, which allows you to add functionality.

This leads to the concept of middleware. Middleware improves the handling between systems by simplifying handling several aspects of the request, adding functionality, or simplifying their usage.

Middleware is a word that can refer to different concepts depending on the context of its usage. When used in an HTTP server environment, it typically refers to plugins that enhance or simplify the handling of requests.

A typical example of middleware is logging each received request in a standard manner. The middleware will receive the request, produce a log, and hand the request to the next level.

Another example is managing whether the user is logged or not. There's a standard Django middleware that will detect any session stored in cookies and will search in the database for the associated user. It will then fill the `request.user` object with the proper user.

Another example, enabled by default in Django, checks the CSRF token on `POST` requests. If the CSRF token is not present or it's incorrect, the request will be immediately intercepted and it will return `403 FORBIDDEN`, before accessing the View code.

We introduced the idea of CSRF and tokens in *Chapter 2*.

Middleware can access the request both when it's received and the response when it's ready, so they can work on either side or both sides in coordination:

- Logging middleware that generates a log with the path and method of the received request can generate it before the request is sent to the View.
- Logging middleware that also logs the status code needs to have the information of the status code, so it will need to do it once the View is finished and the response is ready.
- Logging middleware that logs the time it took to generate the request will need to first register the time when the request was received, and what time it is when the response is ready, to log the difference. This requires code both before and after the View.

Middleware is defined in this way:

```
def example_middleware(get_response):
    # The example_middleware wraps the actual middleware

    def middleware(request):
        # Any code to be executed before the view
        # should be located here

        response = get_response(request)

        # Code to be executed after the view
        # should be located here

        return response

    return middleware
```

The structure to return a function allows the initialization of chained elements. The input `get_reponse` can be another middleware function or could be the final view. This allows this kind of structure:

```
chain = middleware_one(middleware_two(my_view))
final_response = chain(request)
```

The order of the middleware is also important. For example, logging should happen before any middleware that can stop the request, as if done in reverse order, any rejected request (for example, not adding a proper CSRF) won't be logged.

Generally, middleware functions have some recommendations on where they should be located. Some are more sensitive to their position than others. Check the documentation for each one.

Middleware can be easily added, either custom-made or by using third-party options. There are a lot of packages that create their own middleware functions for useful features in Django. When considering adding a new feature, spend some time searching to see if there's something already available.

Django REST framework

While Django was designed originally to support HTML interfaces, its functionality has been expanded, both as new features inside the Django project itself, as well as other external projects that enhance Django.

One of particular interest is Django REST framework. We will use it as an example of the available possibilities.

Django REST framework is not only a popular and powerful module. It also uses a lot of conventions that are common across REST frameworks in multiple programming languages.

For our example, we will implement some of the endpoints that we defined in *Chapter 2*. We will use the following endpoints, to follow the whole lifecycle of a micropost.

Endpoint	**Method**	**Action**
`/api/users/<username>/collection`	`GET`	Retrieve all the microposts from a user
`/api/users/<username>/collection`	`POST`	Create a new micropost for the user
`/api/users/<username>/collection/<micropost_id>`	`GET`	Retrieve a single micropost
`/api/users/<username>/collection/<micropost_id>`	`PUT, PATCH`	Update a micropost
`/api/users/<username>/collection/<micropost_id>`	`DELETE`	Delete a micropost

The basic principle behind Django REST framework is to create different classes that encapsulate the exposed resources as URLs.

The extra concept is that objects will be transformed from an internal Model into an external JSON object and vice versa through a *serializer*. The serializer will handle the creation and validate that the external data is correct.

A serializer can't only transform a Model object, but any kind of internal Python class. You can use them to create "virtual objects" that can pull information from multiple Models.

A peculiarity of Django REST framework is that the serializer is the same for input and output. In other frameworks, there are different modules for the way in and out.

Models

We first need to introduce the models to store the information. We will use a `Usr` Model for the users and a `Micropost` Model.

```
from django.db import models
class Usr(models.Model):
    username = models.CharField(max_length=50)


class Micropost(models.Model):
    user = models.ForeignKey(Usr, on_delete=models.CASCADE,
                             related_name='owner')
    text = models.CharField(max_length=300)
    referenced = models.ForeignKey(Usr, null=True,
                                   on_delete=models.CASCADE,
                                   related_name='reference')
    timestamp = models.DateTimeField(auto_now=True
```

The `Usr` model is very straightforward, only storing the username. The `Micropost` Model stores a string of text and the user that created the micropost. Optionally, it can store a referenced user.

Note that the relations have their own named back reference, `reference` and `owner`. They are created by default by Django so you can search where a `Usr` is referenced, for example.

Note also that the `text` allows for 300 characters, instead of the 255 that we said in the API. This is to allow a bit of extra space in the database. We will still protect against more characters later.

URL routing

With this information, we create two different views, one for each URL that we need to create. They'll be called `MicropostsListView` and `MicropostView`. Let's take a look first at how the URLs are defined in the `urls.py` file:

```
from django.urls import path

from . import views

urlpatterns = [
    path('users/<username>/collection', views.MicropostsListView.as_
view(),
         name='user-collection'),
    path('users/<username>/collection/<pk>', views.MicropostView.as_
view(),
         name='micropost-detail'),
]
```

Note that there are two URLs, that correspond to this definition:

```
/api/users/<username>/collection
/api/users/<username>/collection/<micropost_id>
```

And each is mapped to the corresponding view.

Views

Each view inherits from the proper API endpoint, the collection one from `ListCreateAPIView`, which defines the actions for `LIST` (`GET`) and `CREATE` (`POST`):

```
from rest_framework.generics import ListCreateAPIView
from .models import Micropost, Usr
from .serializers import MicropostSerializer


class MicropostsListView(ListCreateAPIView):
    serializer_class = MicropostSerializer

    def get_queryset(self):
        result = Micropost.objects.filter(
             user__username=self.kwargs['username']
        )
```

```
        return result

    def perform_create(self, serializer):
        user = Usr.objects.get(username=self.kwargs['username'])
        serializer.save(user=user)
```

We will check the serializer later. The class requires defining the queryset that it will use to retrieve the information when the `LIST` part of the class is called. Because our URL includes the username, we need to identify it:

```
    def get_queryset(self):
        result = Micropost.objects.filter(
            user__username=self.kwargs['username']
        )
        return result
```

`self.kwargs['username']` will retrieve the username defined in the URL.

For the `CREATE` part, we need to overwrite the `perform_create` method. This method receives a serializer parameter that already contains the validated parameters.

We need to obtain the username and user from the same `self.kwargs` to be sure to add it to the creation of the `Micropost` object.

```
    def perform_create(self, serializer):
        user = Usr.objects.get(username=self.kwargs['username'])
        serializer.save(user=user)
```

The new object is created combining both the user and the rest of the data, added as part of the `save` method for the serializer.

The individual View follows a similar pattern, but there's no need to overwrite the creation:

```
from rest_framework.generics import ListCreateAPIView
from .models import Micropost, Usr
from .serializers import MicropostSerializer

class MicropostView(RetrieveUpdateDestroyAPIView):
    serializer_class = MicropostSerializer

    def get_queryset(self):
        result = Micropost.objects.filter(
```

```
            user__username=self.kwargs['username']
        )
        return result
```

In this case, we allow more operations: `RETRIEVE` (`GET`), `UPDATE` (`PUT` and `PATCH`), and `DESTROY` (`DELETE`).

Serializer

The serializer transforms from the Python object of the Model to the JSON result and the other way around. The serializer is defined like this:

```
from .models import Micropost, Usr
from rest_framework import serializers

class MicropostSerializer(serializers.ModelSerializer):
    href = MicropostHyperlink(source='*', read_only=True)
    text = serializers.CharField(max_length=255)
    referenced = serializers.SlugRelatedField(queryset=Usr.objects.all(),
                                              slug_field='username',
                                              allow_null=True)
    user = serializers.CharField(source='user.username', read_only=True)

    class Meta:
        model = Micropost
        fields = ['href', 'id', 'text', 'referenced', 'timestamp',
'user']
```

`ModelSerializer` will automatically detect the fields in the model defined in the `Meta` subclass. We specified the fields to be included in the `fields` section. Note that, apart from the ones that are directly translated, `id` and `timestamp`, we include others that will change (`user`, `text`, `referenced`) and an extra one (`href`). The directly translated ones are straightforward; we don't need to do anything there.

The `text` field is described again as a `CharField`, but this time, we limit the maximum number of characters.

The `user` field is also redescribed as a `CharField`, but using the source parameter we define it as the username of the referenced user. The field is defined as `read_only`.

`referenced` is similar to it, but we need to define it as `SlugRelatedField`, so it understands that's a reference. A slug is a string that references the value. We define that the `slug_field` is the username of the reference, and add the queryset to allow searching for it.

The `href` field requires an extra defined class to create a proper URL reference. Let's take a detailed look:

```
from .models import Micropost, Usr
from rest_framework import serializers
from rest_framework.reverse import reverse

class MicropostHyperlink(serializers.HyperlinkedRelatedField):
    view_name = 'micropost-detail'

    def get_url(self, obj, view_name, request, format):
        url_kwargs = {
            'pk': obj.pk,
            'username': obj.user.username,
        }
        result = reverse(view_name, kwargs=url_kwargs, request=request,
                         format=format)
        return result

class MicropostSerializer(serializers.ModelSerializer):
    href = MicropostHyperlink(source='*', read_only=True)
    ...
```

`view_name` describes the URL that will be used. The `reverse` call transforms the parameters into the proper full URL. This is wrapped in the `get_url` method. This method receives mainly the `obj` parameter with the full object. This full object is defined in the `source='*'` call to the `MicropostHyperlink` class in the serializer.

The combination of all these factors makes the interface work correctly. Django REST framework can also create an interface to help you visualize the whole interface and use it.

For example, a list will look like this:

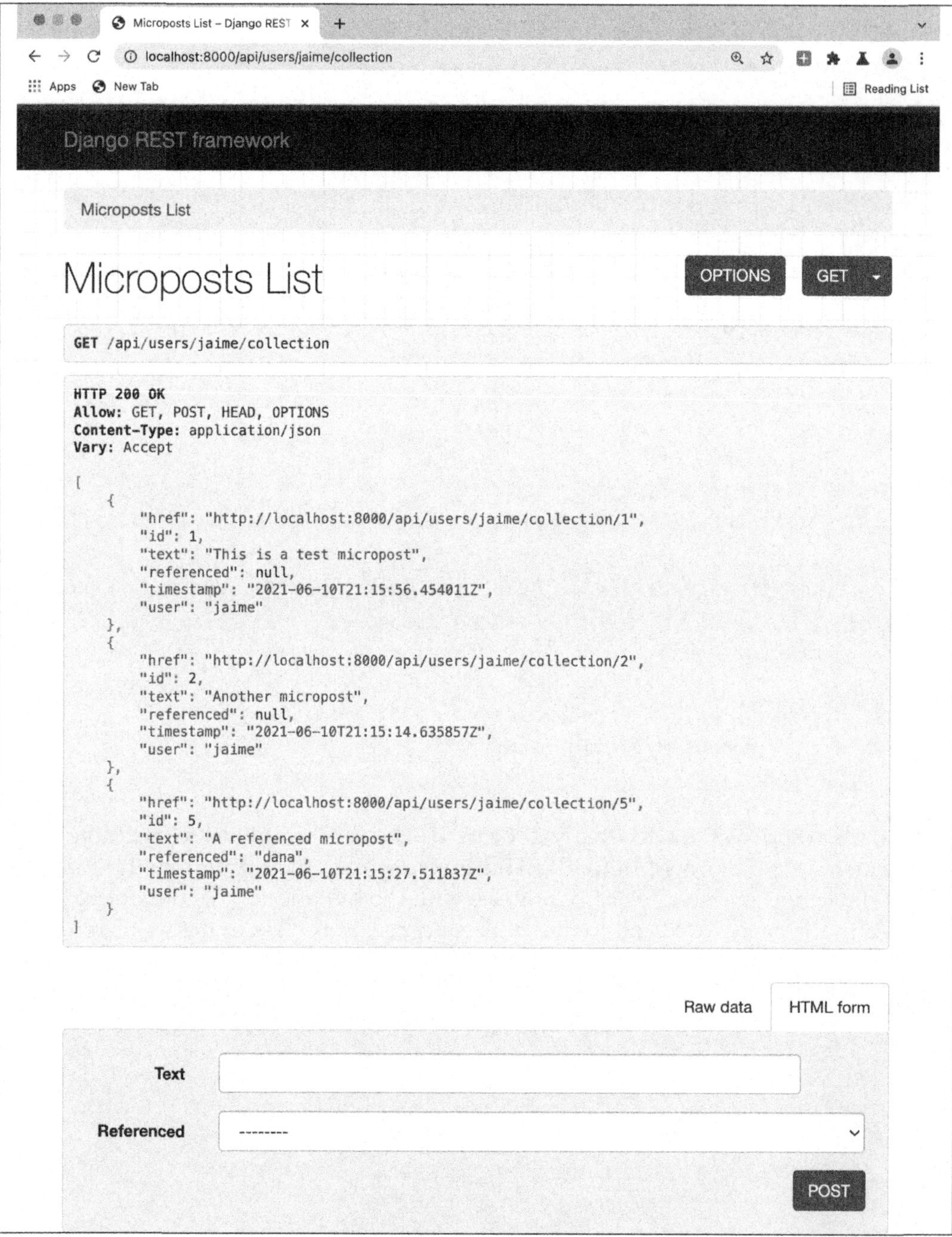

Figure 6.4: Microposts List

And a micropost page will look like this, which allows you to test different actions like `PUT`, `PATCH`, `DELETE`, and `GET`.

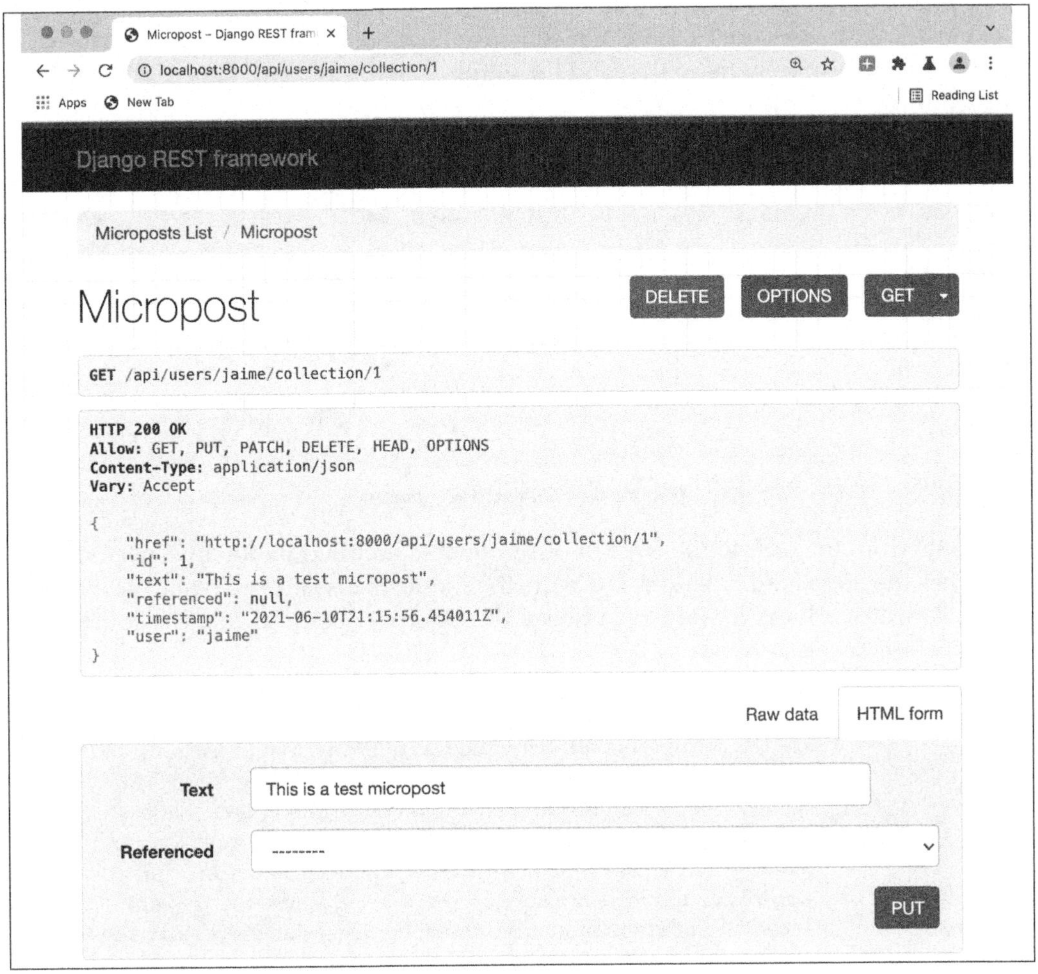

Figure 6.5: Microposts page

Django REST framework is very powerful and can be used in different ways to be sure that it behaves exactly as you expect. It has its own quirks, and it tends to be a little temperamental with the parameters until everything is configured just right. At the same time, it allows you to customize the interface in every aspect. Be sure to read the documentation carefully.

You can find the whole documentation here: `https://www.django-rest-framework.org/`.

External layers

On top of the web server, there is the possibility to continue the link by adding extra levels that work on the HTTP layer. This allows you to load balance between multiple servers and increase the total throughput of the system. This can be chained into multiple layers, if necessary.

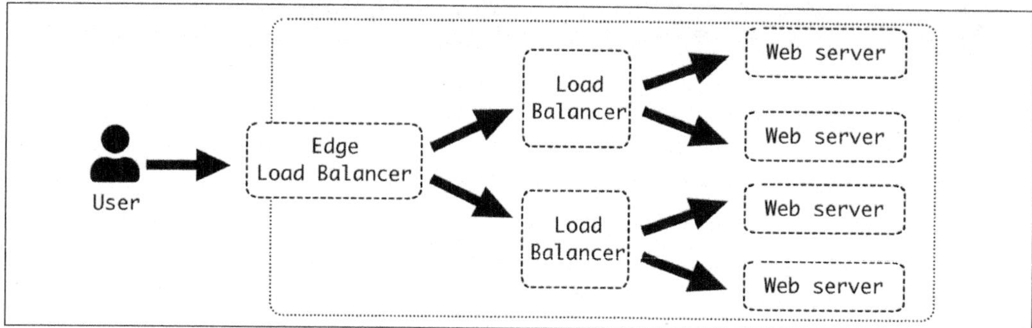

Figure 6.6: Chained load balancers

The route from the user to the edge of our system is handled by the internet, but once it reaches the edge load balancer, it directs the requests inside the system. The edge load balancer works as a gateway between the external networks and the controlled environment of our network.

The edge load balancer is normally the only one that handles HTTPS connection, allowing the rest of the system to use only HTTP. This is convenient as HTTP requests are easier to cache and handle. HTTPS requests are encoded end to end and cannot be properly cached or analyzed. The internal traffic is protected from external access and should have robust policies to be sure that only approved engineers are able to access it and access logs to audit accesses. But at the same time, it can be easily debugged, and any traffic problems can be solved much more easily.

The configuration of the network can greatly vary, and in lots of cases multiple load balancers are not required, and the edge load balancer can handle multiple web servers directly. The capacity in this case is key, as a load balancer has a limit on the number of requests that it can take.

Some key load balancers can be set up as specialized hardware to ensure that they have the capacity to handle the required number of requests.

This multi-layered structure allows you to introduce caching at any point of the system. This can improve the performance of the system, though it needs to be treated with care to be sure that it's adequate. After all, one of the most difficult problems in software development is the proper handling of the cache and its invalidation.

Summary

In this chapter, we went into the details about how web servers work, and the different layers that are involved.

We started by describing the fundamental details of the request-response and web server architecture. Then, we moved on to describe a system with three layers, using nginx as the front web server and uWSGI to handle multiple Python workers that run Django code.

We started with the web server itself, which allows you to serve HTTP, directly return the static content stored in files, and route it towards the next layer. We analyzed the different configuration elements, including enabling header forwarding and logging.

We continued by describing how uWSGI works and how it's able to create and set up different processes that interact through the WSGI protocol in Python. We described how to set up the interaction with the previous level (the nginx web server) and the next level (the Python code). We also described how the workers can be restarted in an orderly way, and how they can be automatically recycled periodically to mitigate certain kinds of problems.

We described how Django works to define a web application, and how the requests and responses flow through the code, including how the middleware can be used to chain elements in the flow. We also introduced Django REST framework as a way to create RESTful APIs and show how our example introduced in *Chapter 2* can be implemented through the views and serializers provided by Django REST framework.

Finally, we described how the structure can be extended by layers on top to be sure to distribute the load across multiple servers and scale the system.

We will next describe event-driven systems.

Join our book's Discord space

Join the book's Discord workspace for a monthly *Ask me Anything* session with the author: `https://packt.link/PythonArchitechture`

7

Event-Driven Structures

Request-response is not the only software architecture that can be used in a system. There can also be requests that don't require an immediate response. Perhaps there's no interest in a response, as the task can be done without the caller being required to wait, or perhaps it takes a long time and the caller doesn't want to be waiting for it. In any case, there's the option to, from the point of view of the caller, just send a message and proceed.

This message is called an *event*, and there are multiple uses for this kind of system. In this chapter, we will introduce the concept, and we will describe in detail one of the most popular uses of it: creating asynchronous tasks that are executed in the background while the caller of the task continues uninterrupted.

In the chapter, we will describe the basics of asynchronous tasks, including the details of queueing systems and how to generate automatically scheduled tasks.

We will use Celery as an example of a popular task manager in Python that has multiple capabilities. We will show specific examples of how to perform common tasks. We will also explore Celery Flower, a tool that creates a web interface to monitor and control Celery and has an HTTP API that allows you to control that interface, including sending new tasks to execute.

In this chapter, we'll cover the following topics:

- Sending events
- Asynchronous tasks
- Subdividing tasks

- Scheduled tasks
- Queue effects
- Celery

Let's start by describing the basics of event-driven systems.

Sending events

Event-driven structures are based on the fire-and-forget principle. Instead of sending data and waiting until the other part returns a response, it just sends data and continues executing.

This makes it different from the request-response architecture that we saw in the previous chapter. A request-response process will wait until an appropriate response is generated. Meanwhile, the execution of more code will stop, as the new data produced by the external system is required to continue.

In an event-driven system, there's no response data, at least not in the same sense. Instead, an event containing the request will be sent, and the task will just continue. Some minimal information could be returned to ensure that the event can be tracked later.

Event-driven systems can be implemented with request-response servers. This doesn't make them a pure request-response system. For example, a RESTful API that creates an event and returns an event ID. Any work is not done yet, and the only detail returned is an identifier to be able to check the status of any follow-up tasks.

This is not the only option, as this event ID may be produced locally, or even not be produced at all.

The difference is that the task itself won't be done in the same moment, so getting back from generating the event will be very fast. The event, once generated, will travel to a different system that will transmit it towards its destination.

This system is called a *bus* and works to make messages flow through the system. An architecture can use a single bus that acts as a central place to send messages across systems, or it can use multiple ones.

In general, it's advisable to use a single bus to communicate all the systems. There are multiple tools that allow us to implement multiple logical partitions, so the messages are routed to and from the right destinations.

Each of the events will be inserted into a *queue*. A queue is a logical FIFO system that will transmit the events from the entry point to the defined next stage. At that point, another module will receive the event and process it.

This new system is listening to the queue and extracts all the received events to process them. This worker can't communicate directly with the sender of the event through the same channel, but it can interact with other elements, like shared databases or exposed endpoints, and can even send more events into queues to further process the results.

The systems at each end of the queue are called the *publisher* and the *subscriber*.

Multiple subscribers can tend the same queue, and they'll be extracting events in parallel. Multiple publishers can also produce events into the same queue. The capacity of the queue will be described by the number of events that can be processed, and enough subscribers should be provided so the queue can be processed quickly enough.

Typical tools that can work as a bus are RabbitMQ, Redis, and Apache Kafka. While it is possible to use a tool "as is," there are multiple libraries that will help you work with these tools to create your own way of handling sending messages.

Asynchronous tasks

A simple event-driven system is one that allows you to execute asynchronous tasks.

The events produced by an event-driven system describe a particular task to execute. Normally, each task will require some time to execute, which makes it impractical to be executed directly as part of the publisher code flow.

The typical example is a web server that needs to respond to the user in a reasonable time. Some HTTP timeouts can produce errors if an HTTP request takes too long, and generally it is not a great experience to respond in more than a second or two.

These operations that take a long time may involve tasks like encoding video into a different resolution, analyzing images with a complex algorithm, sending 1,000 emails to customers, deleting a million registers in bulk, copying data from an external database into a local one, generating reports, or pulling data from multiple sources.

The solution is to send an event to handle this task, generate a task ID, and return the task ID immediately. The event will be sent to a message queue that will deliver it to a back-end system. The back-end system will then execute the task, which can take as long as it needs to execute.

Meanwhile, the task ID can be used to monitor the progress of the execution. The back-end task will update the status of the execution in shared storage, like a database, so when it's completed, the web front-end can inform the user. This shared storage can also store any produced results that may be interesting.

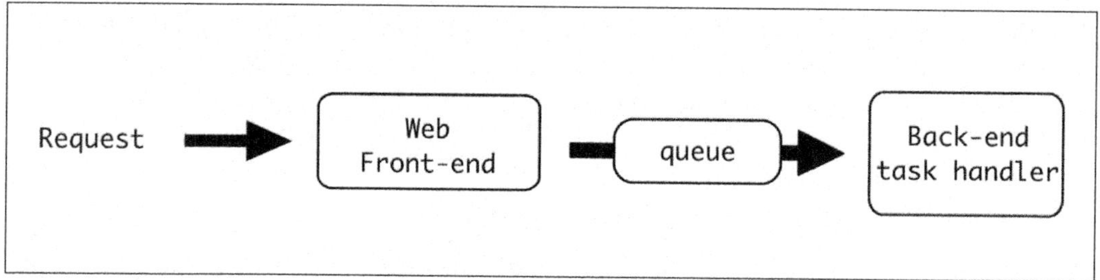

Figure 7.1: The flow of an event

Because the status of the task is stored in a database that's accessible by the front-end web server, the user can ask for the status of the task at any point by identifying it through the task ID.

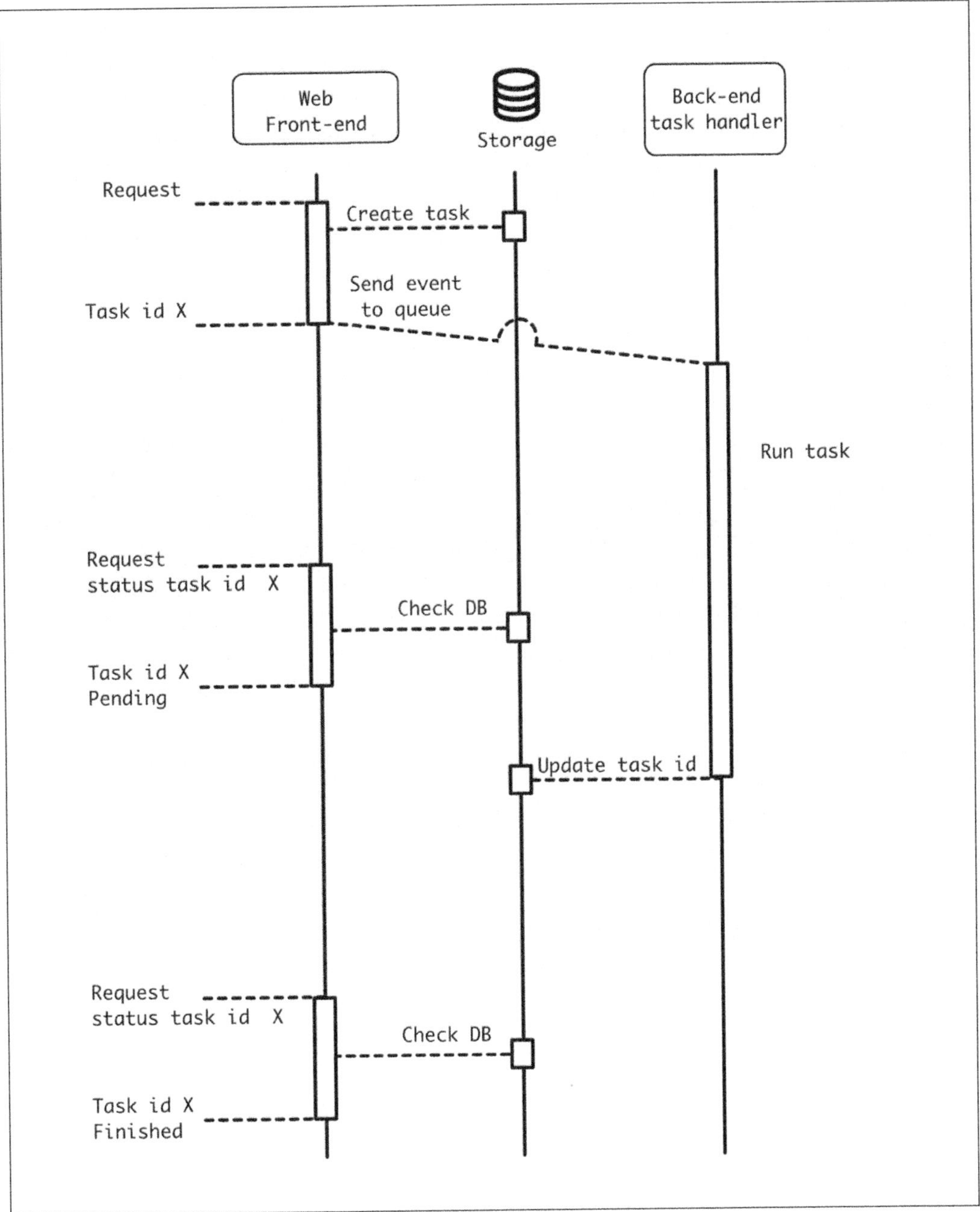

Figure 7.2: Checking the progress of an async task with shared storage

The back-end system can produce intermediate updates if necessary, showing when 25% or 50% of the task has been completed. This will need to be stored in the same shared storage.

This process is a simplification, though. The queue is usually capable of returning whether a task has been finished or not. The shared storage/database will be required only if the task is required to return some data. A database works fine for small results, but if big elements like documents are produced as part of the task, this may not be a valid option and a different kind of storage may be required.

For example, if a task is to generate a report, the back-end will store it in document storage like AWS S3 so it's available to be downloaded by the user later.

A shared database is not the only way to be sure that the web server front-end is capable of receiving information. The web server can expose an internal API that allows the back-end to send back information. This is, to all effects, the same as sending the data to a different external service. The back-end will need to access the API, configure it, and perhaps be authenticated. The API can be created exclusively for the back-end or can be an API for general usage that also accepts the specific data that the back-end system will produce.

Sharing access to a database between two different systems can be difficult, as the database will need to be in sync for both systems. We need to detach the systems so they can be deployed independently and without breaking backward compatibility. Any change in the schema will require extra care to ensure that the system can perform at any point, without interruption. Exposing an API and keeping the database under the full control of the front-end service is a good solution, but keep in mind that requests originating from the back-end will compete with external requests, so we need enough capacity for both.

In this case, all the information, task IDs, statuses, and results can remain inside the web server's internal storage.

Remember that the queue is likely to store the task ID and the status of the task. This may be replicated for convenience in the internal storage.

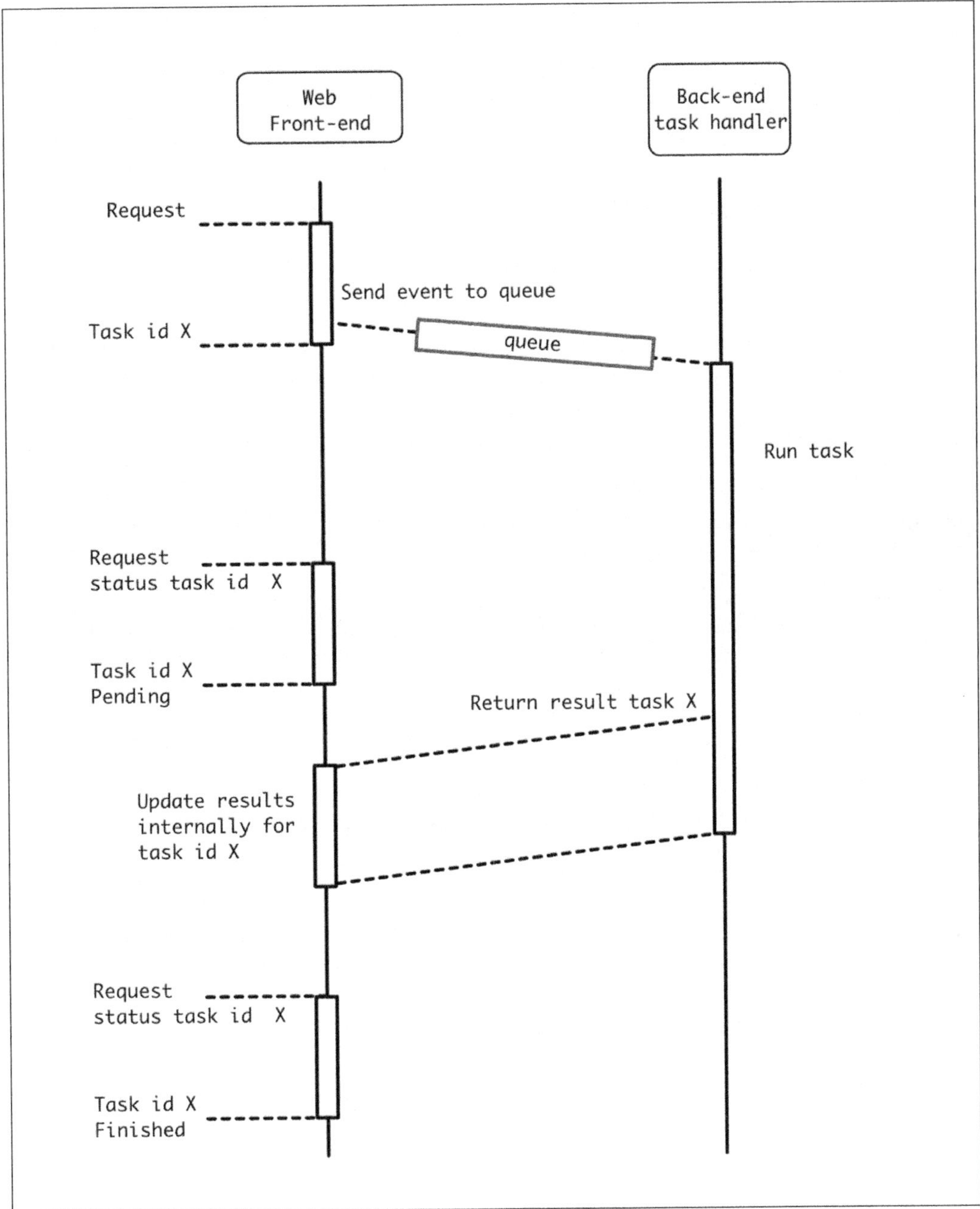

Figure 7.3: Sending back information to the source service

Remember that this API doesn't have to be directed to the same front-end. It can also call any other service, internal or external, generating a complex flow between elements. It even creates its own events that will be reintroduced into the queue to produce other tasks.

Subdividing tasks

It's entirely possible to generate more tasks from an initial one. This is done by creating the right event inside a task and sending it to the right queue.

This allows a single task to distribute its load and parallelize its action. For example, if a task generates a report and sends it by email to a group of recipients, the task can first generate the report and then send the emails in parallel by creating new tasks that will focus only on creating the emails and attaching the report.

This spreads the load over multiple workers, speeding up the process. Another advantage is that individual tasks will be shorter, which makes them easier to control, monitor, and operate.

Some task managers may permit the creation of workflows where tasks are distributed, and their results are returned and combined. This can be used in some cases, but in practice it is less useful than it initially appears, as it introduces extra waiting and we can end up with the task taking a longer time.

But easy wins are bulk tasks performing similar actions on multiple elements without the need to combine the results, which are quite commonly encountered.

Keep in mind, though, that this will make the initial task finish quickly, making the initial task's ID status a bad way to check whether the whole operation has been completed. The initial task may return the IDs of the new tasks if they need to be monitored.

The process can be repeated, if necessary, with subtasks creating their own subtasks. Some tasks may require creating huge amounts of information in the background, so subdividing them may make sense, but it will also increase the complexity of following the flow of the code, so use this technique sparingly and only when it creates a clear advantage.

Scheduled tasks

Asynchronous tasks don't need to be generated directly by a frontend and direct action by a user, but can also be set to run at specific times, through a schedule.

Some examples of scheduled tasks include generating daily reports during night hours, updating information hourly via an external API, precaching values so they are quickly available later, generating a schedule for next week at the start of the week, and sending reminder emails every hour.

Most task queues will allow the generation of scheduled tasks, indicating it clearly in their definition, so they will be triggered automatically.

We will see later in the chapter how to generate a scheduled task for Celery.

Some scheduled tasks can be quite big, such as each night sending emails to thousands of recipients. It's very useful to divide a scheduled task, so a small scheduled task is triggered just to add all the individual tasks to the queue that will be processed later. This distributes the load and allows the task to finish earlier, making full use of the system.

In the example of sending emails, a single task triggers every night, reading the configuration and creating a new task for each email found. Then the new tasks will receive the email, compose the body by pulling from external information, and send it.

Queue effects

An important element of asynchronous tasks is the effect that introducing a queue may have. As we've seen, the background tasks are slow, meaning that any worker running them will be busy for some time.

Meanwhile, more tasks can be introduced, which may mean that the queue starts building up.

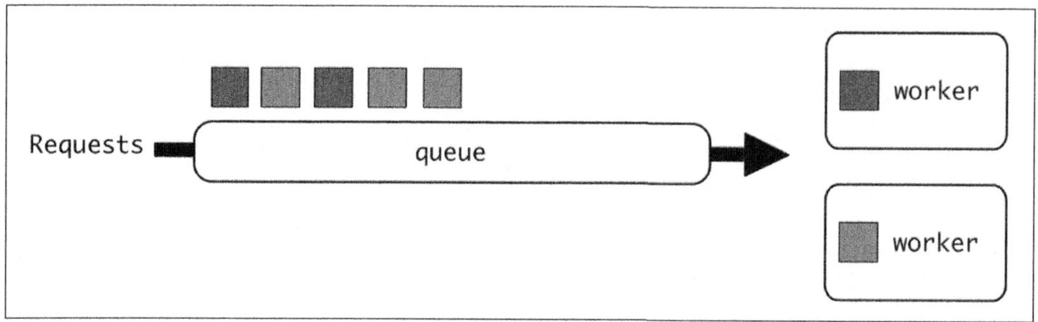

Figure 7.4: Single queue

On the one hand, this can be a capacity problem. If the number of workers is not sufficient to handle the average number of tasks introduced in the queue, the queue will build up until it reaches its limit, and new tasks will be rejected.

But typically, the load doesn't work like a constant influx of tasks. Instead, there are times when there are no tasks to execute, and other times when there's a sudden spike in the number of tasks to be executed, filling the queue. Also, there's a need to calculate the right number of workers to keep running to be sure that the waiting period for those spikes, where a task gets delayed because all the workers are busy, is not causing problems.

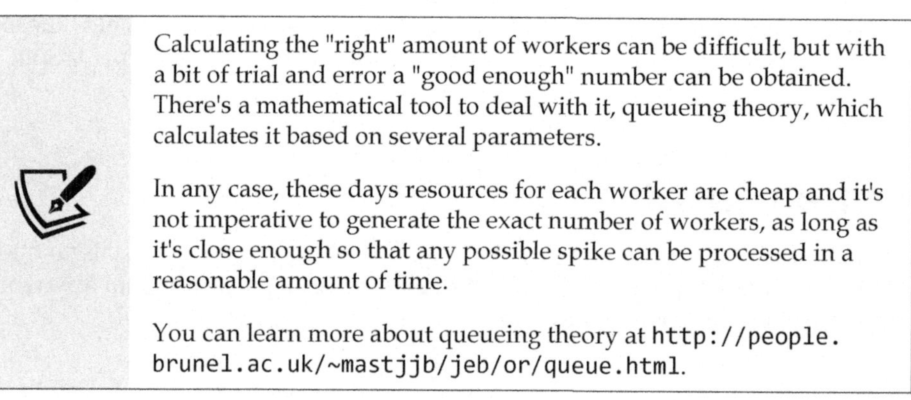

Calculating the "right" amount of workers can be difficult, but with a bit of trial and error a "good enough" number can be obtained. There's a mathematical tool to deal with it, queueing theory, which calculates it based on several parameters.

In any case, these days resources for each worker are cheap and it's not imperative to generate the exact number of workers, as long as it's close enough so that any possible spike can be processed in a reasonable amount of time.

You can learn more about queueing theory at `http://people.brunel.ac.uk/~mastjjb/jeb/or/queue.html`.

An extra difficulty, as we saw with scheduled tasks, is that at a specific time, a considerable number of tasks can be triggered at the same time. This can saturate the queue at a particular time, requiring perhaps an hour to digest all the tasks, for example, creating daily reports, ingesting new updates in an external API every 4 hours, or aggregating data for the week.

This means that, for example, if 100 tasks to create background reports are added, they will block a task to generate a report sent by a user, which will produce a bad experience. The user will have to wait for far too long if they ask for the report a few minutes after the scheduled tasks were fired.

A possible solution is to use multiple queues, with different workers pulling from them.

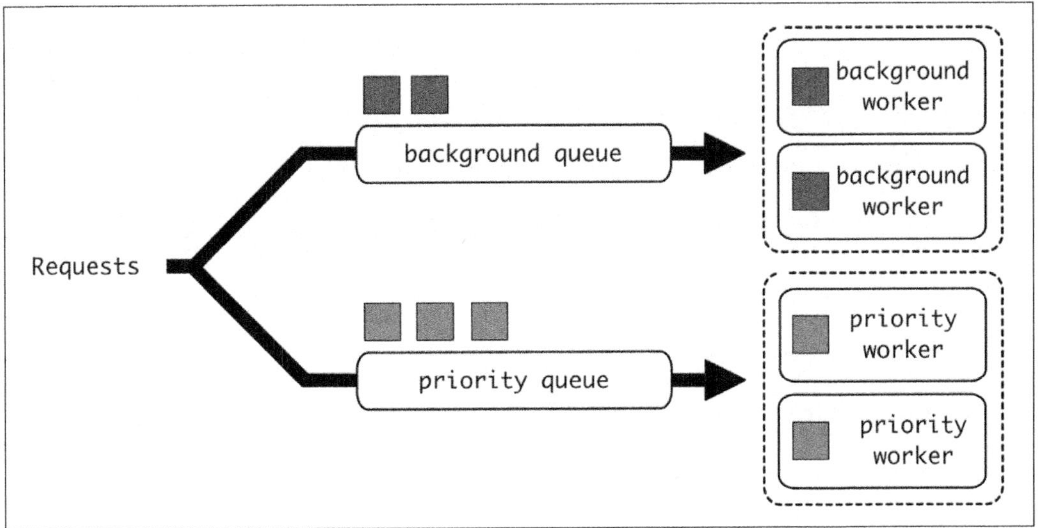

Figure 7.5: Priority and background queue

This makes those different tasks go to different workers, making it possible to reserve capacity for certain tasks to run uninterrupted. In our example, the background reports can go to their own dedicated workers, and the user reports have their own workers as well. This, though, wastes capacity. If the background reports run only once a day, once the 100 tasks are processed, the workers will be idle for the rest of the day, even if there's a long queue in the worker serving the user reports.

Instead of that, a mixed approach can be used.

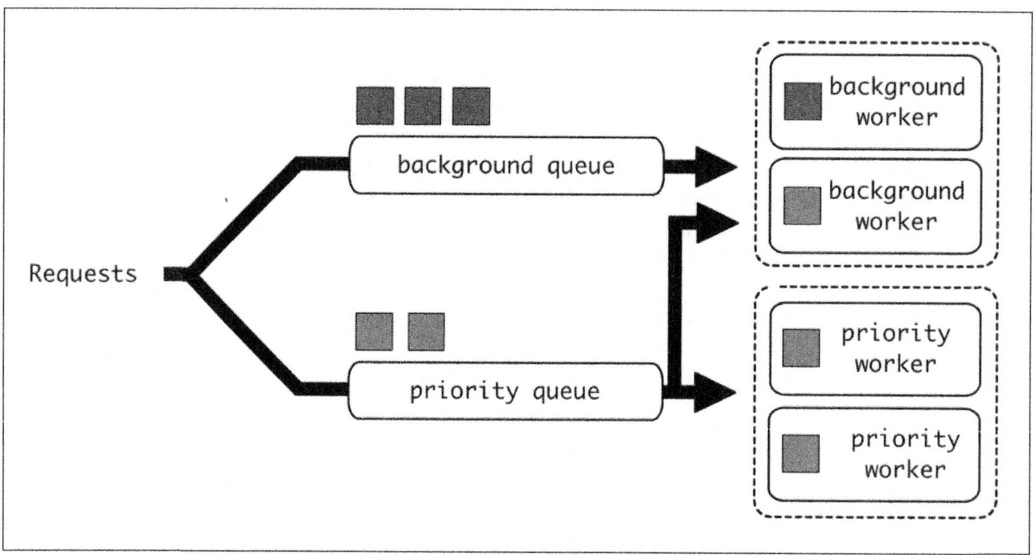

Figure 7.6: Regular worker pulling from multiple queues

In this case, the user report worker will continue with the same approach, but the background report worker will pull tasks from both queues. In this case, we limit the capacity for background reports, but at the same time, we increase it for the user report tasks when there's available capacity.

We reserve capacity for the user report tasks, which are priority, and make the rest of the workers pull from all available tasks, including priority and non-priority tasks.

To be able to divide work into these two queues, the tasks need to be divided carefully:

- *Priority tasks*. They are started on behalf of the user. They are time sensitive. They are fast to execute, so latency is important.
- *Background tasks*. Normally started by automated systems and scheduled tasks. They are less time sensitive. They can run for long periods, so higher latency is easier to accept.

The balance between them should be maintained. If too many tasks are labeled as priority, the queue will be quickly filled, rendering it pointless.

There's always the temptation to generate multiple queues to set up different priorities and reserve capacity for each of them. This is normally not a good idea, as they will waste capacity. The most efficient system is one with a single queue, as all capacity will be always used. There is a problem of priority, though, as it makes some tasks take too long. More than two queues overcomplicates and risks wasting capacity where many workers are idle most of the time, while other queues are filled. The simplicity of two queues helps develop the discipline of deciding between only two options and makes it easy to understand why we want multiple queues.

The number of priority workers can be tweaked based on the number and frequency of spikes and expected turnaround time. Only enough priority workers to cover regular traffic at the times where there are big spikes in background tasks are required, as long as those spikes are predictable.

Good metrics are critical for monitoring and understanding the behavior of the queue. We will talk more about metrics in *Chapter 13, Metrics*.

An alternative is to generate a priority system based on specific priorities, like numbers. That way, a task with priority 3 will be executed before a task with priority 2, and that before a task with priority 1, and so on. The great advantage of having priorities is that the workers can be working all the time, without wasting any capacity.

But this approach has some problems:

- A lot of queue backends don't support it efficiently. To keep a queue sorted by priority costs more than just assigning tasks to a plain queue. In practice, it may not produce as good results as you expect, requiring many tweaks and adjustments.
- It means you need to deal with priority inflation. It's very easy for teams to start increasing the priority of tasks over time, especially if multiple teams are involved. The decision on what task should return first could get complicated and pressure can grow the priority numbers over time.

While it can appear that a sorted queue is ideal, the simplicity of two levels (priority and background) makes it very easy to understand the system and generates easy expectations when developing and creating new tasks. It's way easier to tweak and understand and will generate better results with less work.

Single code for all workers

When having different workers pulling from different queues, the worker could have different codebases, making one with priority tasks and another with background tasks.

Note that for this to work, it will require strict separation of tasks. More about this a bit later.

This is generally not advisable, as it will differentiate the codebase and require maintaining two code bases in parallel, with some problems:

- It's likely that some tasks or task parts will be either priority or background, depending on what system or user triggers them. For example, reports that can be either produced on the fly for a user, or daily as part of a batch process to finally send them by mail. The report generation should remain common, so any change is applied to both.
- Handling two codebases instead of one is more inconvenient. A big part of the general code is shared, so updates will need to be run independently.
- A unique codebase can handle all kinds of tasks. That makes it possible to have a worker that handles both priority and background tasks. Two codebases will require strict task separation, not using the extra capacity available in the background workers to help with priority tasks.

It is better to use a single worker when building, and through the configuration decide to receive messages from one queue or both. This simplifies the architecture for local development and testing.

This may not be adequate when the nature of the tasks may create conflicts. For example, if some of the tasks require big dependencies or specialized hardware (as could be the case with some AI-related tasks) this may require that specific tasks run in dedicated workers, making it impractical for them to share the same codebase. These cases are rare, and unless they are encountered, it's better to try to consolidate and use the same worker for all tasks.

Cloud queues and workers

The main characteristic of cloud computing is that services can be started and stopped dynamically, allowing us to use only the resources required at a particular moment. This allows the system to increase and decrease capacity quickly.

In cloud environments, it's possible that the number of workers extracting events from a queue can be modified. That alleviates the problems with resourcing that we discussed above. Do we have a full queue? Increase the number of workers on demand! Ideally, we could even spawn a single worker for each event that spawns a task, making the system infinitely scalable.

This, obviously, is easier said than done, as there are some issues with trying to dynamically create workers on the spot:

- The start-up time can add significant time to the execution of the task, even to the point of being longer than the execution time of the task itself. Depending on how heavy the creation of a worker is, starting it can take a significant amount of time.

  In the traditional cloud setting, the lowest granularity required to start a new virtual server, which is relatively heavy, takes at least a couple of minutes. With newer tools, such as containers, this can be sped up sensibly, but the underlying principle will remain, as at some point in time a new virtual server will need to be spawned.
- A single new virtual worker may be too big for a single worker, making it inefficient to spawn one for each task. Again, containerized solutions can help by making it easier to separate between creating a new container and requiring spinning up a new virtual server in the cloud service.
- Any cloud service should have limits. Each new worker created costs money and cloud services can get very expensive if scaled up without control. Without certain control on the cost side of things, this can grow to be a problem due to high, unexpected costs. Normally this can happen by accident, with some explosion of workers due to some problem on the system, but there's also a security attack, called Cash Overflow, aimed at making a service run as expensively as possible to force the owner of the service to stop it or even bankrupt them.

Because of these problems, normally a solution will need to work in sort of a batched way, allowing extra space to grow and generating extra virtual servers only when they are required to reduce the queue. In the same way, when the extra capacity is not required any more, it will be removed.

Extra care should be taken to be sure that all the workers located in the same virtual server are idle before stopping it. This is done automatically by stopping the servers gracefully, so they'll finish any remaining tasks, start no new ones, and finish when everything is done.

The process should be similar to this:

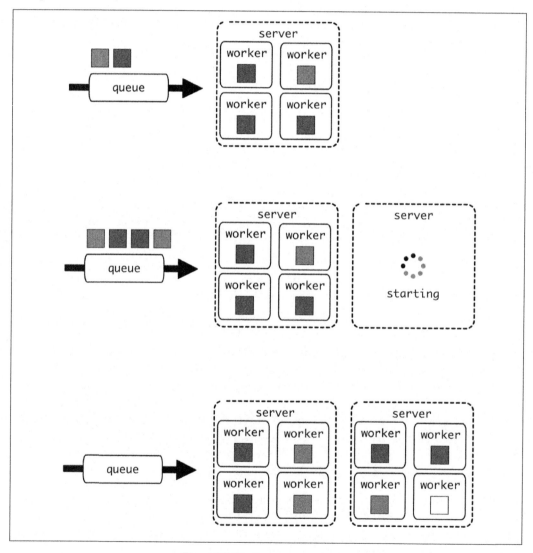

Figure 7.7: Starting up a new server

Knowing exactly when a new server should be spawned depends greatly on the requirements for latency, traffic, and the speed of creating a new server (if the server starts quickly, perhaps it can be less aggressive in scaling up).

A good starting point is to create a new server each time the queue has a number of tasks equal to or greater than the number of workers in a single server. That triggers a new server that will be able to handle those tasks. If the creation is triggered with fewer tasks than that, it will create a server that is not quite filled. If the start-up time is very long, this can be reduced to ensure that the new server is up before there's a significant queue building up. But this will require experimentation and testing for a specific system.

Celery

Celery is the most popular task queue created in Python. It allows us to create new tasks easily and can handle the creation of the events that trigger new tasks.

Celery requires to work to set up a *broker*, which will be used as a queue to handle the messages.

In Celery parlance, the broker is the message queue, while the *backend* is reserved for interacting with a storage system to return information.

The code that creates the message will add it to the broker, and the broker will pass it to one of the connected workers. When everything happens with Python code, where the `celery` package can be installed, it's simple to operate. We'll see later how to operate it in other cases.

Celery can use multiple systems as brokers. The most popular are Redis and RabbitMQ.

In our examples, we will use Redis as it can be used for the broker and the backend, and it's widely available in cloud systems. It's also quite scalable and handles big loads easily.

Using a backend is optional, as tasks don't need to define a return value, and it's very common that asynchronous tasks don't directly return response data other than the status of the task. The key word here is "directly"; sometimes, a task will generate an external result that can be accessible, but not through the Celery system.

Some examples of these values are reports that can be stored in other storage facilities, emails sent during task processing, and pre-caching of values, where there is not a direct result, but there's new data generated and stored in other places.

The returning value needs also to be small enough that it can be stored in the system working as the backend. Also, if strong persistence is used, it's recommended that a database is used as the backend.

We will use the example present on GitHub: `https://github.com/PacktPublishing/Python-Architecture-Patterns/tree/main/chapter_07_event_driven/celery_example`. We will use the example to create a task to retrieve, from an external API, pending `TO DO` actions by some users, and generate an email to send as a reminder.

Remember to install the required dependencies by running `pip install -r requirements.txt`.

Let's take a look at the code.

Configuring Celery

The code is divided into two files: `celery_tasks.py`, which describes the tasks, and `start_task.py`, which connects with the queue and enqueues a task.

At the start of each, we need to configure the broker to use. In this case, we will use a Redis server running in the `localhost`:

```
from celery import Celery

app = Celery('tasks', broker='redis://localhost')
```

As a prerequisite, we need to set up a Redis server running in our expected `localhost` address. An easy way of doing so, if you have Docker installed, is to start a container:

```
$ docker run -d -p 6379:6379 redis
```

This starts the standard Redis container that will expose the service over the standard port, 6379. That will connect automatically with the previous broker URL of `redis://localhost`.

This is all the configuration that's required, and it will allow both sides, the publisher and the subscriber, to connect to the queue.

Celery worker

We will use `https://jsonplaceholder.typicode.com/` to simulate calling an external API. This testing site exposes an accessible REST endpoint to retrieve some mock information. You can see their definition, but basically, we will access the `/todos` and `/users` endpoints. The `/todos` endpoint exposes actions stored by the users, so we will query them to retrieve pending actions, and combine this with the information in the `/users` endpoint.

The `celery_tasks.py` worker defines a main task, `obtain_info`, and a secondary task, `send_email`. The first one pulls the information from the API and decides what emails need to be sent. The second then sends the email.

The sending of the email is just mocked to avoid complicating the system and needing to handle mocked email addresses. It's left as an exercise for the reader.

The file starts with the configuration of the queue and imports:

```
from celery import Celery
import requests
from collections import defaultdict

app = Celery('tasks', broker='redis://localhost')
logger = app.log.get_default_logger()
BASE_URL = 'https://jsonplaceholder.typicode.com'
```

The `logger` definition permits the use of native Celery logs that will be streamed into the Celery configuration for logs. By default, this is the standard output.

Let's take a look at the `obtain_info` task. Note the `@app.task` that defines the function as a Celery task:

```
@app.task
def obtain_info():
```

```
    logger.info('Stating task')
    users = {}
    task_reminders = defaultdict(list)
    # Call the /todos endpoint to retrieve all the tasks
    response = requests.get(f'{BASE_URL}/todos')
    for task in response.json():
        # Skip completed tasks
        if task['completed'] is True:
            continue

        # Retrieve user info. The info is cached to only ask
        # once per user
        user_id = task['userId']
        if user_id not in users:
            users[user_id] = obtain_user_info(user_id)

        info = users[user_id]

        # Append the task information to task_reminders, that
        # aggregates them per user
        task_data = (info, task)
        task_reminders[user_id].append(task_data)

    # The data is ready to process, create an email per
    # each user
    for user_id, reminders in task_reminders.items():
        compose_email(reminders)

    logger.info('End task')
```

We wrap the function with `INFO` logs to provide context to the task execution. First, it calls the `/todos` endpoint on this line, which then goes through each task independently, skipping any completed task.

```
    response = requests.get(f'{BASE_URL}/todos')
    for task in response.json():
        if task['completed'] is True:
            continue
```

Then, it checks the information for the user and puts it into the info variable. Because this information can be used multiple times in the same loop, it is cached in the users dictionary. Once the info is cached, it's not asked for again:

```
        user_id = task['userId']
        if user_id not in users:
            users[user_id] = obtain_user_info(user_id)

        info = users[user_id]
```

The individual task data is added to a list created to store all the tasks for a user. The task_reminders dictionary is created as a defaultdict(list), meaning that the first time a particular user_id is accessed, if it's not present, it will be initialized as an empty list, allowing a new element to be appended.

```
        task_data = (info, task)
        task_reminders[user_id].append(task_data)
```

Finally, the stored elements in task_reminders are iterated to compose the resulting email:

```
    for user_id, reminders in task_reminders.items():
        compose_email(reminders)
```

Two follow-up functions are called: obtain_user_info and compose_email.

obtain_user_info retrieves the information directly from the /users/{user_id} endpoint and returns it:

```
def obtain_user_info(user_id):
    logger.info(f'Retrieving info for user {user_id}')
    response = requests.get(f'{BASE_URL}/users/{user_id}')
    data = response.json()
    logger.info(f'Info for user {user_id} retrieved')
    return data
```

compose_email takes the information in the task list, which includes a group of user_info, task_info, extracts the title information for each task_info, then the email from the matched user_info, and then calls the send_email task:

```
def compose_email(remainders):
    # remainders is a list of (user_info, task_info)
```

```
    # Retrieve all the titles from each task_info
    titles = [task['title'] for _, task in remainders]

    # Obtain the user_info from the first element
    # The user_info is repeated and the same on each element
    user_info, _ = remainders[0]
    email = user_info['email']
    # Start the task send_email with the proper info
    send_email.delay(email, titles)
```

As you can see, the `send_email` task includes a `.delay` call, which enqueues this task with the appropriate parameters. `send_email` is another Celery task. It is very simple as we are just mocking the email delivery. It just logs its parameters:

```
@app.task
def send_email(email, remainders):
    logger.info(f'Send an email to {email}')
    logger.info(f'Reminders {remainders}')
```

Triggering tasks

The `start_task.py` script contains all the code to trigger the task. This is a simple script that imports the task from the other file.

```
from celery_tasks import obtain_info

obtain_info.delay()
```

Note that it inherits all the configuration from `celery_tasks.py` when doing the import.

Importantly, it calls the task with `.delay()`. This sends the task to the queue so the worker can pull it out and execute it.

Note that if you call the task directly with `obtain_info()`, you'll execute the code directly, instead of submitting the task to the queue.

Let's see now how both files interact.

Connecting the dots

To be able to set both parts, the publisher and the consumer, first start the worker calling style:

```
$ celery -A celery_tasks worker --loglevel=INFO -c 3
```

Note: Some of the modules used, such as Celery, might not be compatible with Windows systems. More information can be found at `https://docs.celeryproject.org/en/stable/faq.html#does-celery-support-windows`.

This starts the `celery_tasks` module (the `celery_tasks.py` file) with the `-A` parameter. It sets the log level to `INFO` and starts three workers with the `-c 3` parameter. It will display a starting log similar to this one:

```
$ celery -A celery_tasks worker --loglevel=INFO -c 3


   v5.1.1 (sun-harmonics)

macOS-10.15.7-x86_64-i386-64bit 2021-06-22 20:14:09

[config]
.> app:         tasks:0x110b45760
.> transport:   redis://localhost:6379//
.> results:     disabled://
.> concurrency: 3 (prefork)
.> task events: OFF (enable -E to monitor tasks in this worker)

[queues]
.> celery           exchange=celery(direct) key=celery


[tasks]
  . celery_tasks.obtain_info
  . celery_tasks.send_email

[2021-06-22 20:14:09,613: INFO/MainProcess] Connected to redis://
localhost:6379//
[2021-06-22 20:14:09,628: INFO/MainProcess] mingle: searching for
neighbors
[2021-06-22 20:14:10,666: INFO/MainProcess] mingle: all alone
```

Note that it displays the two available tasks, `obtain_info` and `send_email`. In another window, we can send tasks calling the `start_task.py` script:

```
$ python3 start_task.py
```

This will trigger the task in the Celery worker, producing logs (edited for clarity and brevity). We will explain the logs in the next paragraphs.

```
[2021-06-22 20:30:52,627: INFO/MainProcess] Task celery_tasks.obtain_
info[5f6c9441-9dda-40df-b456-91100a92d42c] received
[2021-06-22 20:30:52,632: INFO/ForkPoolWorker-2] Stating task
[2021-06-22 20:30:52,899: INFO/ForkPoolWorker-2] Retrieving info for
user 1
...
[2021-06-22 20:30:54,128: INFO/MainProcess] Task celery_tasks.send_
email[08b9ed75-0f33-48f8-8b55-1f917cfdeae8] received
[2021-06-22 20:30:54,133: INFO/MainProcess] Task celery_tasks.send_
email[d1f6c6a0-a416-4565-b085-6b0a180cad37] received
[2021-06-22 20:30:54,132: INFO/ForkPoolWorker-1] Send an email to
Sincere@april.biz
[2021-06-22 20:30:54,134: INFO/ForkPoolWorker-1] Reminders ['delectus
aut autem', 'quis ut nam facilis et officia qui', 'fugiat veniam
minus', 'laboriosam mollitia et enim quasi adipisci quia provident
illum', 'qui ullam ratione quibusdam voluptatem quia omnis', 'illo
expedita consequatur quia in', 'molestiae perspiciatis ipsa', 'et
doloremque nulla', 'dolorum est consequatur ea mollitia in culpa']
[2021-06-22 20:30:54,135: INFO/ForkPoolWorker-1] Task celery_tasks.
send_email[08b9ed75-0f33-48f8-8b55-1f917cfdeae8] succeeded in
0.004046451000021989s: None
[2021-06-22 20:30:54,137: INFO/ForkPoolWorker-3] Send an email to
Shanna@melissa.tv
[2021-06-22 20:30:54,181: INFO/ForkPoolWorker-2] Task celery_tasks.
obtain_info[5f6c9441-9dda-40df-b456-91100a92d42c] succeeded in
1.5507660419999638s: None
...
[2021-06-22 20:30:54,141: INFO/ForkPoolWorker-3] Task celery_tasks.
send_email[d1f6c6a0-a416-4565-b085-6b0a180cad37] succeeded in
0.004405897999959052s: None
[2021-06-22 20:30:54,192: INFO/ForkPoolWorker-2] Task celery_tasks.
send_email[aff6dfc9-3e9d-4c2d-9aa0-9f91f2b35f87] succeeded in
0.0012900159999844618s: None
```

Because we started three different workers, the logs are intertwined. Pay attention to the first task, which corresponds to `obtain_info`. This task has been executed in the worker `ForkPoolWorker-2` in our execution.

```
[2021-06-22 20:30:52,627: INFO/MainProcess] Task celery_tasks.obtain_
info[5f6c9441-9dda-40df-b456-91100a92d42c] received
[2021-06-22 20:30:52,632: INFO/ForkPoolWorker-2] Stating task
[2021-06-22 20:30:52,899: INFO/ForkPoolWorker-2] Retrieving info for
user 1
...
[2021-06-22 20:30:54,181: INFO/ForkPoolWorker-2] Task celery_tasks.
obtain_info[5f6c9441-9dda-40df-b456-91100a92d42c] succeeded in
1.5507660419999638s: None
```

While this task is being executed, the `send_email` tasks are also being enqueued and executed by the other workers.

For example:

```
[2021-06-22 20:30:54,133: INFO/MainProcess] Task celery_tasks.send_
email[d1f6c6a0-a416-4565-b085-6b0a180cad37] received
[2021-06-22 20:30:54,132: INFO/ForkPoolWorker-1] Send an email to
Sincere@april.biz
[2021-06-22 20:30:54,134: INFO/ForkPoolWorker-1] Reminders ['delectus
aut autem', 'quis ut nam facilis et officia qui', 'fugiat veniam
minus', 'laboriosam mollitia et enim quasi adipisci quia provident
illum', 'qui ullam ratione quibusdam voluptatem quia omnis', 'illo
expedita consequatur quia in', 'molestiae perspiciatis ipsa', 'et
doloremque nulla', 'dolorum est consequatur ea mollitia in culpa']
[2021-06-22 20:30:54,135: INFO/ForkPoolWorker-1] Task celery_tasks.
send_email[08b9ed75-0f33-48f8-8b55-1f917cfdeae8] succeeded in
0.004046451000021989s: None
```

At the end of the execution, there's a log showing the time it has taken, in seconds.

If only one worker is involved, the tasks will be run consecutively, making it easier to differentiate between tasks.

We can see how the `send_email` tasks start before the end of the `obtain_info` task, and that there are still `send_email` tasks running after the end of the `obtain_info` task, showing how the tasks are running independently.

Scheduled tasks

Inside Celery, we can also generate tasks with a certain schedule, so they can be triggered automatically at the proper time.

To do so, we need to define a task and a schedule. We defined them in the `celery_scheduled_tasks.py` file. Let's take a look:

```
from celery import Celery
from celery.schedules import crontab

app = Celery('tasks', broker='redis://localhost')

logger = app.log.get_default_logger()


@app.task
def scheduled_task(timing):
    logger.info(f'Scheduled task executed {timing}')


app.conf.beat_schedule = {
    # Executes every 15 seconds
    'every-15-seconds': {
        'task': 'celery_scheduled_tasks.scheduled_task',
        'schedule': 15,
        'args': ('every 15 seconds',),
    },

    # Executes following crontab
    'every-2-minutes': {
        'task': 'celery_scheduled_tasks.scheduled_task',
        'schedule': crontab(minute='*/2'),
        'args': ('crontab every 2 minutes',),
    },
}
```

This file starts with the same configuration as the previous example, and we define a small, simple task that just displays when it is executed.

```
@app.task
def scheduled_task(timing):
    logger.info(f'Scheduled task executed {timing}')
```

The interesting bit comes later, as the schedule is configured in the `app.conf.beat_schedule` parameter. We created two entries.

```
app.conf.beat_schedule = {
    # Executes every 15 seconds
    'every-15-seconds': {
        'task': 'celery_scheduled_tasks.scheduled_task',
        'schedule': 15,
        'args': ('every 15 seconds',),
    },
```

The first one defines an execution of the proper task every 15 seconds. The task needs to include the module name (`celery_scheduled_tasks`). The `schedule` parameter is defined in seconds. The `args` parameter contains any parameter to pass for the execution. Note that it's defined as a list of parameters. In this case, we create a tuple with a single entry, as there's only one argument.

The second entry defines the schedule instead as a crontab entry.

```
    # Executes following crontab
    'every-2-minutes': {
        'task': 'celery_scheduled_tasks.scheduled_task',
        'schedule': crontab(minute='*/2'),
        'args': ('crontab every 2 minutes',),
    },
```

This `crontab` object, which is passed as the `schedule` parameter, executes the task once every two minutes. Crontab entries are very flexible and allow for a wide range of possible actions.

Some examples are as follows:

Crontab entry	Description
`crontab()`	Execute every minute, the lowest possible resolution
`crontab(minute=0)`	Execute every hour, at minute 0
`crontab(minute=15)`	Execute hourly, at minute 15
`crontab(hour=0, minute=0)`	Execute daily, at midnight (in your time zone)
`crontab(hour=6, minute=30, day_of_week='monday')`	Execute every Monday, at 6:30
`crontab(hour='*/8', minute=0)`	Execute every hour divisible by 8 (0, 8, 16). Three times a day, at minute 0 in each case
`crontab(day_of_month=1, hour=0, minute=0)`	Execute on the first of each month, at midnight
`crontab(minute='*/2')`	Execute every minute divisible by 2. Once every two minutes

There are more options, including relating the time to solar times, like dawn and dusk, or custom schedulers, but most use cases will be perfectly fine either once every X seconds or with a crontab definition.

You can check the full documentation here: `https://docs.celeryproject.org/en/stable/userguide/periodic-tasks.html#starting-the-scheduler`.

To start the scheduler, we need to start a specific worker, the `beat` worker:

```
$ celery -A celery_scheduled_tasks beat
celery beat v4.4.7 (cliffs) is starting.
__    -    ... __   -        _
LocalTime -> 2021-06-28 13:53:23
Configuration ->
    . broker -> redis://localhost:6379//
    . loader -> celery.loaders.app.AppLoader
    . scheduler -> celery.beat.PersistentScheduler
    . db -> celerybeat-schedule
    . logfile -> [stderr]@%WARNING
    . maxinterval -> 5.00 minutes (300s)
```

We start the celery_scheduled_tasks worker in the usual way.

```
$ celery -A celery_scheduled_tasks worker --loglevel=INFO -c 3
```

But you can see that there's still no incoming tasks. We need to start celery beat, which is a specific worker that inserts the tasks in the queue:

```
$ celery -A celery_scheduled_tasks beat
celery beat v4.4.7 (cliffs) is starting.
__    -    ... __   -        _
LocalTime -> 2021-06-28 15:13:06
Configuration ->
    . broker -> redis://localhost:6379//
    . loader -> celery.loaders.app.AppLoader
    . scheduler -> celery.beat.PersistentScheduler
    . db -> celerybeat-schedule
    . logfile -> [stderr]@%WARNING
    . maxinterval -> 5.00 minutes (300s)
```

Once celery beat is started, you'll start seeing the tasks being scheduled and executed as expected:

```
[2021-06-28 15:13:06,504: INFO/MainProcess] Received task: celery_
scheduled_tasks.scheduled_task[42ed6155-4978-4c39-b307-852561fdafa8]
[2021-06-28 15:13:06,509: INFO/MainProcess] Received task: celery_
scheduled_tasks.scheduled_task[517d38b0-f276-4c42-9738-80ca844b8e77]
[2021-06-28 15:13:06,510: INFO/ForkPoolWorker-2] Scheduled task
executed every 15 seconds
[2021-06-28 15:13:06,510: INFO/ForkPoolWorker-1] Scheduled task
executed crontab every 2 minutes
[2021-06-28 15:13:06,511: INFO/ForkPoolWorker-2] Task celery_scheduled_
tasks.scheduled_task[42ed6155-4978-4c39-b307-852561fdafa8] succeeded in
0.0016690909999965697s: None
[2021-06-28 15:13:06,512: INFO/ForkPoolWorker-1] Task celery_scheduled_
tasks.scheduled_task[517d38b0-f276-4c42-9738-80ca844b8e77] succeeded in
0.0014504210000154671s: None
[2021-06-28 15:13:21,486: INFO/MainProcess] Received task: celery_
scheduled_tasks.scheduled_task[4d77b138-283c-44c8-a8ce-9183cf0480a7]
[2021-06-28 15:13:21,488: INFO/ForkPoolWorker-2] Scheduled task
executed every 15 seconds
[2021-06-28 15:13:21,489: INFO/ForkPoolWorker-2] Task celery_scheduled_
tasks.scheduled_task[4d77b138-283c-44c8-a8ce-9183cf0480a7] succeeded in
0.0005252540000242334s: None
```

```
[2021-06-28 15:13:36,486: INFO/MainProcess] Received task: celery_
scheduled_tasks.scheduled_task[2eb2ee30-2bcd-45af-8ee2-437868be22e4]
[2021-06-28 15:13:36,489: INFO/ForkPoolWorker-2] Scheduled task
executed every 15 seconds
[2021-06-28 15:13:36,489: INFO/ForkPoolWorker-2] Task celery_scheduled_
tasks.scheduled_task[2eb2ee30-2bcd-45af-8ee2-437868be22e4] succeeded in
0.0004935349999755095s: None
[2021-06-28 15:13:51,486: INFO/MainProcess] Received task: celery_
scheduled_tasks.scheduled_task[c7c0616c-857a-4f7b-ae7a-dd967f9498fb]
[2021-06-28 15:13:51,488: INFO/ForkPoolWorker-2] Scheduled task
executed every 15 seconds
[2021-06-28 15:13:51,489: INFO/ForkPoolWorker-2] Task celery_scheduled_
tasks.scheduled_task[c7c0616c-857a-4f7b-ae7a-dd967f9498fb] succeeded in
0.0004461000000333115s: None
[2021-06-28 15:14:00,004: INFO/MainProcess] Received task: celery_
scheduled_tasks.scheduled_task[59f6a323-4d9f-4ac4-b831-39ca6b342296]
[2021-06-28 15:14:00,006: INFO/ForkPoolWorker-2] Scheduled task
executed crontab every 2 minutes
[2021-06-28 15:14:00,006: INFO/ForkPoolWorker-2] Task celery_scheduled_
tasks.scheduled_task[59f6a323-4d9f-4ac4-b831-39ca6b342296] succeeded in
0.0004902660000425385s: None
```

You can see that both kinds of tasks are scheduled accordingly. In this log, check the times and see that they are 15 seconds apart:

```
[2021-06-28 15:13:06,510: INFO/ForkPoolWorker-2] Scheduled task
executed every 15 seconds
[2021-06-28 15:13:21,488: INFO/ForkPoolWorker-2] Scheduled task
executed every 15 seconds
[2021-06-28 15:13:36,489: INFO/ForkPoolWorker-2] Scheduled task
executed every 15 seconds
[2021-06-28 15:13:51,488: INFO/ForkPoolWorker-2] Scheduled task
executed every 15 seconds
```

The other task happens exactly every 2 minutes. Note that the first execution may not be totally precise. In this case, the schedule was triggered in the later seconds of 15:12 and still got executed later than that. In any case, it will be within the 1-minute resolution window of the crontab.

```
[2021-06-28 15:13:06,510: INFO/ForkPoolWorker-1] Scheduled task
executed crontab every 2 minutes
[2021-06-28 15:14:00,006: INFO/ForkPoolWorker-2] Scheduled task
executed crontab every 2 minutes
```

When creating periodic tasks, keep in mind the different priorities, as we described previously in the chapter.

It is good practice to use a periodic task as a "heartbeat" to check that the system is working correctly. This task can be used to monitor that the tasks in the system are flowing as expected, with no big delays or problems.

This leads to the way of monitoring how the different tasks are being executed, in a better way than just by checking the logs.

Celery Flower

Obtaining good monitoring in Celery is important if you want to understand the executed tasks and find and fix problems. A good tool for that is Flower, which enhances Celery by adding a real-time monitoring web page that allows you to control Celery through the web page and through an HTTP API.

You can check the whole documentation at `https://flower.readthedocs.io/en/latest/`.

It's also very easy to set up and integrate with Celery. First, we need to be sure that the `flower` package is installed. The package is included in the `requirements.txt` after the previous step, but if it's not, you can install it independently using `pip3`.

```
$ pip3 install flower
```

Once it is installed, you can start `flower` with the following command:

```
$ celery --broker=redis://localhost flower -A celery_tasks  --port=5555
[I 210624 19:23:01 command:135] Visit me at http://localhost:5555
[I 210624 19:23:01 command:142] Broker: redis://localhost:6379//
[I 210624 19:23:01 command:143] Registered tasks:
    ['celery.accumulate',
     'celery.backend_cleanup',
     'celery.chain',
     'celery.chord',
     'celery.chord_unlock',
```

```
        'celery.chunks',
        'celery.group',
        'celery.map',
        'celery.starmap',
        'celery_tasks.obtain_info',
        'celery_tasks.send_email']
  [I 210624 19:23:01 mixins:229] Connected to redis://localhost:6379//
```

The command is very similar to starting the Celery workers, but includes the definition of the broker using Redis, as we saw before, with `--broker=redis://localhost`, and specifying the port to expose, `--port=5555`.

The interface is exposed in `http://localhost:5555`.

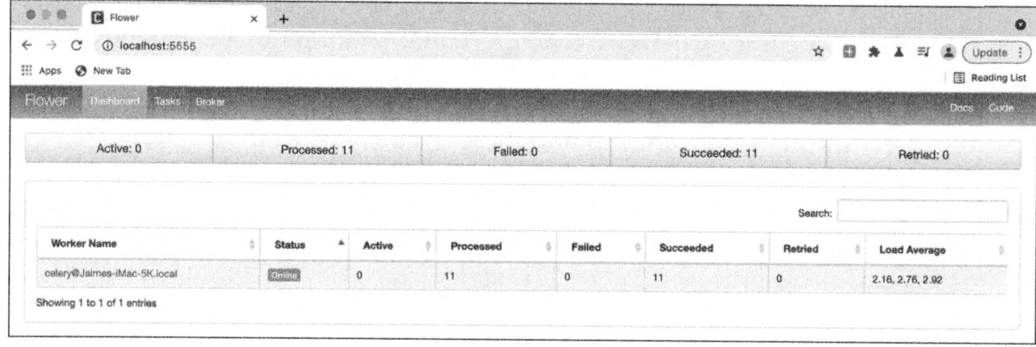

Figure 7.8: Celery Flower interface

The front page shows the different workers in the system. Note that it shows the number of active tasks, as well as processed tasks. In this case, we have 11 tasks corresponding to a whole run of `start_task.py`. You can go to the **Tasks** tab to see the details of each of the tasks executed, which looks like this:

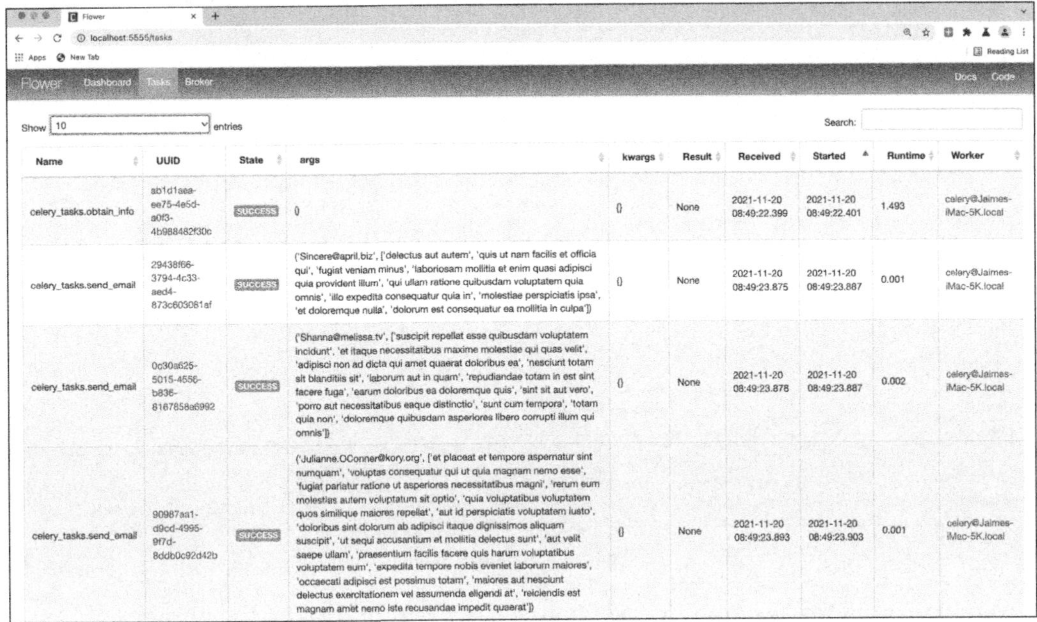

Figure 7.9: Tasks page

You can see information such as the input parameters, the state of the task, the name of the task, and how long it ran for.

Each Celery process will appear independently, even if it's capable of running multiple workers. You can check its parameters on the **Worker** page. See the **Max concurrency** parameter.

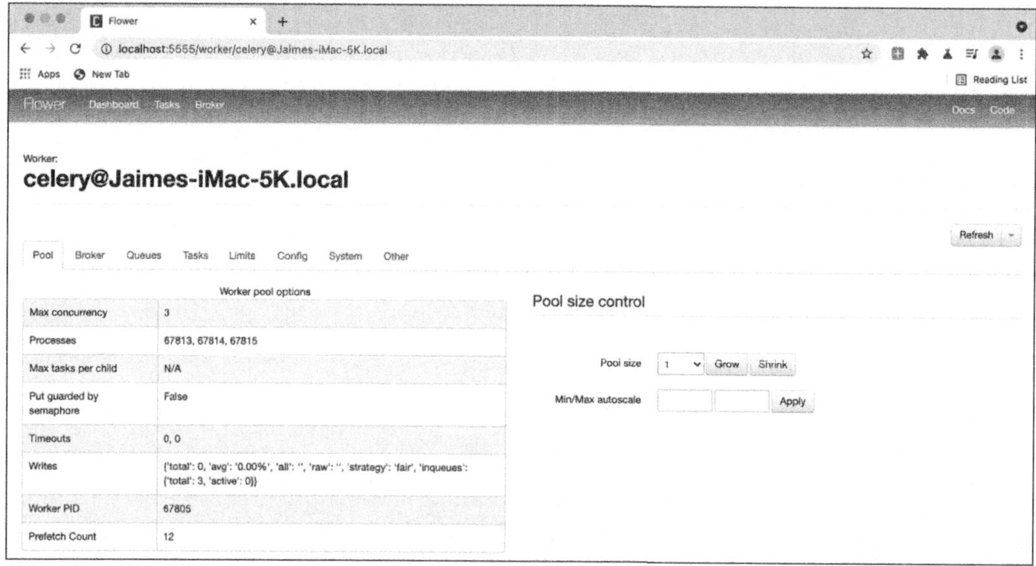

Figure 7.10: Worker page

From here, you can also review and change the configuration of the number of workers per Celery process, set rate limits, and more.

Flower HTTP API

A great addition from Flower is the HTTP API, which allows us to control Flower through HTTP calls. This enables the automatic control of the system and allows us to trigger the tasks directly with an HTTP request. This can be used to call the tasks in any programming language, and greatly increases the flexibility of Celery.

The URL to call a task asynchronously is the following:

```
POST /api/task/async-apply/{task}
```

It requires a POST, and the arguments of the call should be included in the body. For example, make a call with `curl`:

```
$ curl -X POST -d '{"args":["example@email.com",["msg1", "msg2"]]}'
http://localhost:5555/api/task/async-apply/celery_tasks.send_email
{"task-id": "79258153-0bdf-4d67-882c-30405d9a36f0"}
```

The task is executed in the worker:

```
[2021-06-24 22:35:33,052: INFO/MainProcess] Received task: celery_
tasks.send_email[79258153-0bdf-4d67-882c-30405d9a36f0]
[2021-06-24 22:35:33,054: INFO/ForkPoolWorker-2] Send an email to
example@email.com
[2021-06-24 22:35:33,055: INFO/ForkPoolWorker-2] Reminders ['msg1',
'msg2']
[2021-06-24 22:35:33,056: INFO/ForkPoolWorker-2] Task celery_tasks.
send_email[79258153-0bdf-4d67-882c-30405d9a36f0] succeeded in
0.0021811629999999305s: None
```

Using the same API, the status of the task can be retrieved with a GET request:

```
GET /api/task/info/{task_id}
```

For example:

```
$ curl  http://localhost:5555/api/task/info/79258153-0bdf-4d67-882c-
30405d9a36f0
{"uuid": "79258153-0bdf-4d67-882c-30405d9a36f0", "name": "celery_tasks.
send_email", "state": "SUCCESS", "received": 1624571191.674537, "sent":
null, "started": 1624571191.676534, "rejected": null, "succeeded":
1624571191.679662, "failed": null, "retried": null, "revoked": null,
"args": "['example@email.com', ['msg1', 'msg2']]", "kwargs": "{}",
"eta": null, "expires": null, "retries": 0, "worker": "celery@Jaimes-
iMac-5K.local", "result": "None", "exception": null, "timestamp":
1624571191.679662, "runtime": 0.0007789200000161145, "traceback":
null, "exchange": null, "routing_key": null, "clock": 807, "client":
null, "root": "79258153-0bdf-4d67-882c-30405d9a36f0", "root_id":
"79258153-0bdf-4d67-882c-30405d9a36f0", "parent": null, "parent_id":
null, "children": []}
```

Note the `state` parameter, which here shows the task is finished successfully, but it will return `PENDING` if it's not done yet.

This can be used to poll the status of the task until it's completed or it shows an error, as we described earlier in the chapter.

Summary

In this chapter, we have seen what event-driven structures are. We started with a general discussion about how events can be used to create different flows than the traditional request-response structure. We talked about how the events are introduced into queues to be transmitted to other systems. We introduced the idea of a publisher and a subscriber to introduce or extract events from that queue.

We described how this structure could be used to act on asynchronous tasks: tasks that run in the background and allow other elements of the interface to respond quickly. We described how dividing asynchronous tasks into smaller ones can help increase throughput by taking advantage of having multiple subscribers that can execute these smaller tasks. We described how tasks can be added automatically at certain times to allow the execution of predetermined tasks periodically.

As the introduction of tasks can happen with great variability, we discussed some important details of how queues work, the different problems that we can encounter, and strategies to deal with them. We talked about how a simple strategy for a background queue and a priority queue works in most scenarios and warned about overcomplicating it. We also explained that, in the same spirit, it's better to keep the code synchronized among all workers, even in cases when the queues may be different. We also briefly touched on the capabilities of cloud computing as applied to asynchronous workers.

We explained how to use Celery, a popular task manager, to create asynchronous tasks. We covered setting up the different elements, including the back-end broker, how to define a proper worker, and how to generate tasks from a different service. We included a section on how to create scheduled tasks in Celery as well.

We presented Celery Flower, a complement for Celery that includes a web interface with which we can monitor and control Celery. It also includes an HTTP API that allows us to create tasks by sending HTTP requests, allowing any programming language to interact with our Celery system.

Join our book's Discord space

Join the book's Discord workspace for a monthly *Ask me Anything* session with the author: `https://packt.link/PythonArchitechture`

8

Advanced Event-Driven Structures

As we saw in the previous chapter, event-driven architectures are quite flexible and capable of creating complex scenarios. In this chapter, we will see what are the possible event-driven structures that cover more advanced use cases and how to deal with their complexities.

We will see how some common applications like logs and metrics can be thought of as event-driven systems and use them to generate control systems that will feedback into the system producing the events.

We will also discuss, with an example, how to create complex pipelines where different events are being produced and the system is coordinated. We will also move to a more general overview, introducing the bus as a concept to interconnect all the event-driven components.

We will introduce some general ideas on further complex systems to describe some of the challenges that these kinds of big event-driven systems can produce, such as the need to use CQRS techniques to retrieve information that crosses multiple modules. Finally, we will give some notes on how to test the system, paying attention to the different levels of tests.

In this chapter, we'll cover the following topics:

- Streaming events
- Pipelines

- Defining a bus
- More complex systems
- Testing event-driven systems

We will start by describing streams of events.

Streaming events

For some purposes, it can be good to just produce events that capture information and store it for later access. This structure is typical for instrumentation, for example, where we create an event every time there's an error. This event will contain information about things such as where the error was generated, debugging details to be able to understand it, and so on. The event is then sent, and the application continues recovering from the error.

The same can be done for specific parts of the code. For example, to capture an access time to a database, the timing and related data (like the specific query) can be captured and sent in an event.

All those events should be compiled into a location to allow them to be queried and aggregated.

While usually not thought of as event-driven processes, this is pretty much how logs and metrics work. In the case of logs, the events are generally text strings that get fired whenever the code decides to create them. The logs are forwarded to a destination that allows us to search them later.

Logs can be stored in different formats. It's also common to create them in JSON to allow better searching.

These kinds of events are simple but can be very powerful by allowing us to discover what the program is executing in a live system.

This instrumentation may also be used to enable controls or alerts when certain conditions are matched. A typical example of this is to alert us if the number of errors captured by logs crosses a certain threshold.

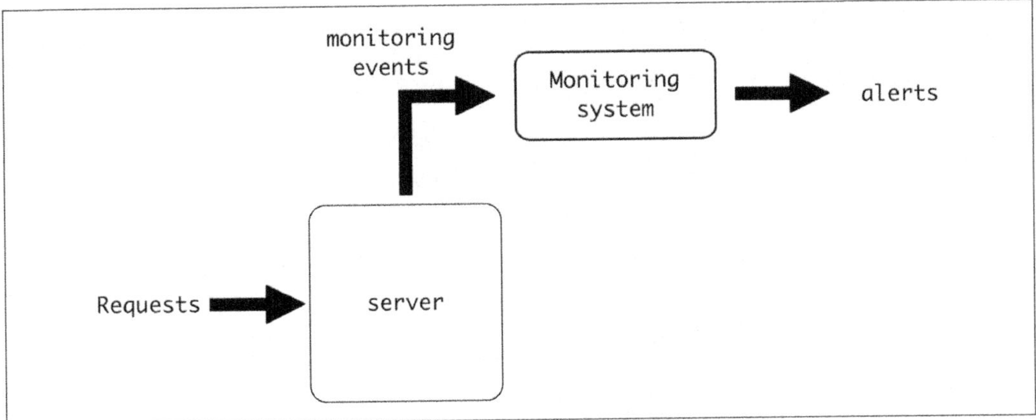

Figure 8.1: Monitoring events flow

This can also be used to produce feedback systems, where the instrumentation monitoring the system can be used to determine whether to change something in the system itself. For example, capturing metrics to determine whether the system needs to scale up or scale down and change the number of servers available based on the amount of requests or other parameters.

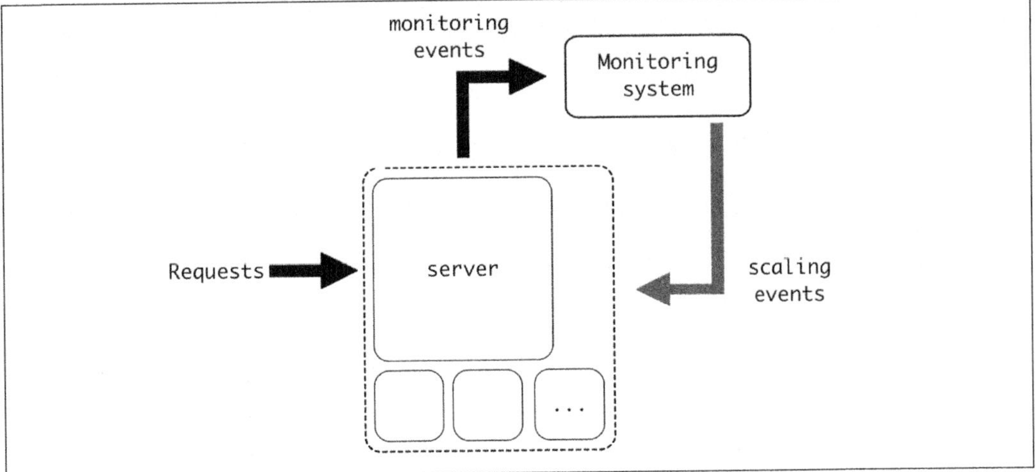

Figure 8.2: Feedback of scaling events

This is not the only way a system can be monitored, though. This method of operation can also be used as a way of detecting quotas, for example, short-circuiting the processing of incoming requests if a certain quota has been exceeded.

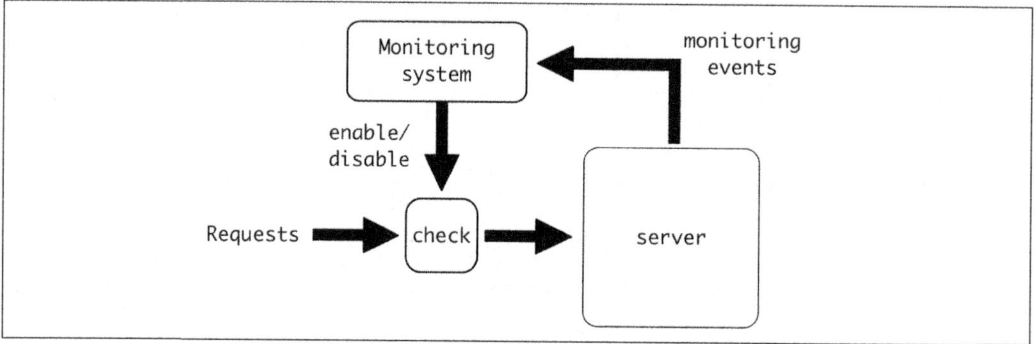

Figure 8.3: Monitor to detect quotas and stop extra requests

This structure is different from the upfront approach of setting a module that controls the system, relying instead on acting only when the threshold is breached, making the calculations in the background. This can reduce the amount of processing required upfront.

For example, for a quota of a maximum number of requests per minute, the process will be something like the following pseudocode:

```
def process_request(request):
    # Search for the owner of the request
    owner = request.owner
    info = retrieve_owner_info_from_db(owner)
    if check_quota_info(info):
        return process_request(request)
    else:
        return 'Quota exceeded'
```

`check_quota_info` will be different in both cases. The upfront approach requires maintaining and storing information about the previous requests:

```
def check_quota_info(info):
    current_minute = get_current_minute()
 if current_minute != info.minute:
     # New minute, start the quota
     info.requests = 0
     info.minute = current_minute
```

```
else:
    info.requests += 1

# Update the information
info.save()


if info.requests > info.quota:
    # Quota exceeded
    return False

# Quota still valid
return False
```

If the validation is done in an external system, based on the events generated, `check_quota_info` doesn't need to store the information, rather just checking whether the quota has been exceeded:

```
def check_quota_info(info):
    # Generate the proper event for a new event
    generate_event('request', info.owner)

 if info.quota_exceeded:
     return False

 # Quota still valid
 return False
```

The whole check is performed in the backend monitoring system, based on the generated events, and then stored in the info. This detaches the logic for whether to apply the quota from the check itself, decreasing the latency. The counterpart is that the detection of the quota having been exceeded may be delayed, allowing some requests to be processed even if they shouldn't be according to the quota.

Ideally, the generated events should already be in use to monitor the requests received. This operation can be very useful as it reuses events generated for other uses, reducing the need to collect extra data.

At the same time, the check can be more complex and doesn't need to be done as each new request comes along. For example, for an hourly quota when multiple requests are received every second, perhaps a check every minute is good enough to ensure the quota is respected. This can save a big deal of processing power compared to checking the conditions every time a request is received.

This, of course, is highly dependent on the specific scales, characteristics, and requests involved in different systems. For some systems, upfront could be a better choice, as it's easier to implement and doesn't require a monitoring system. Always validate whether the options fit into your system before implementing.

We will talk in more detail specifically about logs and metrics in *Chapter 12, Logging*, and *Chapter 13, Metrics*.

Pipelines

The flow of events doesn't have to be contained in a single system. The receiving end of the system can produce its own events, directed to other systems. Events will cascade into multiple systems, generating a process.

This is a similar situation to the one presented previously, but in this case it's a more deliberate process aimed at creating specific data pipelines where the flow between systems is triggered and processed.

A possible example of this is a system to rescale videos into different sizes and formats. When a video is uploaded into the system, it needs to be converted into multiple versions to be used in different situations. A thumbnail should also be created to display the first frame of the video before playing it.

We will do this in three steps. First, a queue will receive the event to start the processing. This will trigger two events in two different queues to process the resize and the thumbnail generation independently. This will be our pipeline.

To store the input and output data, given that they are videos and images, we require external storage. We will use AWS S3, or more precisely, a mock for S3.

AWS S3 is an object storage service provided by Amazon in the cloud, very popular for being both easy to use and very stable. We will use a mock of S3 that will allow us to start a local service that behaves like S3, which will simplify our example.

Here is a high-level diagram of the system:

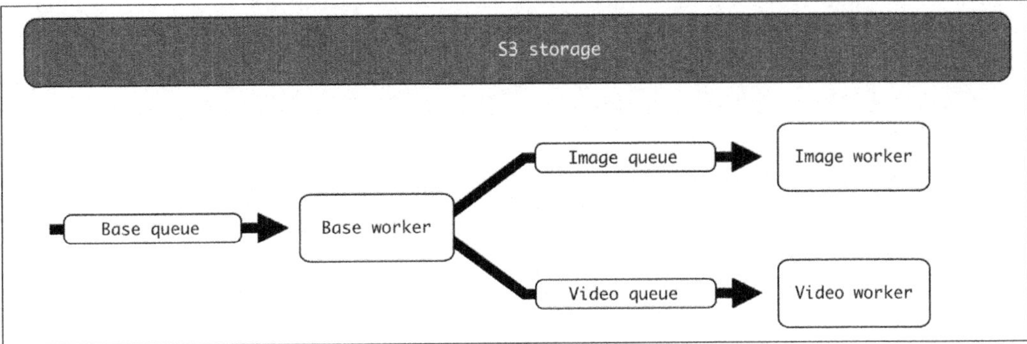

Figure 8.4: Video and image queue

To get started, we need to upload the source video to the mock S3 and start the task. We will also require some way of checking the results. For that, two scripts will be available.

The code is available on GitHub at `https://github.com/PacktPublishing/Python-Architecture-Patterns/tree/main/chapter_08_advanced_event_driven`.

Let's start with the setup configuration.

Preparation

As outlined above, we have two key prerequisites: a queue backend and the mock S3 storage.

For the queue backend, we will use Redis again. Redis is very easy to configure for multiple queues, and we'll see how later. To start the Redis queue, we will again use Docker to download and run the official image:

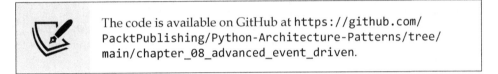

```
$ docker run -d -p 6379:6379 redis
```

This starts a Redis container exposed on the standard port `6379`. Note the `-d` option will keep the container running in the background.

For the mock S3 service, we will use the same approach, starting a container that starts S3 Mock, a system that replicates the S3 API, but stores the files locally. This lets us avoid setting up a real S3 instance, which involves getting an AWS account, paying for our usage, and so on.

S3 Mock is a great option for development testing for S3 storage without using a real connection to S3. We will see later how to connect to the mock with a standard module. The full documentation can be found at `https://github.com/adobe/S3Mock`.

To start S3 Mock, we will also use Docker:

```
$ docker run -d -p 9090:9090 -t adobe/s3mock
```

The container exposes the endpoint on port `9090`. We will direct the S3 requests toward this local port. We will use the `videos` bucket for storing all the data.

We will define three different Celery workers that will perform three different tasks: the base task, image task and video task. Each one will be pulling events from different queues.

This distinction of specific tasks for different workers is done deliberately for explanation purposes. In this example, there's probably not a good reason to make this distinction, as all the tasks can run in the same worker, and new events can be reintroduced in the same queue, and this is recommended, as we saw in the previous chapter. Sometimes, though, there are other conditions that may require a change of approach.

For example, some of the tasks may require specific hardware for AI processing, use way more RAM or CPU power making it impractical to make all workers equal, or other reasons that will necessitate separating the workers. Still, be sure that there's a good reason to make the split. It will complicate the operation and performance of the system.

We will also use some third-party libraries. This includes Celery, as we saw in the previous chapter, but also other libraries, like `boto3`, `click`, and `MoviePy`. All the required libraries are available in the `requirements.txt` file so they can be installed with the following command:

```
$ pip3 install -r requirements.txt
```

Let's start with the first stage of the process, the base task that will redirect to the other two.

Base task

The main task will receive a path that contains the image. It will then create two tasks for the processing of the video resizing and the extraction of the thumbnail.

Here's the code for base_tasks.py:

```
from celery import Celery


app = Celery(broker='redis://localhost/0')
images_app = Celery(broker='redis://localhost/1')
videos_app = Celery(broker='redis://localhost/2')

logger = app.log.get_default_logger()


@app.task
def process_file(path):
    logger.info('Stating task')

    logger.info('The file is a video, needs to extract thumbnail and '
                'create resized version')
    videos_app.send_task('video_tasks.process_video', [path])
    images_app.send_task('image_tasks.process_video', [path])

    logger.info('End task')
```

Note that we are creating three different queues here:

```
app = Celery(broker='redis://localhost/0')
images_app = Celery(broker='redis://localhost/1')
videos_app = Celery(broker='redis://localhost/2')
```

Redis allows us to create different databases easily by referring to them with an integer. So, we create database `0` for the base queue, database `1` for the images queue, and database `2` for the videos queue.

We generate events in these queues with the `.send_task` function. Note that on each queue we send the proper task. We include the path as a parameter.

Note that all parameters for the tasks are defined in the second parameter of `.send_task`. This requires that the parameter is a list of arguments. In this case, we only have a single parameter that needs still to be described as a list with `[path]`.

When the task is triggered, it will enqueue the next tasks. Let's take a look at the image task.

Image task

To generate a thumbnail of the video, we need the help of two third-party modules:

- *boto3*. This common library helps us connect to AWS services. In particular, we will use it to download and upload to our own mocked S3 service.

You can check the whole `boto3` documentation at `https://boto3.amazonaws.com/v1/documentation/api/latest/index.html`. It can be used to control all AWS APIs.

- *MoviePy*. This is a library for working with video. We will extract the first frame as an independent file using this library.

The full `MoviePy` documentation is available at `https://zulko.github.io/moviepy/`.

Both libraries are included in the `requirements.txt` file described earlier in the chapter and included in the GitHub repo. Let's take a look at `image_tasks.py`:

```
from celery import Celery
import boto3
import moviepy.editor as mp
import tempfile

MOCK_S3 = 'http://localhost:9090/'
BUCKET = 'videos'

videos_app = Celery(broker='redis://localhost/1')
```

```
logger = videos_app.log.get_default_logger()


@videos_app.task
def process_video(path):
    logger.info(f'Stating process video {path} for image thumbnail')

    client = boto3.client('s3', endpoint_url=MOCK_S3)
    # Download the file to a temp file
    with tempfile.NamedTemporaryFile(suffix='.mp4') as tmp_file:
        client.download_fileobj(BUCKET, path, tmp_file)

        # Extract first frame with moviepy
        video = mp.VideoFileClip(tmp_file.name)
        with tempfile.NamedTemporaryFile(suffix='.png') as output_file:
            video.save_frame(output_file.name)
            client.upload_fileobj(output_file, BUCKET, path + '.png')

    logger.info('Finish image thumbnails')
```

Note that we define the Celery application with the correct database. We then describe the task. Let's divide it into different steps. We first download the source file defined in `path` into a temporary file:

```
client = boto3.client('s3', endpoint_url=MOCK_S3)
# Download the file to a temp file
with tempfile.NamedTemporaryFile(suffix='.mp4') as tmp_file:
    client.download_fileobj(BUCKET, path, tmp_file)
```

Note that we define the endpoint to connect with `MOCK_S3`, which is our S3 Mock container, exposed on `http://localhost:9090/` as we described before.

Right after it we generate a temporary file to store the downloaded video. We define that the suffix of the temporary file to be `.mp4` so later `VideoPy` can detect properly that the temporary file is a video.

Note the next steps are all inside the `with` block defining the temporary file. If it was defined outside of this block, the file would be closed and not available.

The next step is to load the file in `MoviePy` and then extract the first frame into another temporary file. This second temporary file has a suffix of `.png` to label it as an image:

```
video = mp.VideoFileClip(tmp_file.name)
with tempfile.NamedTemporaryFile(suffix='.png') as output_file:
    video.save_frame(output_file.name)
```

Finally, the file is uploaded to S3 Mock, adding `.png` to the end of the original name:

```
client.upload_fileobj(output_file, BUCKET, path + '.png')
```

Once again, pay attention to the indentation to be sure that the temporary files are available at the different stages.

The task to resize the video follows a similar pattern. Let's take a look.

Video task

The video Celery worker pulls from the video queue and performs similar steps to the image task:

```
from celery import Celery
import boto3
import moviepy.editor as mp
import tempfile

MOCK_S3 = 'http://localhost:9090/'
BUCKET = 'videos'
SIZE = 720

videos_app = Celery(broker='redis://localhost/2')


logger = videos_app.log.get_default_logger()


@videos_app.task
def process_video(path):
    logger.info(f'Starting process video {path} for image resize')

    client = boto3.client('s3', endpoint_url=MOCK_S3)
    # Download the file to a temp file
```

```
    with tempfile.NamedTemporaryFile(suffix='.mp4') as tmp_file:
        client.download_fileobj(BUCKET, path, tmp_file)

        # Resize with moviepy
        video = mp.VideoFileClip(tmp_file.name)
        video_resized = video.resize(height=SIZE)
        with tempfile.NamedTemporaryFile(suffix='.mp4') as output_file:
            video_resized.write_videofile(output_file.name)
            client.upload_fileobj(output_file, BUCKET, path +
f'x{SIZE}.mp4')

    logger.info('Finish video resize')
```

The only difference from the image task is the resizing of the video to a height of 720 pixels and uploading the result:

```
# Resize with moviepy
video = mp.VideoFileClip(tmp_file.name)
video_resized = video.resize(height=SIZE)
with tempfile.NamedTemporaryFile(suffix='.mp4') as output_file:
    video_resized.write_videofile(output_file.name)
```

But the general flow is very similar. Note that it's pulling from a different Redis database, corresponding to the video queue.

Connecting the tasks

To test the system, we need to start all the different elements. Each one is started in a different terminal so we can see their different logs:

```
$ celery -A base_tasks worker --loglevel=INFO
$ celery -A video_tasks worker --loglevel=INFO
$ celery -A image_tasks worker --loglevel=INFO
```

To start the process, we need a video to be processed in the system.

One possibility to find good, free, videos is to use `https://www.pexels.com/`, which has free stock content. For our example run, we will download the 4K video with URL `https://www.pexels.com/video/waves-rushing-and-splashing-to-the-shore-1409899/`.

We will use the following script to upload the video to the S3 Mock storage and start the task:

```
import click
import boto3
from celery import Celery


celery_app = Celery(broker='redis://localhost/0')


    MOCK_S3 = 'http://localhost:9090/'
BUCKET = 'videos'
SOURCE_VIDEO_PATH = '/source_video.mp4'


@click.command()
@click.argument('video_to_upload')
def main(video_to_upload):
# Note the credentials are required by boto3, but we are using
# a mock S3 that doesn't require them, so they can be fake
    client = boto3.client('s3', endpoint_url=MOCK_S3,
                          aws_access_key_id='FAKE_ACCESS_ID',
                          aws_secret_access_key='FAKE_ACCESS_KEY')
    # Create bucket if not set
    client.create_bucket(Bucket=BUCKET)

    # Upload the file
    client.upload_file(video_to_upload, BUCKET, SOURCE_VIDEO_PATH)

    # Trigger the
    celery_app.send_task('base_tasks.process_file', [SOURCE_VIDEO_
PATH])


if __name__ == '__main__':
    main()
```

The start of the script describes the Celery queue, the base queue, that will be the start of the pipeline. We define several values related to the configuration, as we saw in the previous tasks. The only addition is `SOURCE_VIDEO_PATH`, which will host the video in S3 Mock.

In this script we use the same name to upload all files, overwriting it if the script is run again. Feel free to change this if it makes more sense to you to do it differently.

We use the `click` library to generate an easy **command-line interface** (**CLI**). The following lines generate a simple interface that requests the name of the video to upload as the parameter of the function.

```
@click.command()
@click.argument('video_to_upload')
def main(video_to_upload):
          ....
```

`click` is a fantastic option to generate CLIs quickly. You can read more about it in its documentation here: `https://click.palletsprojects.com/`.

The content of the main function simply connects to our S3 Mock, creates the bucket if not set yet, uploads the file to `SOURCE_VIDEO_PATH`, and then sends the task to the queue to start the process:

```
    client = boto3.client('s3', endpoint_url=MOCK_S3)
    # Create bucket if not set
    client.create_bucket(Bucket=BUCKET)

    # Upload the file
    client.upload_file(video_to_upload, BUCKET, SOURCE_VIDEO_PATH)

    # Trigger the
    celery_app.send_task('base_tasks.process_file', [SOURCE_VIDEO_
PATH])
```

Let's run it and see the results.

Running the task

The script can be run after adding the name of the video to upload. Remember that all the libraries in `requirements.txt` need to be installed:

```
$ python3 upload_video_and_start.py source_video.mp4
```

It will take a bit of time to upload the file to S3 Mock. Once called, the first worker to react is the base one. This worker will create two new tasks:

```
[2021-07-08 20:37:57,219: INFO/MainProcess] Received task: base_tasks.
process_file[8410980a-d443-4408-8f17-48e89f935325]
[2021-07-08 20:37:57,309: INFO/ForkPoolWorker-2] Stating task
[2021-07-08 20:37:57,660: INFO/ForkPoolWorker-2] The file is a video,
needs to extract thumbnail and create resized version
[2021-07-08 20:37:58,163: INFO/ForkPoolWorker-2] End task
[2021-07-08 20:37:58,163: INFO/ForkPoolWorker-2] Task base_tasks.
process_file[8410980a-d443-4408-8f17-48e89f935325] succeeded in
0.8547832089971052s: None
```

The other two will start soon after. The image worker will display new logs, starting the image thumbnail creation:

```
[2021-07-08 20:37:58,251: INFO/MainProcess] Received task: image_tasks.
process_video[5960846f-f385-45ba-9f78-c8c5b6c37987]
[2021-07-08 20:37:58,532: INFO/ForkPoolWorker-2] Stating process video
/source_video.mp4 for image thumbnail
[2021-07-08 20:38:41,055: INFO/ForkPoolWorker-2] Finish image
thumbnails
[2021-07-08 20:38:41,182: INFO/ForkPoolWorker-2] Task image_tasks.
process_video[5960846f-f385-45ba-9f78-c8c5b6c37987] succeeded in
42.650344008012326s: None
```

The video worker will take longer as it needs to resize the video:

```
[2021-07-08 20:37:57,813: INFO/MainProcess] Received task: video_tasks.
process_video[34085562-08d6-4b50-ac2c-73e991dbb58a]
[2021-07-08 20:37:57,982: INFO/ForkPoolWorker-2] Starting process video
/source_video.mp4 for image resize
[2021-07-08 20:38:15,384: WARNING/ForkPoolWorker-2] Moviepy - Building
video /var/folders/yx/k970yrd11hb4lmrq4rg5brq80000gn/T/tmp0deg6k8e.mp4.
[2021-07-08 20:38:15,385: WARNING/ForkPoolWorker-2] Moviepy - Writing
video /var/folders/yx/k970yrd11hb4lmrq4rg5brq80000gn/T/tmp0deg6k8e.mp4
[2021-07-08 20:38:15,429: WARNING/ForkPoolWorker-2] t:   0%|          |
0/528 [00:00<?, ?it/s, now=None]
```

```
[2021-07-08 20:38:16,816: WARNING/ForkPoolWorker-2] t:   0%|          |
2/528 [00:01<06:04,  1.44it/s, now=None]
[2021-07-08 20:38:17,021: WARNING/ForkPoolWorker-2] t:   1%|          |
3/528 [00:01<04:17,  2.04it/s, now=None]
...
[2021-07-08 20:39:49,400: WARNING/ForkPoolWorker-2] t:  99%|#########9|
524/528 [01:33<00:00,  6.29it/s, now=None]
[2021-07-08 20:39:49,570: WARNING/ForkPoolWorker-2] t:  99%|#########9|
525/528 [01:34<00:00,  6.16it/s, now=None]
[2021-07-08 20:39:49,874: WARNING/ForkPoolWorker-2] t: 100%|#########9|
527/528 [01:34<00:00,  6.36it/s, now=None]
[2021-07-08 20:39:50,027: WARNING/ForkPoolWorker-2] t: 100%|##########|
528/528 [01:34<00:00,  6.42it/s, now=None]
[2021-07-08 20:39:50,723: WARNING/ForkPoolWorker-2] Moviepy - Done !
[2021-07-08 20:39:50,723: WARNING/ForkPoolWorker-2] Moviepy - video
ready /var/folders/yx/k970yrd11hb4lmrq4rg5brq80000gn/T/tmp0deg6k8e.mp4
[2021-07-08 20:39:51,170: INFO/ForkPoolWorker-2] Finish video resize
[2021-07-08 20:39:51,171: INFO/ForkPoolWorker-2] Task video_tasks.
process_video[34085562-08d6-4b50-ac2c-73e991dbb58a] succeeded in
113.18933968200872s: None
```

To retrieve the results, we will use the `check_results.py` script, which downloads the contents of the S3 Mock storage:

```
import boto3

MOCK_S3 = 'http://localhost:9090/'
BUCKET = 'videos'

client = boto3.client('s3', endpoint_url=MOCK_S3)

for path in client.list_objects(Bucket=BUCKET)['Contents']:
    print(f'file {path["Key"]:25} size {path["Size"]}')

    filename = path['Key'][1:]

    client.download_file(BUCKET, path['Key'], filename)
```

By running it, we download the files into the local directory:

```
$ python3 check_results.py
file /source_video.mp4          size 56807332
file /source_video.mp4.png      size 6939007
file /source_video.mp4x720.mp4 size 8525077
```

You can check the resulting files and confirm that they have been generated correctly. Note that `source_video.mp4` will be the same as your input video.

This example demonstrates how to set up a relatively complex pipeline where different queues and workers are triggered in a coordinated fashion. Note that while we directly used Celery to send the tasks to the queues, we could also have used Celery Flower and an HTTP request to do this.

Defining a bus

While we talked about the queue backend system, this hasn't been truly expanded to the concept of a bus. The term *bus* originates from the hardware buses that transmit data between different components of a hardware system. This makes them a central, multisource, and multidestination part of the system.

A software bus is a generalization of this concept that allows us to interconnect several logical components.

In essence, a bus is a component specialized in the transmission of data. This is an ordered communication compared to the usual alternative of connecting directly to the services through a network, without any intermediate component.

As the bus is in charge of data transmission, that means that the sender doesn't need to know much other than the message to transmit and the queue to send it to. The bus itself will transmit to the destination or destinations.

The concept of a bus is closely related to that of the *message broker*. A message broker, though, typically includes more capacities than a pure bus, such as being able to transform messages along the way and use multiple protocols. Message brokers can be very complex and allow a huge amount of customization and decoupling of services. In general, most of the tools to support the usage of a bus will be labeled as message brokers, though some are more powerful than others.

Though we will use the term "bus", some of the capacities will be more closely related to features such as routing messages, which should require tools considered message brokers. Analyze the requirements of your specific use cases and use a tool that can fulfil them.

The bus will be then defined as a central point where all the event-related communication will be directed to. This simplifies the configuration, as the events can be routed to the proper destination without requiring a different endpoint.

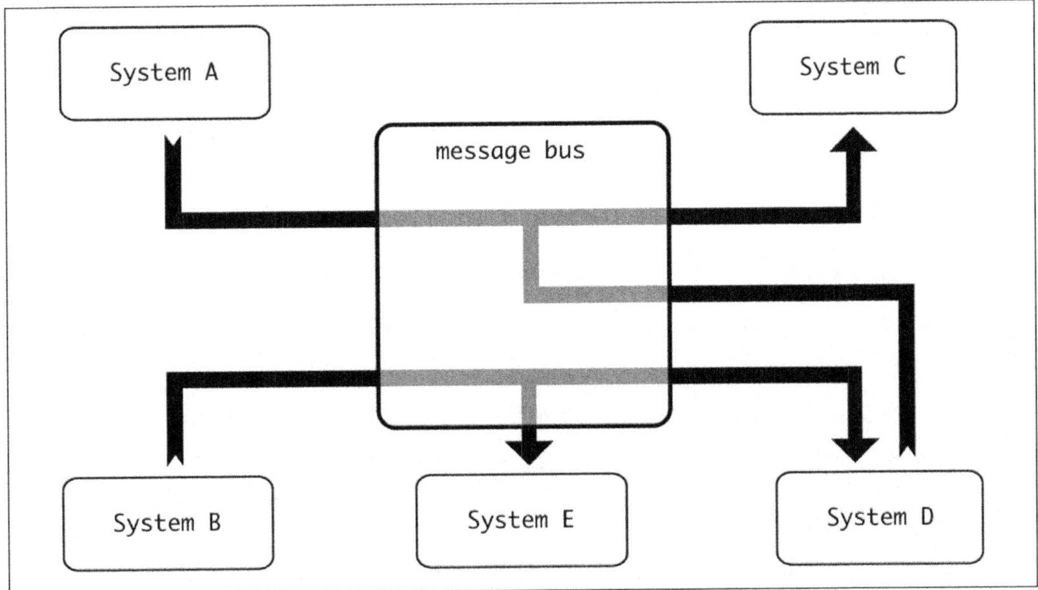

Figure 8.5: Message bussing

Internally, though, the bus will contain different logical divisions that allow the proper routing of messages. These are the queues.

The routing can be complicated, if the bus allows for it, which is the case here.

In our example before, we used Redis as a bus. Though the connection URL is a little different, it can be refactored to make it a bit clearer:

```
# Remember that database 0 is the base queue
BASE_BROKER = 'redis://localhost/0'
Base_app = Celery(broker=BROKER)

# Refactor for base
BROKER_ROOT = 'redis://localhost'
```

```
BROKER_BASE_QUEUE = 0
base_app = Celery(broker=f'{BASE_BROKER}/{BROKER_BASE_QUEUE}')
# To address the image queue
BROKER_ROOT = 'redis://localhost'
BROKER_IMAGE_QUEUE = 1
image_app = Celery(broker=f'{BASE_BROKER}/{BROKER_IMAGE_QUEUE}')
```

This central location makes the configuration of all the different services easy, both for pushing events to the queues and pulling from them.

More complex systems

More complex systems can be created where the events pass through multiple stages and are even designed for easy plugin systems working from the same queue.

This can create complicated setups where the data flows through complex pipelines and is processed by independent modules. These kinds of scenarios are typically seen on instrumentation that aims to analyze and process big quantities of data to try and detect patterns and behaviors.

Imagine, for example, a system that makes bookings for a travel agency. There are a lot of searches and bookings requests that happen in the system, with associated purchases such as car rentals, luggage bags, food, and so on. Each of the actions produces a regular response (search, book, purchase, and so on), but an event describing the action will be introduced into a queue to be processed in the background. Different modules will analyze user behavior with different objectives in mind.

For example, the following modules could be added to this system:

- Aggregate economic results by time, to obtain a global view of how the service is working over time. This can involve details such as purchases per day, revenue, margins, and so on.
- Analyze the behavior of regular users. Follow users to discover their patterns. What are they searching for before booking? Are they using offers? How often are they booking flights? How long is their average trip? Any outliers?
- Be sure that there's enough inventory for purchases. Backorder any required elements, based on the items being purchased in the system. This includes also scheduling enough food for flights, based on pre-purchases.
- Collect information about preferred destinations, based on searches.

- Trigger alerts for things like full flights that could lead to scheduling more planes for those days.

These modules are fundamentally about different things and present a different view on the system. Some are more oriented toward the behavior of users and marketing, while others are more related to logistics. Depending on the size of the system, it could be determined that the modules require a different, dedicated team to take care of each of them independently.

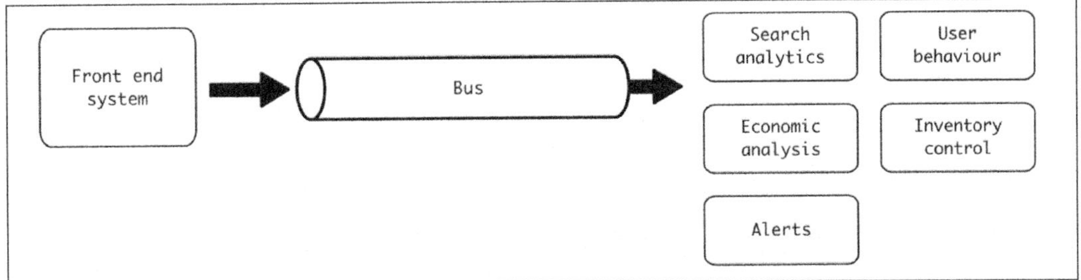

Figure 8.6: Bus from front end system to different modules

Note that each system will likely have its own storage to allow it to store the information. This could also lead to the creation of their own APIs to access this information once collected.

To query the information, the system needs to query the databases of the modules where the data is stored. This can be an independent service, but it will likely be the same system's front end, as it will typically contain all the external interface and permissions handling.

This makes it necessary for the front end system to access the stored information, either by directly accessing the database or by using some API to access it. The front end system should model access to the data, as we saw in *Chapter 3, Data Modeling*, and will very likely require a model definition that abstracts the complex access to the data.

The same event will be sent to the bus, and then the different services will receive it. To be able to do so, you'll need to get a bus that accepts subscriptions from several systems and delivers the same message to all subscribed systems.

This pattern is called *publish/subscribe* or *pub/sub*. The consumers of the events need to subscribe to the *topic*, which is, in pub/sub parlance, is the equivalent of a queue. Most buses accept this system, though it may require some work to configure.

For example, there's a library to allow Celery to work under this system available at `https://github.com/Mulugruntz/celery-pubsub`.

Note that the workers in this case can create more events to be introduced. For example, any module will be able to create an alert, to which the alert system will be notified. For example, if the inventory is too low, it may require a quick alert at the same time it backorders, to be sure that action is taken quickly.

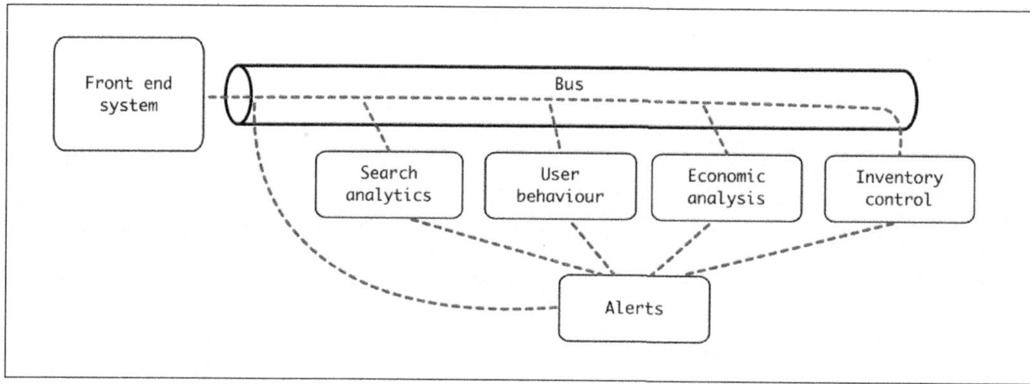

Figure 8.7: Note that communication between the modules and the alerts also is done through the bus

Complex event-driven systems can help you distribute the work between different components. In this example, you can see how the immediate response (booking a flight) is completely independent of the further detailed analysis in the background that can be used for longer-term planning. If all the components were added while the request was served, it could interfere with performance. The backend components can be swapped and upgraded while the front end system is unaffected.

To properly implement this kind of system, the event needs to use a standard format that's easy to adapt and extend, to ensure that any module that receives it can quickly scan through it and discard it if it's not necessary.

A good idea is to use a simple JSON structure like the following:

```
{
  "type": string defining the event type,
  "data": subevent content
}
```

For example, when a search is produced, an event like this will be created:

```
{
  "type": "SEARCH",
  "data": {
    "from": "Dublin",
    "to": "New York",
    "depart_date": 2021-12-31,
    "return_date": null,
    "user": null

  }
}
```

The `type` field makes easy to discard the event if it's not of interest to any module. For example, the `economic analysis` module will discard any `SEARCH` event. Other modules may require further processing. For example, the `user behavior` module will analyze `SEARCH` events where the `user` field in the `data` is set.

Keep in mind that an important element for event-driven systems is that the storage may not be common to all. Perhaps each independent module has its own database. You'll need to use the techniques for CQRS that we discussed in *Chapter 3, Data Modeling*, to model data in these modules. In essence, you'll need to ask differently to read and to save new data, as writing new data requires the generation of events; and you'll need to model them as a business unit. What's more, the model may need to merge information from multiple modules in some cases. For example, if there's a query in the system that requires obtaining some economic information for a user, it needs to query both the `user behavior` module and the `economic analysis` module, while presenting the information as a unique model of `EconomicInfoUser`.

When information is frequently accessed, it may make sense to duplicate it in several places. This goes against the single responsibility principle (that every feature should be the sole responsibility of a single module), but the alternative is to create complicated methods of access to get information that's commonly used. Be careful when designing and dividing the system to avoid these problems.

The flexible data structure will allow for new events to be generated, adding more information and allowing for controlled changes across the modules by enforcing the backward compatibility of changes. Then the different teams can work in parallel, improving the system without stepping on each other's toes too much.

But ensuring that they behave correctly can be complicated, as there are multiple parts that interact with each other.

Testing event-driven systems

Event-driven systems are very flexible and, in certain situations, can be incredibly useful in detaching different elements. But this flexibility and detachment can make them difficult to test to ensure that everything works as expected.

In general, unit tests are the fastest tests to generate, but the detached nature of event-driven systems makes them not very useful to properly test the reception of events. Sure, the events can be simulated, and the general behavior of receiving an event can be tested. But the problem is: how can we ensure that the event has been properly generated? And at the right moment?

The only option is to use integration tests to check the behavior of the system. But these tests are more expensive to design and run.

There's always an endless debate about naming tests, what exactly a unit test is compared to an integration test, system test, acceptance test, and so on. To avoid getting into too deep a discussion here, at it's not the objective of the book, we will use the term *unit test* to describe tests that can only be run in a single module, and *integration test* to refer to those that require two or more modules interacting with each other to be successful. Unit tests will mock any dependence, but integration tests will actually call the dependence to be sure that the connection between modules works correctly.

These two levels are significantly different in terms of the cost for each test written. Way more unit tests can be written and run than integration tests in the same period of time.

For example, in our previous example, to test that a purchase of food correctly triggers an alert, we need to:

1. Generate a call to purchase a food item.
2. Produce the appropriate event.
3. Handle the event in the inventory control. The current inventory should be configured as low, which will produce an alert event.
4. Handle the alert event properly.

All these steps require configuration to be done in three different systems (the front-end system, the inventory control module, and the alert module), along with setting up the bus to connect them. Ideally, this test will require the system to be able to start up with an automation system to automate the tests. That requires every module involved to be automatable.

As we can see, this is a high bar in setting up and running tests, though it is still worth doing. To achieve a sane balance between integration and unit tests, we should grow them and apply some strategy to be sure that we have reasonable coverage for both.

Unit tests are cheap, so every case should have healthy coverage by unit tests, where the external modules are mocked. This includes cases such as different input formats, different configurations, all flows, errors, and so on. Good unit tests should cover most possibilities from an isolation point of view, mocking the input of data and any sent event.

For example, continuing the inventory control example, many unit tests can control the following requisites, all by changing the input request:

- Purchase of an element with high inventory.
- Purchase of an element with low inventory. This should produce an alert event.
- Purchase of a non-existing element. This should generate an error.
- Event with invalid format. This should generate an error.
- Purchase of an element with zero inventory. This should generate an alert event.
- More cases, such as different kinds of purchases, formats, and so on.

Integration tests, on the other hand, should have only a few tests, mostly covering the "happy path". The *happy path* means that a regular representative event is being sent and processed, but doesn't produce expected errors. The objective of an integration test is to confirm that all the parts are connecting and working as expected. Given that integration tests are more expensive to run and operate, aim to implement only the most important, and keep an eye out for any test that isn't worth maintaining and can be pruned.

We described, in the above discussion on integration tests, a happy path scenario. The event triggers a handle in the inventory and generates an alert that's also handled. For integration tests, this is preferred over not generating an alert, as it stresses the system more.

Though it depends on the system, the ratio of unit to integration test should be heavily weighted toward unit tests, sometimes by 20 times or more (meaning 1 integration test for 20 unit tests).

Summary

In this chapter, we have seen more event-driven systems with a variety of advanced and complex architectures that can be designed. We have presented some of the flexibility and power that event-driven design can bring to a design, but also the challenges attached to event-driven design.

We started by presenting common systems such as logs and metrics as event-driven systems, as they are, and considered how looking at them in this way allows us to create alerting and feedback systems that can be used to control the source of the events.

We also presented an example with Celery of a more complex pipeline, including the usage of multiple queues and shared storage to generate multiple coordinated tasks, such as resizing a video and extracting a thumbnail.

We presented the idea of a bus, a shared access point for all events in the system, and looked at how we can generate more complex systems where events are delivered to multiple systems and cascade into complex actions. We also discussed the challenges of solving these complex interactions, both in terms of requiring the use of CQRS techniques to model information that can be read after the write is generated through events, and the demands in terms of testing at different levels with unit and integration tests.

In the next chapter, we will see the two main architectures for complex systems: monolithic and microservices.

Join our book's Discord space

Join the book's Discord workspace for a monthly *Ask me Anything* session with the author: `https://packt.link/PythonArchitechture`

9
Microservices vs Monolith

In this chapter, we will present and comment on two of the most common architectures for complex systems. Monolithic architecture creates a single block where the whole system is contained, and is simple to operate. Microservices architecture, on the other hand, divides the system into smaller microservices that talk to each other, aiming to allow different teams to take ownership of different elements, and helping big teams to work in parallel.

We will discuss when to choose each one, based on its different characteristics. We will also go through the teamwork aspect of them, as they have different requirements in terms of how the work needs to be structured.

Remember that the architecture is not only related to tech, but to a significant degree to how communication is structured! Refer to *Chapter 1, Introduction to Software Architecture*, for a further discussion of Conway's Law.

A common pattern is to migrate from an old monolithic architecture to a microservices one. We will talk about the stages involved in such a change.

We will also introduce Docker as a way of containerizing services, something very useful when it comes to creating microservices, but that can also be applied to monoliths. We will containerize the web application presented in *Chapter 5, The Twelve-Factor App Methodology*.

Finally, we will briefly describe how to deploy and operate multiple containers using an orchestration tool, and describe the most popular one these days – Kubernetes.

In this chapter, we'll cover the following topics:

- Monolithic architecture
- The microservices architecture
- Which architecture to choose
- Moving from a monolith to microservices
- Containerizing services
- Orchestration and Kubernetes

Let's start by talking in more depth about monolithic architecture.

Monolithic architecture

When a system is designed organically, the tendency is to generate a single unitary block of software that contains the whole functionality of the system.

This is a logical progression. When a software system is designed, it starts small, typically with a simple functionality. But, as the software is used, it grows in terms of its usage and starts getting requests for new functionality to complement the existing ones. Unless there are sufficient resources and planning to structure the growth, the path of least resistance will be to keep adding everything into the same code structure, with little modularity.

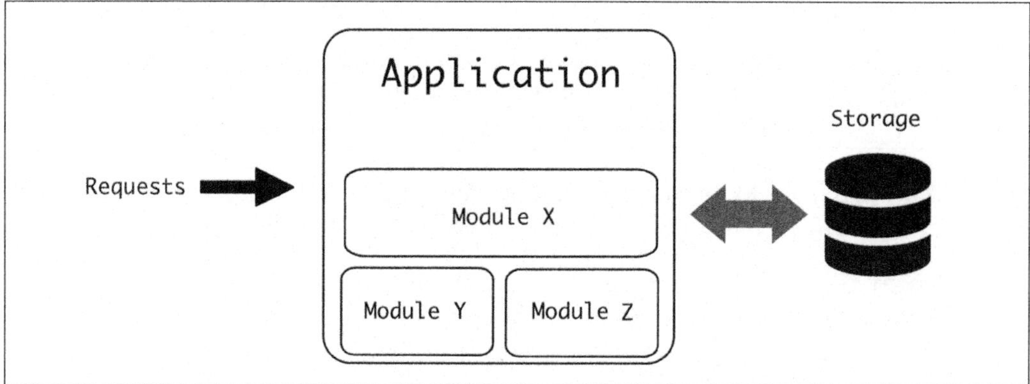

Figure 9.1: A monolithic application

This process ensures that all the code and functionality are tied together in a single block, hence the name *monolithic architecture*.

And, by extension, software that follows this pattern is called a monolith.

Although this kind of structure is quite common, in general, monolithic structures have a better modularity and internal structure. Even if the software is composed of a single block, it can be divided logically into different parts, assigning different responsibilities to different modules.

For example, in previous chapters we discussed the MVC architecture. This is a monolithic architecture. The Models, Views, and Controllers are all under the same process, but there is a definitive structure in place that differentiates the responsibilities and functions.

Monolithic architecture is not synonymous with a lack of structure.

The defining characteristic of a monolith is that all the calls between modules are through *internal* APIs, within the same process. This affords the advantage of being very flexible. The strategy for deploying a new version of the monolith is also easy. Restarting the process will ensure full deployment.

Keep in mind that a monolithic application can have multiple copies running. For example, a monolithic web application can have multiple copies of the same software running in parallel, with a load balancer sending requests to all of them. A restart, in this case, will be in multiple stages.

The version of the monolith is easy to know, as all the code is part of the same structure. The code, if it's under source control, will all be under the same repo.

The microservices architecture

The microservices architecture was developed as an alternative to having a single block containing all the code.

A system following a microservices architecture is *a collection of loosely coupled specialized services that work in unison to provide a comprehensive service*. Let's divide the definition up in order to be clearer:

1. A **collection of specialized services**, meaning that there are different and well-defined modules
2. **Loosely coupled**, so each microservice can be independently deployed and developed
3. That **work in unison**. Each microservice needs to communicate with others
4. To **provide a comprehensive service**, meaning that the whole system creates a full system that has a clear motive and functionality

Compared with a monolith, instead of grouping the whole software under the same process, it uses multiple, separate functional parts (each microservice) that communicate through well-defined APIs. These elements can be in different processes and typically are moved out from different servers to allow proper scaling of the system.

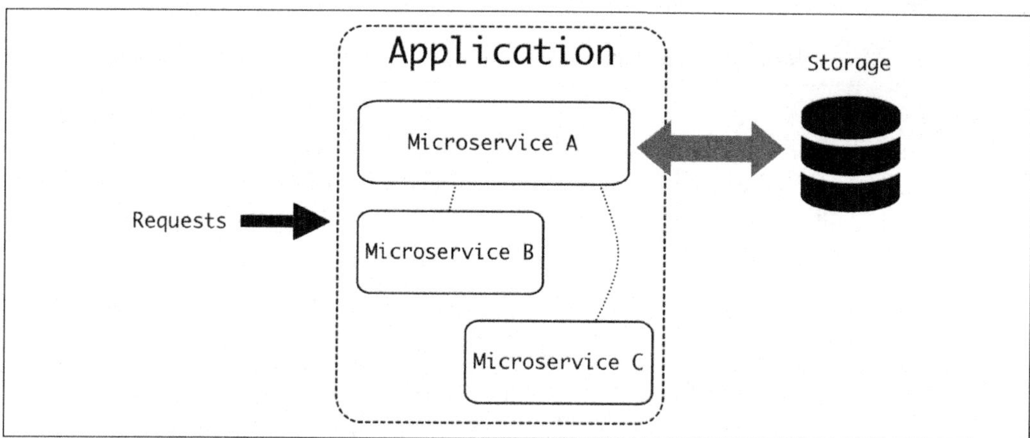

Figure 9.2: Note that not all microservices will be connected to the storage. Each microservice may have its own individual storage

The defining characteristic is that the calls between different services are all through *external* APIs. These APIs act as a clear, defined barrier between functionalities. Because of this, microservices architecture requires advanced planning and needs to define clearly the differences between components.

In particular, microservices architecture requires a good upfront design to be sure that the different elements connect together correctly, as any problem that is cross-service will be costly to work with.

A system that follows the microservices architecture doesn't happen organically, but it's the result of a plan created beforehand and executed carefully. This architecture is not typically started for systems from scratch, but instead, they are migrated from a previously existing, successful, monolithic architecture.

Which architecture to choose

There's a tendency to think that a more evolved architecture, like the microservices architecture, is better, but that's an oversimplification. Each one has its own set of strengths and weaknesses.

The first one is the fact that almost every small application will start as a monolithic application. This is because it is the most natural way to start a system. Everything is at hand, the number of modules is reduced, and it's an easy starting point.

Microservices, on the other hand, require the creation of a plan to divide the functionality carefully into different modules. This task may be complicated, as some designs may prove inadequate later on.

Keep in mind that no design can be totally future-proof. Any perfectly valid architectural decision may prove incorrect a year or two later when changes in the system require adjustments. While it is a good question to think about the future, trying to cover every possibility is futile. The proper balance between designing for the current feature and designing for the future vision of the system is a constant challenge in software architecture.

This requires quite a lot of work to be done beforehand, which requires an investment in the microservices architecture.

That said, as monoliths grow, they can start presenting problems just through the sheer size of the code. The main characteristic of a monolithic architecture is that all the code is found together, and it can start presenting a lot of connections that can cause developers to be confused. Complexity can be reduced by good practices and constant vigilance to ensure good internal structure, but that requires a lot of work in place by existing developers to enforce it. When dealing with a big and complex system, it may be easier to present clear and strict boundaries just by dividing different areas into different processes.

The modules can also require different specific knowledge, making it natural to assign different team members to different areas. To create a proper sense of ownership of the modules, they can have different opinions in terms of code standards, an adequate programming language for the job, ways of performing tasks, and so on; for example, a photosystem that has an interface for uploading photos and an AI system for categorizing them. While the first module will work as a web service, the abilities required for training and handling an AI model to categorize the data will be very different, making the module separation natural and productive. Both of them in the same code base may generate problems by trying to work at the same time.

Another problem of monolithic applications is the inefficient utilization of resources, as each deployment of the monolith carries over every copy of every module. For example, the RAM required will be determined for the worst-case scenario across multiple modules. When there are multiple copies of the monolith, that will waste a lot of RAM preparing for worst-case scenarios that will likely be rare. Another example is the fact that, if any module requires a connection to the database, a new connection will be created, whether that's used or not.

In comparison, using microservices can adjust each service according to its own worst-case use case, and independently control the number of replicas for each. When viewed as a whole, that can lead to big resource saves in big deployments.

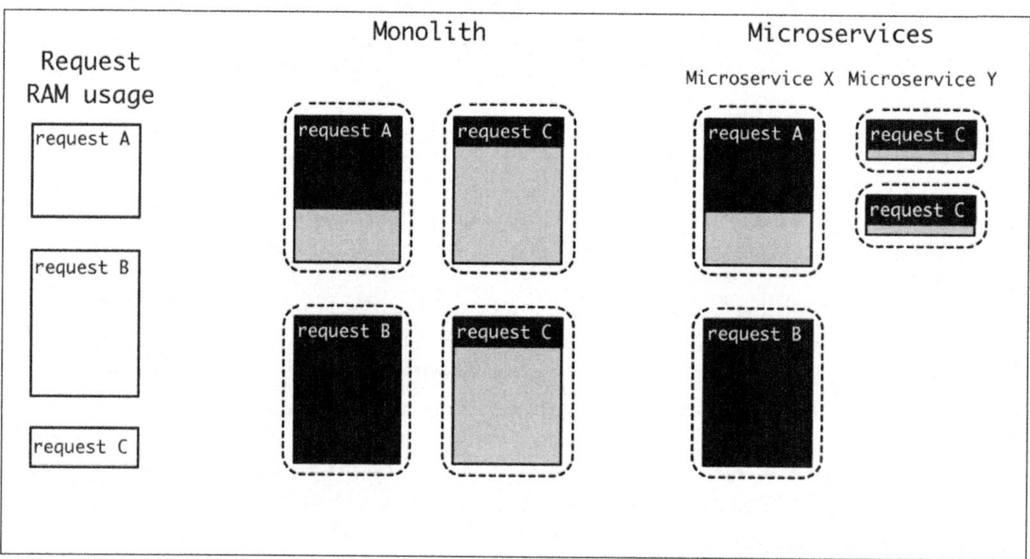

Figure 9.3: Notice that using different microservices allows us to reduce RAM usage by dividing requests into different microservices, while in a monolithic application, the worst-case scenario drives RAM utilization

Deployments also work very differently between monoliths and microservices. As the monolithic application needs to be deployed in a single go, every deployment is, effectively, a task for the whole team. If the team is small, creating a new deployment and ensuring that the new features are properly coordinated between modules and not interfering incorrectly is not very complicated. However, as the teams grow bigger, this can present a serious challenge if the code is not strictly structured. In particular, a bug in a small part of the system may bring down the whole system completely, as any critical error in the monolith affects the whole of the code.

Monolith deployments require coordination between modules, meaning that they need to work with each other, which normally leads to teams working closely together until the feature is ready to be released, and require some sort of supervision until the deployment is ready. This is noticeable when several teams are working on the same code base, with competing goals, and this blurs the ownership and responsibility of deployments.

By comparison, different microservices are deployed independently. The API should be stable and backward compatible with older releases, and that's one of the strong requisites that need to be enforced. However, the boundaries are very clear, and in the event of a critical bug, the worst that can happen is that the particular microservice goes down, while other unrelated microservices continue unaffected.

This makes the system work in a "degraded state," as compared to the "all-or-none" approach of the monolith. It limits the scope of a catastrophic failure.

Of course, certain microservices may be more critical than others, making them worthy of extra attention and care regarding their stability. But, in that case, they can be defined as critical in advance, with stricter stability rules enforced.

Of course, in both cases, solid testing techniques can be used to increase the quality of the software released.

In comparison with the monolith, microservices can be deployed independently, without coordinating closely with other services. This brings independence to the teams working on them and allows for faster, continuous deployments that require less central coordination.

The keyword here is *less* coordination. Coordination is still required, but the objective of a microservices architecture is necessarily that each microservice can be independently deployed and owned by a team, so the majority of changes can be dictated exclusively by the owner without requiring a process of warning other teams.

Monolithic applications, because they communicate with other modules through internal operations, mean that they typically can perform these operations much faster than through the external APIs. This allows a very high level of interaction between modules without paying a significant performance price.

There is an overhead related to the usage of external APIs and communication through a network that can produce a noticeable delay, especially if there are too many internal requests made to different microservices. Careful consideration is required to try to avoid repeating external calls and to limit the number of services that can be contacted in a single task.

In some cases, the usage of tools to abstract the contact with other microservices may produce extra calls that will be absolutely necessary. For example, a task to process a document needs to obtain some user information, which requires calling a different microservice. The name is required at the start of the document, and the email at the end of it. A naïve implementation may produce two requests to obtain the information instead of requesting it all in a single go.

Another interesting advantage of microservices is the independence of technical requirements. In a monolithic application, problems may arise as a result of requiring different versions of libraries for different modules. For example, updating the version of Python requires the whole code base to be prepared for that. These library updates can be complicated as different modules may have different requirements, and one module can effectively mingle with another by requiring an upgrade of the version of a certain library that's used by both.

Microservices, on the other hand, contain their own set of technical requirements, so there's not this limitation. Because of the external APIs used, different microservices can even be programmed in different programming languages. This allows the use of specialized tools for different microservices, tailoring each one for each purpose and thereby avoiding conflicts.

Just because different microservices can be programmed in different languages doesn't mean that they should. Avoid the temptation of using too many programming languages in a microservices architecture as this will complicate maintenance and make it difficult for a member of a different team to be able to help, thereby creating more isolated teams.

Having one or two default languages and frameworks available and then allowing special justified cases is a sensible way to proceed.

As we see, most of the characteristics of microservices make it more suited for a bigger operation, when the number of developers is high enough that they need to be split into different teams and coordination needs to be more explicit. The high change of pace in a big application also requires better ways to deploy and work independently, in general.

A small team can self-coordinate very well and will be able to work quickly and efficiently in a monolith.

This is not to say that a monolith can be very big. Some are. But, in a general sense, microservices architecture only makes sense if there are enough developers such that different teams are working in the same system and are required to achieve a good level of independence between them.

A side note about similar designs

While the decision of monolith versus microservices is normally discussed in the context of web services, it's not exactly a new idea and it's not the only environment where there are similar ideas and structures.

The kernel of an OS can also be monolithic. In this case, a kernel structure is called monolithic if it all operates within kernel space. A program running in kernel space in a computer can access the whole memory and hardware directly, something that is critical for the usage of an OS, while at the same time, this is dangerous as it has big security and safety implications. Because the code in kernel space works so closely with the hardware, any failure here can result in the total failure of the system (a kernel panic). The alternative is to run in user space, which is the area where a program only has access to its own data, and has to interact explicitly with the OS to retrieve information.

For example, a program in user space that wants to read from a file needs to make a call to the OS, and the OS, in kernel space, will access the file, retrieve the information, and return it to the requested program, copying to a part of the memory where the program can access.

The idea of the monolithic kernel is that it can minimize this movement and context switch between different kernel elements, such as libraries or hardware drivers.

The alternative to a monolithic kernel is called a microkernel. In a microkernel structure, the kernel part is greatly reduced and elements such as filesystems, hardware drivers, and network stacks are executed in user space instead of in kernel space. This requires these elements to communicate by passing messages through the microkernel, which is less efficient.

At the same time, it can improve the modularity and security of the elements, as any crash in user space can be restarted easily.

There was a famous argument between Andrew S. Tanenbaum and Linus Torvalds about what architecture is better, given that Linux was created as a monolithic kernel. In the long run, kernels have evolved toward hybrid models, where they take aspects of both elements, incorporating microkernel ideas into existing monolithic kernels for flexibility.

Discovering and analyzing related architectural ideas can help to improve the tools at the disposal of a good architect and improve architectural understanding and knowledge.

The key factor – team communication

A key element of the difference between microservices and monolithic architecture is the difference in the communication structure that they support.

If the monolithic application has grown organically from a small project, as usually happens, the internal structure can become messy, and requires developers with experience in the system who can change and adapt it for any change. In bad cases, the code can become very chaotic and be more and more complicated to work with.

Increasing the size of the development team becomes complicated, as each engineer requires a lot of contextual information, and learning how to navigate the code is difficult. The older teammates who have been around can help to train new team members, but they'll act as bottlenecks, and mentoring is a slow process that has limits. Each new member of the team will require a significant amount of training time until they can be productive in fixing bugs and adding new features.

Teams also have a maximum natural size limit. Managing a team with too many members, without dividing it into smaller groups, is difficult.

The ideal size of a team depends on a lot of different factors, but between 5 and 9 is generally considered the ideal size to work efficiently.

Teams that are bigger than that tend to self-organize into their own smaller groups, losing focus as a unit and creating small information silos where parts of the team are not aware of what's going on.

Teams with fewer members create too much overhead in terms of management and communication with other teams. They will be able to work faster with a slightly bigger size.

If the growing size of the code requires it, this is the time to employ all the techniques that we are describing in this book to generate more structure, architecting the system. This will involve defining modules with clear responsibilities and clear boundaries. This division allows the team to be divided into groups and allows them to work at creating ownership and explicit goals for each team.

This allows the teams to work in parallel without too much interference, so the extra members can increase the throughput in terms of features. As we commented before, clear boundaries will help in defining the work for each team.

In a monolith, however, these limitations are *soft*, as the whole system is accessible. Sure, there is a certain discipline in terms of focusing on certain areas, and the tendency will be that one team will be able to access everything, and will tweak and bend internal APIs.

This characteristic is not necessarily a bad thing, especially on a smaller scale. This way of working with a small, focused team can produce fantastic results, as they'll be able to adjust quickly all the related parts of the software. The drawback is that the members of the team need to be highly experienced and know their way around the software, which normally becomes more and more difficult over time.

When moving to a microservices architecture, the division of work becomes way more explicit. The APIs between teams become hard limitations and there is a need for more work upfront to communicate between teams. The trade-off is that teams are way more independent, as they can:

- Own the microservice completely without other teams coding in the same code base
- Deploy independently from other teams

As the code base will be smaller, new members of the team will be able to learn it quickly and be productive earlier. Because the external APIs to interact with other microservices will be explicitly defined, a higher level of abstraction will be applied, making it easier to interact.

Note this also means that different teams will know less about the internals of other microservices compared with monolithic applications when there's at least a superficial knowledge of it. This can create some friction when moving people from one team to another.

As we saw in the first chapter, Conway's law is something to keep in mind when making architectural decisions that affect communication within the organization. Let's remember that this software law states that the structure of the software will replicate the communication structure of the organization.

A good example of Conway's law is the creation of DevOps practices. The older way of dividing work was to have different teams, one related to developing new features, and another in charge of deploying and operating the software. The abilities required for each task are different, after all.

The risk of this structure is the "I don't know what it is / I don't know where it runs" division, which can cause the team responsible for developing new features to be unaware of bugs and problems associated with operating the software, while the operations team finds changes with little reaction time, and identifies bugs without understanding the inside operation of the software.

This division is still in place in many organizations, but the idea behind DevOps is that the same team that develops the software is responsible for deploying it, thereby creating a virtuous feedback loop where developers are aware of the complexities of the deployment and can react and fix bugs in production and improve the operation of the software.

Note that this normally involves creating a multi-functional team with people who both understand operations and development, though they don't necessarily need to be the same. Sometimes, an external team is responsible for creating a set of common tools for other teams to use in their operations.

This is a big change, and changing from the older structure to the DevOps one involves mixing teams in a way that can be very disruptive for the corporate culture. As we've tried to highlight here, this involves people changes, which are slow and have a significant amount of pain associated with them. For example, there may be a good operations culture where they share their knowledge and have fun together, and now they'll need to break up those teams and integrate them with new people.

This kind of process is difficult and should be planned carefully, understanding both its human and social scale.

Communication within the same team is different from the communication between different teams. Communicating with other teams is always more difficult and costlier. This is probably easy to say, but the implications of it for teamwork are big. Examples include the following:

- Because APIs to be used externally from the team are going to be used by other engineers without the same level of expertise in the internals, it makes sense to make them generic and easy to use, as well as creating proper documentation.
- If a new design follows the structure of already existing teams, it will be easier to implement than the other way around. Architectural changes that lie between teams require organizational changes. Changing the structure of an organization is a long and painful process. Anyone who has been involved in a company reorganization can attest to that. These organizational changes will be reflected in the software naturally, so ideally a plan will be generated to allow for it.
- Two teams working in the same service will create problems because each team will try to pull it to their own goals. This is a situation that can happen with some common libraries or with "core" microservices that are used by multiple teams. Try to enforce clear owners for them to be sure that a single team is in charge of any changes.

Explicit owners establish clarity about who is responsible for changes and new features. Even if something is implemented by someone else, the owner should be responsible for approving it and giving direction and feedback. They should also be prepared to have a long-term vision and handle any technical debt.

- Given that different physical locations and time zones naturally impose their own communication barrier, they normally are used to set up different teams, describing their own structured communication, like the API definition, between time zones.

Working remotely has increased significantly as a result of the COVID-19 crisis. This has also created the need to structure communication differently compared with a team working together in the same room. This has developed and improved communication skills, which can lead to better ways of organizing work. In any case, team division is not only a matter of being physically located in the same place but creating the bonds and structure to work as a team.

Communication aspects of development are an important part of the work and should not be underestimated. Keep in mind that changes to them are "people changes," which are more difficult to implement than tech changes.

Moving from a monolith to microservices

A usual case is the need to migrate from an existing monolithic architecture to a new microservices one.

The main reason for wanting to implement this change is the size of the system. As we've discussed before, the main advantage of a microservice system is the creation of multiple independent parts that can be developed in parallel, enabling the development to be scaled and the pace increased by allowing more engineers to work at the same time.

This is a move that makes sense if the monolith has grown to exceed a manageable size and there are enough problems with releases, interfering features, and stepping on each other's toes. But, at the same time, it's a very huge and painful transition to perform.

Challenges for the migration

While the final result may be much better than a monolithic application that shows its age, migrating to a new architecture is a big undertaking. We'll now look at some of the challenges and problems that we can expect in the process:

- Migrating to microservices will require a huge amount of effort, actively changing the way the organization operates, and will require a big upfront investment until it starts to pay off. The transition time will be painful and will require compromises between the speed of migration and the regular operation of the service, as stopping the operation completely won't be an option. It will require a good deal of meetings and documentation to plan and communicate the migration to everyone. It needs to have active support at the executive level to ensure full commitment to get it done, with a clear understanding of why it is being done.
- It also requires a profound cultural change. As we've seen above, the key element of microservices is the interaction between teams, which will change significantly compared with the way of operating in a monolithic architecture. This will likely involve changing teams and changing tools. Teams will have to be stricter in their usage and documentation of external APIs.

They'll need to be more formal in their interaction with other teams and probably take attributions they didn't have before. In general, people don't like change, and that could be responded to in the form of resistance by members of some teams. Be sure that these elements are taken into account.

- Another challenge is the training aspect. New tools will surely be used (we will cover Docker and Kubernetes later in this chapter), so some teams will likely need to adapt to use them. Managing a cluster of services can be complicated to wrap one's head around, and it will likely involve different tools than the ones used previously. For example, local developers will likely be very different. Learning how to operate and work with containers, if going down that route, will take some time. This requires planning and the need to support team members until they are comfortable with the new system.

A very clear example of this is the extra complexity for debugging a request coming into the system, as it can be jumping around different microservices. Previously, this request was probably easier to track in the monolith. Understanding how a request moves and finding subtle bugs produced by that can be difficult. To be certain of fixing this, they will likely need to be replicated and fixed in local development, which, as we've seen, will entail the use of different tools and systems.

- Dividing the existing monolith into different services requires careful planning. A bad division between services can make two services tightly coupled, thereby not allowing independent deployment. This can result in a situation where practically any change to one service will require a change in the other, even if, theoretically, this could be done independently. This creates duplication of work, as routinely working on a single feature requires multiple microservices to be changed and deployed. Microservices can be mutated later and boundaries redefined, but there's a high cost associated with that. The same care should be taken later when adding new services.
- There's an overhead in creating microservices, as there is some work that gets replicated on each service. That overhead gets compensated for by allowing independent and parallel development. But, to take full advantage of that, you need numbers. A small development team of up to 10 people can coordinate and handle a monolith very efficiently. It's only when the size grows and independent teams are formed that migrating to microservices starts to make sense. The bigger the company, the more it makes sense.

- A balance between allowing each team to make their own decisions and standardize some common elements and decisions is necessary. If teams have too little direction, they'll keep reinventing the wheel over and over. They'll also end up creating knowledge silos where the knowledge in a section of the company is wholly non-transferable to another team, making it difficult to learn lessons collectively. Solid communication between teams is required to allow consensus and the reuse of common solutions. Allow controlled experimentation, label it as such, and get the lessons learned across the board so that the other teams benefit. There will be tension between shared and reusable ideas and independent, multiple-implementation ideas.

Be careful when introducing shared code across services. If the code grows, it will make services dependent on each other. This can reduce the independence of the microservices.

- Following the Agile principles, we know that working software is more important than extensive documentation. However, in microservices, it's important to maximize the usability of each individual microservice to reduce the amount of support between teams. That involves some degree of documentation. The best approach is to create self-documenting services.
- As we've discussed earlier, each call to a different microservice can increase the delay of responses, as multiple layers will have to be involved. This can produce latency problems, with external responses taking longer. They will also be affected by the performance and capacity of the internal network connecting the microservices.

A move to microservices should be taken with care and by carefully analyzing its pros and cons. It is possible that it will take years to complete the migration in a mature system. But for a big system, the resulting system will be much more agile and easy to change, allowing you to tackle technical debt effectively and to empower developers to take full ownership and innovate, structuring communication and delivering a high-quality, reliable service.

A move in four acts

The migration from one architecture to another should be considered in four steps:

1. **Analyze** the existing system carefully.
2. **Design** to determine what the desired destination is.

3. **Plan**. Create a route to move, step by step, from the current system to the vision designed in the first stage.
4. **Execute** the plan. This stage will need to be done slowly and deliberately, and at each step, the design and plan will need to be re-evaluated.

Let's look at each of the steps in greater detail.

1. Analyze

The very first step is to have a good understanding of our starting point with the existing monolith. This may appear trivial, but the fact is that it is quite conceivable that no particular person has a good understanding of all the details of the system. It may require information gathering, compilation, and digging deep to understand the intricacies of the system.

The existing code can be described as *legacy code*. While a debate is currently taking place on exactly what code can be categorized as legacy, the main property of it is code that is already in place and doesn't follow the best and new practices that new code has.

In other words, legacy code is old code from some time ago and that is very likely not up to date with current practices. However, legacy code is critical, as it is in use and probably key for the day-to-day operations of the organization.

The main objective of this phase should be to determine whether a change will actually be beneficial and get a preliminary idea of what microservices will result from the migration. Performing this migration is a big commitment, and it's always a good idea to double-check that tangible benefits will result. Even if, at this stage, it won't be possible to estimate the effort required, it will start shaping the size of the task.

This analysis will benefit greatly from good metrics and actual data showing the number of requests and interactions that are actually being produced in the system. This can be achieved through good monitoring, and adding metrics and logs to the system to allow the current behavior to be measured. This can lead to insights about what parts are commonly used, and, even better, parts that are almost never used and can perhaps be deprecated and removed. Monitoring can continue to be used to ensure that the process is going according to plan.

We will discuss monitoring in more detail in *Chapter 11, Package Mangement*, and *Chapter 12, Logging*.

This analysis can be almost instant if the system is already well-architected and properly maintained, but may extend to months of meetings and digging into code if the monolith is a mess of chaotic code. However, this stage will allow us to build on solid foundations, knowing what the current system is.

2. Design

The next stage of the process is to generate a vision in terms of what the system will look like after breaking the monolith up into multiple microservices.

Each microservice needs to be considered in isolation, and as part of the rest. Think in terms of what makes sense to separate. Some questions that may help you to structure the design are as follows:

- What microservices should be created? Can you describe each microservice with a clear objective and area to control?
- Is there any critical or core microservice that requires more attention or special requirements? For example, higher security or performance requirements.
- How will the teams be structured to cover the microservices? Are there too many for the team to support? If that's the case, can multiple requests or areas be joined as part of the same microservice?
- What are the prerequisites of each microservice?
- What new technologies will be introduced? Is any training required?
- Are microservices independent? What are the dependencies between microservices? Is there any microservice that is accessed more than others?
- Can microservices be deployed independently from each other? What's the process if a new change is introduced that requires a change in a dependent dependency?
- What microservices are going to be exposed externally? What microservices are only exposed internally?
- Is there any prerequisite in terms of required API limitations? For example, is there any service that requires specific APIs, such as a SOAP connection?

Other things that can be useful in informing the design can be to draw expected flow diagrams of requests that need to interact with multiple microservice, so as to analyze the expected movement between services.

Special care should be taken regarding whatever storage is decided for each microservice. In general, storage for one microservice should not be shared with another, to isolate the data.

This has a very concrete application, that is, to not access a database or other kind of raw storage directly by two or more microservices. Instead, one microservice should control the format and expose the data, and allow changes to the data by an accessible API.

For example, let's imagine that there are two microservices, one that controls reports and another that controls users. For certain reports, we may need to access the user information to pull, for example, the name and email of a user who generated a report. We can break the microservice's responsibility by allowing the report service to access directly a database that contains user information.

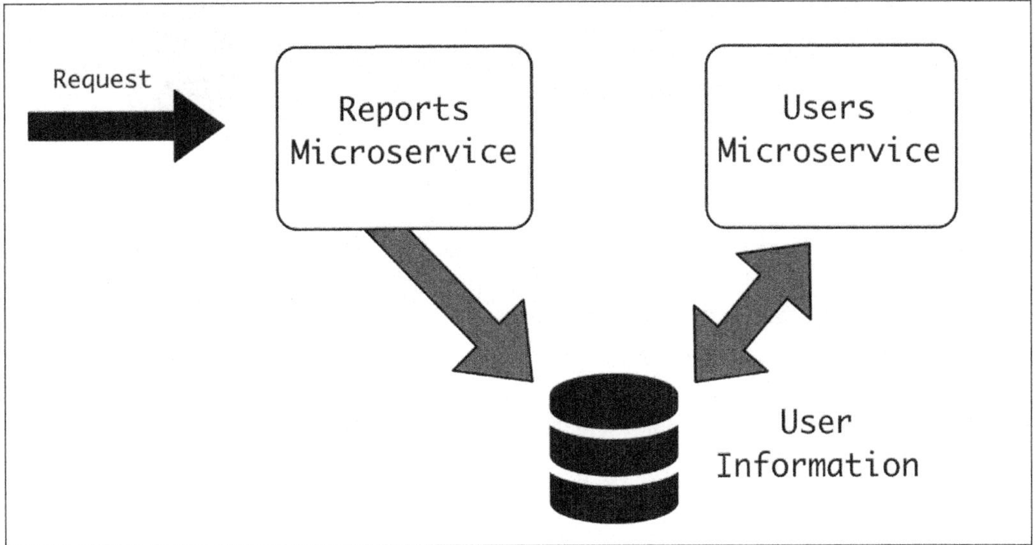

Figure 9.4: An example of incorrect usage, accessing the information directly from storage

Instead, the report service needs to access the user microservice through an API and pull the data. That way, each microservice is responsible for its own storage and format.

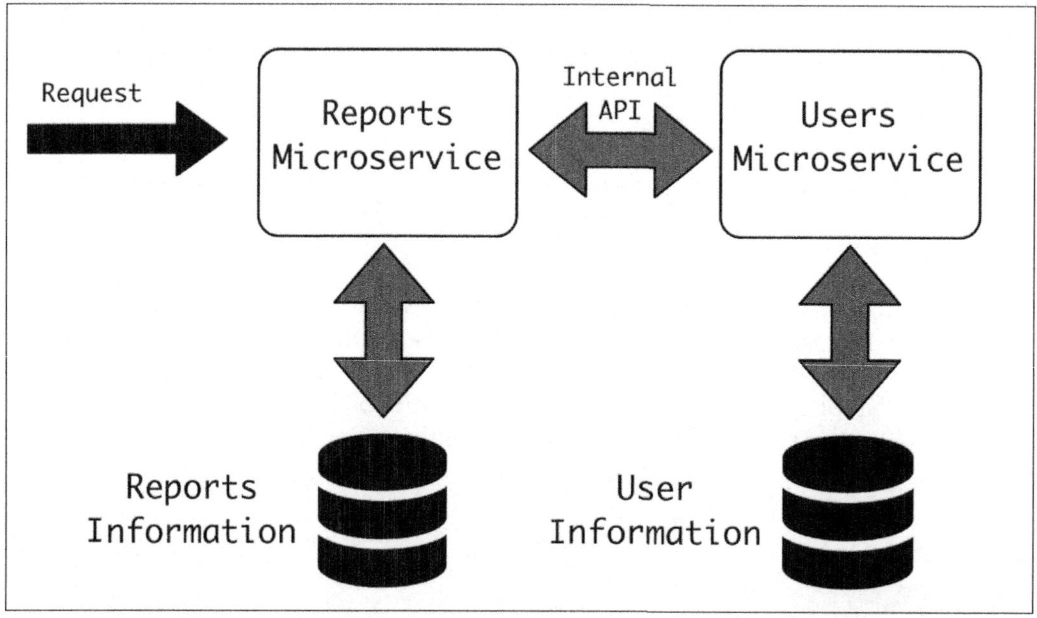

Figure 9.5: This is the correct structure. Each microservice keeps its own independent storage. This way, any information is only shared through well-defined APIs

As we commented before, creating a flow diagram of some requests will help enforce this separation and find possible points of improvement; for example, returning data from an API that is not required until later in the process.

While a prerequisite is not to mix storage, and to retain separation, you can use the same backend service to provide support for different microservices. The same database server can handle two or more logical databases that can store different information.

Generally, though, most microservices won't require their own data to be stored and can work in a completely stateless way, relying instead on other microservices to store the data.

At this stage, there's no need to design detailed APIs between microservices, but some general ideas on what services handle what data and what the required flows between microservices are would be beneficial.

3. Plan

Once the general areas are clear, it's time to get into more detail and start planning how the system is going to be changed from the starting point to the end line.

The challenge here is to iteratively move into the new system while the system simultaneously remains functional at all times. New features are likely being introduced, but let's park that for the moment and talk only about the migration itself.

To be able to do so, we need to use what is known as the **strangler pattern**. This pattern aims to gradually replace parts of the system with new ones until the entire previous system is "strangled" and can be removed safely. This pattern gets applied iteratively, slowly, migrating the functionality from the old system to the new one in small increments.

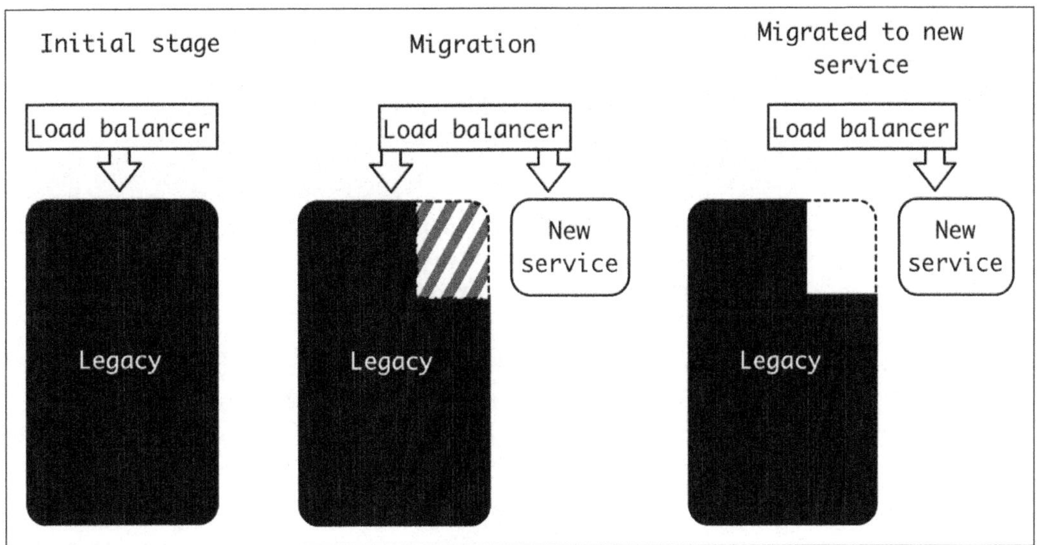

Figure 9.6: The strangler pattern

To create new microservices, there are three possible strategies:

- Replace the functionality with new code that substitutes the old code, functionally producing the same result. Externally, the code reacts exactly the same to external requests, but internally, the implementation is new. This strategy allows you to start from scratch and fix some of the oddities of the old code. It can even be done in newer tools such as frameworks or even programming languages.

At the same time, this approach can be very time-consuming. If the legacy system is undocumented and/or untested, it can be difficult to guarantee the same functionality. Also, if the functionality covered by this microservice is changing quickly, it may enter a game of catch-up between the new system and the old one, where there's no time to replicate any new functionality.

This approach makes the most sense where the legacy parts to be replicated are small and obsolete, like using a tech stack that is considered to be deprecated.

- Divide the functionality, copying and pasting code that exists in the monolith into a new microservice structure. If the existing code is in good shape and structured, this approach is relatively fast, only requiring some internal calls to be replaced with external API calls.

It may be necessary to include in the monolith new access points to ensure that a new microservice can call back to obtain some information.

It's also possible that the monolith needs to be refactored to clarify elements and divide them into a structure that's more in line with the new system.

  This process can also be made iterative by first starting with a single functionality migrated to the new microservice, and then, one by one, moving the code until the functionality is completely migrated. At that point, it is safe to delete the code from the old system.

- A **combination** of both divide and replace. Some parts of the same functionality can likely be copied directly, but for others, a new approach is preferred.

This will inform each microservice plan, although we will need to create a global view to determine which microservices to create in what order.

Here are some useful points to think about to determine what the best course of action is:

- What microservices need to be available first, taking into account dependencies that will be produced.

- An idea of what the biggest pain points are, and whether working on them is a priority. Pain points are the code or other elements that are changed frequently and the current way of dealing with them in a monolith makes them difficult. This can produce great benefits following migration.
- What are the difficult points and the cans of worms? There will likely be some. Acknowledge that they exist and minimize their impact on other services. Note that they may be the same as the pain points, or they may differ. For example, old systems that are very stable are difficult points, but not painful as per our definition, as they don't change.
- Now for a couple of quick wins that will keep the momentum of the project going. Show the advantages to your teams and stakeholders quickly! This will also allow everyone to understand the new mode of operation you want to move to and start working that way.
- An idea of the training that teams will require and what the new elements are that you want to introduce. Also, whether any skills are lacking in your team - you may be planning to hire.
- Any team changes and ownership of the new services. It's important to consider feedback from the teams so that they can express their concerns regarding any oversights during the creation of the plan. Involve the team and value their feedback.

Once we have a plan on how we are going to proceed, it's time to do it.

4. Execute

Finally, we need to act on our plan to start the move from the outdated monolith to the new wonderful land of microservices!

This will actually be the longest stage of the four, and arguably the most difficult. As we said before, the objective is to keep the service running all throughout the process.

The key element for a successful transition is to maintain **backward compatibility**. This means that the system keeps behaving like the monolithic system from an external point of view. That way, we can change the internals in terms of how the system works without affecting customers.

Ideally, the new architecture will allow us to be faster, meaning the only perceived change will be that the system is more responsive!

This is obviously easier said than done. Software development in a production environment has been referred to as starting an automobile race driving a Ford T and crossing the finishing line in a Ferrari, changing every single piece of it without stopping. Fortunately, software is so flexible that this is something we can even discuss.

To be able to make the change, from the monolith to the new microservice or microservices that handle the same functionality, the key tool is to use a load balancer at the top level, right on the ingress of requests. This is especially useful if the new microservice is directly replacing the requests. The load balancer can take the intake of requests and redirect them to the proper service, in a controlled manner.

We will assume that all incoming requests are HTTP requests. A load balancer can handle other kinds of requests, but HTTP is by far the most common.

This can be used to migrate the requests from the monolith slowly to the new microservice that should receive this request. Keep in mind that the load balancer can be configured by a different URL to direct the request to a different service, so it can use that small granularity to distribute the load properly across the different services.

The process will look a little like this. First, the load balancer is directing all the requests to the legacy monolith. Once the new microservice is deployed, the requests can be load-balanced by introducing the new microservice. Initially, the balance should only be forwarding a few requests to the new system, to be sure that the behavior is the same.

Slowly, over time, it can grow until all requests are migrated. For example, the first week can only move 10% of the requests, the second week 30%, the third week 50%, and then 100% of all requests the week after.

The migration period is 4 weeks. During that time, no new features and changes should be introduced as the interface needs to be stable between the legacy monolith and the new microservice. Be sure that all the parties involved are aware of the plan and each of the steps.

At that point, the handling of the requests in the legacy monolith is unused and can be removed to cleanup if this makes sense.

This process is similar to the strangler pattern that we discussed before, but in this case applied to individual requests. The load balancer will be an invaluable ally for implementing the pattern in full form, extending this procedure in a greater mode, as we are adding more functionality and slowly migrating it to be certain that any problem can be detected early and without affecting a large number of requests.

Execution phases

The whole execution plan should consist of three phases:

1. **The pilot phase.** Any plan will need to be tested with care. The pilot phase will be when the plan is checked in terms of its feasibility and the tools tested. A single team should lead this effort, to be sure that they are focused on it, and can learn and share quickly. Try to start on a couple of small services and low-hanging fruit, so that the improvement is obvious for the team. Good candidates are non-critical services, so if there's a problem, it doesn't present a big impact. This phase will allow you to prepare for the migration and to make adjustments and learn from inevitable mistakes.
2. **Consolidation phase.** At this point, the basics of the migration are understood, but there's still a lot of code to migrate. The pilot team can then start training other teams and spread the knowledge, so everyone understands how it should proceed. By this time, the basic infrastructure will be in place, and hopefully the most obvious issues have been corrected or at least there's a good understanding of how to deal with them.

   To help with the spreading of knowledge, documenting standards will help teams to coordinate and depend less on asking the same questions over and over. Enforcing a list of prerequisites for a new microservice to be deployed and running in production will give clarity on what is required. Be sure also to keep a feedback channel, so new teams can share their findings and improve the process.

   This phase will probably see some plan changes, as reality will overcome whatever plan has been laid out in advance. Be sure to adapt and keep an eye on the objective while navigating through the problems.

   At this phase, the pace will be increased, as the uncertainty is being reduced as more and more code is migrated. At some point, creating and migrating a new microservice will be routine for the team.

3. **Final phase**. In this phase, the monolithic architecture has been split, and any new development is done in the microservices. There may still be some remains of the monolith that are regarded as unimportant or low priority. If that's the case, the boundaries should be clear to contain the old way of doing things.

   Now, teams can take full ownership of their microservices and start taking more ambitious tasks, such as replacing a microservice completely by creating an equivalent one in another programming language or changing the architecture by merging or splitting microservices. This is the end stage where, from now on, you live in a microservices architecture. Be sure to celebrate it with the team accordingly.

That's roughly the process. Of course, this may be a long and arduous process that can span many months or even years. Be sure to keep a sustainable pace and a long-term view on the objective to be able to continue until the goal is reached.

Containerizing services

The traditional way of operating services is to use a server using a full OS, such as Linux, and then install on it all the required packages (for example, Python or PHP) and services (for example, nginx, uWSGI). The server acts as the unit, so each physical machine needs to be independently maintained and managed. It also may not be optimal from the point of view of hardware utilization.

This can be improved by replacing the physical server with virtual machines, so a single physical server can handle multiple VMs. This helps with hardware utilization and flexibility, but still requires each server to be managed as an independent physical machine.

Multiple tools help with this management, for example, configuration management tools such as Chef or Puppet. They can manage multiple servers and guarantee that they have installed the proper versions and are running the proper services.

Containers bring a different approach to this area. Instead of using a full-fledged computer (a server), with an installed OS, packages, and dependencies, and then installing your software on top of that, which mutates more often than the underlying system, it creates a package (the container image) that brings it all.

The container has its own filesystem, including the OS, dependencies, packages, and code, and is deployed as a whole. Instead of having a stable platform and running services on top of them, containers run as a whole, self-containing everything required. The platform (host machine) is a thin layer that only needs to be able to run the containers. Containers share the same kernel with the host, making them very efficient to run, compared with VMs, which may require simulating the whole server.

This allows, for example, different containers to be run in the same physical machine and have each container run a different OS, with different packages, and different versions of the code.

Sometimes, containers are thought of as "lightweight virtual machines." This is not correct. Instead, think of them as *a process wrapped in its own filesystem*. This process is the main process of the container, and when it finishes, the container stops running.

The most popular tool for building and running containers is Docker (`https://www.docker.com/`). We will now examine how to operate with it.

To install Docker, you can go to the documentation at `https://docs.docker.com/get-docker/` and follow the instructions. Use version 20.10.7 or later.

Once installed, you should be able to check the version running and get something similar to the following:

```
$ docker version
Client:
 Cloud integration: 1.0.17
 Version:           20.10.7
 API version:       1.41
 Go version:        go1.16.4
 Git commit:        f0df350
 Built:             Wed Jun  2 11:56:22 2021
 OS/Arch:           darwin/amd64
 Context:           desktop-linux
 Experimental:      true

Server: Docker Engine - Community
 Engine:
```

```
  Version:            20.10.7
  API version:        1.41 (minimum version 1.12)
  Go version:         go1.13.15
  Git commit:         b0f5bc3
  Built:              Wed Jun  2 11:54:58 2021
  OS/Arch:            linux/amd64
  Experimental:       false
 containerd:
  Version:            1.4.6
  GitCommit:          d71fcd7d8303cbf684402823e425e9dd2e99285d
 runc:
  Version:            1.0.0-rc95
  GitCommit:          b9ee9c6314599f1b4a7f497e1f1f856fe433d3b7
 docker-init:
  Version:            0.19.0
  GitCommit:          de40ad0
```

Now we need to build a container image that we can run.

Building and running an image

The container image is the whole filesystem and instructions to run when it's started. To start using containers we need to build the proper images that form the basis of the system.

Remember the description presented previously, that a container is a process surrounded by its own filesystem. Building the image creates this filesystem.

An image is created by applying a `Dockerfile`, a recipe that creates the image by executing different layers, one by one.

Let's see a very simple `Dockerfile`. Create a file called `sometext.txt` containing some small example text, and another file called `Dockerfile.simple` containing the following text:

```
FROM ubuntu
RUN mkdir -p /opt/
COPY sometext.txt /opt/sometext.txt
CMD cat /opt/sometext.txt
```

The first line, `FROM`, will start the image by using the Ubuntu image.

There are many images that you can use as a starting point. You have all the usual Linux distributions, such as Ubuntu, Debian, and Fedora, but also images for full-fledged systems such as storage systems (MySQL, PostgreSQL, and Redis) or images to work with specific tools, such as Python, Node.js, or Ruby. Check Docker Hub (`https://hub.docker.com`) for all the available images.

An interesting starting point is to use the Alpine Linux distribution, which is designed to be small and focused on security. Check out `https://www.alpinelinux.org` for further information.

One of the main advantages of containers is the ability to use and share already created containers, either directly or as a starting point to enhance them. Nowadays, it is very common to create and push a container to Docker Hub to allow others to use it directly. That's one of the great things about containers! They are very easy to share and use.

The second line runs a command inside the container. In this case, it creates a new subdirectory in `/opt`:

```
RUN mkdir -p /opt/
```

Next, we copy the current `sometext.txt` file inside, in the new subdirectory:

```
COPY sometext.txt /opt/sometext.txt
```

Finally, we define the command to execute when the image is run:

```
CMD cat /opt/sometext.txt
```

To build the image, we run the following command:

```
docker build -f <Dockerfile> --tag <tag name> <context>
```

In our case, we use the defined Dockerfile and `example` as a tag. The context is `.` (current directory), which defines the root point in terms of where to refer to all the `COPY` commands:

```
$ docker build -f Dockerfile.sample --tag example .
[+] Building 1.9s (8/8) FINISHED
 => [internal] load build definition from Dockerfile.sample
 => => transferring dockerfile: 92B
 => [internal] load .dockerignore
 => => transferring context: 2B
```

```
 => [internal] load metadata for docker.io/library/ubuntu:latest
 => [1/3] FROM docker.io/library/ubuntu@sha256:82becede498899ec668628e7
cb0ad87b6e1c371cb8a1e597d83a47fac21d6af3
 => [internal] load build context
 => => transferring context: 82B
 => CACHED [2/3] RUN mkdir -p /opt/
 => CACHED [3/3] COPY sometext.txt /opt/sometext.txt
 => exporting to image
 => => exporting layers
 => => writing image sha256:e4a5342b531e68dfdb4d640f57165b704b1132cd18b
5e2ba1220e2d800d066cb
```

If we list the available images, you will be able to see the `example` one:

```
$ docker images
REPOSITORY      TAG         IMAGE ID        CREATED         SIZE
example         latest      e4a5342b531e    2 hours ago     72.8MB
ubuntu          latest      1318b700e415    47 hours ago    72.8MB
```

We can now run the container, which will execute the `cat` command inside:

```
$ docker run example
Some example text
```

The container will stop the execution as the command finishes. You can see the stopped containers using the `docker ps -a` command, but a stopped container is generally not very interesting.

A common exception to this is that the resulting filesystem is stored onto disk, so the stopped container may have interesting files generated as part of the command.

While this way of running containers can be useful sometimes to compile binaries or other kinds of operations of a similar kind, normally, it's more common to create `RUN` commands that are always running. In that case, it will run until stopped externally, as the command will run forever.

Building and running a web service

A web service container is the most common type of microservice, as we have seen. To be able to build and run one, we need to have the following parts:

- Proper infrastructure that runs the web service to a port in the container
- Our code, which will run

Following the usual architecture presented in previous chapters, we will use the following tech stack:

- Our code will be written in Python and use Django as the web framework
- The Python code will be executed through uWSGI
- The service will be exposed in port 8000 through an nginx web server

Let's take a look at the different elements.

The code is available at `https://github.com/PacktPublishing/Python-Architecture-Patterns/tree/main/chapter_09_monolith_microservices/web_service`.

The code is structured in two main directories and one file:

- `docker`: This subdirectory contains the files related to the operation of Docker and other infrastructure.
- `src`: The source code of the web service itself. The source code is the same as we saw in *Chapter 5, The Twelve-Factor App Methodology*.
- `requirements.txt`: The file with the Python requirements for running the source code.

The Dockerfile image is located in the `./docker` subdirectory. We will follow it to explain how the different parts connect:

```
FROM ubuntu AS runtime-image

# Install Python, uwsgi and nginx
RUN apt-get update && apt-get install -y python3 nginx uwsgi uwsgi-
plugin-python3
```

```
RUN apt-get install -y python3-pip

# Add starting script and config
RUN mkdir -p /opt/server
ADD ./docker/uwsgi.ini /opt/server
ADD ./docker/nginx.conf /etc/nginx/conf.d/default.conf
ADD ./docker/start_server.sh /opt/server

# Add and install requirements
ADD requirements.txt /opt/server
RUN pip3 install -r /opt/server/requirements.txt

# Add the source code
RUN mkdir -p /opt/code
ADD ./src/ /opt/code

WORKDIR /opt/code

# compile the static files
RUN python3 manage.py collectstatic --noinput

EXPOSE 8000
CMD ["/bin/sh", "/opt/server/start_server.sh"]
```

The first part of the file starts the container from the standard Ubuntu Docker image and install the basic requirements: Python interpreter, nginx, uWSGI, and a couple of complementary packages – the uWSGI plugin to run `python3` code and `pip` to be able to install Python packages:

```
FROM ubuntu AS runtime-image

# Install Python, uwsgi and nginx
RUN apt-get update && apt-get install -y python3 nginx uwsgi uwsgi-
plugin-python3
RUN apt-get install -y python3-pip
```

The next stage is to add all the required scripts and config files to start the server and configure uWSGI and nginx. All these files are in the `./docker` subdirectory and are stored inside the container in `/opt/server` (except for the nginx configuration that is stored in the default `/etc/nginx` subdirectory).

We ensure that the start script is executable:

```
# Add starting script and config
RUN mkdir -p /opt/server
ADD ./docker/uwsgi.ini /opt/server
ADD ./docker/nginx.conf /etc/nginx/conf.d/default.conf
ADD ./docker/start_server.sh /opt/server
RUN chmod +x /opt/server/start_server.sh
```

The Python requirements are installed next. The `requirements.txt` file is added and then installed through the `pip3` command:

```
# Add and install requirements
ADD requirements.txt /opt/server
RUN pip3 install -r /opt/server/requirements.txt
```

Some Python packages may need certain packages to be installed in the container in the first stage to be sure that some tools are available; for example, installing certain database connection modules will require the proper client libraries to be installed.

We add the source code to `/opt/code` next. With the `WORKDIR` command, we execute any `RUN` command in that subdirectory and then run `collectstatic` with the Django `manage.py` command to generate the static files in the proper subdirectory:

```
# Add the source code
RUN mkdir -p /opt/code
ADD ./src/ /opt/code

WORKDIR /opt/code

# compile the static files
RUN python3 manage.py collectstatic --noinput
```

Finally, we describe the exposed port (8000) and the `CMD` to run to start the container, the `start_server.sh` script copied previously:

```
EXPOSE 8000
CMD ["/bin/bash", "/opt/server/start_server.sh"]
```

uWSGI configuration

The uWSGI configuration is very similar to the one presented in *Chapter 5, The Twelve-Factor App Methodology*:

```
[uwsgi]
plugins=python3
chdir=/opt/code
wsgi-file = microposts/wsgi.py
master=True
socket=/tmp/uwsgi.sock
vacuum=True
processes=1
max-requests=5000
uid=www-data
# Used to send commands to uWSGI
master-fifo=/tmp/uwsgi-fifo
```

The only difference is the need to include the `plugins` parameter to indicate that it runs the `python3` plugin (this is because the Ubuntu-installed `uwsgi` package doesn't have it activated by default). Also, we will run the process with the same user as nginx, to allow them to communicate through the `/tmp/uwsgi.sock` socket. This is added with `uid=www-data`, with `www-data` being the default nginx user.

nginx configuration

The nginx configuration is also very similar to the one presented in *Chapter 5, The Twelve-Factor App Methodology*:

```
server {
    listen 8000 default_server;
    listen [::]:8000 default_server;


    root /opt/code/;

    location /static/ {
        autoindex on;
        try_files $uri $uri/ =404;
    }
```

```
    location / {
        proxy_set_header Host $host;
        proxy_set_header X-Real-IP $remote_addr;
        uwsgi_pass unix:///tmp/uwsgi.sock;
        include uwsgi_params;
    }

}
```

The only difference is the exposed port, which is `8000`. Note that the root directory is `/opt/code`, making the static file directory `/opt/code/static`. This needs to be in sync with the configuration from Django.

Start script

Let's take a look at the script that starts the service, `start_script.sh`:

```
#!/bin/bash

_term() {
  # See details in the uwsgi.ini file and
  # in http://uwsgi-docs.readthedocs.io/en/latest/MasterFIFO.html
  # q means "graceful stop"
  echo q > /tmp/uwsgi-fifo
}

trap _term TERM

nginx
uwsgi --ini /opt/server/uwsgi.ini &

# We need to wait to properly catch the signal, that's why uWSGI is
started
# in the background. $! is the PID of uWSGI
wait $!
# The container exits with code 143, which means "exited because
SIGTERM"
# 128 + 15 (SIGTERM)
# http://www.tldp.org/LDP/abs/html/exitcodes.html
# http://tldp.org/LDP/Bash-Beginners-Guide/html/sect_12_02.html
echo "Exiting, bye!"
```

The core of the start is at the center, in these lines, nginx:

```
uwsgi --ini /opt/server/uwsgi.ini &
wait $!
```

This starts both `nginx` and `uwsgi`, and waits until the `uwsgi` process is not running. In Bash, `$!` is the PID of the last process (the `uwsgi` process).

When Docker attempts to stop a container, it will first send a `SIGTERM` signal to the container. That's why we create a `trap` command that captures this signal and executes the `_term()` function. This function sends a graceful stop command to the `uwsgi` queue, as we described in *Chapter 5, The Twelve-Factor App Methodology*, which ends the process in a graceful manner:

```
_term() {
  echo q > /tmp/uwsgi-fifo
}

trap _term TERM
```

If the initial `SIGTERM` signal is not successful, Docker will stop the container killing it following a grace period, but that will risk having a non-graceful end for the process.

Building and running

We can now build the image and run it. To build the image, we perform a similar command as before:

```
$ docker build -f docker/Dockerfile --tag example .
[+] Building 0.2s (19/19) FINISHED
 => [internal] load build definition from Dockerfile
 => => transferring dockerfile: 85B
 => [internal] load .dockerignore
 => => transferring context: 2B
 => [internal] load metadata for docker.io/library/ubuntu:latest
 => [ 1/14] FROM docker.io/library/ubuntu
 => [internal] load build context
 => => transferring context: 4.02kB
 => CACHED [ 2/14] RUN apt-get update && apt-get install -y python3 
nginx uwsgi uwsgi-plugin-pytho
 => CACHED [ 3/14] RUN apt-get install -y python3-pip
 => CACHED [ 4/14] RUN mkdir -p /opt/server
 => CACHED [ 5/14] ADD ./docker/uwsgi.ini /opt/server
 => CACHED [ 6/14] ADD ./docker/nginx.conf /etc/nginx/conf.d/default.
conf
```

```
 => CACHED [ 7/14] ADD ./docker/start_server.sh /opt/server
 => CACHED [ 8/14] RUN chmod +x /opt/server/start_server.sh
 => CACHED [ 9/14] ADD requirements.txt /opt/server
 => CACHED [10/14] RUN pip3 install -r /opt/server/requirements.txt
 => CACHED [11/14] RUN mkdir -p /opt/code
 => CACHED [12/14] ADD ./src/ /opt/code
 => CACHED [13/14] WORKDIR /opt/code
 => CACHED [14/14] RUN python3 manage.py collectstatic --noinput
 => exporting to image
 => => exporting layers
 => => writing image sha256:7be9ae2ab0e16547480aef6d32a11c2ccaa3da4aa5e
fbfddedb888681b8e10fa
 => => naming to docker.io/library/example
```

To run the service, start the container, mapping its port `8000` to a local port, for example, `local 8000`:

```
$ docker run -p 8000:8000 example
[uWSGI] getting INI configuration from /opt/server/uwsgi.ini
*** Starting uWSGI 2.0.18-debian (64bit) on [Sat Jul 31 20:07:20 2021]
***
compiled with version: 10.0.1 20200405 (experimental) [master revision
0be9efad938:fcb98e4978a:705510a708d3642c9c962beb663c476167e4e8a4] on 11
April 2020 11:15:55
os: Linux-5.10.25-linuxkit #1 SMP Tue Mar 23 09:27:39 UTC 2021
nodename: b01ce0d2a335
machine: x86_64
clock source: unix
pcre jit disabled
detected number of CPU cores: 2
current working directory: /opt/code
detected binary path: /usr/bin/uwsgi-core
setuid() to 33
chdir() to /opt/code
your memory page size is 4096 bytes
detected max file descriptor number: 1048576
lock engine: pthread robust mutexes
thunder lock: disabled (you can enable it with --thunder-lock)
uwsgi socket 0 bound to UNIX address /tmp/uwsgi.sock fd 3
Python version: 3.8.10 (default, Jun  2 2021, 10:49:15)  [GCC 9.4.0]
*** Python threads support is disabled. You can enable it with
--enable-threads ***
Python main interpreter initialized at 0x55a60f8c2a40
your server socket listen backlog is limited to 100 connections
```

```
your mercy for graceful operations on workers is 60 seconds
mapped 145840 bytes (142 KB) for 1 cores
*** Operational MODE: single process ***
WSGI app 0 (mountpoint='') ready in 1 seconds on interpreter
0x55a60f8c2a40 pid: 11 (default app)
*** uWSGI is running in multiple interpreter mode ***
spawned uWSGI master process (pid: 11)
spawned uWSGI worker 1 (pid: 13, cores: 1)
```

After doing this, you can access your local address, `http://localhost:8000`, and access the service; for example, accessing the URL `http://localhost:8000/api/users/jaime/collection`:

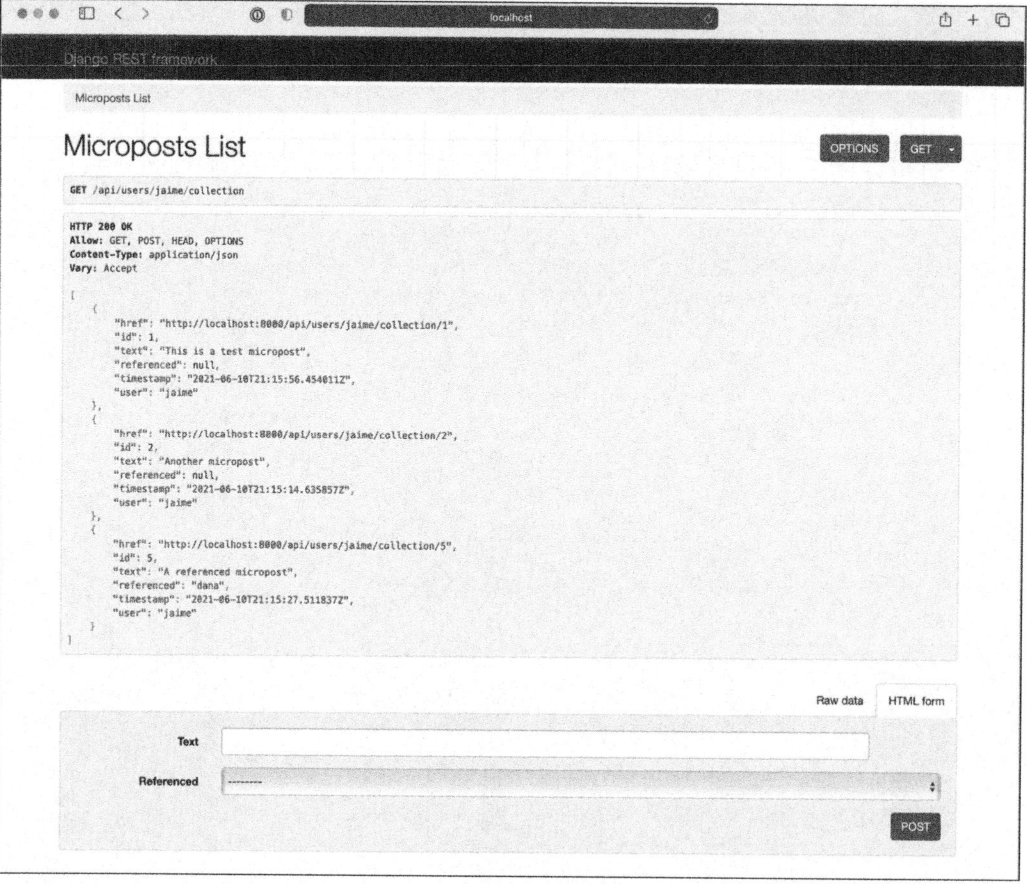

Figure 9.7: Microposts list

You'll see the access log in the screen where you started the container:

```
[pid: 13|app: 0|req: 2/2] 172.17.0.1 () {42 vars in 769 bytes} [Sat Jul
31 20:28:56 2021] GET /api/users/jaime/collection => generated 10375
bytes in 173 msecs (HTTP/1.1 200) 8 headers in 391 bytes (1 switches on
core 0)
```

The container can be stopped gracefully using the `docker stop` command. To do so, you'll need to first discover the container ID using `docker ps`:

```
$ docker ps
CONTAINER ID   IMAGE     COMMAND                  CREATED
STATUS          PORTS                                       NAMES
b01ce0d2a335   example   "/bin/bash /opt/serv…"   23 minutes ago   Up
23 minutes   0.0.0.0:8000->8000/tcp, :::8000->8000/tcp   hardcore_chaum
$ docker stop b01ce0d2a335
b01ce0d2a335
```

The container log will show the details when capturing the `SIGTERM` signal sent by Docker and will then exit:

```
Caught SIGTERM signal! Sending graceful stop to uWSGI through the
master-fifo
Exiting, bye!
```

To be able to set this example, we made some conscious decisions to simplify the operation compared with a typical service.

Caveats

Remember to check *Chapter 5*, *The Twelve-Factor App Methodology*, to see the defined API and understand it better.

The `DEBUG` mode in the Django `settings.py` file is set to `True`, which allows us to see more information when, for example, 404 or 500 errors are triggered. This parameter should be disabled in production as it can give away critical information.

The `STATIC_ROOT` and `STATIC_URL` parameters need to be coordinated between Django and nginx to point to the same place. That way, the `collectstatic` command will store the data in the same place where nginx will pick it up.

The most important detail is the use of a SQLite database instead of an internal one. This database is stored in the `src/db.sqlite3` file, in the filesystem of the container. This means that if the container is stopped and restarted, any changes will be destroyed.

The `db.sqlite3` file in the GitHub repo contains some information that has been stored for convenience, two users, `jaime` and `dana`, each with a couple of microposts. The API so far hasn't been defined in such a way to create new users, so it needs to relay into creating them using Django tools or manipulating the SQL directly. These users are added for demonstration purposes.

As an exercise, create a script that seeds the database with information as part of the build process.

In general, this database usage is not well suited for production usage, requiring connection to a database external to the container. This obviously requires an available external database, which complicates the setup.

Now that we know how to use containers, we can perhaps start another Docker container with a database, such as MySQL, for a better configuration.

A containerized database is not a great idea for production. In general, containers are great for stateless services that change often, as they can be started and stopped easily. Databases tend to be very stable and there are a lot of services that make provisions for managed databases. The advantages that containers bring are simply not relevant for a typical database.

That doesn't mean that there are usages out of production. It is a great option for local development, for example, as it allows the creation of a replicable local environment easily.

If we want to create more than one container and connect them, like a web server and a database that acts as a backend for storing the data, instead of starting all the containers individually, we can use orchestration tools.

Orchestration and Kubernetes

Managing multiple containers and connecting them is known as orchestrating them. Microservices that are deployed in containers will have to orchestrate them to be sure that the multiple microservices are interconnecting.

This concept includes details such as discovering where the other containers are, dependencies between services, and generating multiple copies of the same container.

Orchestration tools are very powerful, as well as complex, and require that you become familiar with a lot of terms. To explain them fully is beyond the scope of this book, but we will point to some and give a short introduction. Please refer to the linked documentation in the sections below for more information.

There are several tools that can perform orchestration, the two most common ones being `docker-compose` and Kubernetes.

`docker-compose` is part of the general offering by Docker. It works very well for small deployments or local development. It defines a single YAML file that contains the definition of the different services, and the name that they can use. It can be used to replace a lot of `docker build` and `docker run` commands, as it can define all the parameters in the YAML file.

You can check the documentation for Docker Compose here: `https://docs.docker.com/compose/`.

Kubernetes is aimed at bigger deployments and clusters and allows the generation of a full logical structure for containers to define how they connect to one another, thereby allowing abstraction to the underlying infrastructure.

Any physical (or virtual) server configured in Kubernetes is called a **node**. All nodes define the cluster. Each node is handled by Kubernetes, and Kubernetes will create a network between the nodes and assign the different containers to each of them, attending to the available space on them. This means that the number, location, or kind of node doesn't need to be handled by the services.

Instead, the applications in the cluster are distributed in the logical layer. Several elements can be defined:

- **Pod**. A Pod is the minimal unit defined in Kubernetes, and it is defined as a group of containers that runs as a unit. Normally, Pods will consist of just one container, but in some cases, they may comprise several. Everything in Kubernetes runs in Pods.
- **Deployment**. A collection of Pods. The Deployment will define the number of replicas that are needed, and create the proper number of Pods. Each Pod for the same deployment can live in different nodes, but that's under the control of Kubernetes.

Because the Deployment controls the number of Pods, if a Pod crashes, the Deployment will restart it. Also, the Deployment can be manipulated to change the number, for example, by creating autoscalers. If the image to be deployed in the Pods is changed, the Deployment will create new Pods with the right image and remove the old ones accordingly, based on rolling updates or other strategies.

- **Service**. A label that can be used to route requests to certain Pods, acting as a DNS name. Normally, this will point to the Pods created for deployment. This allows other Pods in the system to send requests to a known place. The requests will be load-balanced between the different Pods.
- **Ingress**. External access to a service. This will map an incoming DNS to a service. Ingresses allow applications to be exposed externally. An external request will go through the process of entering through an Ingress, being directed to a Service, and then handled by a specific pod.

Some components can be described in a Kubernetes cluster, such as `ConfigMaps`, defining key-value pairs that can be used for configuration purposes; `Volumes` to share storage across Pods; and `Secrets` to define secret values that can be injected into Pods.

Kubernetes is a fantastic tool that can handle pretty big clusters with hundreds of nodes and thousands of Pods. It's also a complex tool that requires you to learn how it can be used and has a significant learning curve. It's pretty popular these days, and there's plenty of documentation about it. The official documentation can be found here: `https://kubernetes.io/docs/home/`.

Summary

In this chapter, we described both the monolithic and microservices architectures. We started by presenting the monolithic architecture and how it tends to be a "default architecture," generated organically as an application is designed. Monoliths are created as unitary blocks that contain all the code within a single block.

In comparison, the microservices architecture divides the functionality of the whole application into smaller parts so that they can be worked in parallel. For this strategy to work, it needs to define clear boundaries and document how to interconnect the different services. Compared with the monolithic architecture, microservices aim to generate more structured code and control big code bases by dividing them into smaller, more manageable systems.

We discussed what the best architecture is and how to choose whether to design a system as a monolith or as microservices. Each approach has its pros and cons, but in general, systems start as monolithic and the move to divide the code base into smaller microservices comes after the code base and the number of developers working on it reaches a certain size.

The difference between the two architectures is not just technical. It largely involves how developers working on the system need to communicate and divide the teams. We discussed the different aspects to take into account, including the structure and size of the teams.

Since migrating from an old monolithic architecture to a new microservices one is such a common case, we talked about how to approach the work, analyze it, and perform it, using a four-stage roadmap: Analyze, Design, Plan, and Execute.

We then discussed how containerizing services (and, in particular, microservices) can be helpful. We explored how to use Docker as a tool to containerize services and its multiple advantages and uses. We included an example of containerizing our example web service, as described in *Chapter 5, The Twelve-Factor App Methodology*.

Finally, we described briefly the usage of an orchestration tool to coordinate and intercommunicate between multiple containers, and the most popular, Kubernetes. We then covered a brief introduction to Kubernetes.

You can get more information about microservices and how to perform a migration from a monolithic architecture to a microservices one in the book *Hands-On Docker for Microservices with Python*, from the author of this book, which expands on these concepts and goes into greater depth.

Join our book's Discord space

Join the book's Discord workspace for a monthly *Ask me Anything* session with the author: `https://packt.link/PythonArchitechture`

Part III

Implementation

Designing is an important stage to have a plan of action, but really the meat of the developing process is in the implementation.

Implementing the general architecture design will require multiple smaller design decisions about how the code needs to be structured and developed. It doesn't matter how good the design is, the execution is critical and will validate or adjust the prepared plan.

A solid implementation, then, requires developers to be skeptical about their own coding abilities and code needs to be tested thoroughly before it can be considered "done." This is a normal operation, and when done constantly, it produces good cascading effects, not only improving the quality of the code and reducing the number of problems but also increasing the capacity of the team to foresee weak points and harden them to be sure that, once in operation, the software is reliable and works with as few problems as possible.

We will see how to approach testing, including the use of **Test-Driven Design (TDD)**, a practice that puts testing at the center of the development process.

Sometimes some code aspects need to be shared multiple times to be reused. A powerful tool in the Python world is the easy creation and sharing of modules that can be implemented. We will see how to structure, create, and maintain standard Python modules, including uploading them into PyPI, the standard Python repository of third-party packages.

This section of the book includes the following chapters:

- *Chapter 10, Testing and TDD*, explaining different approaches to testing, the Test-Driven Design methodology, and tools to write tests easily
- *Chapter 11, Package Management*, describing how to structure code to be shared to use in different parts of the system or to share it with the broader community

10
Testing and TDD

No matter how good a developer is, they'll write code that doesn't always perform correctly. This is unavoidable, as no developer is perfect. But it's also because the expected results are sometimes not the ones that one would think of while immersed in coding.

Designs rarely go as expected and there's always a discussion going back and forth while they are being implemented, until refining them and getting them correct.

> *Everyone has a plan until they get punched in the mouth. – Mike Tyson*

Writing software is notoriously difficult because of its extreme plasticity, but at the same time, we can use software to double-check that the code is doing what it is supposed to do.

Be aware that, as with any other code, tests can have bugs as well.

Writing tests allows you to detect problems while the code is fresh and with some sane skepticism to verify that the expected results are the actual results. We will see during the chapter how to write tests easily, as well as different strategies to write different tests for capturing different kinds of problems.

We will describe how to work under TDD, a methodology that works by defining the tests first, to ensure that the validation is as independent of the actual code implementation as possible.

We will also show how to create tests in Python using common unit test frameworks, the standard `unittest` module, and the more advanced and powerful `pytest`.

Note this chapter is a bit longer than others, mostly due to the need to present example code.

In this chapter, we'll cover the following topics:

- Testing the code
- Different levels of testing
- Testing philosophy
- Test-Driven Development
- Introduction to unit testing in Python
- Testing external dependencies
- Advanced pytest

Let's start with some basic concepts about testing.

Testing the code

The first question when discussing testing the code is a simple one: What exactly do we mean by testing the code?

While there are multiple answers to that, in the broadest sense, the answer could be "*any procedure that probes the application to check that it works correctly before it reaches the final customers.*" In this sense, any formal or informal testing procedure will fulfil the definition.

The most relaxed approach, which is sometimes seen in small applications with one or two developers, is to not create specific tests but to do informal "full application runs" checking that a newly implemented feature works as expected.

This approach may work for small, simple applications, but the main problem is ensuring that older features remain stable.

But, for high-quality software that is big and complex enough, we need to be a bit more careful about the testing. So, let's try to come up with a more precise definition of testing: *Testing is any documented procedure, preferably automated, that, from a known setup, checks the different elements of the application work correctly before it reaches the final customers.*

If we check the differences with the previous definition, there are several key words. Let's check each of them to see the different details:

- **Documented**: Compared with the previous version, the aim should be that the tests are documented. This allows you to reproduce them precisely if necessary and allows you to compare them to discover blind spots.

  There are multiple ways that a test can be documented, either by specifying a list of steps to run and expected results or by creating code that runs the test. The main idea is that a test can be analyzed, be run several times by different people, be changed if necessary, and have a clear design and result.
- **Preferably automated**: Tests should be able to be run automatically, with as little human intervention as possible. This allows you to trigger Continuous Integration techniques to run many tests over and over, creating a "safety net" that is able to catch unexpected errors as early as possible. We say "preferably" because perhaps some tests are impossible or very costly to totally automate. In any case, the objective should be to have the vast majority of tests automated, to allow computers to do the heavy lifting and save precious human time. There are also multiple software tools that allow you to run tests, which can help.
- **From a known setup**: To be able to run tests in isolation, we need to know what the status of the system should be before running the test. That ensures that the result of a test will not create a certain state that could interfere with the next test. Before and after a test, certain cleanup may be required.

  This can make running tests in batches slower, compared with not worrying about the initial or end status, but it will create a solid foundation to avoid problems.

As a general rule, and especially in automated tests, the order in which the tests are executed should be irrelevant, to avoid cross-contamination. This is easier said than done, and in some cases, the order of tests can create problems. For example, test A creates an entry that test B reads. If test B is run in isolation, it will fail as it expects the entry created by A. These cases should be fixed, as they can greatly complicate debugging. Also, being able to run tests independently allows them to be parallelized.

- **Different elements of the application**: Most tests should not address the whole application, but smaller parts of it. We will talk more later about the different levels of testing, but tests should be specific about what are they testing and cover different elements, as tests covering more ground will be costlier.

A key element of testing is to have a good return on investment. Designing and running tests takes time, and that time needs to be well spent. Any test needs to be maintained, which should be worth it. Over the whole chapter, we will be commenting on this important aspect of testing.

> There's an important kind of testing that we are not covering with this definition, which is called *exploratory testing*. These tests are typically run by QA engineers, who use the final application without a clear preconceived idea but try to pre-emptively find problems. If the application has a customer-facing UI, this style of testing can be invaluable in detecting inconsistencies and problems that are not detected in the design phase.
>
> For example, a good QA engineer will be able to say that the color of a button on page X is not the same as the button on page Y, or that the button is not evident enough to perform an action, or that to perform a certain action there's a prerequisite that's not evident or possible with the new interface. Any **user experience** (**UX**) check will probably fall into this category.
>
> By its nature, this kind of testing cannot be "designed" or "documented," as it ultimately comes down to interpretation and a good eye to understand whether the application *feels correct*. Once a problem is detected, then it can be documented to be avoided.
>
> While this is certainly useful and recommended, this style of testing is more an art than an engineering practice and we won't be discussing it in detail.

This general definition helps to start the discussion, but we can be more concrete about the different tests defined by how much of the system is under test, during each test.

Different levels of testing

As we described before, tests should cover different elements of the system. This means that a test can address a small or big part of the system (or the whole system), trying to reduce its range of action.

When testing a small part of the system, we reduce the complexity of the test and scope. We need to call only that small part of the system, and the setup is easier to start with. In general, the smaller the element to test, the faster and easier it is to test it.

We will define three different levels or kinds of tests, from small to big scopes:

- **Unit tests**, for tests that check only part of a service
- **Integration tests**, for tests that check a single service as a whole
- **System tests**, for tests that check multiple services working together

Names can actually vary quite a lot. In this book, we won't be very strict with definitions, instead defining soft limits and suggesting finding a balance that works for your specific project. Don't be shy to take decisions on the proper level for each test and define your own nomenclature, and always keep in mind how much effort it takes to create tests to be sure that they are always worth it.

The definition of the levels can be a little blurred. For example, integration and unit tests can be defined side by side, and the difference between them could be more academic in that case.

Let's start describing each of the levels in more detail.

Unit tests

The smallest kind of test is also the one where most effort is typically invested, the *unit test*. This kind of test checks the behavior of a small unit of code, not the whole system. This unit of code could be as small as a single function or test a single API endpoint, and so on.

As we said above, there's a lot of debate on how big a unit test should actually be, based on what the "unit" is and whether it is actually a unit. For example, in some cases, people will only call a test a unit test if it involves a single function or class.

Because a unit test checks a small part of the functionality, it can be very easy to set up and quick to run. Therefore, making new unit tests is quick and can thoroughly test the system, checking that the small individual pieces that make the whole system work as expected.

The objective of unit tests is to check in depth the behavior of a defined feature of a service. Any external requests or elements should be simulated, meaning that they are defined as part of the test. We will cover unit tests in more detail later in the chapter, as they are the key elements of the TDD approach.

Integration tests

The next level is the integration test. This is checking the whole behavior of a service or a couple of services.

The main goal of integration testing is to be sure that the different services or different modules inside the same service can work with each other. While in unit tests, external requests are simulated, integration tests use the real service.

The simulation of external APIs may still be required. For example, simulating an external payment provider for the tests. But, in general, as many real services should be used for integration tests as possible, as the point of the test is to test that the different services work together.

It's important to note that, commonly, different services will be developed by different developers or even different teams, and they can diverge in their understanding of how a particular API is implemented, even in the event of a well-defined spec.

The setup in integration tests is more complex than in unit tests, as more elements need to be properly set up. This makes integration tests slower and more expensive than unit tests.

Integration tests are great to check that different services work in unison, but there are some limitations.

Integration tests are normally not as thorough as unit tests, focusing on checking basic functionality and following a *happy path*. A happy path is a concept in testing meaning that the test case should produce no errors or exceptions.

Expected errors and exceptions are normally tested in unit tests, since they are also elements that can fail. That doesn't mean that every single integration test should follow a happy path; some integration errors may be worth checking, but in general, a happy path tests the expected general behavior of the feature. They will compose the bulk of the integration tests.

System tests

The final level is the system level. System tests check that all the different services work correctly together.

A requirement for this kind of test is that there are actually multiple services in the system. If not, they are not different from tests at the lower levels. The main objective of these tests is to check that the different services can cooperate, and the configuration is correct.

System tests are slow and difficult to implement. They require the whole system to be set up, with all the different services properly configured. Creating that environment can be complicated. Sometimes, it's so difficult that the only way of actually performing any system tests is to run them in the live environment.

The environment configuration is an important part of what these tests check. That may make them important to run on each environment that is under test, including the live environment.

While this is not ideal, sometimes it is unavoidable and can help to improve confidence after deployments, to ensure that the new code is working correctly. In that case, given the constraints, only a minimum amount of tests should be run, as the live environment is critical. The tests to run should also exercise the maximum amount of common functionality and services to detect any critical problem as fast as possible. This set of tests is sometimes called *acceptance tests* or *smoke tests*. They may be run manually, as a way of ensuring that everything looks correct.

Of course, smoke tests can be run not only on the live environment and can work as a way to ensure that other environments are working correctly.

Smoke tests should be very clear, well documented, and designed carefully to cover the most critical parts of the whole system. Ideally, they should also be read-only, so they don't leave useless data after their execution.

Testing philosophy

A key element of everything involved with testing is another question: *Why test?* What are we trying to achieve with it?

As we've seen, testing is a way of ensuring that the behavior of the code is the expected one. The objective of testing is to detect possible problems (sometimes called *defects*) before the code is published and used by real users.

There's a subtle difference between *defects* and *bugs*. Bugs are a kind of defect where the software behaves in a way that it's not expected to. For example, certain input produces an unexpected error. Defects are more general. A defect could be that a button is not visible enough, or that the logo on a page is not the correct one. In general, tests are way better at detecting bugs than other defects, but remember what we said about exploratory testing.

A defect that goes undetected and gets deployed into a live system is pretty expensive to repair. First of all, it needs to be detected. In a live application with a lot of activity, detecting a problem can be difficult (though we will talk about it in *Chapter 16, Ongoing Architecture*), but even worse, it will normally be detected by a user of the system using the application. It's possible that the user won't properly communicate the problem back, so the problem is still present, creating problems or limiting activity. The detecting user might abandon the system, or at the very least their confidence in the system will decrease.

Any reputational cost will be bad, but it can also be difficult to extract enough information from the user to know exactly what happened and how to fix it. This makes the cycle between detecting the problem and fixing it long.

Any testing system will improve the ability to fix defects earlier. Not only can we create a specific test that simulates exactly the same problem, but we can also create a framework that executes tests regularly to have a clear approach to how to detect and fix problems.

Different testing levels have different effects on this cost. In general, any problem that can be detected at the unit test level is going to be cheaper to fix there, and the cost increases from there. Designing and running a unit test is easier and faster than doing the same with an integration test, and an integration test is cheaper than a system test.

The different test levels could be understood as different layers capturing possible problems. Each layer will capture different problems if they appear. The closer to the start of the process (design and unit tests while coding), the cheaper it is to create a dense net that will detect and alert for problems. The cost of fixing a problem increases the farther away it is from the controlled environment at the start of the process.

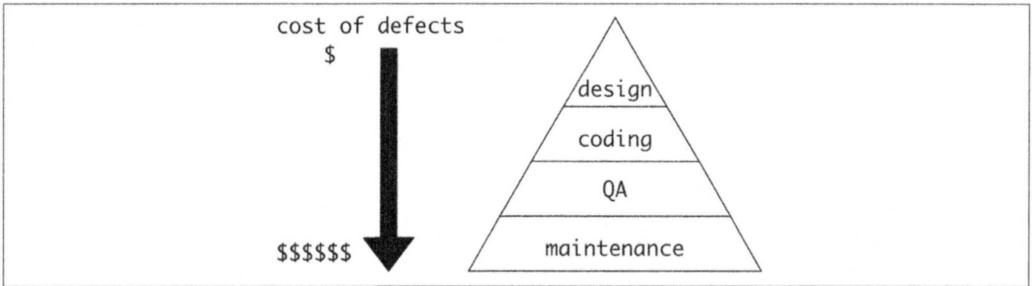

Figure 10.1: The cost of fixing defects increases the later they get detected

Some defects are impossible to detect at the unit test level, like the integration of different parts. That's where the next level comes into play. As we've seen, the worst scenario is not detecting a problem and it affecting real users on the live system.

But having tests is not only a good way of capturing problems once. Because a test can still remain, and be run on new code changes, it also creates a safety net while developing to be sure that creating new code or modifying the code does not affect the old functionality.

This is one of the best arguments for running tests automatically and constantly, as per Continuous Integration practices. The developer can focus on the feature being developed, while the Continuous Integration tool will run every test, alerting early if there's a problem with some test. A problem with previously introduced functionality that is failing is called a *regression*.

Regression problems are quite common, so having good test coverage is great to prevent them going undetected. Specific tests covering previous functionality to ensure that it keeps running as expected can be introduced. These are regression tests, and sometimes they are added after we have detected a regression problem.

Another benefit of having good tests that check the behavior of the system is that the code itself can be changed heavily, knowing that the behavior will remain the same. These changes can be made to restructure the code, clean it, and in general improve it. These changes are called *refactoring* the code, changing how the code is written without changing the expected behavior of it.

Now, we should answer the question "what is a good test?" As we discussed, writing a test is not free, there's an effort involved, and we need to be sure that it's worth it. How can we create good ones?

How to design a great test

Designing good tests requires a certain mindset. The objective while designing the code that covers certain functionality is to make the code fulfill that functionality while at the same time being efficient, writing clear code that could even be described as elegant.

The objective of the test is to be sure that the functionality sticks to the expected behavior, and that all the different problems that can arise produce results that make sense.

Now, to be able to really put the functionality to the test, the mindset should be to stress the code as much as possible. For example, let's imagine a function `divide(A, B)`, that divides two integers between -100 and 100: `A` between `B`.

While approaching the test, we need to check what the limits are of this, trying to check that the function is performing properly with the expected behavior. For example, the following tests could be created:

Action	Expected behavior	Comments
`divide(10, 2)`	`return 5`	Basic case
`divide(-20, 4)`	`return -5`	Divide one negative and one positive integer
`divide(-10, -5)`	`return 2`	Divide two negative integers
`divide(12, 2)`	`return 5`	Not exact division
`divide(100, 50)`	`return 2`	Maximum value of A
`divide(101, 50)`	`Produce an input error`	Value of A exceeding the maximum
`divide(50, 100)`	`return 0`	Maximum value of B
`divide(50, 101)`	`Produce an input error`	Value of B exceeding the maximum

`divide(10, 0)`	`Produce an exception`	Divide by zero
`divide('10', 2)`	`Produce an input error`	Invalid format for parameter A
`divide(10, '2')`	`Produce an input error`	Invalid format for parameter B

Note how we are testing different possibilities:

- The usual behavior of all the parameters is correct, and the division works correctly. This includes both positive and negative numbers, exact division, and inexact division.
- Values within the maximum and minimum values: We check that the maximum values are hit and correct, and the next value is properly detected.
- Division by zero: A known limitation on functionality that should produce a predetermined response (exception).
- Wrong input format.

We can really create a lot of test cases for simple functionality! Note that all these cases can be expanded. For example, we can add `divide(-100, 50)` and `divide(100, -50)` cases. In those cases, the question is the same: are those tests adding better detection of problems?

The best test is the test that really stresses the code and ensures that it's working as expected, trying very hard to cover the most difficult use cases. Making the tests ask difficult questions of the code under test is the best way of preparing your code for the real action. A system under load will see all kinds of combinations, so the best preparation for that is to create tests that try as hard as possible to find problems, to be able to solve them before moving to the next phase.

This is analogous to football training, where a series of very demanding exercises are presented to be sure that the trainee will be able to perform later, during the match. Be sure that your training regime is hard enough to properly prepare for demanding matches!

The proper balance between the number of tests and not having tests that cover functionality already checked by an existing test (for example, creating a big table dividing numbers with a lot of divisions) may depend greatly on the code under test and practices in your organization. Some critical areas may require more thorough testing as a failure there could be more important.

For example, any external API should test any input with care and be really defensive about that, as external users may abuse external APIs. For example, testing what happens when strings are input in integer fields, infinity or `NaN` (Not a Number) values are added, payload limits are exceeded, the maximum size of a list or page is exceeded, etc.

By comparison, interfaces that are mostly internal will require less testing, as the internal code is less likely to abuse the API. For example, if the `divide` function is only internal, it might not be required to test that the input format is incorrect, just to check that the limits are respected.

Note that tests are done independently from the implementation of the code. A test definition is done purely from an external view of the function to test, without requiring knowing what's inside. This is called *black-box testing*. A heathy test suite always starts with this approach.

A critical ability to develop as a developer writing tests is to detach from the knowledge of the code itself and approach tests independently.

Testing can be so detached that it may use independent people just to create the tests, like a QA team performing tests. Unfortunately, this is not a possible approach for unit tests, which will likely be created by the same developers that write the code itself.

In some cases, this external approach won't be enough. If the developer knows that there's some specific area where there could be problems, it may be good to complement it with tests that check functionality that is not apparent from an external point of view.

For example, a function that calculates a result based on some input may have an internal point where the algorithm changes to calculate it using different models. This information doesn't need to be known by the external user, but it will be good to add a couple of checks that the transition works correctly.

This kind of testing is called *white-box testing*, in comparison to the black-box approach discussed early.

It's important to remember that, in a test suite, white-box tests should always be secondary to black-box tests. The main objective is to test the functionality from an external perspective. White-box testing may be a good addition, especially in some aspects, but it should have a lower priority.

Developing the ability to be able to create good black-box tests is important and should be transmitted to the team.

Black-box testing tries to avoid a common problem where the same developer writes both the code and the test and then checks that the interpretation of the feature implemented in the code works as expected, instead of checking that it works as it should when looking from an external endpoint. We will take a look later at TDD, which tries to ensure tests are created without the implementation in mind by writing the tests before writing the code.

Structuring tests

In terms of structure, especially for unit tests, a nice way to structure tests is using the **Arrange Act Assert** (**AAA**) pattern.

This pattern means the test is in three different phases:

- **Arrange**: Prepare the environment for the tests. This includes all the setup to get the system right at the point before performing the next step, at a stable moment.
- **Act**: Perform the action that is the objective of the test.
- **Assert**: Check that the result of the action is the expected one.

The test gets structured as a sentence like this:

GIVEN (Arrange) an environment known, the **ACTION** (Act) produces the specified **RESULT** (Assert)

This pattern is also sometimes called *GIVEN, WHEN, THEN* as each step can be described in those terms.

Note that this structure aims for all the tests to be independent, and for each to test a single thing.

A common different pattern is to group act steps in tests, testing multiple functionalities in a single test. For example, test that writing a value is correct and then check that the search for the value returns the proper value. This won't follow the AAA pattern. Instead, to follow the AAA pattern, two tests should be created, the first one to validate that the write works correctly and the second where the value is created as part of the setup in the Arrange step before doing the search.

Note that this structure can be used whether the tests are executed through code or run manually, though they'll be used more for automated tests. When running them manually, the Arrange stage can take a long time to produce for each test, leading to a lot of time spent on that. Instead, manual tests are normally grouped together in the pattern that we describe above, executing a series of Act and Assert and using the input in the previous stage as setup for the next. This creates a dependency in requiring to run tests in a specific sequence, which is not great for unit test suites, but it can be better for smoke tests or other environments where the Arrange step is very expensive.

In the same way, if the code to test is purely functional (meaning that only the input parameters are the ones that determine its state, like the `divide` example above), the Arrange step is not required.

Let's see an example of code created with this structure. Imagine that we have a method that we want to test, called `method_to_test`. The method is part of a class called `ClassToTest`.

```
def test_example():
    # Arrange step
    # Create the instance of the class to test
    object_to_test = ClassToTest(paramA='some init param',
                                 paramB='another init param')


    # Act step
    response = object_to_test.method_to_test(param='execution_param')
```

```
    # Assert step
    assert response == 'expected result'
```

Each of the steps is very clearly defined. The first one prepares, in this case, an object in the class that we want to test. Note that we may need to add some parameters or some preparation so the object is in a known starting point so the next steps work as expected.

The Act step just generates the action that is under test. In this case, call the `method_to_test` method for the prepared object with the proper parameter.

Finally, the Assert step is very straightforward and just checks the response is the expected one.

In general, both the Act and Assert steps are simple to define and write. The Arrange step is where most of the effort of the test will normally be.

Another common pattern that appears using the AAA pattern for tests is to create common functions for testing in Arrange steps. For example, creating a basic environment, which could require a complex setup, and then having multiple copies where the Act and Assert steps are different. This reduces the repetition of code.

For example:

```
def create_basic_environment():
    object_to_test = ClassToTest(paramA='some init param',
                                 paramB='another init param')
    # This code may be much more complex and perhaps have
    # 100 more lines of code, because the basic environment
    # to test requires a lot of things to set up
    return object_to_test

def test_exampleA():
    # Arrange
    object_to_test = create_basic_environment()

    # Act
    response = object_to_test.method_to_test(param='execution_param')

    # Assert
    assert response == 'expected result B'
```

```
def test_exampleB():
    # Arrange
    object_to_test = create_basic_environment()

    # Act
    response = object_to_test.method_to_test(param='execution_param')

    # Assert
    assert response == 'expected result B'
```

We will see later how we can structure multiple tests that are very similar to avoid repetition, which is a problem when having big test suites. Having big test suites is important to create good test coverage, as we saw above.

Repetition in tests is, up to a certain point, unavoidable and even healthy to a certain degree. When changing the behavior of some part of the code because there are changes, the tests need to be changed accordingly to accommodate the changes. This change helps to weigh the size of the changes and avoid making big changes lightly, as the tests will work as a reminder of the affected functionality.

Nonetheless, mindless repetition is not great, and we will see later some options to reduce the amount of code to be repeated.

Test-Driven Development

A very popular technique to approach programming is **Test-Driven Development** or **TDD**. TDD consists of putting tests at the center of the developing experience.

This builds on some of the ideas that we exposed earlier in the chapter, though working on them with a more consistent view.

The TDD flow to develop software works as follows:

1. New functionality is decided on to be added to the code.
2. A new test is written to define the new functionality. Note that this is done *before* the code.
3. The test suite is run to show that it's failing.
4. The new functionality is then added to the main code, focusing on simplicity. Only the required feature, without extra details, should be added.

5. The test suite is run to show that the new test is working. This may need to be done several times until the code is ready.
6. The new functionality is ready! Now the code can be refactored to improve it, avoiding duplication, rearranging elements, grouping it with previously existing code, etc.

The cycle can start again for any new functionality.

As you can see, TDD is based on three main ideas:

- **Write the tests before writing the code**: This prevents the problem of creating a test that is too tightly coupled with the current implementation, forcing the developer to think about the test and the feature before jumping into writing it. It also forces the developer to check that the test actually fails before the feature is written, being sure that a problem later on will be detected. This is similar to the black box testing approach that we described earlier in the *How to design a great test* section.
- **Run the tests constantly**: A critical part of the process is running the whole test suite to check that all the functionality in the system is correct. This is done over and over, every time that a new test is created, but also while the functionality is being written. Running the tests is an essential part of developing in TDD. This ensures that all functionality is always checked and that the code works as expected at all times so any bug or discrepancy can be solved quickly.
- **Work in very small increments**: Focus on the task at hand, so each step builds and grows a test suite that is big and covers the whole functionality of the code in depth.

This big test suite creates a safety net that allows you to perform refactors of the code often, big and small, therefore improving the code constantly. Small increments mean small tests that are specific and need to be thought about before adding the code.

An extension of this idea is a focus on writing only the code that's required for the task at hand and not more. This is sometimes referred to as the **YAGNI** principle (**You Ain't Gonna Need It**). The intention of this principle is to prevent overdesigning or creating code for "foreseeable requests in the future," which, in practice, have a high probability of never materializing and, even worse, makes the code more difficult to change in other directions. Given that software development is notoriously difficult to plan in advance, the emphasis should be on keeping things small and not getting too far ahead of yourself.

These three ideas interact constantly during the development cycle, and it keeps the tests at the center of the development process, hence the name of the practice.

Another important advantage of TDD is that putting the focus so heavily on the tests means that how the code is going to be tested is thought about from the start, which helps in designing code that's easily testable. Also, reducing the amount of code to write, focusing on it being strictly required to pass the test reduces the probability of overdesign. The requirement to create small tests and work in increments also tends to generate modular code, in small units that are combined together but are able to be tested independently.

The general flow is to be constantly working with new failing tests, making them pass and then refactoring, sometimes called the "*red/green/refactor*" pattern: red when the test is failing and green when all tests are passing.

Refactoring is a critical aspect of the TDD process. It is strongly encouraged, to constantly improve the quality of the existing code. One of the best outcomes of this way of working is the generation of very extensive test suites that cover each detail of the code functionality, meaning that refactoring code can be done knowing that there's a solid ground that is going to capture any problems introduced by changing the code and adding bugs.

Improving the code's readability, usability, and so on, by refactoring is known to have a good impact in terms of improving the morale of developers and increasing the pace at which changes can be introduced, as the code is kept in good shape.

In general, and not only in TDD, allowing time to clean up old code and improve it is critical to maintain a good pace for changes. Old code that is stale tends to be more and more difficult to work with, and over time it will require way more effort to change it to make more changes. Encouraging healthy habits to care about the current state of the code and allowing time to perform maintenance improvements is critical for the long-term sustainability of any software system.

Another important aspect of TDD is the requirement of speedy tests. As tests are always running following TDD practices, the total execution time is quite important. The time that it takes for each test should be considered carefully, as the growing size of the test suite will make it take longer to run.

There's a general threshold where focus gets lost, so running tests taking longer than around 10 seconds will make them not "part of the same operation," risking the developer thinking about other stuff.

Obviously, running the whole test suite in under 10 seconds will be extremely difficult, especially as the number of tests grows. A full unit test suite for a complex application can consist of 10,000 tests or more! In real life, there are multiple strategies that can help alleviate this fact.

The whole test suite doesn't need to be run all the time. Instead, any test runner should allow you to select a range of tests to run, allowing you to reduce the number of tests to run on each run while the feature is in development. This means running only the tests that are relevant for the same module, for example. It can even mean running a single test, in certain cases, to speed up the result.

Of course, at some point, the whole test suite should be run. TDD is actually aligned with Continuous Integration, as it is also based on running tests, this time automatically once the code is checked out into a repo. The combination of being able to run a few tests locally to ensure that things are working correctly while developing with the whole test suite running in the background once the code is committed to the repo is great.

Anyway, as the time taken to run tests is important in TDD, observing the duration of tests is important, and generating tests that can run quickly is key to being able to work in the TDD way. This is mainly achieved by creating tests that cover small portions of the code, and therefore the time to set up can be kept under control.

TDD practices work best with unit tests. Integration and system tests may require a big setup that is not compatible with the speed and tight feedback loop required for TDD to work.

Fortunately, as we saw before, unit testing is where the bulk of testing is typically focused on most projects.

Introducing TDD into new teams

Introducing TDD practices in an organization can be tricky, as they change the way to perform actions that are quite basic, and go a bit against the usual way of working (writing tests after writing the code).

When considering introducing TDD into a team, it's good to have an advocate that can act as a point of contact for the rest of the team and solve the questions and problems that may arise through creating tests.

TDD is very popular in environments where pair programming is also common, so it's another possibility to have someone drive a session while training the other developers and introducing the practice.

> Remember, the key element of TDD is the mindset of forcing the developer to think first about how a particular feature is going to be tested before starting to think about the implementation. This mindset doesn't come naturally and needs to be trained and practiced.

It may be challenging to apply TDD techniques with already existing code, as pre-existing code can be difficult to test in this configuration, especially if the developers are new to the practice. TDD works great for new projects, though, as a test suite for new code will be created at the same time as the code. A mixed approach of starting a new module inside an existing project, so most code is new and can be designed using TDD techniques, reduces the problem of dealing with legacy code.

If you want to see if TDD can be effective for new code, try to start small, using some small project with a small team to be sure that it's not too disruptive and that the principles can be properly digested and applied. There are some developers that really love to use TDD principles, as it fits their personality and how they approach the process of developing. Remember that this is not necessarily how everyone will feel and that starting with these practices requires time, and perhaps it won't be possible to apply them 100% as the previous code might limit it.

Problems and limitations

TDD practices are very popular and widely followed in the industry, though they have their limits. One is the problem of big tests that take too long to run. These tests may be unavoidable in certain situations.

Another is the difficulty of fully taking this approach if it is not done from the beginning, as parts of the code will already be written, and perhaps new tests should be added, violating the rule of creating the tests before the code.

Another problem is designing new code while the features to be implemented are fluid and not fully defined. This requires experimentation, for example, to design a function to return a color that contrasts with an input color, for example, to present a contrast color based on a theme selectable by the user. This function may require inspection to see if it "looks right," which can require tweaking that's difficult to achieve with a preconfigured unit test.

Not a problem specifically with TDD, but something to be careful about is to remember to avoid dependencies between tests. This can happen with any test suite, but given the focus on creating new tests, it's a likely problem if the team is starting with TDD practices. Dependencies can be introduced by requiring tests to run in a particular order, as the tests can contaminate the environment. This is normally not done on purpose, but it's done inadvertently while writing multiple tests.

A typical effect on that will be that some tests fail if run independently, as their dependencies are not run in that case.

In any case, remember that TDD is not necessarily something that it's all or nothing, but a set of ideas and practices that can help you design code that's well tested and high quality. Not every single test in the system needs to be designed using TDD, but a lot of them can be.

Example of the TDD process

Let's imagine that we need to create a function that:

- For values lower than 0, returns zero
- For values greater than 10, returns 100
- For values between, it returns the power of two of the value. Note that for the edges, it returns the power of two of the input (0 for 0 and 100 for 10)

To write the code in full TDD fashion, we start with the smallest possible test. Let's create the smallest skeleton and the first test.

```
def parameter_tdd(value):
    pass


assert parameter_tdd(5) == 25
```

We run the test, and get an error with the test failing. Right now, we will use pure Python code, but later in the chapter, we'll see how to run tests more efficiently.

```
$ python3 tdd_example.py
Traceback (most recent call last):
  File ".../tdd_example.py", line 6, in <module>
```

```
    assert parameter_tdd(5) == 25
AssertionError
```

The implementation of the use case is quite straightforward.

```
def parameter_tdd(value):
    return 25
```

Yes, we are actually returning a hardcoded value, but that's really all that is required to pass the first tests. Let's run the tests now and you'll see no errors.

```
$ python3 tdd_example.py
```

But now we add tests for the lower edge. While these are two lines, they can be considered the same test, as they're checking that the edge is correct.

```
assert parameter_tdd(-1) == 0
assert parameter_tdd(0) == 0
assert parameter_tdd(5) == 25
```

Let's run the tests again.

```
$ python3 tdd_example.py
Traceback (most recent call last):
  File ".../tdd_example.py", line 6, in <module>
    assert parameter_tdd(-1) == 0
AssertionError
```

We need to add code to handle the lower edge.

```
def parameter_tdd(value):
    if value <= 0:
        return 0

    return 25
```

When running the test, we see that it's running the tests correctly. Let's add parameters now to handle the upper edge.

```
assert parameter_tdd(-1) == 0
assert parameter_tdd(0) == 0
assert parameter_tdd(5) == 25
assert parameter_tdd(10) == 100
assert parameter_tdd(11) == 100
```

This triggers the corresponding error.

```
$ python3 tdd_example.py
Traceback (most recent call last):
  File ".../tdd_example.py", line 12, in <module>
    assert parameter_tdd(10) == 100
AssertionError
```

Let's add the higher edge.

```
def parameter_tdd(value):
    if value <= 0:
        return 0

    if value >= 10:
        return 100

    return 25
```

This runs correctly. We are not confident that all the code is fine, and we really want to be sure that the intermediate section is correct, so we add another test.

```
assert parameter_tdd(-1) == 0
assert parameter_tdd(0) == 0
assert parameter_tdd(5) == 25
assert parameter_tdd(7) == 49
assert parameter_tdd(10) == 100
assert parameter_tdd(11) == 100
```

Aha! Now it shows an error, due to the initial hardcoding.

```
$ python3 tdd_example.py
Traceback (most recent call last):
  File "/.../tdd_example.py", line 15, in <module>
    assert parameter_tdd(7) == 49
AssertionError
```

So let's fix it.

```
def parameter_tdd(value):
    if value <= 0:
        return 0
```

```
    if value >= 10:
        return 100

    return value ** 2
```

This runs all the tests correctly. Now, with the safety net of the tests, we think we can refactor the code a little bit to clean it up.

```
def parameter_tdd(value):
    if value < 0:
        return 0

    if value < 10:
        return value ** 2

    return 100
```

We can run the tests all through the process and be sure that the code is correct. The final result may be different based on what the team considers good code or what is more explicit, but we have our test suite that will ensure that the tests are consistent, and the behavior is correct.

The function here is quite small, but this shows what the flow is when writing code in the TDD style.

Introduction to unit testing in Python

There are multiple ways to run tests in Python. One, as we have seen above, a bit crude, is to execute code with multiple asserts. A common one is the standard library `unittest`.

Python unittest

`unittest` is a module included in the Python standard library. It is based on the concept of creating a testing class that groups several testing methods. Let's write a new file with the tests written in the proper format, called `test_unittest_example.py`.

```
import unittest
from tdd_example import parameter_tdd
```

```
class TestTDDExample(unittest.TestCase):

    def test_negative(self):
        self.assertEqual(parameter_tdd(-1), 0)

    def test_zero(self):
        self.assertEqual(parameter_tdd(0), 0)

    def test_five(self):
        self.assertEqual(parameter_tdd(5), 25)

    def test_seven(self):
        # Note this test is incorrect
        self.assertEqual(parameter_tdd(7), 0)

    def test_ten(self):
        self.assertEqual(parameter_tdd(10), 100)

    def test_eleven(self):
        self.assertEqual(parameter_tdd(11), 100)


if __name__ == '__main__':
    unittest.main()
```

Let's analyze the different elements. The first ones are the imports on top.

```
import unittest
from tdd_example import parameter_tdd
```

We import the `unittest` module and the function to test. The most important part comes next, which defines the tests.

```
class TestTDDExample(unittest.TestCase):

    def test_negative(self):
        self.assertEqual(parameter_tdd(-1), 0)
```

The class `TestTDDExample` groups the different tests. Notice that it's inheriting from `unittest.TestCase`. Then, methods that start with `test_` will produce the independent tests. Here, we will show one. Internally, it calls the function and compares the result with 0, using the `self.assertEqual` function.

Notice that `test_seven` is defined incorrectly. We do this to produce an error when running it.

Finally, we add this code.

```
if __name__ == '__main__':
    unittest.main()
```

This runs the tests automatically if we run the file. So, let's run the file:

```
$ python3 test_unittest_example.py
...F..
======================================================================
FAIL: test_seven (__main__.TestTDDExample)
----------------------------------------------------------------------
Traceback (most recent call last):
  File ".../unittest_example.py", line 17, in test_seven
    self.assertEqual(parameter_tdd(7), 0)
AssertionError: 49 != 0

----------------------------------------------------------------------
Ran 6 tests in 0.001s

FAILED (failures=1)
```

As you can see, it has run all six tests, and shows any errors. Here, we can clearly see the problem. If we need more detail, we can run with `-v showing` showing each of the tests that are being run:

```
$ python3 test_unittest_example.py -v
test_eleven (__main__.TestTDDExample) ... ok
test_five (__main__.TestTDDExample) ... ok
test_negative (__main__.TestTDDExample) ... ok
test_seven (__main__.TestTDDExample) ... FAIL
test_ten (__main__.TestTDDExample) ... ok
```

```
test_zero (__main__.TestTDDExample) ... ok

======================================================================
FAIL: test_seven (__main__.TestTDDExample)
----------------------------------------------------------------------
Traceback (most recent call last):
  File ".../unittest_example.py", line 17, in test_seven
    self.assertEqual(parameter_tdd(7), 0)
AssertionError: 49 != 0

----------------------------------------------------------------------
Ran 6 tests in 0.001s

FAILED (failures=1)
```

You can also run a single test or combination of them using the `-k` option, which searches for matching tests.

```
$ python3 test_unittest_example.py -v -k test_ten
test_ten (__main__.TestTDDExample) ... ok

----------------------------------------------------------------------
Ran 1 test in 0.000s

OK
```

`unittest` is extremely popular and can accept a lot of options, and it's compatible with virtually every framework in Python. It's also very flexible in terms of ways of testing. For example, there are multiple methods to compare values, like `assertNotEqual` and `assertGreater`.

There's a specific assert function that works differently, which is `assertRaises`, used to detect when the code generates an exception. We will take a look at it later when testing mocking external calls.

It also has `setUp` and `tearDown` methods to execute code before and after the execution of each test in the class.

Be sure to take a look at the official documentation: `https://docs.python.org/3/library/unittest.html`.

While `unittest` is probably the most popular test framework, it's not the most powerful one. Let's take a look at it.

Pytest

Pytest simplifies writing tests even further. One common complaint about `unittest` is that it forces you to set a lot of `assertCompare` calls that are not obvious. It also needs to structure the tests, adding a bit of boilerplate code, like the `test` class. Other problems are not as obvious, but when creating big test suites, the setup of different tests can start to get complicated.

A common pattern is to create classes that inherit from other test classes. Over time, that can grow legs of its own.

Pytest instead simplifies the running and defining of tests, and captures all the relevant information using standard `assert` statements that are easier to read and recognize.

In this section, we will use `pytest` in the simplest way. Later in the chapter, we will cover more interesting cases.

Be sure to install `pytest` through pip in your environment.

```
$ pip3 install pytest
```

Let's see how to run the tests defined in the `unittest`, in the file `test_pytest_example.py`.

```
from tdd_example import parameter_tdd


def test_negative():
```

```
    assert parameter_tdd(-1) == 0


def test_zero():
    assert parameter_tdd(0) == 0


def test_five():
    assert parameter_tdd(5) == 25


def test_seven():
    # Note this test is deliberatly set to fail
    assert parameter_tdd(7) == 0


def test_ten():
    assert parameter_tdd(10) == 100


def test_eleven():
    assert parameter_tdd(11) == 100
```

If you compare it with the equivalent code in `test_unittest_example.py`, the code is significantly leaner. When running it with `pytest`, it also shows more detailed, colored information.

```
$ pytest test_unittest_example.py
================= test session starts =================
platform darwin -- Python 3.9.5, pytest-6.2.4, py-1.10.0, pluggy-0.13.1
collected 6 items

test_unittest_example.py ...F..                    [100%]

===================== FAILURES ======================
______________ TestTDDExample.test_seven ______________

self = <test_unittest_example.TestTDDExample testMethod=test_seven>

    def test_seven(self):
>       self.assertEqual(parameter_tdd(7), 0)
```

```
E       AssertionError: 49 != 0

test_unittest_example.py:17: AssertionError
=============== short test summary info ===============
FAILED test_unittest_example.py::TestTDDExample::test_seven
============= 1 failed, 5 passed in 0.10s =============
```

As with unittest, we can see more information with -v and run a selection of tests with -k.

```
$ pytest -v test_unittest_example.py
========================= test session starts ==========================
platform darwin -- Python 3.9.5, pytest-6.2.4, py-1.10.0, pluggy-0.13.1
-- /usr/local/opt/python@3.9/bin/python3.9
cachedir: .pytest_cache
collected 6 items

test_unittest_example.py::TestTDDExample::test_eleven PASSED       [16%]
test_unittest_example.py::TestTDDExample::test_five PASSED         [33%]
test_unittest_example.py::TestTDDExample::test_negative PASSED     [50%]
test_unittest_example.py::TestTDDExample::test_seven FAILED        [66%]
test_unittest_example.py::TestTDDExample::test_ten PASSED          [83%]
test_unittest_example.py::TestTDDExample::test_zero PASSED        [100%]

=============================== FAILURES ===============================
______________________ TestTDDExample.test_seven ______________________

self = <test_unittest_example.TestTDDExample testMethod=test_seven>

    def test_seven(self):
>       self.assertEqual(parameter_tdd(7), 0)
E       AssertionError: 49 != 0

test_unittest_example.py:17: AssertionError
====================== short test summary info =======================
FAILED test_unittest_example.py::TestTDDExample::test_seven -
AssertionErr...
===================== 1 failed, 5 passed in 0.08s =====================

$ pytest test_pytest_example.py -v -k test_ten
========================= test session starts ==========================
```

```
platform darwin -- Python 3.9.5, pytest-6.2.4, py-1.10.0, pluggy-0.13.1
-- /usr/local/opt/python@3.9/bin/python3.9
cachedir: .pytest_cache
collected 6 items / 5 deselected / 1 selected

test_pytest_example.py::test_ten PASSED                            [100%]

=================== 1 passed, 5 deselected in 0.02s ===================
```

And it's totally compatible with `unittest` defined tests, which allows you to combine both styles or migrate them.

```
$ pytest test_unittest_example.py
========================= test session starts =========================
platform darwin -- Python 3.9.5, pytest-6.2.4, py-1.10.0, pluggy-0.13.1
collected 6 items

test_unittest_example.py ...F..                                    [100%]

============================== FAILURES ===============================
______________________ TestTDDExample.test_seven ______________________

self = <test_unittest_example.TestTDDExample testMethod=test_seven>

    def test_seven(self):
>       self.assertEqual(parameter_tdd(7), 0)
E       AssertionError: 49 != 0

test_unittest_example.py:17: AssertionError
====================== short test summary info ======================
FAILED test_unittest_example.py::TestTDDExample::test_seven -
AssertionErr...
===================== 1 failed, 5 passed in 0.08s =====================
```

Another great feature of `pytest` is easy autodiscovery to find files that start with `test_` and run inside all the tests. If we try it, pointing at the current directory, we can see it runs both `test_unittest_example.py` and `test_pytest_example.py`.

```
$ pytest .
========================= test session starts =========================
platform darwin -- Python 3.9.5, pytest-6.2.4, py-1.10.0, pluggy-0.13.1
collected 12 items
```

```
test_pytest_example.py ...F..                                          [50%]
test_unittest_example.py ...F..                                       [100%]

================================ FAILURES =================================
_______________________________ test_seven ________________________________

    def test_seven():
        # Note this test is deliberatly set to fail
>       assert parameter_tdd(7) == 0
E       assert 49 == 0
E        +  where 49 = parameter_tdd(7)

test_pytest_example.py:18: AssertionError
______________________ TestTDDExample.test_seven ______________________

self = <test_unittest_example.TestTDDExample testMethod=test_seven>

    def test_seven(self):
>       self.assertEqual(parameter_tdd(7), 0)
E       AssertionError: 49 != 0

test_unittest_example.py:17: AssertionError
======================= short test summary info =======================
FAILED test_pytest_example.py::test_seven - assert 49 == 0
FAILED test_unittest_example.py::TestTDDExample::test_seven -
AssertionErr...
==================== 2 failed, 10 passed in 0.23s =====================
```

We will continue talking about more features of `pytest` during the chapter, but first, we need to go back to how to define tests when the code has dependencies.

Testing external dependencies

When building unit tests, we talked about how it's based around the concept of isolating a unit in the code to test it independently.

This isolation concept is key, as we want to focus on small sections of the code to create small, clear tests. Creating small tests also helps in keeping the tests fast.

In our example above, we tested a purely functional function, `parameter_tdd`, that had no dependencies. It was not using any external library or any other function. But inevitably, at some point, you'll need to test something that depends on something else.

The question in this case is *should the other component be part of the test or not?*

This is not an easy question to answer. Some developers think that all unit tests should be purely about a single function or method, and therefore, any dependency should not be part of the test. But, on a more practical level, there are sometimes pieces of code that form a unit that it's easier to test in conjunction than separately.

For example, think about a function that:

- For values lower than 0, returns zero.
- For values greater than 100, returns 10.
- For values between, it returns the square root of the value. Note that for the edges, it returns the square root of them (0 for 0 and 10 for 100).

This is very similar to the previous function, `parameter_tdd`, but this time we need the help of an external library to produce the square root of a number. Let's take a look at the code.

It's divided into two files. `dependent.py` contains the definition of the function.

```
import math


def parameter_dependent(value):
    if value < 0:
        return 0

    if value <= 100:
        return math.sqrt(value)

    return 10
```

The code is pretty similar to the code in the `parameter_tdd` example. The module `math.sqrt` returns the square root of a number.

And the tests are in `test_dependent.py`.

```
from dependent import parameter_dependent


def test_negative():
    assert parameter_dependent(-1) == 0


def test_zero():
    assert parameter_dependent(0) == 0


def test_twenty_five():
    assert parameter_dependent(25) == 5


def test_hundred():
    assert parameter_dependent(100) == 10


def test_hundred_and_one():
    assert parameter_dependent(101) == 10
```

In this case, we are completely using the external library and testing it at the same time that we are testing our code. For this simple example, this is a perfectly valid option, though that may not be the case for other cases.

The code is available in GitHub at `https://github.com/PacktPublishing/Python-Architecture-Patterns/tree/main/chapter_10_testing_and_tdd`.

For example, the external dependency could be making external HTTP calls that need to be captured to prevent making them while running tests and to have control over the returned values, or other big pieces of functionality that should be tested in isolation.

To detach a function from its dependencies, there are two different approaches. We will show them using `parameter_dependent` as a baseline.

Again, in this case, the tests work perfectly fine with the dependency included, as it's simple and doesn't produce side effects like external calls, etc.

We will see next how to mock the external calls.

Mocking

Mocking is a practice that internally replaces the dependencies, replacing them with fake calls, under the control of the test itself. This way, we can introduce a known response for any external dependency, and not call the actual code.

Internally, mocking is implemented using what is known as *monkey-patching*, which is the dynamic replacement of existing libraries with alternatives. While this can be achieved in different ways in different programming languages, it's especially popular in dynamic languages like Python or Ruby. Monkey-patching can be used for other purposes than testing, though it should be used with care, as it can change the behavior of libraries and can be quite disconcerting for debugging.

To be able to mock the code, in our test code, we need to prepare the mock as part of the Arrange step. There are different libraries to mock calls, but the easiest is to use the `unittest.mock` library included as part of the standard library.

The easiest usage of `mock` is to patch an external library:

```
from unittest.mock import patch
from dependent import parameter_dependent


@patch('math.sqrt')
def test_twenty_five(mock_sqrt):
    mock_sqrt.return_value = 5
    assert parameter_dependent(25) == 5
    mock_sqrt.assert_called_once_with(25)
```

The `patch` decorator intercepts the calls to the defined library, `math.sqrt`, and replaces it with a `mock` object that passes to the function, here called `mock_sqrt`.

This object is a bit special. It basically allows any calls, accesses almost any method or attributes (except predefined ones), and keeps returning a mock object. This makes the mock object something really flexible that will adapt to whatever code surrounds it. When necessary, the returning value can be set calling `.return_value`, as we show in the first line.

We are, in essence, saying that calls to `mock_sqrt` will return the value 5. So, we are preparing the output of the external call, so we can control it.

Finally, we check that we called the mock `mock_sqrt` once, with the input `(25)` using the method `assert_called_once_with`.

In essence, we are:

- Preparing the mock so it replaces `math.sqrt`
- Setting the value that it will return when called
- Checking that the call works as expected
- Double-checking that the mock was called with the right value

For other tests, for example, we can check that the mock was not called, indicating that the external dependence wasn't called.

```
@patch('math.sqrt')
def test_hundred_and_one(mock_sqrt):
    assert parameter_dependent(101) == 10
    mock_sqrt.assert_not_called()
```

There are multiple `assert` functions that allow you to detect how the mock has been used. Some examples:

- The `called` attribute returning `True` or `False` based on whether the mock has been called or not, allowing you to write:

  ```
  assert mock_sqrt.called is True
  ```

- The `call_count` attribute returning the number of times a mock has been called.
- The `assert_called_with()` method to check the number of times that it has been called. It will raise an exception if the last call is not produced in the specified way.

- The `assert_any_call()` method to check whether any of the calls have been produced in the specified way.

With that information, the full file for testing, `test_dependent_mocked_test.py`, will be like this.

```
from unittest.mock import patch
from dependent import parameter_dependent


@patch('math.sqrt')
def test_negative(mock_sqrt):
    assert parameter_dependent(-1) == 0
    mock_sqrt.assert_not_called()


@patch('math.sqrt')
def test_zero(mock_sqrt):
    mock_sqrt.return_value = 0
    assert parameter_dependent(0) == 0
    mock_sqrt.assert_called_once_with(0)


@patch('math.sqrt')
def test_twenty_five(mock_sqrt):
    mock_sqrt.return_value = 5
    assert parameter_dependent(25) == 5
    mock_sqrt.assert_called_with(25)


@patch('math.sqrt')
def test_hundred(mock_sqrt):
    mock_sqrt.return_value = 10
    assert parameter_dependent(100) == 10
    mock_sqrt.assert_called_with(100)


@patch('math.sqrt')
def test_hundred_and_one(mock_sqrt):
    assert parameter_dependent(101) == 10
    mock_sqrt.assert_not_called()
```

If the mock needs to return different values, you can define the `side_effect` attribute of the mock as a list or tuple. `side_effect` is similar to `return_value`, but it has a few differences, as we'll see.

```
@patch('math.sqrt')
def test_multiple_returns_mock(mock_sqrt):
    mock_sqrt.side_effect = (5, 10)
    assert parameter_dependent(25) == 5
    assert parameter_dependent(100) == 10
```

`side_effect` can also be used to produce an exception, if needed.

```
import pytest
from unittest.mock import patch
from dependent import parameter_dependent

@patch('math.sqrt')
def test_exception_raised_mock(mock_sqrt):
    mock_sqrt.side_effect = ValueError('Error on the external library')
    with pytest.raises(ValueError):
        parameter_dependent(25)
```

The `with` section asserts that the expected `Exception` is raised in the block. If not, it shows an error.

In `unittest`, checking a raised exception can be done with a similar `with` block.

```
with self.assertRaises(ValueError):

    parameter_dependent(25)
```

Mocking is not the only way to handle dependencies for tests. We will see a different approach next.

Dependency injection

While mocking replaces the dependency without the original code noticing, by patching it externally, dependency injection is a technique to make that dependency explicit when calling the function under test, so it can be replaced with a testing substitute.

In essence, it's a way of designing the code that makes dependencies explicit by requiring them as input parameters.

Dependency injection, while useful for testing, is not only aimed at that. By adding the dependencies explicitly, it also reduces the need for a function to know how to initialize a particular dependency, instead relying on the interface of the dependency. It creates a separation between "initializing" a dependency (which should be taken care of externally) and "using" it (which is the only part that the dependent code will do). This differentiation will become clearer later when we see an OOP example.

Let's see how this changes the code under test.

```
def parameter_dependent(value, sqrt_func):
    if value < 0:
        return 0

    if value <= 100:
        return sqrt_func(value)

    return 10
```

Notice how now the `sqrt` function is an input parameter.

If we want to use the `parameter_dependent` function in a normal scenario, we will have to produce the dependency, for example.

```
import math

def test_good_dependency():
    assert parameter_dependent(25, math.sqrt) == 5
```

And if we want to perform tests, we can do it by replacing the `math.sqrt` function with a specific function, and then using it. For example:

```
def test_twenty_five():

    def good_dependency(number):
        return 5

    assert parameter_dependent(25, good_dependency) == 5
```

We can also provoke an error if calling the dependency to ensure that in some tests the dependency is not used, for example.

```
def test_negative():

    def bad_dependency(number):
        raise Exception('Function called')

    assert parameter_dependent(-1, bad_dependency) == 0
```

Note how this approach is more explicit than mocking. The code to test becomes, in essence, totally functional as it doesn't have external dependencies.

Dependency injection in OOP

Dependency injection can also be used with OOP. In this case, we can start with code that is like this.

```
class Writer:

    def __init__(self):
        self.path = settings.WRITER_PATH

    def write(self, filename, data):
        with open(self.path + filename, 'w') as fp:
            fp.write(data)



class Model:

    def __init__(self, data):
        self.data = data
        self.filename = settings.MODEL_FILE
        self.writer = Writer()

    def save(self):
        self.writer.write(self.filename, self.data)
```

As we can see, the settings class stores different elements that are required on where the data will be stored. The model receives some data and then saves it. The code in operation will require minimal initialization.

```
model = Model('test')
model.save()
```

The model receives some data and then saves it. The code in operation requires minimal initialization, but at the same time, it's not explicit.

To use dependency injection principles, the code will need to be written in this way:

```
class WriterInjection:

    def __init__(self, path):
        self.path = path

    def write(self, filename, data):
        with open(self.path + filename, 'w') as fp:
            fp.write(data)


class ModelInjection:

    def __init__(self, data, filename, writer):
        self.data = data
        self.filename = filename
        self.writer = writer

    def save(self):
        self.writer.write(self.filename, self.data)
```

In this case, every value that is a dependency is provided explicitly. In the definition of the code, the settings module is not present anywhere, but instead, that will be specified when the class is instantiated. The code will now need to define the configuration directly.

```
writer = WriterInjection('./')
model = ModelInjection('test', 'model_injection.txt', writer)
model.save()
```

We can compare how to test both cases, as seen in the file `test_dependency_injection_test.py`. The first test is mocking, as we saw before, the `write` method of the `Writer` class to assert that it has been called correctly.

```
@patch('class_injection.Writer.write')
def test_model(mock_write):

    model = Model('test_model')
    model.save()

    mock_write.assert_called_with('model.txt', 'test_model')
```

Compared to that, the dependency injection example doesn't require a mock through monkey-patching. It just creates its own `Writer` that simulates the interface.

```
def test_modelinjection():

    EXPECTED_DATA = 'test_modelinjection'
    EXPECTED_FILENAME = 'model_injection.txt'

    class MockWriter:

        def write(self, filename, data):
            self.filename = filename
            self.data = data

    writer = MockWriter()
    model = ModelInjection(EXPECTED_DATA, EXPECTED_FILENAME,
                           writer)
    model.save()

    assert writer.data == EXPECTED_DATA
    assert writer.filename == EXPECTED_FILENAME
```

This second style is more verbose, but it shows some of the differences when writing code in this way:

- No monkey-patching mock is required. Monkey-patching can be quite fragile, as it's meddling with internal code that's not supposed to be exposed. While in testing this interference is not the same as doing it for regular code running, it's still something that can be messy and have unintended effects, especially if the internal code changes in some unforeseen way.

Keep in mind that mocks will likely involve, at some point, relating to second-level dependencies, which can start having strange or complicated effects requiring you to spend time handling that extra complexity.

- The way of writing the code is different in itself. Code produced with dependency injection is, as we've seen, more modular and composed of smaller elements. This tends to create smaller and more combinable modules that play along together, with fewer unknown dependencies, as they are always explicit.
- Be careful, though, as this requires a certain amount of discipline and mental framing to produce truly loosely coupled modules. If this is not considered when designing the interfaces, the resulting code will instead be artificially divided, resulting in tightly coupled code across different modules. Developing this discipline requires certain training; do not expect it to come naturally to all developers.
- The code can sometimes be more difficult to debug, as the configuration will be separated from the rest of the code, sometimes making it difficult to understand the flow of the code. The complexity can be produced at the interaction of classes, which may be more difficult to understand and test. Typically, the upfront effort to develop code in this style is a bit greater as well.

Dependency injection is a very popular technique in certain software circles and programming languages. Mocking is more difficult in less dynamic languages than Python, and also different programming languages have their own sets of ideas on how to structure code. For example, dependency injection is very popular in Java, where there are specific tools to work in this style.

Advanced pytest

While we've described the basic functionalities for `pytest`, we barely scratched the surface in terms of the number of possibilities that it presents to help generate testing code.

Pytest is a big and comprehensive tool. It is worth learning how to use it. Here, we will only scratch the surface. Be sure to check the official documentation at `https://docs.pytest.org/`.

Without being exhaustive, we will see some useful possibilities of the tool.

Grouping tests

Sometimes it is useful to group tests together so they are related to specific things, like modules, or to run them in unison. The simplest way of grouping tests together is to join them into a single class.

For example, going back to the test examples before, we could structure tests into two classes, as we see in `test_group_classes.py`.

```
from tdd_example import parameter_tdd


class TestEdgesCases():

    def test_negative(self):
        assert parameter_tdd(-1) == 0

    def test_zero(self):
        assert parameter_tdd(0) == 0

    def test_ten(self):
        assert parameter_tdd(10) == 100

    def test_eleven(self):
        assert parameter_tdd(11) == 100


class TestRegularCases():

    def test_five(self):
        assert parameter_tdd(5) == 25

    def test_seven(self):
        assert parameter_tdd(7) == 49
```

This is an easy way to divide tests and allows you to run them independently:

```
$ pytest -v test_group_classes.py
======================== test session starts ========================
platform darwin -- Python 3.9.5, pytest-6.2.4, py-1.10.0, pluggy-0.13.1
-- /usr/local/opt/python@3.9/bin/python3.9
collected 6 items
```

```
test_group_classes.py::TestEdgesCases::test_negative PASSED       [16%]
test_group_classes.py::TestEdgesCases::test_zero PASSED           [33%]
test_group_classes.py::TestEdgesCases::test_ten PASSED            [50%]
test_group_classes.py::TestEdgesCases::test_eleven PASSED         [66%]
test_group_classes.py::TestRegularCases::test_five PASSED         [83%]
test_group_classes.py::TestRegularCases::test_seven PASSED       [100%]

========================= 6 passed in 0.02s ==========================

$ pytest -k TestRegularCases -v test_group_classes.py
========================= test session starts ========================
platform darwin -- Python 3.9.5, pytest-6.2.4, py-1.10.0, pluggy-0.13.1
-- /usr/local/opt/python@3.9/bin/python3.9
collected 6 items / 4 deselected / 2 selected

test_group_classes.py::TestRegularCases::test_five PASSED         [50%]
test_group_classes.py::TestRegularCases::test_seven PASSED       [100%]

================== 2 passed, 4 deselected in 0.02s ===================
$ pytest -v test_group_classes.py::TestRegularCases
========================= test session starts ========================
platform darwin -- Python 3.9.5, pytest-6.2.4, py-1.10.0, pluggy-0.13.1
-- /usr/local/opt/python@3.9/bin/python3.9
cachedir: .pytest_cache
rootdir: /Users/jaime/Dropbox/Packt/architecture_book/chapter_09_
testing_and_tdd/advanced_pytest
plugins: celery-4.4.7
collected 2 items

test_group_classes.py::TestRegularCases::test_five PASSED         [50%]
test_group_classes.py::TestRegularCases::test_seven PASSED       [100%]

========================= 2 passed in 0.02s ==========================
```

Another possibility is to use markers. Markers are indicators that can be added through a decorator in the tests, for example, in `test_markers.py`.

```
import pytest
from tdd_example import parameter_tdd

@pytest.mark.edge
```

```
def test_negative():
    assert parameter_tdd(-1) == 0

@pytest.mark.edge
def test_zero():
    assert parameter_tdd(0) == 0

def test_five():
    assert parameter_tdd(5) == 25

def test_seven():
    assert parameter_tdd(7) == 49

@pytest.mark.edge
def test_ten():
    assert parameter_tdd(10) == 100

@pytest.mark.edge
def test_eleven():
    assert parameter_tdd(11) == 100
```

See that we are defining a decorator, `@pytest.mark.edge`, on all the tests that checks the edge of the values.

If we execute the tests, we can use the parameter `-m` to run only the ones with a certain tag.

```
$ pytest -m edge -v test_markers.py
======================== test session starts ========================
platform darwin -- Python 3.9.5, pytest-6.2.4, py-1.10.0, pluggy-0.13.1
-- /usr/local/opt/python@3.9/bin/python3.9
collected 6 items / 2 deselected / 4 selected

test_markers.py::test_negative PASSED                              [25%]
test_markers.py::test_zero PASSED                                  [50%]
test_markers.py::test_ten PASSED                                   [75%]
test_markers.py::test_eleven PASSED                               [100%]

========================= warnings summary =========================
test_markers.py:5
```

```
  test_markers.py:5: PytestUnknownMarkWarning: Unknown pytest.mark.edge
- is this a typo?  You can register custom marks to avoid this warning
- for details, see https://docs.pytest.org/en/stable/mark.html
    @pytest.mark.edge

test_markers.py:10
...

-- Docs: https://docs.pytest.org/en/stable/warnings.html
============ 4 passed, 2 deselected, 4 warnings in 0.02s =============
```

The warning `PytestUnknownMarkWarning: Unknown pytest.mark.edge` is produced if the marker edge is not registered.

Be aware that the GitHub code includes the `pytest.ini` code. You won't see the warning if the `pytest.ini` file is present, for example, if you clone the whole repo.

This is very useful for finding typos, like accidentally writing `egde` or similar. To avoid this warning, you'll need to add a `pytest.ini` config file with the definition of the markers, like this.

```
[pytest]
markers =
       edge: tests related to edges in intervals
```

Now, running the tests shows no warning.

```
$ pytest -m edge -v test_markers.py
========================= test session starts ==========================
platform darwin -- Python 3.9.5, pytest-6.2.4, py-1.10.0, pluggy-0.13.1
-- /usr/local/opt/python@3.9/bin/python3.9
cachedir: .pytest_cache
rootdir: /Users/jaime/Dropbox/Packt/architecture_book/chapter_09_
testing_and_tdd/advanced_pytest, configfile: pytest.ini
plugins: celery-4.4.7
collected 6 items / 2 deselected / 4 selected

test_markers.py::test_negative PASSED                            [25%]
test_markers.py::test_zero PASSED                                [50%]
```

```
test_markers.py::test_ten PASSED                                        [75%]
test_markers.py::test_eleven PASSED                                     [100%]

================== 4 passed, 2 deselected in 0.02s ===================
```

Note that markers can be used across the full test suite, including multiple files. That allows for making markers to identify common patterns across the tests, for example, creating a quick test suite with the most important tests to run with the marker `basic`.

There are also some predefined markers with some built-in features. The most common ones are `skip` (which will skip the test) and `xfail` (which will reverse the test, meaning that it expects it to fail).

Using fixtures

The use of fixtures is the preferred way to set up tests in `pytest`. A fixture, in essence, is a context created to set up a test.

Fixtures are used as input for the test functions, so they can be set up and create specific environments for the test to be created.

For example, let's take a look at a simple function that counts the number of occurrences of a character in a string.

```
def count_characters(char_to_count, string_to_count):
    number = 0
    for char in string_to_count:
        if char == char_to_count:
            number += 1

    return number
```

That's a pretty simple loop that iterates through the string and counts the matching characters.

This is equivalent to using the function `.count()` for a string, but this is included to present a working function. It could be refactored afterward!

A regular test to cover the functionalities could be as follows.

```
def test_counting():
    assert count_characters('a', 'Barbara Ann') == 3
```

Pretty straightforward. Now let's see how we can define a fixture to define a setup, in case we want to replicate it.

```
import pytest

@pytest.fixture()
def prepare_string():
    # Setup the values to return
    prepared_string = 'Ba, ba, ba, Barbara Ann'

    # Return the value
    yield prepared_string

    # Teardown any value
    del prepared_string
```

First of all, the fixture is decorated with `pytest.fixture` to mark it as such. A fixture is divided into three steps:

- **Setup**: Here, we simply defined a string, but this will probably be the biggest part, where the values are prepared.
- **Return the value**: If we use the `yield` functionality, we will be able to go to the next step; if not, the fixture will finish here.
- **Teardown and clean up values**: Here, we simply delete the variable as an example, though this will happen automatically later.

Later, we will see a more complex fixture. Here, we are just presenting the concept.

Defining the fixture this way will allow us to reuse it easily in different test functions, just using the name as the input parameter.

```
def test_counting_fixture(prepare_string):
    assert count_characters('a', prepare_string) == 6


def test_counting_fixture2(prepare_string):
    assert count_characters('r', prepare_string) == 2
```

Note how the `prepare_string` parameter is automatically providing the value that we defined with `yield`. If we run the tests, we can see the effect. Even more, we can use the parameter `--setup-show` to see the setup and tear down all of the fixtures.

```
$ pytest -v test_fixtures.py -k counting_fixture --setup-show
======================== test session starts ========================
platform darwin -- Python 3.9.5, pytest-6.2.4, py-1.10.0, pluggy-0.13.1
-- /usr/local/opt/python@3.9/bin/python3.9
plugins: celery-4.4.7
collected 3 items / 1 deselected / 2 selected

test_fixtures.py::test_counting_fixture
        SETUP    F prepare_string
        test_fixtures.py::test_counting_fixture (fixtures used:
prepare_string)PASSED
        TEARDOWN F prepare_string
test_fixtures.py::test_counting_fixture2
        SETUP    F prepare_string
        test_fixtures.py::test_counting_fixture2 (fixtures used:
prepare_string)PASSED
        TEARDOWN F prepare_string

=================== 2 passed, 1 deselected in 0.02s ===================
```

This fixture was very simple and did not do anything that couldn't be done defining the string, but fixtures can be used to connect to a database or prepare files, taking into account that they can clean them up at the end.

For example, complicating the same example a bit, instead of counting from a string, it should count from a file, so the function needs to open a file, read it, and count the characters. The function will be like this.

```
def count_characters_from_file(char_to_count, file_to_count):
    '''
    Open a file and count the characters in the text contained
    in the file
    '''
    number = 0
    with open(file_to_count) as fp:
        for line in fp:
            for char in line:
                if char == char_to_count:
                    number += 1

    return number
```

The fixture should then create a file, return it, and then remove it as part of the teardown. Let's take a look at it.

```
import os
import time
import pytest


@pytest.fixture()
def prepare_file():
    data = [
        'Ba, ba, ba, Barbara Ann',
        'Ba, ba, ba, Barbara Ann',
        'Barbara Ann',
        'take my hand',
    ]
    filename = f'./test_file_{time.time()}.txt'
    # Setup the values to return
    with open(filename, 'w') as fp:
        for line in data:
```

```
            fp.write(line)

    # Return the value
    yield filename

    # Delete the file as teardown
    os.remove(filename)
```

Note that in the filename, we define the name adding the timestamp when it's generated. This means that each of the files that will be generated by this fixture will be unique.

```
    filename = f'./test_file_{time.time()}.txt'
```

The file then gets created and the data is written.

```
    with open(filename, 'w') as fp:
        for line in data:
            fp.write(line)
```

The name of the file, which, as we've seen, is unique, gets yielded. Finally, the file is deleted in the teardown.

The tests are similar to the previous ones, as most of the complexity is stored in the fixture.

```
def test_counting_fixture(prepare_file):
    assert count_characters_from_file('a', prepare_file) == 17


def test_counting_fixture2(prepare_file):
    assert count_characters_from_file('r', prepare_file) == 6
```

When running it, we see it works as expected, and we can check that the teardown step deletes the testing files after each test.

```
$ pytest -v test_fixtures2.py
========================= test session starts =========================
platform darwin -- Python 3.9.5, pytest-6.2.4, py-1.10.0, pluggy-0.13.1
-- /usr/local/opt/python@3.9/bin/python3.9
collected 2 items
```

```
test_fixtures2.py::test_counting_fixture PASSED                        [50%]
test_fixtures2.py::test_counting_fixture2 PASSED                       [100%]

========================== 2 passed in 0.02s ==========================
```

Fixtures don't need to be defined in the same file. They can also be stored in a special file called `conftest.py`, which will automatically be shared by `pytest` across all the tests.

Fixtures can also be combined, they can be set to be used automatically, and there are already built-in fixtures to work with temporal data and directories or capture output. There are also a lot of plugins for useful fixtures in PyPI, installable as third-party modules, covering functionality like connecting to databases or interacting with other external resources. Be sure to check the Pytest documentation and to search before implementing your own fixture to see if you can leverage an already existing module: `https://docs.pytest.org/en/latest/explanation/fixtures.html#about-fixtures`.

In this chapter, we only scratched the surface in terms of the possibilities of `pytest`. It is a fantastic tool and one that I encourage you to learn about. It will pay off greatly to efficiently run tests and design them in the best possible way. Testing is a critical part of a project and it's one of the development stages where developers spend most of their time.

Summary

In this chapter, we went through the whys and hows of tests to describe how a good testing strategy is required to produce high-quality software and prevent problems once the code is in use by customers.

We started by describing the general principles behind testing, how to make tests that provide more value than their cost, and the different levels of testing to ensure this. We saw the three main levels of tests, which we called unit tests (parts of a single component), system tests (the whole system), and integration tests in the middle (a whole component or several components, but not all).

We continued by describing different strategies to ensure that our tests are great ones, and how to structure them using the Arrange-Act-Assert pattern, for ease of writing and understanding them after they are written.

Later, we described in detail the principles behind Test-Driven Development, a technique that puts tests at the center of development, which mandates writing the tests before the code, working in small increments, and running the tests over and over to create a good test suite that protects against unexpected behavior. We also analyzed the limits and caveats of working in a TDD fashion and provided an example of what the flow looks like.

We continued by presenting ways of creating unit tests in Python, both using the standard `unittest` module and by introducing the more powerful `pytest`. We also presented a section with advanced usage of `pytest` to show a bit of what this great third-party module is capable of.

We described how to test external dependencies, something that is critically important when writing unit tests to isolate functionality. We also described how to mock dependencies and how to work under the dependency injection principles.

Join our book's Discord space

Join the book's Discord workspace for a monthly *Ask me Anything* session with the author: `https://packt.link/PythonArchitechture`

11
Package Management

When working in complex systems, especially in microservices or similar architectures, there is sometimes a need to share code so it's available at different, unconnected parts of the system. That's normally code that will help to abstract some functions, which can vary greatly, from security purposes (for example, calculating a signature in a way that's understood by other systems that will have to verify it), to connecting to databases or external APIs, or even helping to monitor the system consistently.

Instead of reinventing the wheel each time, we can reuse the same code multiple times to be certain that it's properly tested and validated, and consistent throughout the entire system. Some modules may be interesting to share not only across the organization but even outside it, creating a standard module others can take advantage of.

Others have done that before, and a lot of common use cases, such as connecting to existing databases, using network resources, accessing OS features, understanding files in all kinds of formats, calculating common algorithms and formulas, in all kinds of domains, creating and operating AI models, and a long list of other cases besides, are available.

To enhance the sharing and utilization of all those abilities, modern programming languages have their own ways of creating and sharing packages, so the usefulness of the language multiplies greatly.

In this chapter, we will discuss the use of packages, mostly from a Python perspective, covering when and how to decide to create a package. We will explore the different options available, from a simple structure to packages that include code compiled so that it can be optimized for specific tasks.

In this chapter, we'll cover the following topics:

- The creation of a new package
- Trivial packaging in Python
- The Python packaging ecosystem
- Creating a package
- Cython
- Python package with binary code
- Uploading your package to PyPI
- Creating your own private index

Let's start by defining what code could be a candidate to create a package.

The creation of a new package

In any software, there will be snippets of code that could be shared across different parts of the code. When working with small, monolithic applications, this can be as easy as creating some internal modules or functions that can share functionality by calling it directly.

Over time, this common function or functions could be grouped together under a module to clarify that they are to be used across the application.

Avoid the temptation to use the name `utils` for a module with code expected to be used in different positions. While this is very common, it is also not very descriptive and a bit lazy. How does someone know if a function is in the `utils` module? Instead of that, try to use a descriptive name.

If it's not possible, divide it into submodules, so you can create something like `utils.communication` or `utils.math` to avoid this effect.

This will work fine up to a certain size. Some of the problems that can arise as the code grows and becomes more complex are as follows:

- Create a more generic API to interact with the module, aimed at greater flexibility in terms of module utilization. This can involve creating a more defensive style of programming, to be sure that the module is used as expected and return proper errors.

- Specific documentation needs to be provided for the module so that developers who are not familiar with the module are able to use it.
- Ownership of the module may need to be clarified and its own maintainers specified. This can take the form of a stricter code review before changing the code, with some developer or developers designated as the point of contact for the module.
- The most critical one, the functionality of the module, is required to be present in two or more independent services or code bases. If this happens, instead of just copying/pasting the code across different code bases, it makes sense to create an independent module that can be imported. This could be a deliberate option upfront, to standardize certain operations (for example, produce and verify signed messages across multiple services) or it could be an afterthought following successful implementation of the functionality in one code base that it could be handy to have in other services of the system. For example, instrumenting the communication messages to you generates a log. This log can be useful in other services, so, from the original service, it gets migrated to others.

In general, the module starts getting its own entity, and not only as a shared location for incorporating code that is going to be shared. At that time, it starts to make sense to treat it as an independent library more than a module attached to a particular code base.

Once the decision to create some code as an independent package has been taken, several aspects should be considered:

- As we've seen before, the most important is the ownership of the new package. Packages exist in the boundaries between different teams and groups, as they are used by different ones. Be sure to provide clear ownership regarding any package to be sure that the team responsible for it is reachable, both for any possible inquiries and for setting its own maintenance.
- Any new package will require time to develop new features and adjustments, especially as the package is in use, probably stretching its limits as it's used in multiple services and in more ways. Be sure to take this into account and adjust the load of the team responsible accordingly. This will be very dependent on how mature the package is and how many new features are required.
- In the same way, be sure to budget time to maintain the package. Even if there are no new features, bugs will be detected and other general maintenance, such as updating the dependencies on account of security fixes or compatibility with new OS versions, will need to be continued.

All these elements should be taken into account. In general, it is advisable to create some sort of roadmap where the team responsible can define what the objectives are and a time frame to achieve them.

The bottom line is that a new package is a new project. You need to treat it as such.

We will focus on creating a new package in Python, but the basics are similar when creating other packages in other languages.

Trivial packaging in Python

In Python, it is easy to create a package to be imported by just adding a subdirectory to the code. While this is simple, it can be adequate initially, as the subdirectory can be copied. For example, the code can be added directly to the source control system, or it can even be installed by compressing the code and uncompressing it in place.

This is not a long-term solution, as it won't handle multiple versions, dependencies, and so on, but it can work in some cases as a first step. At least initially, all the code to be packetized needs to be stored in the same subdirectory.

The structure of the code for a module in Python can be worked out as a subdirectory with a single entry point. For example, when creating a module called `naive_package` with the following structure:

```
└── naive_package
    ├── __init__.py
    ├── module.py
    └── submodule
        ├── __init__.py
        └── submodule.py
```

We can see that the module contains a submodule, so let's start there. The submodule directory contains two files, the `submodule.py` file with the code, and an empty `__init__.py` file to allow the other file to be imported, as we will see later.

`__init__.py` is a special Python file that indicates that the directory contains Python code and can be imported externally. It symbolizes the directory itself, as we will see later.

The content of `submodule.py` is this example function:

```
def subfunction():
    return 'calling subfunction'
```

The top level is the module itself. We have the `module.py` file, which defines the `some_function` function that calls the submodule:

```
from .submodule.submodule import subfunction


def some_function():
    result = subfunction()
    return f'some function {result}'
```

The `import` line has a detail, a dot in the form of the submodule located in the same directory. This is specific syntax in Python 3 for being more precise when importing. Without the dot, it will try to import from the library instead.

You can learn more about relative imports in PEP-328, which describes it, here: `https://www.python.org/dev/peps/pep-0328/`. **PEPs** (**Python Enhancement Proposals**) are documents describing new features relating to the Python language or information related to the community. It is the official channel for proposing changes and advancing the language.

The rest of the function calls `subfunction` and combines the result to return a string of text.

The `__init__.py` file, in this case, is not empty, but instead, it imports the `some_function` function:

```
from .module import some_function
```

Note again the relative `import` as indicated by the preceding dot. This allows having the `some_function` function available as part of the top level of the `naive_package` module.

We can now create a file to call the module. We'll write the `call_naive_package.py` file, which needs to be at the same level as the `native_package` directory:

```
from naive_package import some_function


print(some_function())
```

This file just calls the module-defined function and prints the result:

```
$ python3 call_naive_package.py
some function calling subfunction
```

This method of handling a module to be shared is not recommended, but this small module can help us understand how to create a package and what the structure of a module is. The first step to detaching a module and creating an independent package will be to create a single subdirectory that has a clear API, including clear entry points to use it.

But to get a better solution, we will need to be able to create a full Python package from there. Let's take a look at what that means exactly.

The Python packaging ecosystem

Python has a very active ecosystem of third-party open source packages that covers a wide variety of topics and enables the power of any Python program to be enhanced. You can take advantage of installing them by using `pip`, which is installed automatically for any new Python install.

For example, to install the package named `requests`, a package allowing the compilation of easier and more powerful HTTP requests, the command is:

```
$ pip3 install requests
```

`pip` searches in the Python Package Index automatically to see whether the package is available and if it is, it will download it and install it.

Note that the `pip` command could take the form of `pip3`. This depends on the installation of Python in your system. We will use them indistinctly.

We will see more detailed usage on `pip` later in the chapter, but first, we need to discuss the main source where the packages are downloaded.

PyPI

The Python Package Index (PyPI, normally pronounced as *Pie-P-I*, as opposed to *Pie-Pie*) is the official source of packages in Python and can be checked at `https://pypi.org`:

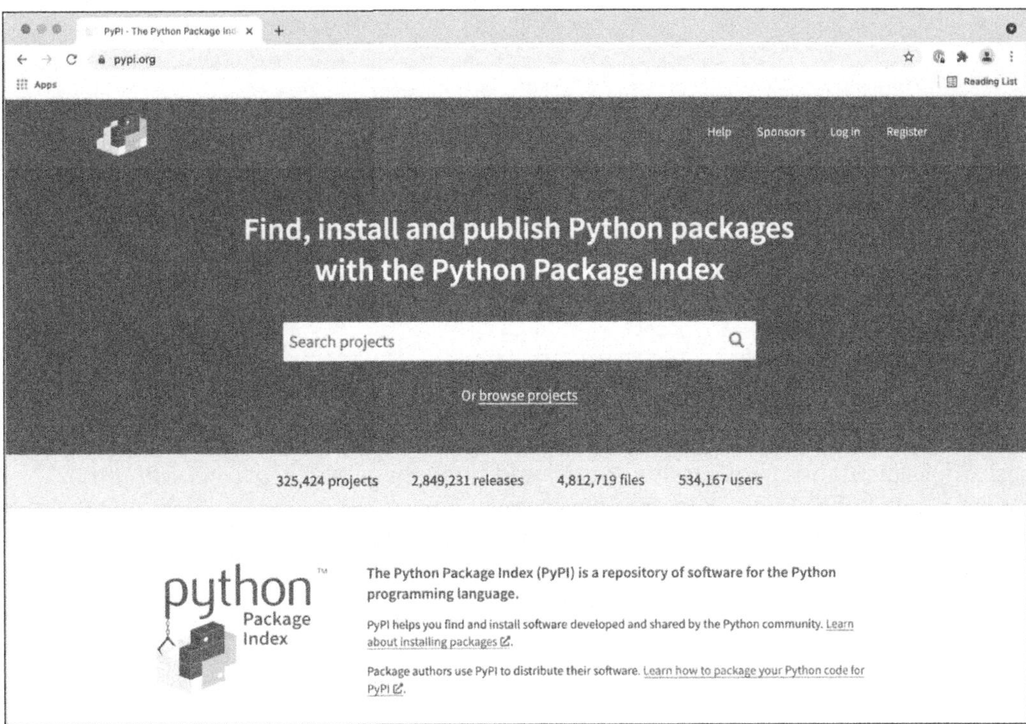

Figure 11.1: pypi.org main page

On the PyPI web page, the search enables specific packages to be found along with useful information, including available packages with partial matches. They can also be filtered.

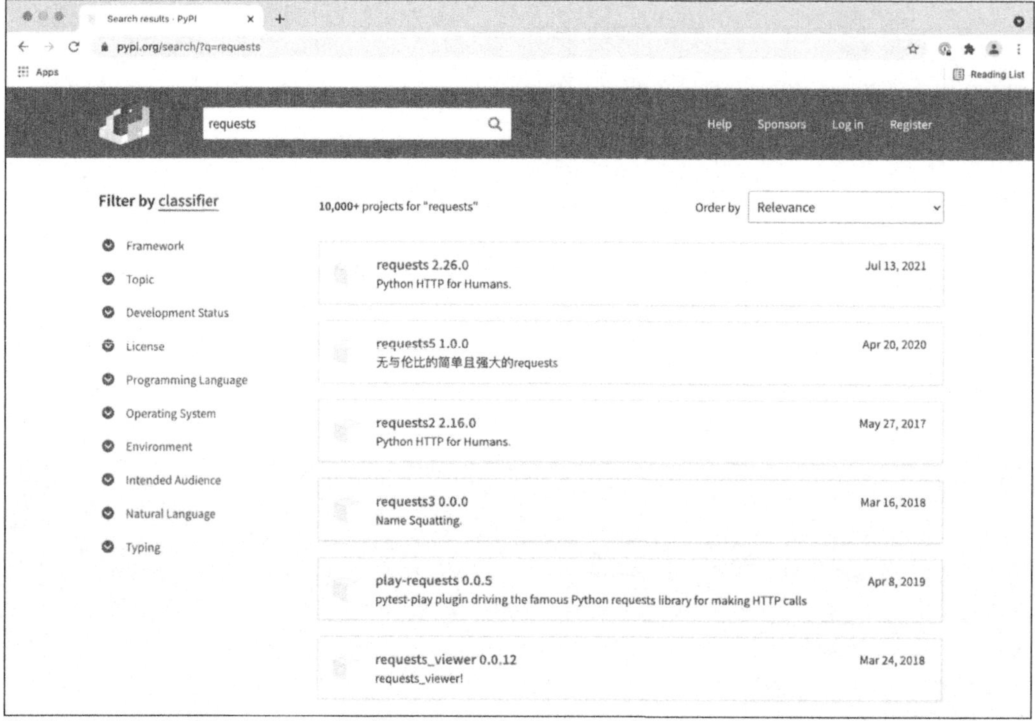

Figure 11.2: Searching for packages

Once the individual package is specified, more information can be found regarding brief documentation, links to the source and home page of the project, and other similar kinds of licenses or maintainers.

The home page and documentation page are very significant for big packages, as they will include much more information about how to use the package. Smaller packages will normally only include the documentation on this page, but it's always worth checking their page for the source as it may link to a GitHub page with details about bugs and the possibility of submitting patches or reports.

The page for `requests` looks like this at the time of writing this book:

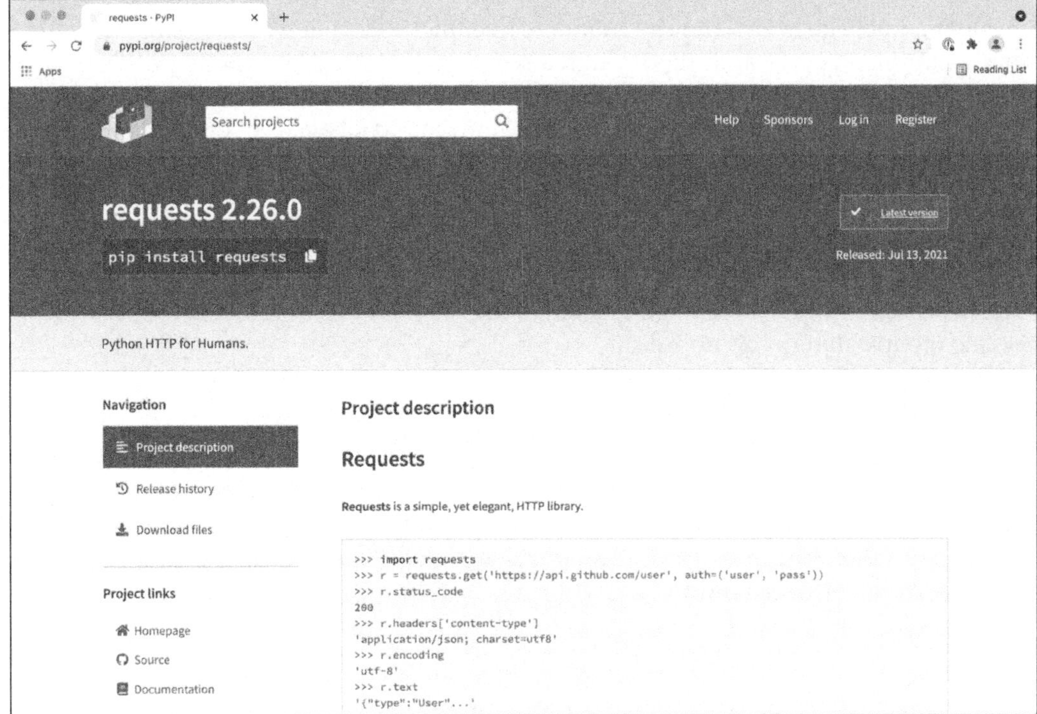

Figure 11.3: Detailed info about a module

Searching directly in PyPI can help locate some interesting modules, and in some cases, will be quite straightforward, such as finding a module to connect to a database (for example, searching by the name of the database). This, though, normally involves a significant amount of trial and error, as the name may not be indicative of how good a module will be for your use case.

Spending some time on the internet searching for the best module for a use case is a great idea and it will improve the chances of finding the right package for your use case.

A great source of knowledge in this case is StackOverflow (`https://stackoverflow.com/`), which contains a lot of questions and answers that can be used to ascertain interesting modules. A general Google search will also help.

In any case, given the number of available packages for Python, of varying quality and maturity, it's always worthwhile setting aside some time to research alternatives.

Packages are not curated in any way by `pypi.org`, as it's publicly available to anyone to submit their packages, although malicious ones will be eliminated. How popular a package is will require more indirect methods, such as searching how many downloads or searching through a searcher online to see whether other projects are using it. Ultimately, it will require the performance of some Proof-of-Concept programs to analyze whether the candidate packages cover all the required functionalities.

Virtual environments

The next element in the packaging chain is the creation of virtual environments to isolate the installation of modules.

When dealing with installing packages, using the default environments in the system leads to the packages being installed there. This means that the general installation of the Python interpreter will be affected by this.

This can lead to problems, as you may install packages that have side effects when using the Python interpreter for other purposes, as dependencies in the packages may interfere with each other.

For example, if the same machine has a Python program that requires the `package1` package and another Python program that requires `package2`, and they are both incompatible, that will create a conflict. Installing both `package1` and `package2` won't be possible.

Note that this can also happen through version incompatibility, especially in the dependencies of the packages, or in the dependencies of dependencies. For example, `package1` requires dependency version 5 to be installed, and `package2` requires dependency version 6 or higher. They won't be able to run in conjunction with one another.

The solution to this problem is to create two different environments, so each package and its dependencies are stored independently – independently from each other, but also independently from the system Python interpreter, so it won't affect any possible system activity that depends on the Python system interpreter.

To create a new virtual environment, you can use the standard module **`venv`**, included in all installations of Python 3 after 3.3:

```
$ python3 -m venv venv
```

This creates the venv subdirectory, which contains the virtual environment. The environment can be activated using the following `source` command:

Please note that we have used a name for the created virtual environment, `venv`, which is the same as the name of the module. That's not necessary. Virtual environments can be created with any name. Be sure to use a name that's descriptive in your use case.

```
$ source ./venv/bin/activate
(venv) $ which python
./venv/bin/python
(venv) $ which pip
./venv/bin/python
```

You can see that the `python` interpreter and `pip` that get executed is the one located in the virtual environment, and not the system one, and also the indication in the prompt that the virtual environment, `venv`, is active.

The virtual environment also has its own library, so any installed packages will be stored here, and not in the system environment.

The virtual environment can be deactivated by calling the `deactivate` command. You can see that the `(venv)` indication disappears.

Once in the virtual environment, any call to `pip` will install the packages in the virtual environment, so they are independent of any other environment. Each program can then be executed within its own virtual environment.

In cases where the virtual environment cannot be activated directly through the command line and the command needs to be executed directly, for example, for cronjob cases, you can call the `python` interpreter directly in the virtual environment by its full path, such as `/path/to/venv/python/your_script.py`.

With a proper environment, we can use pip to install the different dependencies.

Preparing an environment

Creating a virtual environment is the first stage, but we need to install all dependencies for our software.

To be able to replicate the environment in all situations, the best is to create a requirements file that defines all dependencies that should be installed. `pip` allows working with a file, normally called `requirements.txt`, to install dependencies.

This is an excellent way of creating a replicable environment that can be started from scratch when necessary.

For example, let's take a look at the following `requirements.txt` file:

```
requests==2.26.0
pint==0.17
```

The file can be downloaded from GitHub at `https://github.com/PacktPublishing/Python-Architecture-Patterns/blob/main/chapter_11_package_management/requirements.txt`.

Note the format is `package==version`. This specifies the exact version to use for the package, which is the recommended way of installing dependencies. That avoids the problem of using just `package`, which will install the latest version, and which can lead to an upgrade that's not planned, which may break compatibility.

Other options, such as `package>=version`, to specify a minimum version are available.

The file can be installed in the virtual environment (remember to activate it) using the following command:

```
(venv) $ pip install -r requirements.txt
```

After that, all the specified requirements will be installed in the environment.

Note that the dependencies of your specified dependencies may not be totally pinned down to specific versions. This is because the dependencies have their own definition, which can produce unknown upgrades on second-level dependencies when a new package is delivered.

To avoid having that problem, you can create an initial installation with your first-level dependencies, and then obtain all the dependencies that have been installed with the `pip freeze` command:

```
(venv) $ pip freeze
certifi==2021.5.30
chardet==3.0.4
charset-normalizer==2.0.4
idna==2.10
packaging==21.0
Pint==0.17
pyparsing==2.4.7
requests==2.26.0
urllib3==1.26.6
```

You can use the output to update the `requirements.txt` directly, so the next installation will have all the second-level dependencies also pinned down.

Note that adding new requirements will require the same process to be generated, to install first, then run `freeze`, and then update the `requirements.txt` file with the ouput.

A note on containers

When working in a container manner, the distinction between the system interpreter and the program interpreter is more diluted, as the container has its own OS wrapped, thereby enforcing a strong separation.

In the traditional way of deploying services, they are installed and run in the same server, making it necessary to keep a separation between the interpreter due to the restrictions that we talked about previously.

By using containers, we have already created a wrap around each of the services into their own OS filesystem, which means that we can skip the creation of a virtual environment. The container acts as a virtual environment in this case, enforcing separation between different containers.

As we've discussed previously in *Chapter 8, Advanced Event-Driven Structures*, when talking about containers, each container should serve only a single service, coordinating different containers to generate different servers. That way, it eliminates the case of having to share the same interpreter.

This means that we can ease some of the restrictions that we would normally impose in a traditional setting, and care just about one environment, being able to take less care about polluting the system environment. There's only one environment, so we can play with it more freely. If we need more services or environments, we can always create more containers.

Python packages

A Python module ready to use is, in essence, a subdirectory with certain Python code. This subdirectory gets installed in the proper library's subdirectoy, and the interpreter searches in this subdirectory. The directory is called `site-packages`.

This subdirectory is available in the virtual environment, if you are using one. You can check the following subdirectory: `venv/lib/python3.9/site-packages/`.

To distribute it, the subdirectory is packaged into two different files, either `Egg` files or `Wheel` files. Importantly, though, `pip` can only install `Wheel` files.

Source packages can also be created. In this case, the file is a tar file that contains all the code.

`Egg` files are considered deprecated, as their format is older and it's basically a zipped file containing some metadata. `Wheel` files have several advantages:

- They are better defined and allow for more use cases. There's a specific PEP, PEP-427 (`https://www.python.org/dev/peps/pep-0427/`), that defines the format. `Egg` files were never officially defined.
- They can be defined to have better compatibility, allowing the creation of `Wheel` files that are compatible between different versions of Python, including Python 2 and Python 3.
- `Wheel` files can include already compiled binary code. Python allows the inclusion of libraries that are written in C, but these libraries need to target the proper hardware architecture. In `Egg` files, the source files were included and compiled at install time, but that required the proper compilation tools and environment in the installation machine, and this could easily result in compilation issues.

- Instead of that, `Wheel` files can be precompiled with binary files. The `Wheel` file has better-defined compatibility based on hardware architecture and the OS, so the right `Wheel` file will be downloaded and installed, if available. This makes the installation faster, as no compilation needs to be performed in the installation, and removes the need for compilation tools available in the target machine. A `Wheel` file with a source file can also be created to allow its installation in machines not already precompiled, though in this case, it will require a compiler.
- `Wheel` files can be cryptographically signed, while `Eggs` don't support this option. That adds an extra layer to avoid compromised and modified packages.

Right now, the standard for packaging in Python is `Wheel` files, and they should be preferred as a general rule. `Egg` files should be limited to older packages that haven't been upgraded to the new format.

Egg files can be installed with the older `easy_install` script, although this is no longer included in the latest versions of Python. Check the documentation for setup tools on how to use `easy_install`: `https://setuptools.readthedocs.io/en/latest/deprecated/easy_install.html`.

We will see now how to create your own package.

Creating a package

Even if, in most cases, we will use third-party packages, at some point, it is possible that you'll need to create your own package.

To do so, you need to create a `setup.py` file, which is the base of the package, describing what is inside it. Base package code will look like this:

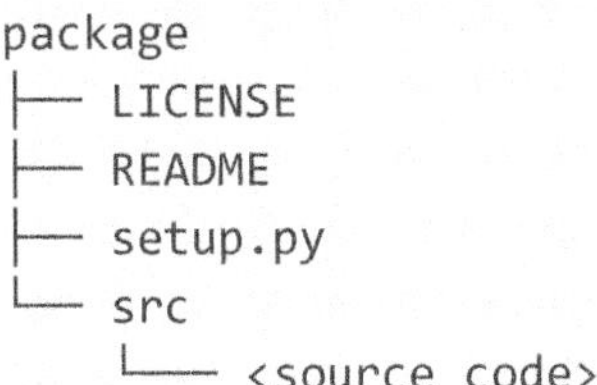

```
package
├── LICENSE
├── README
├── setup.py
└── src
    └─── <source code>
```

The `LICENSE` and `README` files are not mandatory but are good to include for adding information about the package. The `LICENSE` file will be included automatically in the package.

Choosing your own open source license can be difficult. You can use the web (`https://choosealicense.com/`), which shows different options and explains them. We will use the MIT license as an example.

The `README` file is not included, but we will include its content in a full description of the package as part of the build process, as we will see later.

The code of the process is the `setup.py` file. Let's take a look at an example:

```
import setuptools

with open('README') as readme:
    description = readme.read()


setuptools.setup(
    name='wheel-package',
    version='0.0.1',
    author='you',
    author_email='me@you.com',
    description='an example of a package',
    url='http://site.com',
    long_description=description,
    classifiers=[
        'Programming Language :: Python :: 3',
        'Operating System :: OS Independent',
        'License :: OSI Approved :: MIT License',
    ],
    package_dir={'': 'src'},
    install_requires=[
        'requests',
    ],
    packages=setuptools.find_packages(where='src'),
    python_requires='>=3.9',
)
```

The `setup.py` file essentially contains the `setuptools.setup` function, which defines the package. It defines the following:

- `name`: The name of the package.
- `version`: The version of the package. It will be used when installing a particular version or when ascertaining which is the latest version.
- `author` and `author_email`: It is good to include these to receive any possible bug reports or requests.
- `description`: A short description.
- `url`: The URL for the project.
- `long_description`: A longer description. Here, we are reading the `README` file, storing the content in the `description` variable:

  ```
  with open('README') as readme:
      description = readme.read()
  ```

  An important detail of `setup.py` is that it is dynamic, so we can use code to determine the values of any parameter.

- `classifier`: Categories for allowing packages to be categorized in different areas, such as the kinds of licenses and languages, or if the package is supposed to work with a framework like Django. You can check the full list of classifiers at the following link: `https://pypi.org/classifiers/`.
- `package_dir`: The subdirectory where the code of the package is located. Here, we specify `src`. By default, it will use the same directory as `setup.py`, but it's better to make the division so as to keep the code tidy.
- `install_requires`: Any dependency that needs to be installed with your package. Here, we are adding `requests` as an example. Note that any second-order dependencies (dependencies of `requests`) will be installed as well.
- `packages`: Using the `setuptools.find_packages` function, include everything that's in the `src` directory.
- `python_requires`: Define what Python interpreters are compatible with the package. In this case, we define it for Python 3.9 or higher.

Once the file is ready, you can run the `setup.py` script directly, for example, to check that the data is correct:

```
$ python setup.py check
running check
```

This command will verify that the `setup.py` definition is correct and that no mandatory elements are missing.

Development mode

The `setup.py` file can be used to install the package in `develop` mode. This installs the package in the current environment in a linked way. This means that any changes to the code will be applied directly to the package after the interpreter is restarted, making it easy to change and work with tests. Remember to run it while inside the virtual environment:

```
(venv) $ python setup.py develop
running develop
running egg_info
writing src/wheel_package.egg-info/PKG-INFO
writing dependency_links to src/wheel_package.egg-info/dependency_
links.txt
writing requirements to src/wheel_package.egg-info/requires.txt
writing top-level names to src/wheel_package.egg-info/top_level.txt
reading manifest file 'src/wheel_package.egg-info/SOURCES.txt'
adding license file 'LICENSE'
...
Using venv/lib/python3.9/site-packages
Finished processing dependencies for wheel-package==0.0.1
```

The developed version can be uninstalled easily to clean up the environment:

```
(venv) $ python setup.py develop --uninstall
running develop
Removing  /venv/lib/python3.9/site-packages/wheel-package.egg-link
(link to src)
Removing wheel-package 0.0.1 from easy-install.pth file
```

You can read more about development mode in the official documentation here: `https://setuptools.readthedocs.io/en/latest/userguide/development_mode.html`.

This step installs the package directly in the current environment and can be used to run tests and validate that the package is working as expected once installed. Once this is done, we can prepare the package itself.

Pure Python package

To create a package, we first need to define what kind of package we want to create. As we described before, we have three options: a source distribution, an `Egg`, or a `Wheel`. Each one is defined by a different command in `setup.py`.

To create a source distribution, we will use `sdist` (source distribution):

```
$ python setup.py sdist
running sdist
running egg_info
writing src/wheel_package.egg-info/PKG-INFO
writing dependency_links to src/wheel_package.egg-info/dependency_
links.txt
writing requirements to src/wheel_package.egg-info/requires.txt
writing top-level names to src/wheel_package.egg-info/top_level.txt
reading manifest file 'src/wheel_package.egg-info/SOURCES.txt'
adding license file 'LICENSE'
writing manifest file 'src/wheel_package.egg-info/SOURCES.txt'
running check
creating wheel-package-0.0.1
creating wheel-package-0.0.1/src
creating wheel-package-0.0.1/src/submodule
creating wheel-package-0.0.1/src/wheel_package.egg-info
copying files to wheel-package-0.0.1...
copying LICENSE -> wheel-package-0.0.1
copying README.md -> wheel-package-0.0.1
copying setup.py -> wheel-package-0.0.1
copying src/submodule/__init__.py -> wheel-package-0.0.1/src/submodule
copying src/submodule/submodule.py -> wheel-package-0.0.1/src/submodule
copying src/wheel_package.egg-info/PKG-INFO -> wheel-package-0.0.1/src/
wheel_package.egg-info
copying src/wheel_package.egg-info/SOURCES.txt -> wheel-package-0.0.1/
src/wheel_package.egg-info
copying src/wheel_package.egg-info/dependency_links.txt -> wheel-
package-0.0.1/src/wheel_package.egg-info
copying src/wheel_package.egg-info/requires.txt -> wheel-package-0.0.1/
src/wheel_package.egg-info
copying src/wheel_package.egg-info/top_level.txt -> wheel-
package-0.0.1/src/wheel_package.egg-info
Writing wheel-package-0.0.1/setup.cfg
creating dist
Creating tar archive
removing 'wheel-package-0.0.1' (and everything under it)
```

The `dist` package is available in the newly created `dist` subdirectory:

```
$ ls dist
wheel-package-0.0.1.tar.gz
```

To generate a proper `Wheel` package, we need to install the `wheel` module first:

```
$ pip install wheel
Collecting wheel
  Using cached wheel-0.37.0-py2.py3-none-any.whl (35 kB)
Installing collected packages: wheel
Successfully installed wheel-0.37.0
```

This adds the `bdist_wheel` command to the available commands in `setup.py`, which generates a `wheel`:

```
$ python setup.py bdist_wheel
running bdist_wheel
running build
running build_py
installing to build/bdist.macosx-11-x86_64/wheel
...
adding 'wheel_package-0.0.1.dist-info/LICENSE'
adding 'wheel_package-0.0.1.dist-info/METADATA'
adding 'wheel_package-0.0.1.dist-info/WHEEL'
adding 'wheel_package-0.0.1.dist-info/top_level.txt'
adding 'wheel_package-0.0.1.dist-info/RECORD'
removing build/bdist.macosx-11-x86_64/wheel
```

And the `wheel` file is available, once more, in the `dist` subdirectory:

```
$ ls dist
wheel_package-0.0.1-py3-none-any.whl
```

Note that it also includes Python version 3.

Wheel packages compatible with both Python 2 and Python 3 can be used. These wheels are called *Universal*. That was useful while doing the transition between both versions. Hopefully, by now, most of the new code in Python is using version 3 and we don't have to worry about that.

All these created packages can be installed directly with pip:

```
$ pip install dist/wheel-package-0.0.1.tar.gz
Processing ./dist/wheel-package-0.0.1.tar.gz
...
```

```
Successfully built wheel-package
Installing collected packages: wheel-package
Successfully installed wheel-package-0.0.

$ pip uninstall wheel-package
Found existing installation: wheel-package 0.0.1
Uninstalling wheel-package-0.0.1:
  Would remove:
    venv/lib/python3.9/site-packages/submodule/*
    venv/lib/python3.9/site-packages/wheel_package-0.0.1.dist-info/*
Proceed (Y/n)? y
  Successfully uninstalled wheel-package-0.0.1

$ pip install dist/wheel_package-0.0.1-py3-none-any.whl
Processing ./dist/wheel_package-0.0.1-py3-none-any.whl
Collecting requests
  Using cached requests-2.26.0-py2.py3-none-any.whl (62 kB)
...
Collecting urllib3<1.27,>=1.21.1
  Using cached urllib3-1.26.6-py2.py3-none-any.whl (138 kB)
...
Installing collected packages: wheel-package
Successfully installed wheel-package-0.0.
```

Note that the dependencies, in this case, `requests`, are installed automatically as well as any second-level dependency, for example, `urllib3`.

The power of the packaging is not only applicable to packages that contain only Python code. One of the most interesting features of `wheels` is the ability to generate pre-compiled packages, which includes compiled code for a target system.

To be able to show that, we need to produce some Python module that contains code that will be compiled. To do so, we need to take a small detour.

Cython

Python is capable of creating C and C++ language extensions that are compiled and interact with the Python code. Python itself is written in C, so this is a natural extension.

While Python has a lot of great features, pure speed when performing certain operations, such as numerical operations, is not its forte. This is where the C extensions come into their own as they enable low-level code to be accessed, which can be optimized and run faster than Python. Don't underestimate the possibility of creating a small, localized C extension that speeds up critical parts of the code.

Creating a C extension, however, can be difficult. The interface between Python and C is not straightforward, and the memory management required in C may be daunting unless you have significant experience of working with the C language.

If you want to dive deep into the topic and create your own C/C++ extensions, you can start by reading the official documentation at `https://docs.python.org/3/extending/index.html`.

Other options are available, such as creating extensions in Rust. You can check how to do this in the following article: `https://developers.redhat.com/blog/2017/11/16/speed-python-using-rust`.

Fortunately, there are some alternatives to make the task easier. A very good one is Cython.

Cython is a tool that compiles Python code with some extensions in C, so writing a C extension is as simple as writing Python code. The code is annotated to describe the C types for variables, but other than that, it looks pretty similar.

A complete description of Cython and all its possibilities is beyond the scope of this book. We present just a brief introduction. Please check the complete documentation for more information: `https://cython.org/`.

Cython files are stored as `.pyx` files. Let's see an example, which will determine whether a number is a prime number with the help of the `wheel_package_compiled.pyx` file:

```
def check_if_prime(unsigned int number):
    cdef int counter = 2

    if number == 0:
        return False
```

```
    while counter < number:
        if number % counter ==  0:
            return False

        counter += 1

    return True
```

The code is checking whether a positive number is a prime number:

- It returns `False` if the input is zero.
- It tries to divide the number by a number from 2 to the number. If any division is exact, it returns `False` as the number is not a prime number.
- If no division is exact, or the number is lower than 2, it returns `True`.

The code is not exactly Pythonic, as it will be translated into C. It's more efficient to avoid Python calls like `range` or similar. Don't be afraid to test different approaches to see what's faster to execute.

The code is not particularly good; it attempts too many divisions in general. It is just for the purpose of showing example code that may make sense to be compiled and is not too complicated.

Once the `pyx` file is ready, it can be compiled and imported into Python, using Cython. First, we need to install Cython:

```
$ pip install cython
Collecting cython
  Using cached Cython-0.29.24-cp39-cp39-macosx_10_9_x86_64.whl (1.9 MB)
Installing collected packages: cython
Successfully installed cython-0.29.24
```

Now, using `pyximport`, we can import the module directly like a `py` file. Cython will automatically compile it if necessary:

```
>>> import pyximport
>>> pyximport.install()
(None, <pyximport.pyximport.PyxImporter object at 0x10684a190>)
>>> import wheel_package_compiled
```

```
venv/lib/python3.9/site-packages/Cython/Compiler/Main.py:369:
FutureWarning: Cython directive 'language_level' not set, using 2 for
now (Py2). This will change in a later release! File: wheel_package_
compiled.pyx
  tree = Parsing.p_module(s, pxd, full_module_name)
.pyxbld/temp.macosx-11-x86_64-3.9/pyrex/wheel_package_
compiled.c:1149:35: warning: comparison of integers of different signs:
'int' and 'unsigned int' [-Wsign-compare]
    __pyx_t_1 = ((__pyx_v_counter < __pyx_v_number) != 0);
                  ~~~~~~~~~~~~~~~ ^ ~~~~~~~~~~~~~~
1 warning generated.
>>> wheel_package_compiled.check_if_prime(5)
   True
```

You can see that the compiler produces an error because there's a comparison between `unsigned int` and `int` (between `counter` and `number`).

This has been deliberately left to clearly show when the compilation takes place and that any compilation feedback, such as warnings or errors, will be displayed.

Once the code is compiled, Cython creates both a `wheel_package_compiled.c` file, local to the directory, and the compiled `.so` file, which, by default, is stored in `$HOME/.pyxbld`:

Note that this will be specific to your system. Here, we are showing a module compiled for macOS.

```
$ ls ~/.pyxbld/lib.macosx-11-x86_64-3.9/
wheel_package_compiled.cpython-39-darwin.so
```

Using `pyximport` is good for local development, but we can create a package that compiles and packages it as part of the build process.

Python package with binary code

We will use the code we created using Cython to show how to build a package that combines Python code with precompiled code. We will generate a `Wheel` file.

We create a package called `wheel_package_compiled` that extends the previous example package, `wheel_package`, with the code presented to be compiled in Cython.

The code is available in GitHub at `https://github.com/PacktPublishing/Python-Architecture-Patterns/tree/main/chapter_11_package_management/wheel_package_compiled`.

The structure of the package will be like this:

```
wheel_package_compiled
    ├── LICENSE
    ├── README
    ├── src
    │   ├── __init__.py
    │   ├── submodule
    │   │   ├── __init__.py
    │   │   └── submodule.py
    │   ├── wheel_package.py
    │   └── wheel_package_compiled.pyx
    └── setup.py
```

This is the same as the package introduced previously, but with the addition of the `.pyx` file. The `setup.py` file needs to add some changes:

```
import setuptools
from Cython.Build import cythonize
from distutils.extension import Exteldnsion

extensions = [
    Extension("wheel_package_compiled", ["src/wheel_package_compiled.
pyx"]),
]
```

```
with open('README') as readme:
    description = readme.read()


setuptools.setup(
    name='wheel-package-compiled',
    version='0.0.1',
    author='you',
    author_email='me@you.com',
    description='an example of a package',
    url='http://site.com',
    long_description=description,
    classifiers=[
        'Programming Language :: Python :: 3',
        'Operating System :: OS Independent',
        'License :: OSI Approved :: MIT License',
    ],
    package_dir={'': 'src'},
    install_requires=[
        'requests',
    ],
    ext_modules=cythonize(extensions),
    packages=setuptools.find_packages(where='src'),
    python_requires='>=3.9',
)
```

The changes introduced, other than the `name` change for the package, are all related to the new extension:

```
from Cython.Build import cythonize
from distutils.extension import Extension

extensions = [
    Extension("wheel_package_compiled", ["src/wheel_package_compiled.
pyx"]),
]
...
ext_modules=cythonize(extensions),
```

The extension definition targets the name of the module to add, and the location of the source. With the `cythonize` function, we are indicating that we want to use Cython to compile it.

Extension modules are modules compiled in C/C++. In this case, Cython will run the intermediate steps to be sure that the proper `.c` file is the one being compiled.

Once this is configured, we can run the code to generate the wheel, calling `setup.py`:

```
$ python setup.py bdist_wheel
Compiling src/wheel_package_compiled.pyx because it changed.
[1/1] Cythonizing src/wheel_package_compiled.pyx
...
running bdist_wheel
running build
running build_py
...
creating 'dist/wheel_package_compiled-0.0.1-cp39-cp39-macosx_11_0_
x86_64.whl' and adding 'build/bdist.macosx-11-x86_64/wheel' to it
adding 'wheel_package_compiled.cpython-39-darwin.so'
adding 'submodule/__init__.py'
adding 'submodule/submodule.py'
adding 'wheel_package_compiled-0.0.1.dist-info/LICENSE'
adding 'wheel_package_compiled-0.0.1.dist-info/METADATA'
adding 'wheel_package_compiled-0.0.1.dist-info/WHEEL'
adding 'wheel_package_compiled-0.0.1.dist-info/top_level.txt'
adding 'wheel_package_compiled-0.0.1.dist-info/RECORD'
removing build/bdist.macosx-11-x86_64/wheel
```

The compiled `Wheel` is available, as before, in the `dist` subdirectory.

```
$ ls dist
wheel_package_compiled-0.0.1-cp39-cp39-macosx_11_0_x86_64.whl
```

Compared with the `Wheel` created previously, we can see that it adds the platform and hardware architecture (macOS 11 and x86 64 bits, which is the computer used to compile it while writing the book). The `cp39` part shows that it used the Python 3.9 ABI (Application Binary Interface).

The created `Wheel` is ready to use for the same architecture and system. The `Wheel` package directly includes all the compiled code, so the package will install quickly, as only copying files is involved. Also, there will be no need to install compilation tools and dependencies.

When working with packages that need to be installed in multiple architectures or systems, you'll need to create an individual `Wheel` for each case and add the source distribution file to allow other systems to work with it.

But, unless you are creating a general package to be submitted to PyPI, the package will be for self-consumption, and normally you only need to create a `Wheel` file for your specific use case.

Which leads to the same step. What if you want to share your module with the whole Python community?

Uploading your package to PyPI

PyPI is open to accepting packages from any developer. We can create a new account and upload our packages to the official Python repo to allow any project to use it.

One of the great characteristics of open source projects, like Python and its ecosystem, is the ability to use code that is gracefully shared by other developers. While not mandatory, it is always good to give back and to share code that could be of interest to other developers to increase the usefulness of the Python library.

Be a good participant in the Python ecosystem and share code that could be useful to others.

To help with testing and to be sure that we can verify the process, there's a testing site called **TestPyPI** at `https://test.pypi.org/` that can be used to perform tests and to upload your package first.

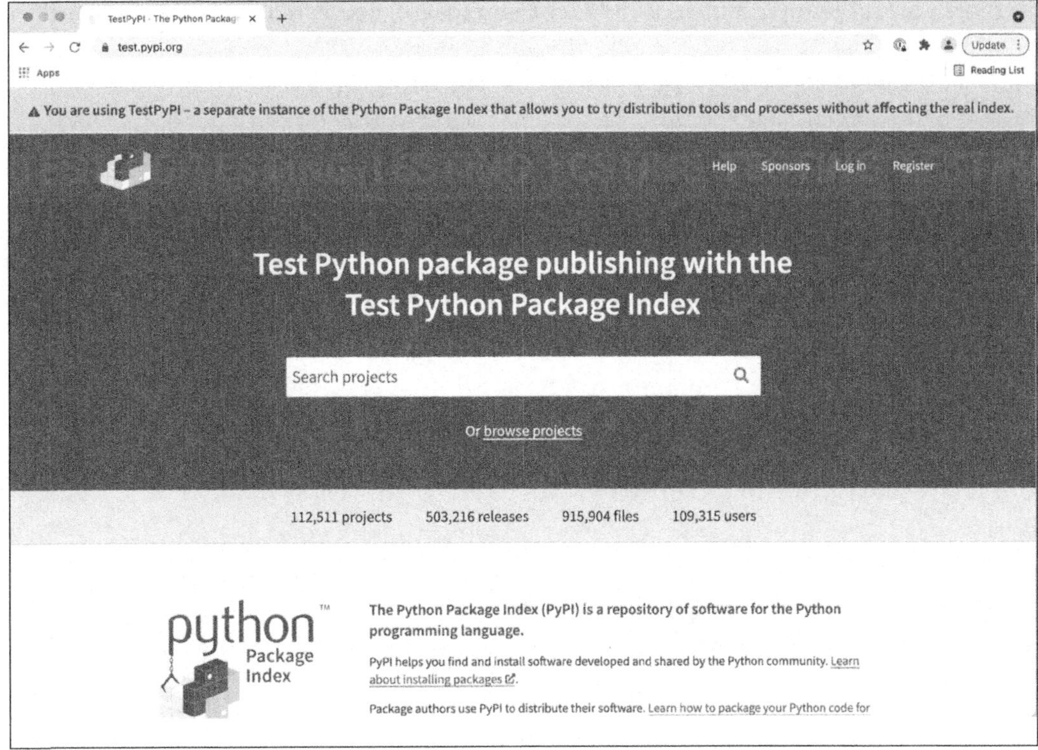

Figure 11.4: TestPyPI main page

The site is the same as the production one but indicates with a banner that it's the testing site.

You can register a new user at `https://test.pypi.org/account/register/`. After that, you'll need to create a new API token to allow the package to be uploaded.

Remember to verify your email. Without a verified email, you won't be able to create an API token.

If there's a problem with the API token or you lose it, you can always delete it and start again.

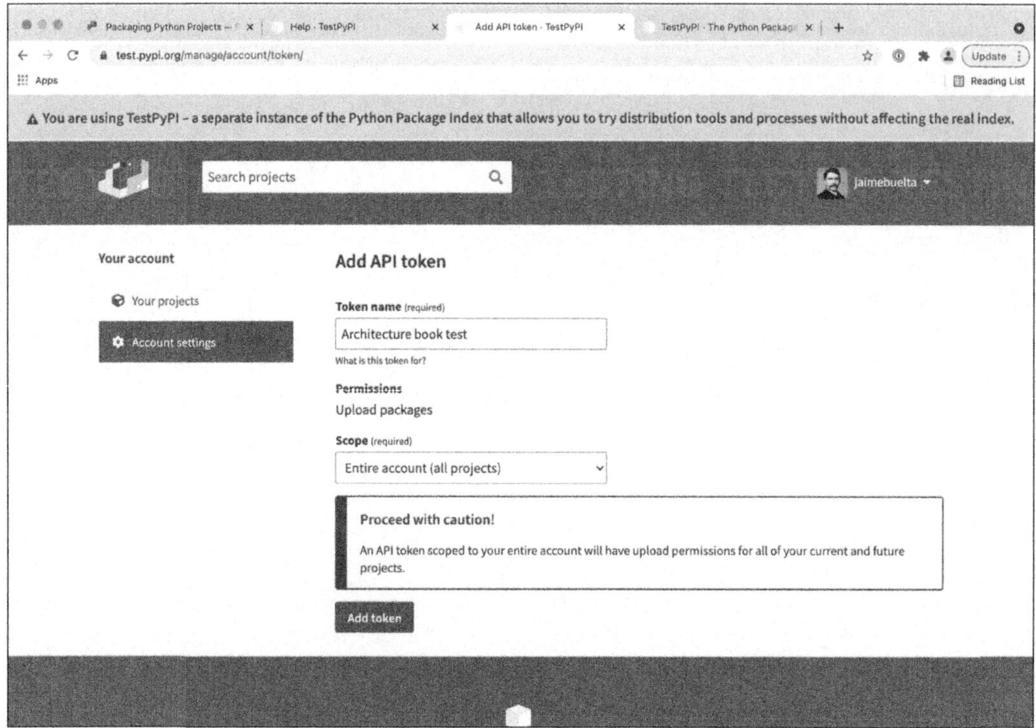

Figure 11.5: You'll need to grant the full scope to upload a new package

Create a new token and copy it to a safe place. The token (which starts with `pypi-`) will only be displayed once for safety reasons, so be careful with it.

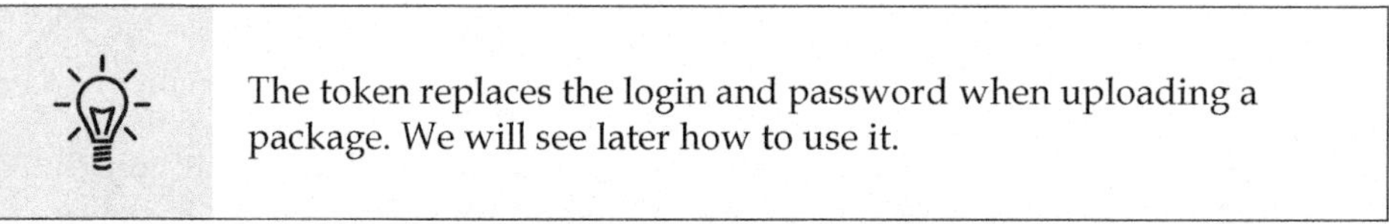

The token replaces the login and password when uploading a package. We will see later how to use it.

The next step is to install the `twine` package, which simplifies the process of uploading. Be sure to install it in our virtual environment:

```
(venv) $ pip install twine
Collecting twine
  Downloading twine-3.4.2-py3-none-any.whl (34 kB)
...
```

```
Installing collected packages: zipp, webencodings, six, Pygments,
importlib-metadata, docutils, bleach, tqdm, rfc3986, requests-toolbelt,
readme-renderer, pkginfo, keyring, colorama, twine
Successfully installed Pygments-2.10.0 bleach-4.1.0 colorama-0.4.4
docutils-0.17.1 importlib-metadata-4.8.1 keyring-23.2.0 pkginfo-1.7.1
readme-renderer-29.0 requests-toolbelt-0.9.1 rfc3986-1.5.0 six-1.16.0
tqdm-4.62.2 twine-3.4.2 webencodings-0.5.1 zipp-3.5.0
```

Now we can upload the packages created in the `dist` subdirectory.

For our example, we will use the same package created previously, but keep in mind that trying to reupload it may not work, as there may already be a package called that in TestPyPI. TestPyPI is not permanent, and regularly deletes packages, but the example uploaded as part of the writing process of the book could still be there. To do your tests, create your own package with a unique name.

We have now built the compiled `Wheel` and the source distribution:

```
(venv) $ ls dist
wheel-package-compiled-0.0.1.tar.gz
wheel_package_compiled-0.0.1-cp39-cp39-macosx_11_0_x86_64.whl
```

Let's upload the packages. We need to indicate that we want to upload to the `testpy` repo. We will use `__token__` as the username and the full token (including the `pypi-` prefix) as the password:

```
(venv) $ python -m twine upload --repository testpypi dist/*
Uploading distributions to https://test.pypi.org/legacy/
Enter your username: __token__
Enter your password:
Uploading wheel_package_compiled-0.0.1-cp39-cp39-macosx_11_0_x86_64.whl
100%|██████████████████████████████████████████████████
████| 12.6k/12.6k [00:01<00:00, 7.41kB/s]
Uploading wheel-package-compiled-0.0.1.tar.gz
100%|██████████████████████████████████████████████████
████| 24.0k/24.0k [00:00<00:00, 24.6kB/s]

View at:
https://test.pypi.org/project/wheel-package-compiled/0.0.1/
```

The package is now uploaded! We can check the page on the TestPyPI website.

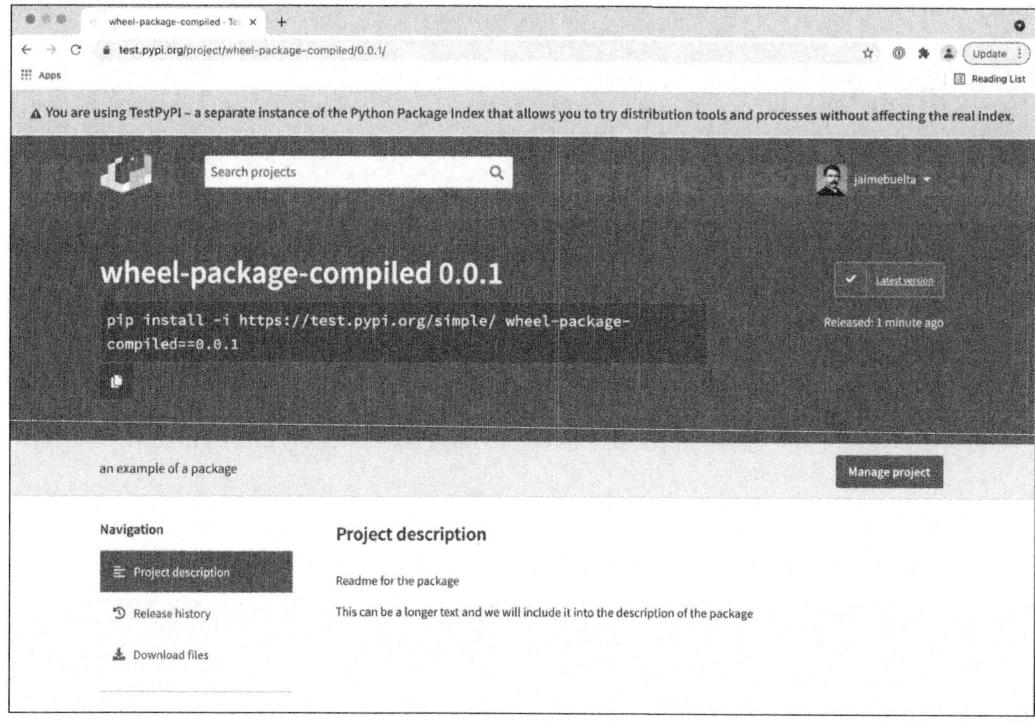

Figure 11.6: Main page for the package

You can verify the uploaded files by clicking **Download files**:

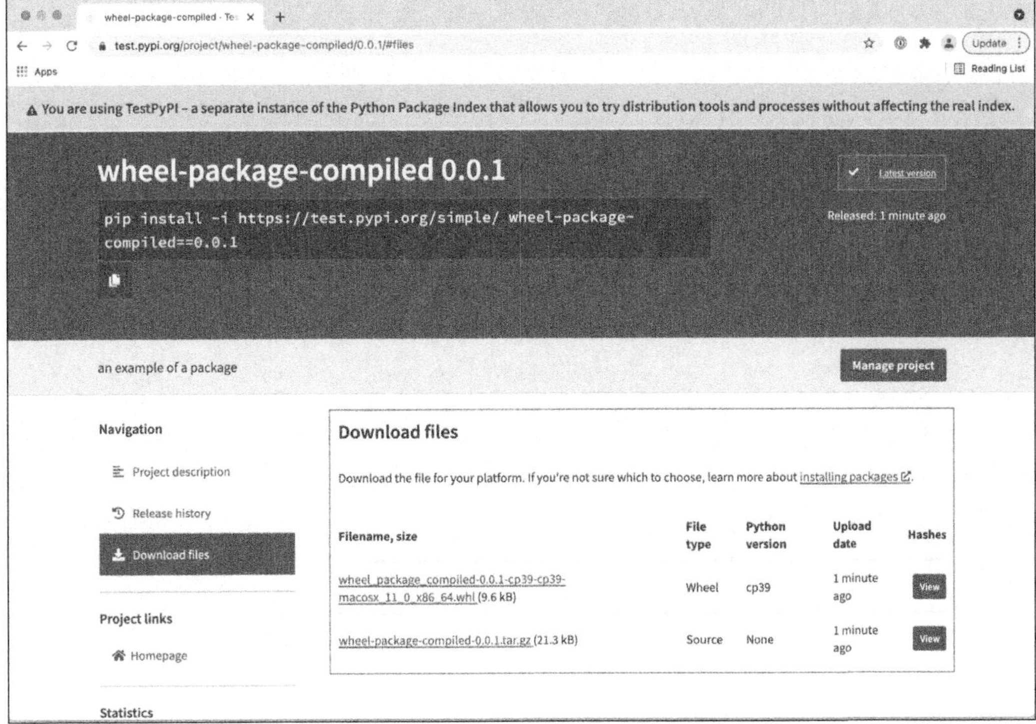

Figure 11.7: Verifying the uploaded files

You can also access the files through the search function:

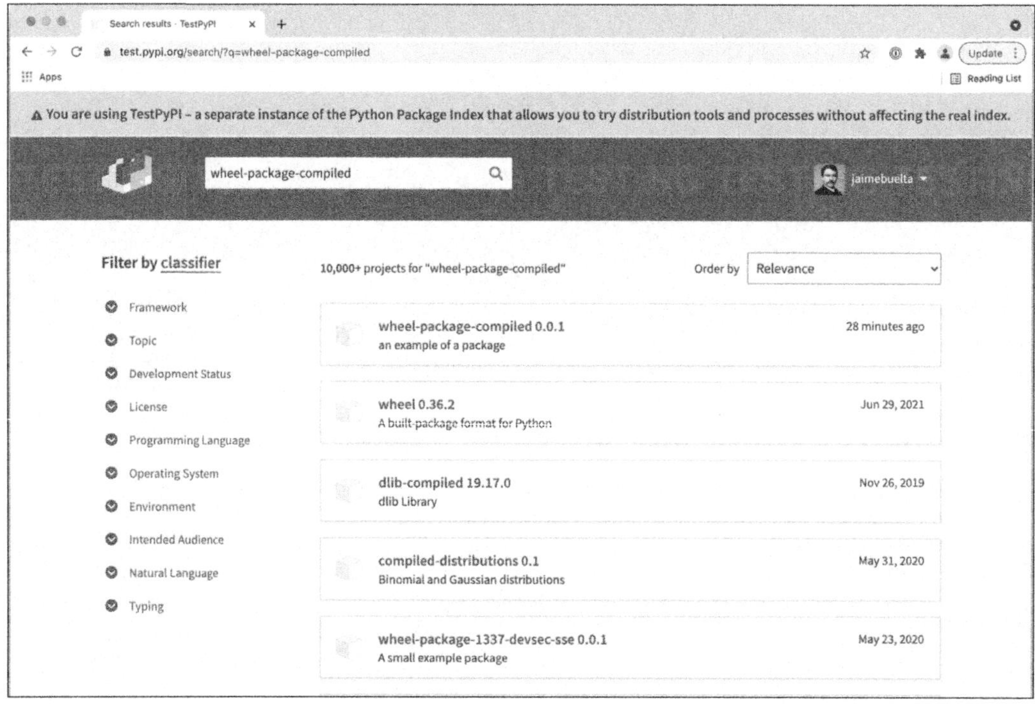

Figure 11.8: The package available in search

You can now download the package directly through `pip`, but you need to indicate that the index to use is the TestPyPI one. To ensure a clean installation, create a new virtual environment as follows:

```
$ python3 -m venv venv2
$ source ./venv2/bin/activate
(venv2) $ pip install --index-url https://test.pypi.org/simple/ wheel-
package-compiled
Looking in indexes: https://test.pypi.org/simple/
Collecting wheel-package-compiled
  Downloading https://test-files.pythonhosted.org/packages/87/c3/88129
8cdc8eb6ad23456784c80d585b5872581d6ceda6da3dfe3bdcaa7ed/wheel_package_
compiled-0.0.1-cp39-cp39-macosx_11_0_x86_64.whl (9.6 kB)
Collecting requests
  Downloading https://test-files.pythonhosted.org/packages/6d/00/8ed
1b6ea43b10bfe28d08e6af29fd6aa5d8dab5e45ead9394a6268a2d2ec/requests-
2.5.4.1-py2.py3-none-any.whl (468 kB)
     |████████████████████████████████| 468 kB 634 kB/s
```

```
Installing collected packages: requests, wheel-package-compiled
Successfully installed requests-2.5.4.1 wheel-package-compiled-0.0.1
```

Note that the version downloaded is the `Wheel` one, as it is the right target for the compiled version. It also correctly downloads the specified `requests` dependency.

You can now test the package through the Python interpreter:

```
(venv2) $ python
Python 3.9.6 (default, Jun 29 2021, 05:25:02)
[Clang 12.0.5 (clang-1205.0.22.9)] on darwin
Type "help", "copyright", "credits" or "license" for more information.
>>> import wheel_package_compiled
>>> wheel_package_compiled.check_if_prime(5)
True
```

The package is now installed and ready to use. The next step is to upload this package to production PyPI instead of TestPyPI. This is totally analogous to the process that we've seen here, creating an account in PyPI and proceeding from there.

But, what if the objective of the package is not to create a publicly available package? It is possible that we need to create our own index with our packages.

Creating your own private index

Sometimes, you'll need to have your own private index, so you can serve your own packages without opening them to the full internet, for internal packages that need to be used across the company, but where it doesn't make sense to upload them to the public PyPI.

You can create your own private index that can be used to share those packages and install them by calling to that index.

To serve the packages, we need to run a PyPI server locally. There are several options in terms of available servers that can be used, but an easy option is `pypiserver` (`https://github.com/pypiserver/pypiserver`).

`pypiserver` can be installed in several ways; we will see how to run it locally, but to serve it correctly, you'll need to install it in a way that's available in your network. Check the documentation to see several options, but a good option is to use the official Docker image available.

To run `pypiserver`, first, install the package using `pip` and create a directory for storing the packages:

```
$ pip install pypiserver
Collecting pypiserver
  Downloading pypiserver-1.4.2-py2.py3-none-any.whl (77 kB)
     |████████████████████████████████| 77 kB 905 kB/s
Installing collected packages: pypiserver
Successfully installed pypiserver-1.4.2
$ mkdir ./package-library
```

Start the server. We use the parameter `-p 8080` to serve it in that port, the directory to store the packages, and `-P . -a .` to facilitate the uploading of packages without authentication:

```
$ pypi-server -P . -a . -p 8080 ./package-library
```

Open a browser and check `http://localhost:8080`.

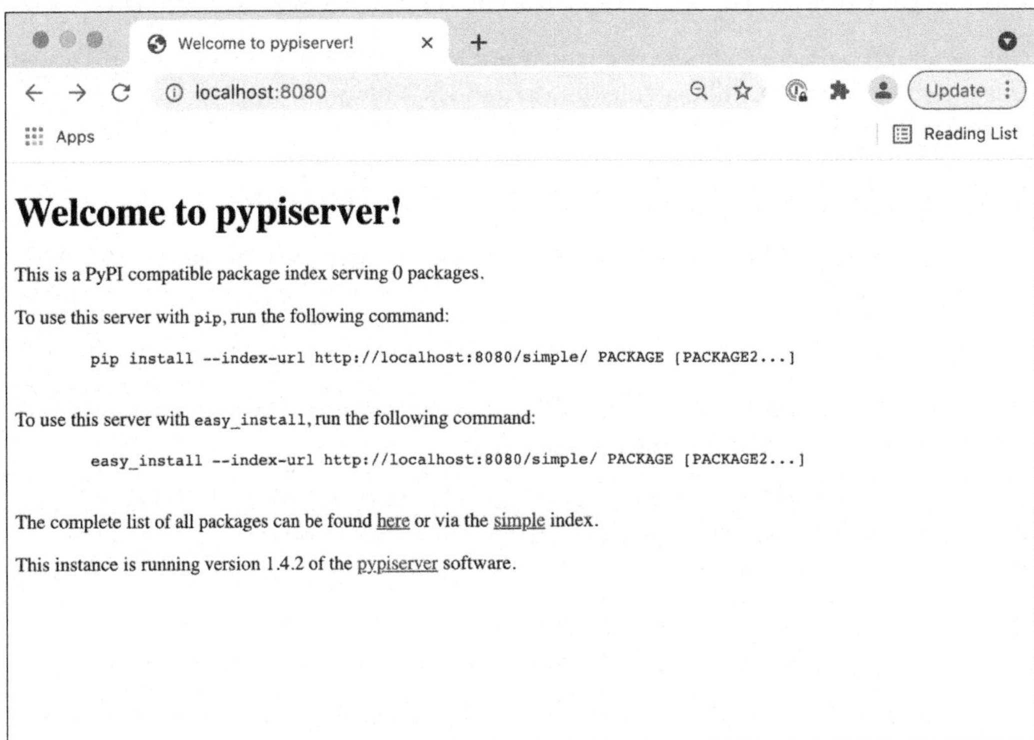

Figure 11.9: Local pypi server

You can check the available packages in this index by going to `http://localhost:8080/simple/`.

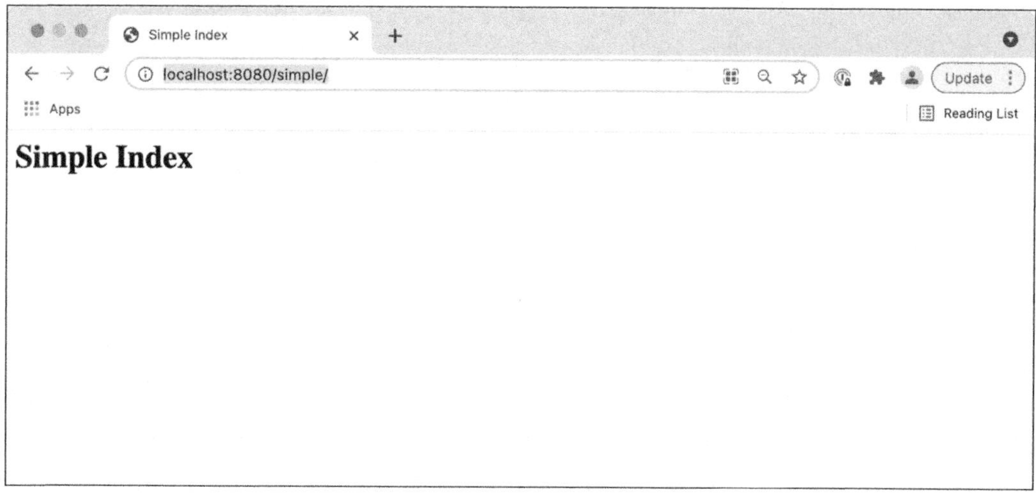

Figure 11.10: Empty index so far

We now need to upload the packages, using `twine` again, but pointing to our private URL. As we are able to upload with no authentication, we can enter an empty username and password:

```
$ python -m twine upload --repository-url http://localhost:8080 dist/*
Uploading distributions to http://localhost:8080
Enter your username:
Enter your password:
Uploading wheel_package_compiled-0.0.1-cp39-cp39-macosx_11_0_x86_64.whl
100%|████████████████████████████████| 12.6k/12.6k [00:00<00:00,
843kB/s]
Uploading wheel-package-compiled-0.0.1.tar.gz
100%|████████████████████████████████| 24.0k/24.0k [00:00<00:00,
2.18MB/s]
```

The index is now showing the package available.

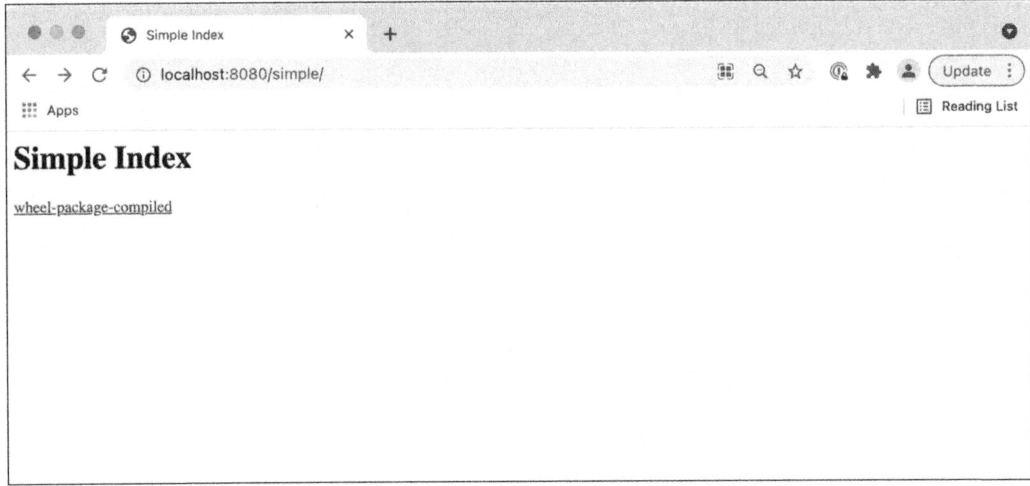

Figure 11.11: Showing the package uploaded

Figure 11.12: All the uploaded files for the package

The files are also uploaded to the `package-library` directory:

```
$ ls package-library
wheel-package-compiled-0.0.1.tar.gz
wheel_package_compiled-0.0.1-cp39-cp39-macosx_11_0_x86_64.whl
```

Any file added to `package-library` will also be served, allowing packages to be added by moving them to the directory, although that could be complicated once the server is deployed properly to the packages over the network.

The package can now be downloaded and installed, pointing to your private index using the `-index-url` parameter:

```
$ pip install --index-url http://localhost:8080 wheel-package-compiled
Looking in indexes: http://localhost:8080
Collecting wheel-package-compiled
  Downloading http://localhost:8080/packages/wheel_package_compiled-0.0.1-cp39-cp39-macosx_11_0_x86_64.whl (9.6 kB)
…
Successfully installed certifi-2021.5.30 charset-normalizer-2.0.4 idna-3.2 requests-2.26.0 urllib3-1.26.6 wheel-package-compiled-0.0.1
$ python
Python 3.9.6 (default, Jun 29 2021, 05:25:02)
[Clang 12.0.5 (clang-1205.0.22.9)] on darwin
Type "help", "copyright", "credits" or "license" for more information.
>>> import wheel_package_compiled
>>> wheel_package_compiled.check_if_prime(5)
True
```

This tests that the module can be imported and executed after installation.

Summary

In this chapter, we described when it's a good idea to create a standard package and the caveats and requirements that we should add to be sure that we are taking a good decision. In essence, creating a new package is creating a new project, and we should give the proper ownership, documentation, and so on, as expected of other projects in the organization.

We described the simplest possible package in Python just by structuring code, but without creating a proper package. This acts as a baseline on how the code should be structured later.

We continued describing what the current packaging environment is and what are the different elements that are part of it, like PyPI, which is the official source for publicly available packages, and how to create virtual environments to not cross-contaminate different environments when requiring different dependencies. We also described the `Wheel` package, which will be the kind of package that we will create later.

Next, we described how to create such a package, creating a `setup.py` file. We described how to install it in development mode to be able to do tests and how to build and get the package ready.

There are some alternatives to creating packages instead of using the standard `setup.py` file. You can take a look at the `Poetry` package (`https://python-poetry.org/`) to see how to manage packages in a more integrated way, especially if the package has many dependencies.

We took a small detour to explain how to generate code to be compiled with Cython, an easy way to create Python extensions writing in Python code with some extensions, to generate C code automatically.

We used Cython code to show how to generate a compiled `Wheel`, allowing the distribution of already precompiled code without needing to be compiled on installation.

We showed how to upload packages to PyPI to distribute publicly (showing how to upload to TestPyPI, allowing the upload of packages to be tested) and described how to create your own individual index so that you can distribute your own packages privately.

Join our book's Discord space

Join the book's Discord workspace for a monthly *Ask me Anything* session with the author: `https://packt.link/PythonArchitechture`

Part IV

Ongoing operations

Our work with an architecture is not finished when a system is up and running. A working application requires ongoing maintenance and effort to keep it running successfully.

Systems will be in a maintenance phase during the longest part of their life cycles. This phase is where we add features, detect and fix defects, and analyze the system's behavior to prevent problems.

To be able to do that successfully, we need to have tools to cover two basic elements:

- *Observability*: This is the capability of knowing what's going on in a live system. Low-observability systems are difficult or even impossible to understand, which makes it difficult to know if there are problems or work out the cause of those problems. In high-observability systems, it's easy to infer the internal state and the events flowing inside the system, which allows for easy detection of the critical structures where problems are being generated.
  The main tools for observing systems are **logs** and **metrics**, which are used in conjunction to allow us to understand the system and analyze its behavior.

  Observability is a property of the system itself. Typically, monitoring is the action of obtaining information about the current or past state of the system. It's all a bit of a naming debate, but technically, you *monitor* the system to collect the *observable* parts of it.

- *Analysis*: To detect problems in more controlled situations, we have two important tools, **debugging** and **profiling**. The first is a staple of the development process, working step by step through code to understand how a piece of code works and ascertain why it's doing what it is doing. Profiling is instrumenting the code to show how it works and, specifically, determine which parts take the most time to execute, to allow you to act on them and improve their performance.
  These two tools work complementarily with one another and allow us to fix and improve different kinds of problems after they've been detected.

In this section, we will also talk about the challenge of making changes while the system is in operation. The only constant in software is change, and balancing existing systems with new functionalities is a critical ability. Part of this task is to coordinate between different teams so they are aware of the implications of their changes and can work as a single unit.

This section comprises of the following chapters:

- Logging
- Metrics
- Profiling
- Debugging
- Ongoing architecture

We will start by understanding how to use logs for monitoring.

12
Logging

One of the basic elements of monitoring and observability is logs. Logs allow us to detect actions that are happening in a running system. That information can be used to analyze the behavior of the system, especially any errors or bugs that may arise, giving us useful insight into what is actually going on.

Using logs correctly is deceptively difficult, though. It's easy to collect too much or too little information, or to log the wrong information. In this chapter, we will see some of the key elements of what to collect, and the general strategy to follow to ensure that logs are used to their best effect.

In this chapter, we'll cover the following topics:

- Log basics
- Producing logs in Python
- Detecting problems through logs
- Log strategies
- Adding logs while developing
- Log limitations

Let's start with the basic principles of logging.

Log basics

Logs are basically messages produced by the system as it runs. These messages are produced by specific pieces of code as they are executed, allowing us to track actions happening in the code.

Logs can be completely generic, like "*Function X is called*" or can include some context of the specifics of the execution, like "*Function X is called with parameter Y.*"

Normally, logs are generated as plaintext messages. While there are other options, pure plaintext is very easy to deal with, can be read easily, is flexible in its format, and can be searched with pure text tools like `grep`. These tools are normally very fast and most developers and sysadmins know how to use them.

As well as the main message text, each log contains some metadata about what system produced the log, what time the log was created, and so on. If the log is in text format, this is normally attached to the start of the line.

A standard and consistent log format helps you with searching, filtering, and sorting the messages. Ensure that you use consistent formats across your different systems.

Another important metadata value is the severity of the log. This allows us to categorize the different logs by their relative importance. The standard severity levels, in order of less to more important, are `DEBUG`, `INFO`, `WARNING`, and `ERROR`.

The `CRITICAL` level is less used, but it's useful to show catastrophic errors.

It's important to categorize the logs with their proper severity and filter out unimportant messages to focus on the more important ones. Each logging facility can be configured to only produce logs at one severity level or more.

It's possible to add custom log levels instead of the predefined ones. This is generally a bad idea and should be avoided in most cases, as the log levels are well understood by all tools and engineers. We will describe later in this chapter how to define a strategy per level to make the best of each level.

In a system serving requests, either as request-response or asynchronously, most of the logs will be generated as part of dealing with a request, which will produce several logs indicating what the request is doing. Because more than one request will normally be undergoing processing at once, the logs will be generated intermixed. For example, consider the following logs:

```
Sept 16 20:42:04.130 10.1.0.34 INFO web: REQUEST GET /login
Sept 16 20:42:04.170 10.1.0.37 INFO api: REQUEST GET /api/login
Sept 16 20:42:04.250 10.1.0.37 INFO api: REQUEST TIME 80 ms
Sept 16 20:42:04.270 10.1.0.37 INFO api: REQUEST STATUS 200
Sept 16 20:42:04.360 10.1.0.34 INFO web: REQUEST TIME 230 ms
Sept 16 20:42:04.370 10.1.0.34 INFO web: REQUEST STATUS 200
```

The preceding logs show two different services, as indicated by the different IP addresses (`10.1.0.34` and `10.1.0.37`) and the two different service types (`web` and `api`). Though this can be enough to separate the requests, it's a good idea to create a single request ID to be able to group the requests in the following way:

```
Sept 16 20:42:04.130 10.1.0.34 INFO web: [4246953f8] REQUEST GET /login
Sept 16 20:42:04.170 10.1.0.37 INFO api: [fea9f04f3] REQUEST GET /api/
login
Sept 16 20:42:04.250 10.1.0.37 INFO api: [fea9f04f3] REQUEST TIME 80 ms
Sept 16 20:42:04.270 10.1.0.37 INFO api: [fea9f04f3] REQUEST STATUS 200
Sept 16 20:42:04.360 10.1.0.34 INFO web: [4246953f8] REQUEST TIME 230
ms
Sept 16 20:42:04.370 10.1.0.34 INFO web: [4246953f8] REQUEST STATUS 200
```

In microservices environments, requests will flow from one service to the other, so it's a good idea to create a request ID that's shared across services so the full cross-service flow can be understood. To do that, the request ID needs to be created by the first service and then transmitted to the next, typically as a header in an HTTP request.

As we saw in *Chapter 5, The Twelve-Factor App Methodology*, in the Twelve-Factor App methodology, logs should be treated as an event stream. This means that the application itself should not be concerned with the storage and treatment of logs. Instead, the logs should be directed to `stdout`. From there, while developing the application, the developer can extract the information while it's running.

In production environments, `stdout` should be captured so that other tools can use it and then routed, annexing any different sources into a single stream, and then stored or indexed for later consulting. These tools should be configured in the production environment, and not in the app itself.

Possible tools for this rerouting include alternatives like Fluentd (`https://github.com/fluent/fluentd`) or even the old favorite combination of a direct to `logger` Linux command to create system logs and then sending those logs to a configured `rsyslog` (`https://www.rsyslog.com/`) server that can forward and aggregate them.

No matter how we collect logs, a typical system will produce a lot of them, and they need to be stored somewhere. While each individual log is small, aggregating thousands of them uses a significant amount of space. Any log system should be configured to have a policy on how much data it should accept to avoid growing indefinitely. In general, a retention policy based on time (such as keeping logs from the last 15 days) is the best approach, as it will be easy to understand. Finding the balance between how far back in the past you need to be able look and the amount of space the system uses is important.

Be sure to check the retention policy when enabling any new log service, be it local or cloud-based, to make sure it's compatible with your defined retention period. You won't be able to analyze anything that happened before the time window. Double-check that the rate of log creation is as expected and that space consumption is not making the effective time window in which you can collect logs smaller. You don't want to find out that you unexpectedly went over quota while you were tracking a bug.

Generating log entries is easy, as we will see in the next section, *Producing logs in Python*.

Producing logs in Python

Python includes a standard module to produce logs. This module is easy to use, with a very flexible configuration, but it can be confusing if you don't understand the way it operates.

A basic program to create logs looks like this. This is available as `basic_logging.py` on GitHub at `https://github.com/PacktPublishing/Python-Architecture-Patterns/tree/main/chapter_12_logging`:

```
import logging

# Generate two logs with different severity levels
logging.warning('This is a warning message')
logging.info('This is an info message')
```

The `.warning` and `.info` methods create logs with the corresponding severity message. The message is a text string.

When executed, it shows the following:

```
$ python3 basic_logging.py
WARNING:root:This is a warning message
```

The logs are, by default, routed to `stdout`, which is what we want, but it is configured not to display `INFO` logs. The format of the logs is also the default, which doesn't include a timestamp.

To add all this information, we need to understand the three basic elements used for logging in Python:

- A *formatter*, which describes how the full log is going to be presented, attaching metadata like the timestamp or the severity.
- A *handler*, which decides how the logs are propagated. It sets the format of the logs through the formatter, as defined above.
- A *logger*, which produces the logs. It has one or more handlers that describe how the logs are propagated.

With this information, we can configure the logs to specify all the details we want:

```
import sys
import logging


# Define the format
FORMAT = '%(asctime)s.%(msecs)dZ:APP:%(name)s:%(levelname)s:%(message)
s'
formatter = logging.Formatter(FORMAT, datefmt="%Y-%m-%dT%H:%M:%S")

# Create a handler that sends the logs to stdout
handler = logging.StreamHandler(stream=sys.stdout)
handler.setFormatter(formatter)
```

```
# Create a logger with name 'mylogger', adding the handler and setting
# the level to INFO
logger = logging.getLogger('mylogger')
logger.addHandler(handler)
logger.setLevel(logging.INFO)


# Generate three logs
logger.warning('This is a warning message')
logger.info('This is an info message')
logger.debug('This is a debug message, not to be displayed')
```

We define the three elements in the same order that we saw before. First the `formatter`, then the `handler`, which sets the `formatter`, and finally the `logger`, which adds the `handler`.

The `formatter` has the following format:

```
FORMAT = '%(asctime)s.%(msecs)dZ:APP:%(name)s:%(levelname)s:%(message)
s'
formatter = logging.Formatter(FORMAT, datefmt="%Y-%m-%dT%H:%M:%S")
```

`FORMAT` is composed in Python `%` format, which is an old way to describe strings. Most elements are described as `%(name)s`, where the final `s` character means string format. Here's a description of each element:

- `asctime` sets the timestamp in a human-readable format. We describe it in the `datefmt` argument to follow the ISO 8601 format. We also add the milliseconds next and a `Z` to get the timestamp in full ISO 8601 form. `%(msecs)d` with a `d` at the end means that we print the value as an integer. This is to limit the value to milliseconds and not show any extra resolution, which is available as a fractional value.
- `name` is the name of the logger, as we will describe later. We add also `APP` to differentiate between different applications.
- `levelname` is the severity of the log, such as `INFO`, `WARNING`, or `ERROR`.
- `message`, finally, is the log message.

Once we have defined the `formatter`, we can move to the `handler`:

```
handler = logging.StreamHandler(stream=sys.stdout)
handler.setFormatter(formatter)
```

The handler is a `StreamHandler`, and we set the destination of the stream to be `sys.stdout`, which is the Python-defined variable that points to `stdout`.

There are more handlers available, like `FileHandler` to send the logs to a file, `SysLogHandler` to send logs to a `syslog` destination, and even more advanced cases like `TimeRotatingFileHandler`, which rotates the logs based on time, meaning it stores the last defined time, and archives older versions. You can see more information of all available handlers in the documentation at `https://docs.python.org/3/howto/logging.html#useful-handlers`.

Once the `handler` is defined, we can create the `logger`:

```
logger = logging.getLogger('mylogger')
logger.addHandler(handler)
logger.setLevel(logging.INFO)
```

The first thing to do is to create a name for the logger, which here we define as `mylogger`. This allows us to divide the logs of the application into subsections. We append the handler using `.addHandler`.

Finally, we define the level to log as `INFO` using the `.setLevel` method. This will display all logs of the level `INFO` and higher, while those lower won't be.

If we run the file, we see the whole configuration coming together:

```
$ python3 configured_logging.py
2021-09-18T23:15:24.563Z:APP:mylogger:WARNING:This is a warning message
2021-09-18T23:15:24.563Z:APP:mylogger:INFO:This is an info message
```

We can see that:

- The time is defined in ISO 8601 format as `2021-09-18T23:15:24.563Z`. This is a combination of the `asctime` and `msec` parameters.
- The `APP` and `mylogger` parameters allow us to filter by application and submodule.
- The severity is displayed. Note that there's a `DEBUG` message that isn't displayed, as the minimum level configured is `INFO`.

The `logging` module in Python is capable of high levels of configuration. Check the official documentation for more information at `https://docs.python.org/3/library/logging.html`.

Detecting problems through logs

For any problem in a running system, there are two kind of errors that can occur: expected and unexpected. In this section, we will see the differences between them in terms of logs and how we handle them.

Detecting expected errors

Expected errors are errors that are detected explicitly by creating an `ERROR` log in the code. For example, the following code produces an `ERROR` log when the accessed URL returns a status code different from `200 OK`:

```
import logging
import requests


URL = 'https://httpbin.org/status/500'

response = requests.get(URL)
status_code = response.status_code
if status_code != 200:
    logging.error(f'Error accessing {URL} status code {status_code}')
```

This code, when executed, triggers an `ERROR` log:

```
$ python3 expected_error.py
ERROR:root:Error accessing https://httpbin.org/status/500 status code
500
```

This is a common pattern to access an external URL and validate that it has been accessed correctly. The block where the log is generated could perform some remediation or a retry, among other things.

Here, we use the `https://httpbin.org` service, a simple HTTP request and response service that can be used to test code. In particular, the `https://httpbin.org/status/<code>` endpoint returns the specified status code, making it easy to generate errors.

This is an example of an expected error. We planned in advance for something that we didn't want to happen, but understood that there's a possibility of it happening. By planning in advance, the code is ready to process the error and capture it adequately.

In this case, we can describe the situation clearly enough, and provide context to understand what is happening. The problem is obvious, even if the solution may not be.

These kinds of errors are relatively easy to deal with since they describe foreseen problems.

For example, the site may be unavailable, there could be an authentication problem, or perhaps the base URL is misconfigured.

Keep in mind that in some cases, it's possible for the code to deal with a certain situation without failing, but for it still to be considered an error. For example, maybe you want to detect if an old authentication system is still in use by someone. This method of adding `ERROR` or `WARNING` logs when deprecated actions are detected can enable you to take actions to remedy the situation.

Other examples of this type of error include connections to databases and data being stored in a deprecated format.

Capturing unexpected errors

But expected errors are not the only ones that can occur. Unfortunately, any running system will surprise you with all kinds of unexpected behavior that will break the code in creative ways. Unexpected errors in Python are normally produced by an exception being raised at some point in the code when that exception won't be captured.

For example, imagine that when making a small change to some code, we introduce a typo:

```
import logging
import requests


URL = 'https://httpbin.org/status/500'

logging.info(f'GET {URL}')
response = requests.ge(URL)
status_code = response.status_code
if status_code != 200:
    logging.error(f'Error accessing {URL} status code {status_code}')
```

Note that in line 8, we introduced a typo:

```
response = requests.ge(URL)
```

The correct `.get` call has been replaced by `.ge`. When we run it, it produces the following error:

```
$ python3 unexpected_error.py
Traceback (most recent call last):
  File "./unexpected_error.py", line 8, in <module>
    response = requests.ge(URL)
AttributeError: module 'requests' has no attribute 'ge'
```

By default in Python, it will show the error and stack trace in the `stdout`. When the code is executed as part of a web server, this is sometimes enough to send these messages as `ERROR` logs, depending on how the configuration is set up.

Any web server will capture and route these messages properly toward the logs and generate a proper 500 status code, indicating that there has been an unexpected error. The server will still be available for the next request.

If you need to create a script that needs to be running endlessly and is protected against any unexpected errors, be sure to use a `try..except` block as it's generic, so any possible exception will be captured and handled.

Any Python exception that's properly captured with a specific `except` block can be considered an expected error. Some of them may require `ERROR` messages to be generated, but others may be captured and handled without requiring such information.

For example, let's adjust the code to make a request every few seconds. The code is available in GitHub at `https://github.com/PacktPublishing/Python-Architecture-Patterns/tree/main/chapter_12_logging`:

```
import logging
import requests
from time import sleep

logger = logging.getLogger()
logger.setLevel(logging.INFO)
```

```
while True:

    try:
        sleep(3)
        logging.info('--- New request ---')

        URL = 'https://httpbin.org/status/500'

        logging.info(f'GET {URL}')
        response = requests.ge(URL)
        scode = response.status_code
        if scode != 200:
            logger.error(f'Error accessing {URL} status code {scode}')
    except Exception as err:
        logger.exception(f'ERROR {err}')
```

The key element is the following endless loop:

```
while True:
    try:
        code
    except Exception as err:
        logger.exception(f'ERROR {err}')
```

The `try..except` block is inside the loop, so even if there's an error, the loop will be uninterrupted. If there's any error, `except Exception` will capture it, no matter what the exception is.

This is sometimes referred to as *Pokemon exception handling*, as in "Gotta catch 'em all." This should be restricted to a kind of "last-resort safety net." In general, not being precise with the exceptions to be captured is a bad idea, as you can hide errors by handling them incorrectly. Errors should never pass silently.

To be sure that not only is the error logged, but also the full stack trace, we log it using `.exception` instead of `.error`. This extends the information over a single text message while logging it with `ERROR` severity.

When we run the command, we get these logs. Be sure to stop it by pressing *Ctrl* + *C*:

```
$ python3 protected_errors.py
INFO:root:--- New request ---
INFO:root:GET https://httpbin.org/status/500
ERROR:root:ERROR module 'requests' has no attribute 'ge'
```

```
Traceback (most recent call last):
  File "./protected_errors.py", line 18, in <module>
    response = requests.ge(URL)
AttributeError: module 'requests' has no attribute 'ge'
INFO:root:--- New request ---
INFO:root:GET https://httpbin.org/status/500
ERROR:root:ERROR module 'requests' has no attribute 'ge'
Traceback (most recent call last):
  File "./protected_errors.py", line 18, in <module>
    response = requests.ge(URL)
AttributeError: module 'requests' has no attribute 'ge'
^C
...
KeyboardInterrupt
```

As you can see, the logs include `Traceback`, which allows us to detect a specific problem by adding information about where the exception was produced.

Any unexpected error should be logged as `ERROR`. Ideally, they should also be analyzed and the code changed to bugfix them or at least transform them into expected errors. Sometimes this is not feasible due to other pressing issues or a low occurrence of the problem, but some strategy should be implemented to make sure there's consistency in the handling of bugs.

A great tool to handle unexpected errors is Sentry (`https://sentry.io/`). This tool creates a trigger for each error on a lot of common platforms, including Python Django, Ruby on Rails, Node, JavaScript, C#, iOS, and Android. It aggregates the errors detected and allows us to work with them more strategically, which is sometimes difficult when just having access to the logs.

Sometimes, unexpected errors will present themselves with enough information about what the problem is, which could be related to an external problem like a network issue or a database problem. The solution may be located outside the realm of the service itself.

Log strategies

A common problem when dealing with logs is deciding on the appropriate severity for each of the individual services. Is this message a `WARNING` or an `ERROR`? Should this statement be added as an `INFO` message or not?

Most of the log severity descriptions have definitions, such as *the program shows a potentially harmful situation* or *the application highlights the progress of the request*. These are vague definitions and difficult to act on in a real-life situation. Instead of using these vague definitions, try to define each level in relationship with any follow-up action that should be taken if the issue is encoutered. This helps to clarify to the developers what to do when a given error log is found. For example: "*Do I want to be informed each and every time this situation happens?*"

The following table shows some examples of the different severity levels and what action could be taken:

Log level	**Action to take**	**Comments**
`DEBUG`	None.	Not tracked. Only useful while developing.
`INFO`	None.	`INFO` logs show generic information about the flow of the actions in the app to help track systems.
`WARNING`	Track the number of logs. Alert on raising levels.	`WARNING` logs track errors that are automatically fixed, like retries to connect to an external service, or fixable format errors in a database. A sudden increase may require investigation.
`ERROR`	Track the number of logs. Alert on raising levels. Review all errors.	`ERROR` logs track errors that can't be recovered. A sudden increase may require immediate action. All of them should be periodically reviewed to fix common occurrences and mitigate them, perhaps moving them to `WARNING` level.
`CRITICAL`	Immediate response.	`CRITICAL` logs indicate a catastrophic failure in the application. A single one indicates the system is not working at all and can't recover.

This sets clear expectations on how to respond. Note this is an example, and you may need to make tweaks and adjustments to adapt this to the needs of your specific organization.

The hierarchy of different severities is very clear, and in our example, there's an acceptance that there'll be a certain number of `ERROR` logs generated. For the development team's sanity, not everything needs to be fixed immediately, but a certain order and prioritization should be enforced.

In production situations, `ERROR` logs will typically be categorized from "we're doomed" to "meh." Development teams should actively either fix "meh" logs or stop the issue from being logged to remove noise from the monitoring tools. That may include lowering the level of logs if they aren't worth checking. You want as few `ERROR` logs as possible, so all of them can be meaningful.

Remember that `ERROR` logs will include unexpected errors that typically require a fix to either resolve the issue completely, or explicitly capture it and reduce its severity if it is not important.

This follow-up is definitely a challenge as applications grow, as the number of `ERROR` logs will increase significantly. It requires time to be spent on proactive maintenance. If this is not taken seriously and it is too often dropped for other tasks, it will compromise the reliability of the application in the medium term.

`WARNING` logs are indications that something may not be working as smoothly as expected, but things are under control, unless there's a sudden increase in the number of logs of this kind. `INFO` logs are just there to give context in the event of a problem, but can be ignored otherwise.

A common mistake is to generate `ERROR` logs in actions where there are incorrect input parameters, such as in web requests when a `400 BAD REQUEST` status code is returned. Some developers will argue that a customer sending a malformed request is an error. But there's nothing that the developer team should do if the request is properly detected and returned. It's business as usual, and the only action may be to return a meaningful message to the requester so they can fix their request.

If this behavior persists in certain critical requests, like repeatedly sending a bad password, a `WARNING` log can be created. There's no point in creating an `ERROR` log when the application is behaving as expected.

In web applications, as a rule of thumb, `ERROR` logs should only be created when the status code is one of the 50X variants (like 500, 502, and 503). Remember that the 40X errors mean that the sender has a problem, while 50X means that the application has the problem, and it's your team's responsibility to fix it.

With common and shared definitions of log levels across the team, all engineers will have a shared understanding of error severity that will help shape meaningful actions toward improving the code.

Allow time for tweaking and adjusting any definition. It's also likely that you'll have to deal with logs created before the definition, which can require work. One of the biggest challenges in legacy systems is creating a proper logging system to categorize problems, as they'll likely be very noisy, making it difficult to distinguish the real problems from annoyances and even non-problems.

Adding logs while developing

Any test runner will capture logs and display it as part of the trace while running tests.

`pytest`, which we introduced in *Chapter 10, Testing and TDD*, will display logs as part of the result of a failing test.

This is a good opportunity to check that the expected logs are being generated while the feature is still in development phase, especially if it's done in a TDD process where the failing tests and errors are produced routinely as part of the process, as we saw in *Chapter 10, Testing and TDD*. Any test that checks an error should also add a corresponding log and, while developing the feature, check that they are being produced.

You can explicitly add to the test a check to validate that the log is being generated by using a tool like `pytest-catchlog` (`https://pypi.org/project/pytest-catchlog/`).

Typically, though, we just take a bit of care and incorporate the practice of checking while using TDD practices as part of the initial check that the test is failing. However, be sure that the developers understand why it's useful to have logs while developing to make the habit stick.

While developing, `DEBUG` logs can be used to add extra information about the code flow that would be excessive for production. In development, this extra information can help fill in the gaps between `INFO` logs and help developers to solidify the habit of adding logs. A `DEBUG` log may be promoted to `INFO` if, during tests, it's found to be useful in tracking problems in production.

Additionally, for special occasions, `DEBUG` logs can be enabled in production in controlled cases to track certain problems that are difficult to understand. Note that this has big implications on the number of generated logs, which can lead to storage problems. Be very cautious here.

Be sensible about the messages displayed in `INFO` and higher severity logs. In terms of information that's displayed, avoid sensitive data such as passwords, secret keys, credit card numbers, and personal information.

Keep an eye in production for any size limitations and how quickly logs are generated. Systems may experience a log explosion in situations when new features are generated, if the number of requests grows, or if the number of workers in the system is increased. These three situations can be produced when systems undergo growth.

It's always a good idea to double-check that the logs are being properly captured and available in different environments. All the configuration to ensure that the logs are properly captured may take a bit of time, so it's better to do this beforehand. This involves capturing unexpected errors and other logs in production and checking that all the plumbing is done correctly. The alternative is to discover that it's not working correctly only after stumbling into a real problem.

Log limitations

Logs are very useful to understand what's happening in a running system, but they have certain limitations that are important to understand:

- *Logs are only as good as their messages.* A good, descriptive message is critical in making logs useful. Reviewing the log messages with a critical eye, and correcting them when needed, is important to save precious time on production problems.
- *Have an appropriate number of logs.* Too many logs can confuse a flow, and too few may not include enough information to allow us to understand the problem. Large numbers of logs also create problems with storage.
- *Logs should work as an indication of the context of the problem, but likely won't pinpoint it.* Trying to generate specific logs that fully explain a bug will be an impossible task. Instead, focus on showing the general flow and surrounding context of the action, so it can be replicated locally and debugged. For example, for a request, make sure to log both the request and its parameters so the situation can be replicated.

- *Logs allow us to follow the execution of a single instance.* When grouped together using a request ID or similar, logs can be grouped by execution, allowing us to follow the flow of a request or task. However, logs don't directly display aggregated information. Logs answer the question, "*what happened in this task?*", but not "*what is going on in the system?*" For that kind of info, it's better to use metrics.

There are tools available to create metrics based on logs. We will talk more about metrics in *Chapter 13, Metrics*.

- *Logs only work retrospectively.* When a problem in a task is detected, logs can only show information that was prepared in advance. That's why it's important to analyze critically and refine the information, removing logs that are not useful and adding others with relevant contextual information to help replicate the problem.

Logs are a fantastic tool, but they need to be maintained to ensure that they can be used to detect bugs and problems and allow us to take action as efficiently as possible.

Summary

In this chapter, we started by presenting the basic elements of logs. We defined how logs contain messages plus some metadata like a timestamp, and considered the different severity levels. We also described the need to define request IDs to group logs related to the same task. We also discussed how, in the Twelve-Factor App methodology, logs should be sent to `stdout` to detach log generation from the process of handling and routing them to the proper destination to allow the collection of all logs in the system.

We then showed how to produce logs in Python using the standard `logging` module, describing the three key elements of the `logger`, the `handler`, and the `formatter`. Next, we showed the two different errors that can be produced in a system: *expected*, understood as errors that were foreseen as possible and are handled; and *unexpected*, meaning those that were not foreseen and occurred out of our control. We then went through the different strategies and cases for these.

We described the different severities and how to generate a strategy for what actions should be taken when a log of a certain severity is detected, instead of categorizing the logs in terms of "how critical they are", which ends up generating vague guidelines and not being very useful.

We discussed several habits to improve the usefulness logs by including them in development in a TDD workflow. This allows developers to consider the information presented in logs while writing tests and producing errors, which presents the perfect opportunity to ensure that the logs generated work correctly.

Finally, we discussed the limitations of logs and how we can deal with them.

In the next chapter, we will look at how to work with aggregated information to find out the general state of the system through the usage of metrics.

Join our book's Discord space

Join the book's Discord workspace for a monthly *Ask me Anything* session with the author: `https://packt.link/PythonArchitechture`

13
Metrics

As well as logging, the other key element of observability is metrics. Metrics allow you to see the general state of the system and observe trends and situations that are mostly caused by multiple, perhaps even many, tasks being executed at the same time.

During this chapter, we will mostly use examples of web services, like request metrics. Do not feel restricted by them; you can generate metrics in all kinds of services!

When monitoring a live system, typically metrics are the main focus, as they allow you to see at a glance whether everything appears to be working correctly. Normally with metrics, it is possible to detect if a system is struggling, for example, for a sudden increase in the number of incoming requests, but also to foresee problems by showing trends, like a small but constant increase in the number of requests. This allows you to act preemptively, without waiting until a problem is serious.

Generating a good metric system to monitor the life of a system is invaluable to be able to react quickly when problems arise. Metrics can also be used as a base for automatic alerts that can help warn about certain conditions taking place, typically something to investigate or correct.

In this chapter, we'll cover the following topics:

- Metrics versus logs
- Generating metrics with Prometheus

- Querying Prometheus
- Proactively working with metrics
- Alerting

First, we will take a look at metrics compared with the other main tool for observability, logs.

Metrics versus logs

As we saw in the previous chapter, logs are text messages produced as code is executed. They are good at giving visibility on each of the specific tasks that the system is performing, but they generate a huge amount of data, which is difficult to digest in bulk. Instead, only small groups of logs are able to be analyzed at any given time.

Normally, the logs analyzed will all be related to a single task. We saw in the previous chapter how to use a request ID for that. But on certain occasions, it may be necessary to check all logs happening in a particular time window to see crossing effects, like a problem in one server that affects all tasks during certain times.

But sometimes the important information is not a specific request, but to understand the behavior of the system as a whole. Is the load of the system growing compared to yesterday's? How many errors are we returning? Is the time it takes to process tasks increasing? Or decreasing?

All those questions are impossible to answer with logs, as they require a broader view, at a higher level. To be able to achieve that, the data needs to be aggregated to be able to understand the system as a whole.

The information to store in metrics is also different. While each recorded log is a text message, each produced metric is a number. These numbers will later be statistically processed to aggregate the information.

We will talk later in the chapter about the different kinds of numbers that can be produced as a metric.

The difference between the amount of information produced in each record means that metrics are much more lightweight compared with logs. To further reduce the amount of data stored, the data is aggregated automatically.

The resolution of metrics may depend on the tool and set configuration. Keep in mind that a higher resolution will require more resources to store all the data. A typical resolution is one minute, which is small enough to present detailed information unless you have a very active system that routinely receives 10 tasks per second or more.

Metrics should capture and analyze information related to performance, such as the average time to process a task. That allows you to detect possible bottlenecks and act quickly in order to improve the performance of the system. This is easier to do in an aggregated way, as information for a single task, like generated logs, may not capture enough information to see the big picture. An important outcome of this is to be able to see trends and detect problems before they grow too big, remediating them early. Compared to this, logs are mostly used after the fact and are difficult to use as a way to take preventive action.

Kinds of metrics

There are different kinds of metrics that can be produced. This can be different depending on the specific tool used to generate the metrics, but in general, there are a few that are common in most systems, like the following:

- **Counter**: A trigger is generated each time something happens. This will be counted and aggregated as a total; for example, in a web service, the number of requests or the number of generated errors. Counters are useful for understanding how many times a certain action happens in the system.
- **Gauge**: A single number across the system. A gauge number can go up or down, but the last value overwrites the previous, as it stores the general state of the system; for example, the number of elements in a queue, or the number of existing workers in the system.
- **Measure**: Events that have a numeric value associated with them. These numbers can be averaged, summed, or aggregated in a certain way. Compared with gauges, the difference is that previous measures are still independent; for example, when we emit a metric with a request time in milliseconds and request size in bytes.

Measures can also work as counters, since each emitted event is, in essence, a counter. For example, tracking the request time will also count the number of requests, as it will be generated once per request. Tools will normally create the associated counter automatically for every measure.

Defining which metric is adequate for the specific value to measure is important. In most cases, they'll be *measures*, to allow storing a value produced by events. *Counters* are normally evident (they are *measures* without values), while *gauges* are normally the ones that are less obvious and can present more of a challenge on when to use them.

Metrics can also be derived from other metrics to generate new ones. For example, we can divide the number of requests that return an error code by the total number of requests to produce an error percentage. Such derived metrics can help you understand information in a meaningful way.

There are also two kinds of metric systems, depending on how the metrics are produced:

- Every time there's a metric produced, an event gets *pushed* toward the metrics collector
- Each system maintains its own metrics internally, which are periodically *pulled* from the metrics collector

Each system has its own pros and cons. Pushing events produces higher traffic and activity, as every individual event is sent immediately, which can cause bottlenecks and delays. Pulling events will only sample the information, and produce lower-resolution data, as it can miss what happened between samples, but it's more stable as the number of requests is not increasing with the number of events.

Both approaches are used, but the current trend is moving toward pulling systems. They reduce the amount of maintenance that is required for pushing systems and are easier to scale.

We will use some examples with Prometheus, a metrics system that uses the pulling approach. The most used exponent of the push approach is Graphite.

Generating metrics with Prometheus

Prometheus is a popular metrics system that is well supported and easy to use. We will use it as an example during the chapter to show how to collect metrics and how it interconnects with other tools to display metrics.

As we saw before, Prometheus uses the *pulling* approach to metrics generation. That means that any system that produces metrics will run its own internal Prometheus client that keeps track of metrics.

For web services, this can be added as an extra endpoint that serves the metrics. This is the approach taken by the `django-prometheus` module, which will automatically collect a lot of common metrics for a Django web service.

We will build up from the Django application code presented in *Chapter 6, Web Server Structures*, to present a working application. Check the code in GitHub at `https://github.com/PacktPublishing/Python-Architecture-Patterns/tree/main/chapter_13_metrics/microposts`.

Preparing the environment

We need to set up the environment to be sure to install all the required packages and dependencies of the code.

Let's start by creating a new virtual environment, as introduced in *Chapter 11, Package Management*, to be sure to create our own isolated sandbox to install packages:

```
$ python3 -m venv venv
$ source venv/bin/activate
```

We can now install the prepared list of requirements, stored in `requirements.txt`. This contains the Django and Django REST framework modules, as seen in *Chapter 6, Web Server Structures*, but also the Prometheus dependency:

```
(venv) $ cat requirements.txt
django
django-rest-framework
django-prometheus
(venv) $ pip install -r requirements.txt
Collecting Django
```

```
  Downloading Django-3.2.7-py3-none-any.whl (7.9 MB)
     |████████████████████████████████| 7.9 MB 5.7 MB/s
...
Installing collected packages: djangorestframework, django-rest-
framework
    Running setup.py install for django-rest-framework ... done
Successfully installed django-rest-framework-0.1.0
djangorestframework-3.12.4
```

To start the server, go to the `micropost` subdirectory and run the `runserver` command:

```
(venv) $ python3 manage.py runserver 0.0.0.0:8000
Watching for file changes with StatReloader
Performing system checks...

System check identified no issues (0 silenced).
October 01, 2021 - 23:24:26
Django version 3.2.7, using settings 'microposts.settings'
Starting development server at http://0.0.0.0:8000/
Quit the server with CONTROL-C.
```

The application is now accessible in the root address: `http://localhost:8000`, for example, `http://localhost:8000/api/users/jaime/collection`.

Note that we started the server at address 0.0.0.0. This opens Django to serve any IP address, and not only requests coming from `localhost`. This is an important detail that will be clarified later.

Note also that the root address will return a 404 error, as no endpoint is defined there.

If you remember from *Chapter 3, Data Modeling*, we added some initial data, so you can access the URLs `http://localhost:8000/api/users/jaime/collection` and `http://localhost:8000/api/users/dana/collection` to see some data.

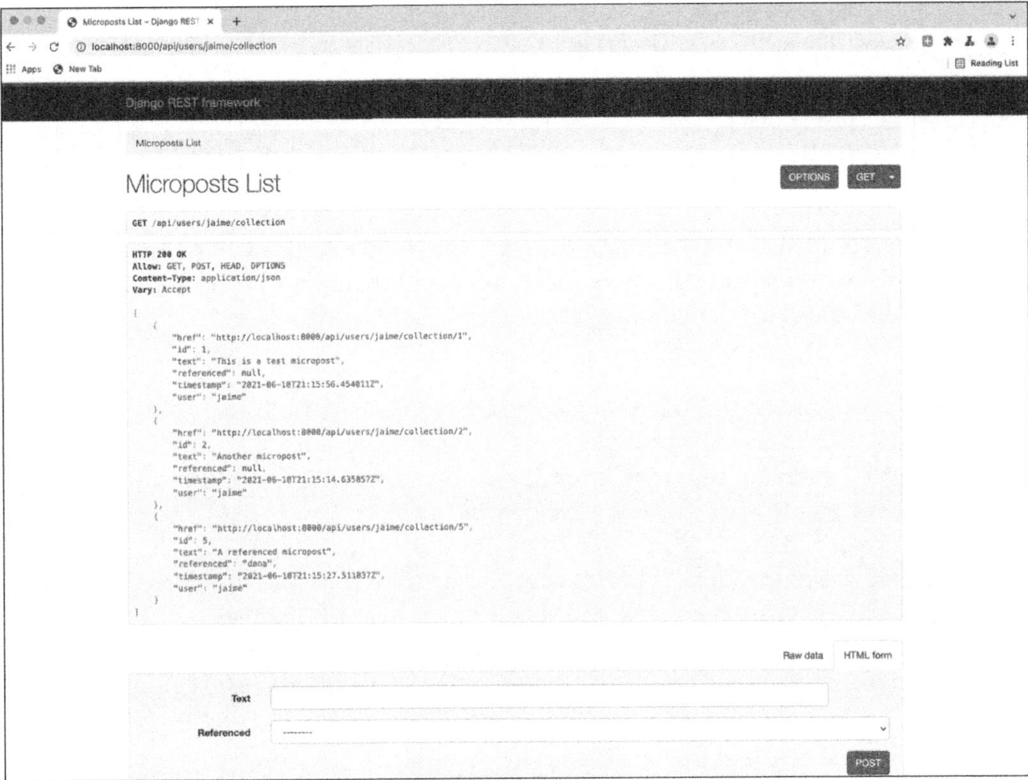

Figure 13.1: Accessing an available URL in the application

Access these pages a couple of times to produce metrics that we can later access.

Configuring Django Prometheus

The configuration of the `django-prometheus` module is done in the `microposts/settings.py` file, where we need to do two things.

First, add the `django-prometheus` application to the installed app list which enables the module:

```
INSTALLED_APPS = [
    'django.contrib.admin',
    'django.contrib.auth',
    'django.contrib.contenttypes',
    'django.contrib.sessions',
```

```
    'django.contrib.messages',
    'django.contrib.staticfiles',
    'django_prometheus',
    'rest_framework',
    'api',
]
```

We also need to include the proper middlewares to track requests. We need to put one middleware at the start of the request process and another at the end, to be sure to capture and measure the whole process:

```
MIDDLEWARE = [
    'django_prometheus.middleware.PrometheusBeforeMiddleware',
    'django.middleware.security.SecurityMiddleware',
    'django.contrib.sessions.middleware.SessionMiddleware',
    'django.middleware.common.CommonMiddleware',
    'django.middleware.csrf.CsrfViewMiddleware',
    'django.contrib.auth.middleware.AuthenticationMiddleware',
    'django.contrib.messages.middleware.MessageMiddleware',
    'django.middleware.clickjacking.XFrameOptionsMiddleware',
    'django_prometheus.middleware.PrometheusAfterMiddleware',
]
```

Check the position of `django.prometheus.middleware.PrometheusBeforeMiddleware` and `django_prometheus.middleware.PrometheusAfterMiddleware`.

We also changed the `ALLOWED_HOSTS` value to be `'*'` and allow requests from any hostname. This detail will be explained a bit later.

With this configuration, the Prometheus collection is now enabled. But we also need a way to access them. Remember, an important element for the Prometheus system is that each application serves its own metric collection.

In this case, we can add an endpoint to the file `microposts/url.py`, which handles the top-level URLs for the system:

```
from django.contrib import admin
from django.urls import include, path

urlpatterns = [
```

```
    path('', include('django_prometheus.urls')),
    path('api/', include('api.urls')),
    path('admin/', admin.site.urls),
]
```

The `path('', include('django_prometheus.urls'))` line sets up a `/metrics` URL that we can now access.

Checking the metrics

The main URL root shows that there's a new endpoint – `/metrics`:

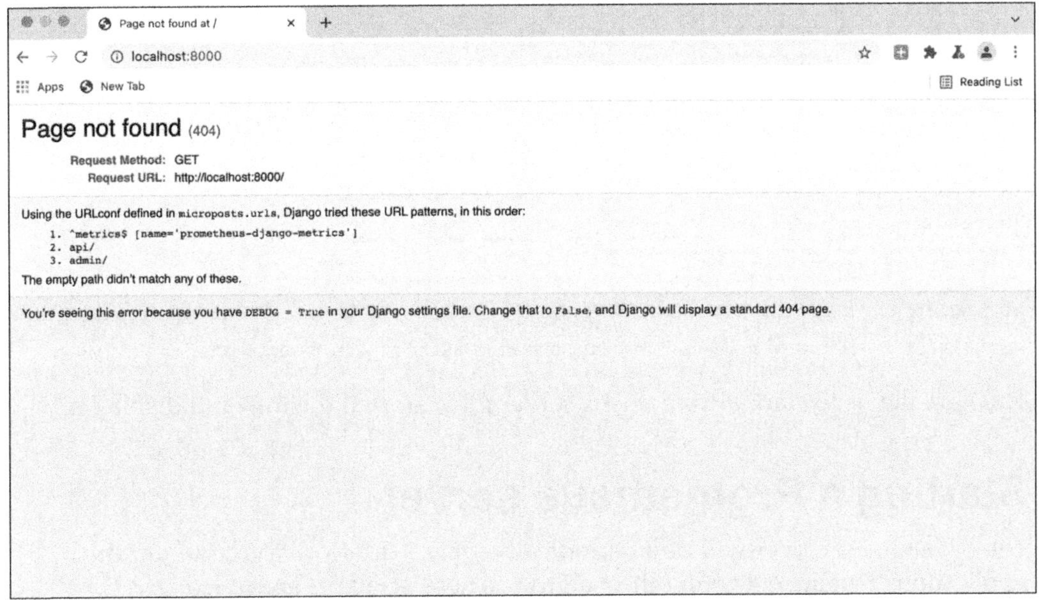

Figure 13.2: This page appears because the DEBUG mode is active. Remember to deactivate it before deploying in production

When accessing the `/metrics` endpoint, it shows all the collected metrics. Note that there are a lot of metrics that are collected. This is all in text format, and it's expected to be collected by a Prometheus metric server.

Be sure to access a few times the endpoints `http://localhost:8000/api/users/jaime/collection` and `http://localhost:8000/api/users/dana/collection` to produce some metrics. You can check how some metrics, like `django_http_requests_total_by_view_transport_method_total{method="GET",transport="http",view="user-collection"}`, are increasing.

localhost:8000/metrics

Apps New Tab Reading List

```
# HELP python_gc_objects_collected_total Objects collected during gc
# TYPE python_gc_objects_collected_total counter
python_gc_objects_collected_total{generation="0"} 14726.0
python_gc_objects_collected_total{generation="1"} 2640.0
python_gc_objects_collected_total{generation="2"} 99.0
# HELP python_gc_objects_uncollectable_total Uncollectable object found during GC
# TYPE python_gc_objects_uncollectable_total counter
python_gc_objects_uncollectable_total{generation="0"} 0.0
python_gc_objects_uncollectable_total{generation="1"} 0.0
python_gc_objects_uncollectable_total{generation="2"} 0.0
# HELP python_gc_collections_total Number of times this generation was collected
# TYPE python_gc_collections_total counter
python_gc_collections_total{generation="0"} 178.0
python_gc_collections_total{generation="1"} 16.0
python_gc_collections_total{generation="2"} 1.0
# HELP python_info Python platform information
# TYPE python_info gauge
python_info{implementation="CPython",major="3",minor="9",patchlevel="7",version="3.9.7"} 1.0
# HELP django_model_inserts_total Number of insert operations by model.
# TYPE django_model_inserts_total counter
# HELP django_model_updates_total Number of update operations by model.
# TYPE django_model_updates_total counter
# HELP django_model_deletes_total Number of delete operations by model.
# TYPE django_model_deletes_total counter
# HELP django_migrations_unapplied_total Count of unapplied migrations by database connection
# TYPE django_migrations_unapplied_total gauge
django_migrations_unapplied_total{connection="default"} 0.0
# HELP django_migrations_applied_total Count of applied migrations by database connection
# TYPE django_migrations_applied_total gauge
django_migrations_applied_total{connection="default"} 19.0
# HELP django_http_requests_before_middlewares_total Total count of requests before middlewares run.
# TYPE django_http_requests_before_middlewares_total counter
django_http_requests_before_middlewares_total 5.0
# HELP django_http_requests_before_middlewares_created Total count of requests before middlewares run.
# TYPE django_http_requests_before_middlewares_created gauge
django_http_requests_before_middlewares_created 1.633130666713357e+09
# HELP django_http_responses_before_middlewares_total Total count of responses before middlewares run.
# TYPE django_http_responses_before_middlewares_total counter
django_http_responses_before_middlewares_total 4.0
# HELP django_http_responses_before_middlewares_created Total count of responses before middlewares run.
# TYPE django_http_responses_before_middlewares_created gauge
django_http_responses_before_middlewares_created 1.6331306667134058e+09
```

Figure 13.3: The raw Prometheus metrics, as collected by the application

The next step is to start a Prometheus server that can pull the info and display it.

Starting a Prometheus server

The Prometheus server will pull periodically for metrics to all the configured applications that are collecting their metrics. These elements are called *targets* by Prometheus.

The easiest way to start a Prometheus server is to start the official Docker image.

We introduced Docker in *Chapter 9, Microservices vs Monolith*. Refer to that chapter for more information.

We need to start the server, but before that, we need to set up the configuration in the `prometheus.yml` file. You can check the example on GitHub: `https://github.com/PacktPublishing/Python-Architecture-Patterns/blob/main/chapter_13_metrics/prometheus.yml`:

```
# my global config
global:
  scrape_interval: 15s # Set the scrape interval to every 15 seconds.
Default is every 1 minute.
  # scrape_timeout is set to the global default (10s).

scrape_configs:
  # The job name is added as a label `job=<job_name>` to any timeseries
scraped from this config.
  - job_name: "prometheus"

    # metrics_path defaults to '/metrics'
    # scheme defaults to 'http'.

    static_configs:
      # The target needs to point to your local IP address
      # 192.168.1.196 IS AN EXAMPLE THAT WON'T WORK IN YOUR SYSTEM
      - targets: ["192.168.1.196:8000"]
```

The config file has two main sections. The first with `global` indicates how often to scrape (to read information from the targets) and other general configuration values.

The second, `scrape_config`, describes what to scrape from, and the main parameter is `targets`. Here, we need to configure all our targets. This one in particular needs to be described by its external IP, which will be the IP from your computer.

This address cannot be `localhost`, as inside the Prometheus Docker container it will resolve as the same container, which is not what you want. You'll need to find out your local IP address.

If you don't know how to find it through ipconfig or ifconfig, you can check out this article on ways to find it: `https://lifehacker.com/how-to-find-your-local-and-external-ip-address-5833108`. Remember that it's your **local address**, not the external one.

This is to ensure that the Prometheus server can access the Django application that's running locally. As you remember, we opened the access allowing connections from any hostname with the option `0.0.0.0` when starting the server and allowing all hosts in the config parameter `ALLOWED_HOSTS`.

Double-check that you can access the metrics in the local IP.

192.168.1.196:8000/metrics

Not Secure | 192.168.1.196:8000/metrics

Apps New Tab

Reading List

```
# HELP python_gc_objects_collected_total Objects collected during gc
# TYPE python_gc_objects_collected_total counter
python_gc_objects_collected_total{generation="0"} 20677.0
python_gc_objects_collected_total{generation="1"} 2915.0
python_gc_objects_collected_total{generation="2"} 99.0
# HELP python_gc_objects_uncollectable_total Uncollectable object found during GC
# TYPE python_gc_objects_uncollectable_total counter
python_gc_objects_uncollectable_total{generation="0"} 0.0
python_gc_objects_uncollectable_total{generation="1"} 0.0
python_gc_objects_uncollectable_total{generation="2"} 0.0
# HELP python_gc_collections_total Number of times this generation was collected
# TYPE python_gc_collections_total counter
python_gc_collections_total{generation="0"} 191.0
python_gc_collections_total{generation="1"} 17.0
python_gc_collections_total{generation="2"} 1.0
# HELP python_info Python platform information
# TYPE python_info gauge
python_info{implementation="CPython",major="3",minor="9",patchlevel="7",version="3.9.7"} 1.0
# HELP django_model_inserts_total Number of insert operations by model.
# TYPE django_model_inserts_total counter
# HELP django_model_updates_total Number of update operations by model.
# TYPE django_model_updates_total counter
# HELP django_model_deletes_total Number of delete operations by model.
# TYPE django_model_deletes_total counter
# HELP django_migrations_unapplied_total Count of unapplied migrations by database connection
# TYPE django_migrations_unapplied_total gauge
django_migrations_unapplied_total{connection="default"} 0.0
# HELP django_migrations_applied_total Count of applied migrations by database connection
# TYPE django_migrations_applied_total gauge
django_migrations_applied_total{connection="default"} 19.0
# HELP django_http_requests_before_middlewares_total Total count of requests before middlewares run.
# TYPE django_http_requests_before_middlewares_total counter
django_http_requests_before_middlewares_total 58.0
# HELP django_http_requests_before_middlewares_created Total count of requests before middlewares run.
# TYPE django_http_requests_before_middlewares_created gauge
django_http_requests_before_middlewares_created 1.633187368153887e+09
# HELP django_http_responses_before_middlewares_total Total count of responses before middlewares run.
# TYPE django_http_responses_before_middlewares_total counter
django_http_responses_before_middlewares_total 57.0
# HELP django_http_responses_before_middlewares_created Total count of responses before middlewares run.
# TYPE django_http_responses_before_middlewares_created gauge
django_http_responses_before_middlewares_created 1.633187368153912e+09
# HELP django_http_requests_latency_including_middlewares_seconds Histogram of requests processing time (including middleware processing time).
# TYPE django_http_requests_latency_including_middlewares_seconds histogram
django_http_requests_latency_including_middlewares_seconds_bucket{le="0.005"} 49.0
django_http_requests_latency_including_middlewares_seconds_bucket{le="0.01"} 50.0
django_http_requests_latency_including_middlewares_seconds_bucket{le="0.025"} 52.0
django_http_requests_latency_including_middlewares_seconds_bucket{le="0.05"} 52.0
django_http_requests_latency_including_middlewares_seconds_bucket{le="0.075"} 52.0
django_http_requests_latency_including_middlewares_seconds_bucket{le="0.1"} 53.0
django_http_requests_latency_including_middlewares_seconds_bucket{le="0.25"} 55.0
django_http_requests_latency_including_middlewares_seconds_bucket{le="0.5"} 55.0
django_http_requests_latency_including_middlewares_seconds_bucket{le="0.75"} 55.0
django_http_requests_latency_including_middlewares_seconds_bucket{le="1.0"} 55.0
django_http_requests_latency_including_middlewares_seconds_bucket{le="2.5"} 56.0
django_http_requests_latency_including_middlewares_seconds_bucket{le="5.0"} 57.0
django_http_requests_latency_including_middlewares_seconds_bucket{le="7.5"} 57.0
```

Figure 13.4: Note the IP used to access; remember that you should use your own local one

With all this information, you are now ready to start the Prometheus server in Docker, using your own config file.

Please note that this command requires you to find the full path to the `prometheus.yml` file. If you are in the same directory, you can address it as `$(pwd)/prometheus.yml`.

For this, run the following `docker` command, adding the whole path to the config file to share it with the new container:

```
$ docker run -p 9090:9090  -v /full/path/to/file/prometheus.yml:/etc/
prometheus/prometheus.yml prom/prometheus
level=info ts=2021-10-02T15:24:17.228Z caller=main.go:400 msg="No
time or size retention was set so using the default time retention"
duration=15d
level=info ts=2021-10-02T15:24:17.228Z caller=main.go:438 msg="Starting
Prometheus" version="(version=2.30.2, branch=HEAD, revision=b30db03f356
51888e34ac101a06e25d27d15b476)"
...
level=info ts=2021-10-02T15:24:17.266Z caller=main.go:794 msg="Server
is ready to receive web requests."
```

The `docker` command is structured in the following way:

- `-p 9090:9090` maps the local 9090 port to the 9090 port inside the container
- `-v /full/path/to/file/prometheus.yml:/etc/prometheus/prometheus.yml` mounts the local file (remember to add the full path or use `$(pwd)/prometheus.yml`) in the expected configuration route for Prometheus
- `docker run prom/Prometheus` is the command to run the `prom/Prometheus` image, which is the official Prometheus image

After the Prometheus server is up and running, the server is accessible at `http://localhost:9090`.

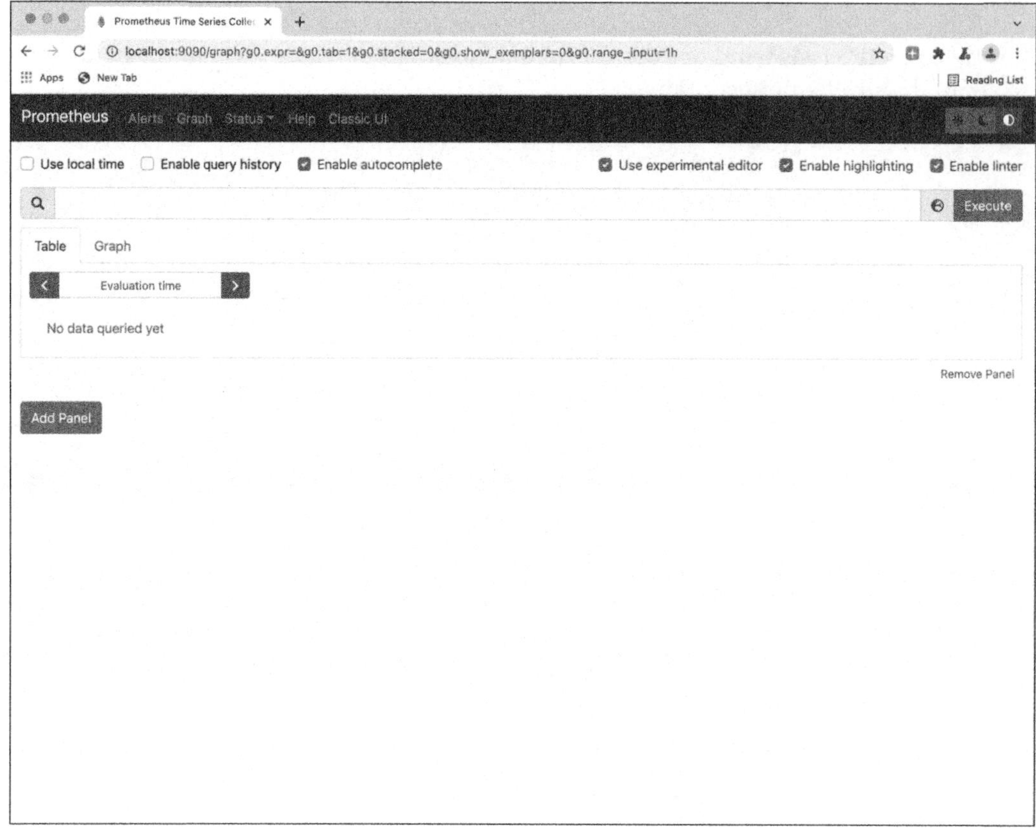

Figure 13.5: The empty graph Prometheus page

From here, we can start querying the system.

Querying Prometheus

Prometheus has its own query system, called PromQL, and ways of operating with metrics that, while powerful, can be a little confusing at the beginning. Part of it is its pull approach to metrics.

For example, requesting one useful metric, like `django_http_requests_latency_seconds_by_view_method_count`, will display how many times each view has been called for each method.

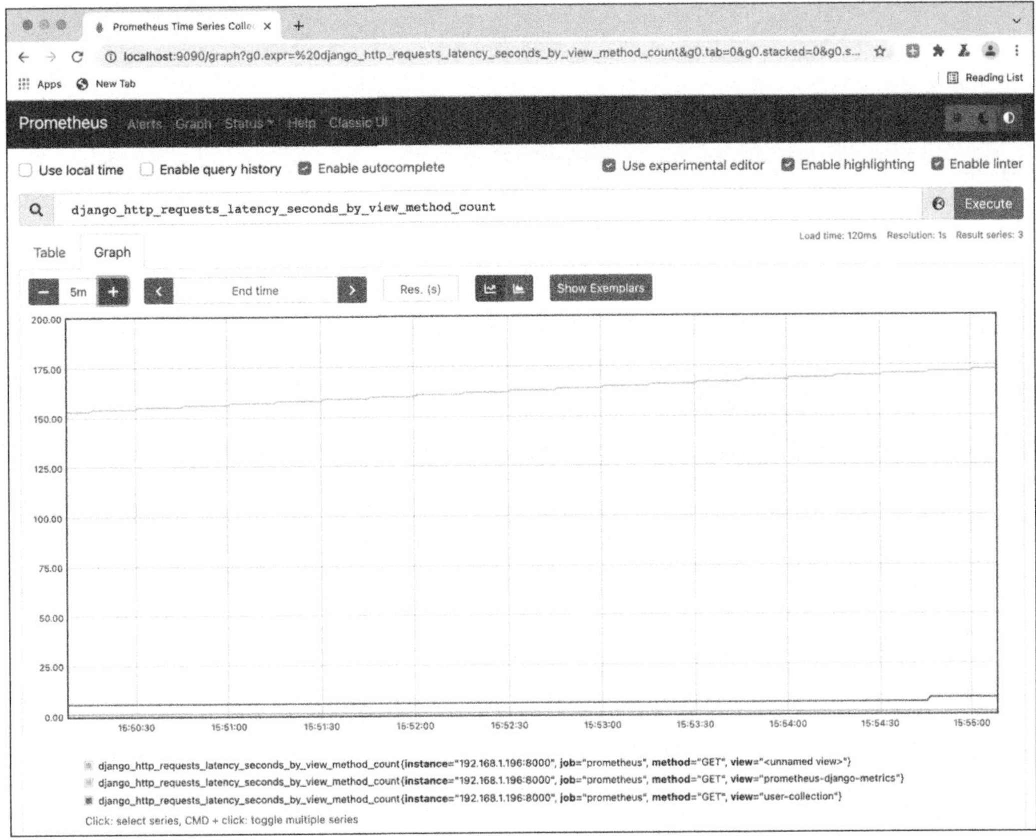

Figure 13.6: Notice how the prometheus-django-metrics view is called more often, as it is called automatically by Prometheus once every 15 seconds to scrape the results

This is presented as an accumulated value that grows over time. This is not very useful, as it's difficult to make sense of what exactly it means.

Instead, the value is more likely to be presented as a `rate`, representing how many requests have been detected per second. For example, with a resolution of 1 minute, `rate(django_http_requests_latency_seconds_by_view_method_count[1m])` shows the following graph instead:

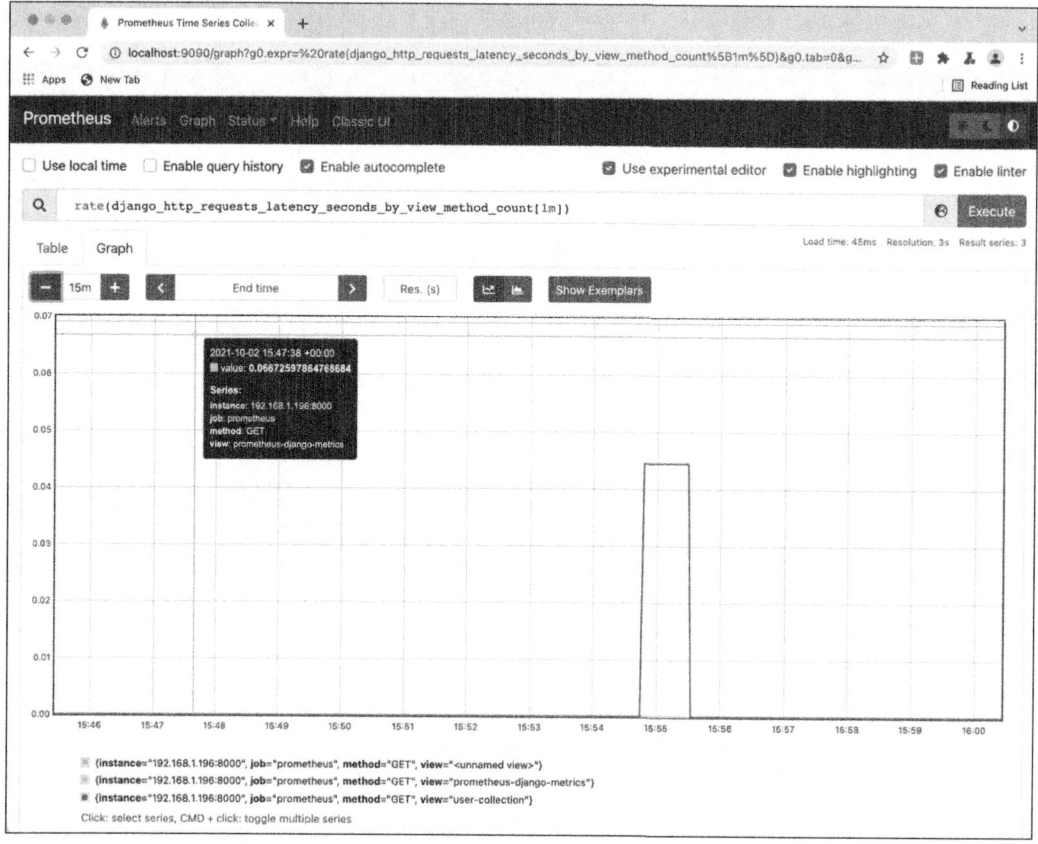

Figure 13.7: Note that the different methods and views are displayed as different lines

As you can see, there's a constant number of requests from `prometheus-django-metrics`, which is Prometheus requesting the metrics information. This happens once every 15 seconds, or approximately 0.066 times per second.

In the graph, there's also another spike of the `user-collection` method happening at 15:55, at the time where we manually generated some requests to the service. As you can see, the resolution is per minute, as described in the rate.

If we want to aggregate all of this in a single graph, we can use the sum operator, specifying what we want to aggregate from. To sum all `GET` requests, for example, with:

```
sum(rate(django_http_requests_latency_seconds_by_view_method_
count[1m])) by (method)
```

This produces this other graph:

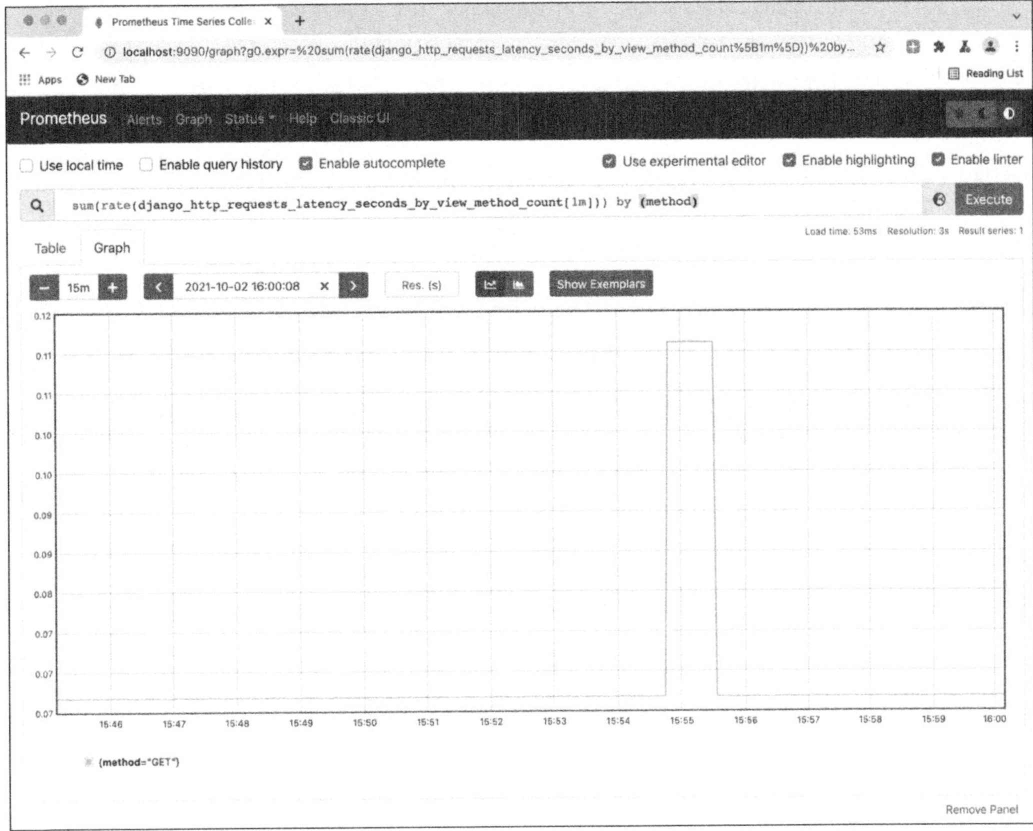

Figure 13.8: Note the bottom value is based on the baseline created by the calls to prometheus-django-metrics

To plot times instead, the metric to use is the `django_http_requests_latency_seconds_by_view_method_bucket` one. The bucket metrics are generated in a way that can be combined with the `histogram_quantile` function to display a particular quantile, which is useful for giving a proper feeling of times.

For example, quantile 0.95 means that the time is the highest of 95% of the requests. This is more useful than creating averages as they can get skewed by high numbers. Instead, you can draw the quantile 0.50 (the maximum time it takes for half of the requests), the quantile 0.90 (the maximum time for most of the requests), and quantile 0.99 for the very top time it takes to return a request. This allows you to get a better picture, as it's different from the situation of growing quantile 0.50 (most requests take longer to return) with growing quantile 0.99 (some slow queries are getting worse).

To plot the 0.95 quantile over a period of 5 minutes, the following query can be generated:

```
histogram_quantile(0.95, rate(django_http_requests_latency_seconds_by_
view_method_bucket[5m]))
```

When you run it, you should receive the following:

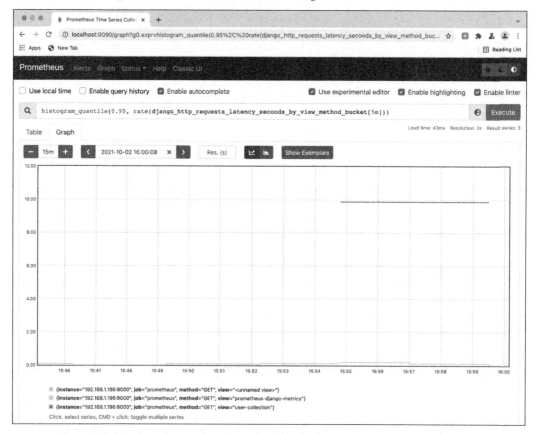

Figure 13.9: Note how the metrics collection is much faster than the user-collection requests

To plot times instead, the metric to use is the `django_http_requests_latency_seconds_by_view_method_bucket` one. The bucket metrics are generated in a way that can be combined with the `histogram_quantile` function to display a particular quantile, which is useful for giving a proper feeling of times.

Metrics can also be filtered to display only specific labels, and a good number of functions to multiply, divide, add, create averages, and all kinds of operations are available.

Prometheus queries can be a bit long and complicated when trying to display the result of several metrics, such as the percentage of successful requests over the total. Be sure to test that the result is what you expect it to be and allocate time to tweak the queries later to keep improving them.

The interface has autocompleted, which can help you find certain metrics.

Prometheus is normally paired with Grafana. Grafana is an open source, interactive visualization tool that can be connected with Prometheus to create rich dashboards. This leverages the collection of metrics and helps visualize the state of the system in a much more understandable way. Describing how to use Grafana is out of scope for this book, but using it to display metrics is highly recommended: `https://grafana.com/`.

Check the Prometheus documentation about queries to find out more: `https://prometheus.io/docs/prometheus/latest/querying/basics/`.

Proactively working with metrics

As we've seen, metrics show an aggregated point of view for the status of the whole cluster. They allow you to detect trending problems, but it's difficult to pinpoint a single spurious error.

This shouldn't stop us from considering them as a critical tool for successful monitoring because they can tell whether the whole system is healthy. In some companies, the most critical metrics are on permanent display on screens so the operations team can see them and react quickly to any sudden problem.

Finding the proper balance of what metrics are the key ones for a service is not as straightforward as it seems, and it will require time and experience, perhaps even trial and error.

There are, though, four metrics for online services that are considered always important. They are:

- **Latency**: How many milliseconds it takes for the system to respond to a request. Depending on the service, sometimes seconds can be used instead. In my experience, milliseconds are typically the adequate time scale, as most web applications take between 50 ms and 1 second to respond, depending on the request. Requests taking longer than 1 second are typically rarer, though there are always some, depending on the system.
- **Traffic**: The number of requests flowing through the system per unit of time, for example, the number of requests per minute.
- **Errors**: The percentage of requests received that return an error.
- **Saturation**: Describing whether the capacity of the cluster has enough headroom. This includes elements as available hard drive space, memory, and so on. For example, there's 15% available RAM in the system.

The main tool to check saturation is the multiple default exporters available to collect most of the hardware information automatically, like memory, CPU, and hard drive space. When using a cloud provider, normally they expose their own set of related metrics, like CloudWatch in AWS.

These metrics can be found in the Google SRE book as *the four golden signals* and are recognized as the most important high-level elements for successful monitoring.

Alerting

When problems are detected through the metrics, an automatic alert should be triggered. Prometheus has an alert system that will raise when a defined metric fulfills the defined alert.

Check out the Prometheus documentation on alerting for more information: `https://prometheus.io/docs/alerting/latest/overview/`.

Normally, alerts will be configured when the value of metrics is crossing some threshold. For example, the number of errors is higher than X, or the time to return a request is too high.

An alert could also be that some element is too low; for example, if the number of requests in a system falls to zero, that could be an indication that the system is down.

The built-in Alertmanager can alert in some ways, like sending an email, but it can also be connected to other tools to perform more complex actions. For example, connecting to an integrated incident solution like Opsgenie (`https://www.atlassian.com/software/opsgenie`) allows you to create alert flows, such as sending emails and SMS, calls.

While alerts can be generated directly from metrics, there are tools that allow you also to generate alerts from logs directly. For example, Sentry (`https://sentry.io/`) will aggregate errors based on logs and can set up thresholds to escalate toward more active alerts, like sending emails.

Another alternative is to derivate metrics from logs using external logging systems. This allows you, for example, to create a counter based on the number of `ERROR` logs, or more complicated metrics. These systems, once more, allow you to trigger alerts based on these derived metrics.

Alerting, as with metrics, is an ongoing process. Some key thresholds won't be evident at the start of the system, and only experience will allow you to discover them. In the same way, it's very likely that some alerts are created that don't require active monitoring, and should be disconnected to ensure that the alerts in the system are on point and have a high signal-to-noise ratio.

Summary

In this chapter, we described what metrics are and how they compare with logs. We described how metrics are useful to analyze the general state of the system, while logs describe specific tasks, being more difficult to describe the aggregated situation.

We enumerated different kinds of metrics that can be produced and described Prometheus, a common metrics system that uses the pull approach on how to capture metrics.

We set an example of how to generate metrics automatically in Django by installing and configuring the `django-prometheus` module, and how to start a Prometheus server that scrapes the generated metrics.

Keep in mind that you can also generate your own custom metrics, not having to only rely on the ones in an external module. Check the Prometheus client to see how, for example, for Python: `https://github.com/prometheus/client_python`.

Next, we described how to query metrics in Prometheus, introducing PromQL, and showed some common examples of how to display metrics, plot `rate` to see clearly how the metrics are changing over time, and how to use the `histogram_quantile` function to work with times.

We also showed in the chapter how to work proactively to detect common problems as soon as possible and what the four golden signals are, as described by Google. Finally, we introduced alerts as a way to be notified when metrics are out of a normal margin. Using alerts is a smart way to be notified without having to manually look at metrics.

Join our book's Discord space

Join the book's Discord workspace for a monthly *Ask me Anything* session with the author: `https://packt.link/PythonArchitechture`

14
Profiling

It is quite common that written code doesn't behave perfectly after being tested with real data. Other than bugs, we can find the problem that the performance of the code is not adequate. Perhaps some requests are taking too much time, or perhaps the usage of memory is too high.

In those cases, it's difficult to know exactly what the key elements are, that are taking the most time or memory. While it's possible to try to follow the logic, normally once the code is released, the bottlenecks will be at points that are almost impossible to know beforehand.

To get information on what exactly is going on and follow the code flow, we can use profilers to dynamically analyze the code and better understand how the code is executed, in particular, where most time is spent. This can lead to adjustments and improvements affecting the most significant elements of the code, driven by data, instead of vague speculation.

In this chapter, we'll cover the following topics:

- Profiling basics
- Types of profilers
- Profiling code for time
- Partial profiling
- Memory profiling

First, we will take a look at the basic principles of profiling.

Profiling basics

Profiling is a dynamic analysis that instruments code to understand how it runs. This information is extracted and compiled in a way that can be used to get a better knowledge of a particular behavior based on a real case, as the code is running as usual. This information can be used to improve the code.

Certain static analysis tools, as opposed to dynamic, can provide insight into aspects of the code. For example, they can be used to detect if certain code is dead code, meaning it's not called anywhere in the whole code. Or, they can detect some bugs, like the usage of variables that haven't been defined before, like when having a typo. But they don't work with the specifics of code that's actually being run. Profiling will bring specific data based on the use case instrumented and will return much more information on the flow of the code.

The normal application of profiling is to improve the performance of the code under analysis. By understanding how it executes in practice, it sheds light on the dynamics of the code modules and parts that could be causing problems. Then, actions can be taken in those specific areas.

Performance can be understood in two ways: either *time performance* (how long code takes to execute) or *memory performance* (how much memory the code takes to execute). Both can be bottlenecks. Some code may take too long to execute or use a lot of memory, which may limit the hardware where it's executed.

We will focus more on time performance in this chapter, as it is typically a bigger problem, but we will also explain how to use a memory profiler.

A common case in software development is that you don't really know what your code is going to do until it gets executed. Clauses to cover corner cases that appear rare may execute much more than expected, and software works differently when there are big arrays, as some algorithms may not be adequate.

The problem is that doing that analysis before having the system running is incredibly difficult, and at most times, futile, as the problematic pieces of code will very likely be completely unexpected.

> *Programmers waste enormous amounts of time thinking about, or worrying about, the speed of noncritical parts of their programs, and these attempts at efficiency actually have a strong negative impact when debugging and maintenance are considered. We should forget about small efficiencies, say about 97% of the time:* **premature optimization is the root of all evil**. *Yet we should not pass up our opportunities in that critical 3%.*
>
> *Donald Knuth – Structured Programing with GOTO Statements - 1974.*

Profiling gives us the ideal tool to *not* prematurely optimize, but to optimize according to real, tangible data. The idea is that you cannot optimize what you cannot measure. The profiler measures so it can be acted upon.

The famous quote above is sometimes reduced to "premature optimization is the root of all evil," which is a bit reductionist and doesn't carry the nuance. Sometimes it's important to design elements with care and it's possible to plan in advance. As good as profiling (or other techniques) may be, they can only go so far. But it's important to understand, on most occasions, it's better to take the simple approach, as performance will be good enough, and it will be possible to improve it later in the few cases when it's not.

Profiling can be achieved in different ways, each with its pros and cons.

Types of profilers

There are two main kinds of time profilers:

- **Deterministic profilers**, through a process of tracing. A deterministic profiler instruments the code and records each individual command. This makes deterministic profilers very detailed, as they can follow up the code on each step, but at the same time, the code is executed slower than without the instrumentation.

- Deterministic profilers are not great to execute continuously. Instead, they can be activated in specific situations, like while running specific tests offline, to find out problems.
- **Statistical profiles**, through sampling. This kind of profiler, instead of instrumenting the code and detecting each operation, awakes at certain intervals and takes a sample of the current code execution stack. If this process is done for long enough, it captures the general execution of the program.

> Taking a sample of the stack is similar to taking a picture. Imagine a train or subway hall where people are moving across to go from one platform to another. Sampling is analogous to taking pictures at periodic intervals, for example, once every 5 minutes. Sure, it's not possible to get exactly who comes from one platform and goes to another, but after a whole day, it will provide good enough information on how many people have been around and what platforms are the most popular.

While they don't give as detailed information as deterministic profiles, statistical profilers are much more lightweight and don't consume many resources. They can be enabled to constantly monitor live systems without interfering with their performance.

Statistical profilers only make sense on systems that are under relative load, as in a system that is not stressed, they'll show that most time is spent waiting.

Statistical profilers can be internal, if the sampling is done directly on the interpreter, or even external if it's a different program that is taking the samples. An external profiler has the advantage that, even if there's any problem with the sampling process, it won't interfere with the program being sampled.

Both profilers can be seen as complementary. Statistical profilers are good tools for understanding the most-visited parts of the code and where the system, aggregated, is spending time. They live in the live system, where the real case usages determine the behavior of the system.

The deterministic profilers are tools for analyzing specific use cases in the petri dish of the developer's laptop, where a specific task that is having some problem can be dissected and analyzed carefully, to be improved.

In some respects, statistical profilers are analogous to metrics and deterministic profilers to logs. One displays the aggregated elements and the other the specific elements. Deterministic profilers, contrary to logs, are not ideal tools for using in live systems without care, though.

Typically, code will present *hotspots*, slow parts of it that get executed often. Finding the specific parts to focus attention on and then act on them is a great way to improve the overall speed.

These hotspots can be revealed by profiling, either by checking the *global* hotspots using a statistical profiler or the *specific* hotspots for a task with a deterministic profiler. The first will display the specific parts of the code that are most used in general, which allows us to understand the pieces that get hit more often and take the most time in aggregate. The deterministic profiler can show, for a specific task, how long it takes for each line of code, and determine what are the slow elements.

We won't look at statistical profilers as they require systems that are under load and they are difficult to create in a test that's fit for the scope of this book. You can check `py-spy` (`https://pypi.org/project/py-spy/`) or `pyinstrument` (`https://pypi.org/project/pyinstrument/`).

Another kind of profiler is the memory profiler. A memory profiler records when memory is increased and decreased, tracking the usage of memory. Profiling memory is typically used to find out memory leaks, which are rare for a Python program, but they can happen.

Python has a garbage collector that releases memory automatically when an object is not referenced anymore. This happens without having to take any action, so compared with programs with manual memory assignment, like C/C++, the memory management is easier to handle. The garbage collection mechanism used for Python is called *reference counting*, and it frees memory immediately once a memory object is not used by anyone, as compared with other kinds of garbage collectors that wait.

In the case of Python, memory leaks can be created by three main use cases, from more likely to least:

- Some objects are still referenced, even if they are not used anymore. This can typically happen if there are long-lived objects that keep small elements in big elements, like lists of dictionaries when they are added and not removed.

- An internal C extension is not managing the memory correctly. This may require further investigation with specific C profiling tools, which is out of scope for this book.
- Complex reference cycles. A reference cycle is a group of objects that reference each other, e.g. object A references B and object B references A. While Python has algorithms to detect them and release the memory nonetheless, there's the small possibility that the garbage collector is disabled or any other bug problem. You can see more information on the Python garbage collector here: `https://docs.python.org/3/library/gc.html`.

The most likely situation for extra usage of memory is an algorithm that uses a lot of memory, and detecting when the memory is allocated can be achieved with the help of a memory profiler.

Memory profiling is typically more complicated and takes more effort than time profiling.

Let's introduce some code and profile it.

Profiling code for time

We will start by creating a short program that will calculate and display all prime numbers up to a particular number. Prime numbers are numbers that are only divisible by themselves and one.

We will start by taking a naïve approach first:

```
def check_if_prime(number):
    result = True

    for i in range(2, number):
        if number % i == 0:
            result = False

    return result
```

This code will take every number from 2 to the number under test (without including it), and check whether the number is divisible. If at any point it is divisible, the number is not a prime number.

To calculate all the way from 1 to 5,000, to verify that we are not making any mistakes, we will include the first prime numbers lower than 100 and compare them. This is on GitHub, available as `primes_1.py` at `https://github.com/PacktPublishing/Python-Architecture-Patterns/blob/main/chapter_14_profiling/primes_1.py`.

```
PRIMES = [1, 2, 3, 5, 7, 11, 13, 17, 19, 23, 29, 31, 37, 41, 43, 47,
53,
          59, 61, 67, 71, 73, 79, 83, 89, 97]
NUM_PRIMES_UP_TO = 5000


def check_if_prime(number):
    result = True

    for i in range(2, number):
        if number % i == 0:
            result = False

    return result


if __name__ == '__main__':
    # Calculate primes from 1 to NUM_PRIMES_UP_TO
    primes = [number for number in range(1, NUM_PRIMES_UP_TO)
              if check_if_prime(number)]
    # Compare the first primers to verify the process is correct
    assert primes[:len(PRIMES)] == PRIMES

    print('Primes')
    print('------')
    for prime in primes:
        print(prime)
    print('------')
```

The calculation of prime numbers is performed by creating a list of all numbers (from 1 to `NUM_PRIMES_UP_TO`) and verifying each of them. Only values that return `True` will be kept:

```
# Calculate primes from 1 to NUM_PRIMES_UP_TO
primes = [number for number in range(1, NUM_PRIMES_UP_TO)
          if check_if_prime(number)]
```

The next line asserts that the first prime numbers are the same as the ones defined in the PRIMES list, which is a hardcoded list of the first primes lower than 100.

```
assert primes[:len(PRIMES)] == PRIMES
```

The primes are finally printed. Let's execute the program, timing its execution:

```
$ time python3 primes_1.py
Primes
------
1
2
3
5
7
11
13
17
19
…
4969
4973
4987
4993
4999
------

Real      0m0.875s
User      0m0.751s
sys 0m0.035s
```

From here, we will start analyzing the code to see what is going on internally and see if we can improve it.

Using the built-in cProfile module

The easiest, faster way of profiling a module is to directly use the included cProfile module in Python. This module is part of the standard library and can be called as part of the external call, like this:

```
$ time python3 -m cProfile primes_1.py
Primes
```

```
------
1
2
3
5
...
4993
4999
------
         5677 function calls in 0.760 seconds

   Ordered by: standard name

   ncalls  tottime  percall  cumtime  percall filename:lineno(function)
        1    0.002    0.002    0.757    0.757 primes_1.
py:19(<listcomp>)
        1    0.000    0.000    0.760    0.760 primes_1.py:2(<module>)
     4999    0.754    0.000    0.754    0.000 primes_1.py:7(check_if_
prime)
        1    0.000    0.000    0.760    0.760 {built-in method
builtins.exec}
        1    0.000    0.000    0.000    0.000 {built-in method
builtins.len}
      673    0.004    0.000    0.004    0.000 {built-in method
builtins.print}
        1    0.000    0.000    0.000    0.000 {method 'disable' of '_
lsprof.Profiler' objects}



Real      0m0.895s
User      0m0.764s
sys 0m0.032s
```

Note this called the script normally, but also presented the profile analysis. The table shows:

- `ncalls`: Number of times each element has been called
- `tottime`: Total time spent on each element, not including sub calls
- `percall`: Time per call on each element (not including sub calls)
- `cumtime`: Cumulative time – the total time spent on each element, including subcalls

- `percall`: Time per call on an element, including subcalls
- `filename:lineno`: Each of the elements under analysis

In this case, the time is clearly seen to be spent in the `check_if_prime` function, which is called 4,999 times, and it takes the practical totality of the time (744 milliseconds compared with a total of 762).

While not easy to see here due to the fact that it's a small script, `cProfile` increases the time it takes to execute the code. There's an equivalent module called `profile` that's a direct replacement but implemented in pure Python, as opposed to a C extension. Please generally use `cProfile` as it's faster, but `profile` can be useful at certain moments, like when trying to extend the functionality.

While this text table can be enough for simple scripts like this one, the output can be presented as a file and then displayed with other tools:

```
$ time python3 -m cProfile -o primes1.prof  primes_1.py
$ ls primes1.prof
primes1.prof
```

Now we need to install the visualizer SnakeViz, installing it through `pip`:

```
$ pip3 install snakeviz
```

Finally, open the file with `snakeviz`, which will open a browser with the information:

```
$ snakeviz primes1.prof
snakeviz web server started on 127.0.0.1:8080; enter Ctrl-C to exit
http://127.0.0.1:8080/snakeviz/%2FUsers%2Fjaime%2FDropbox%2FPackt%2Farc
hitecture_book%2Fchapter_13_profiling%2Fprimes1.prof
```

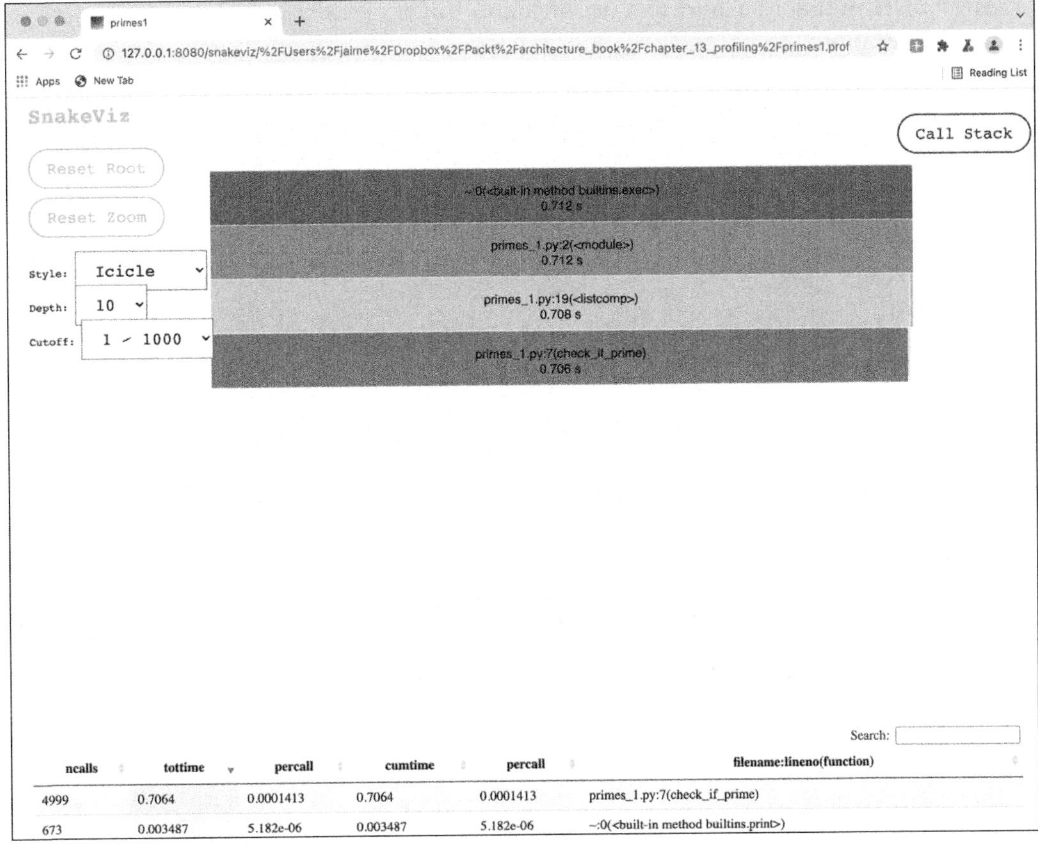

Figure 14.1: Graphical representation of the profiling information. The full page is too big to fit here and has been cropped purposefully to show some of the info.

This graph is interactive, and we can click and hover on different elements to get more information:

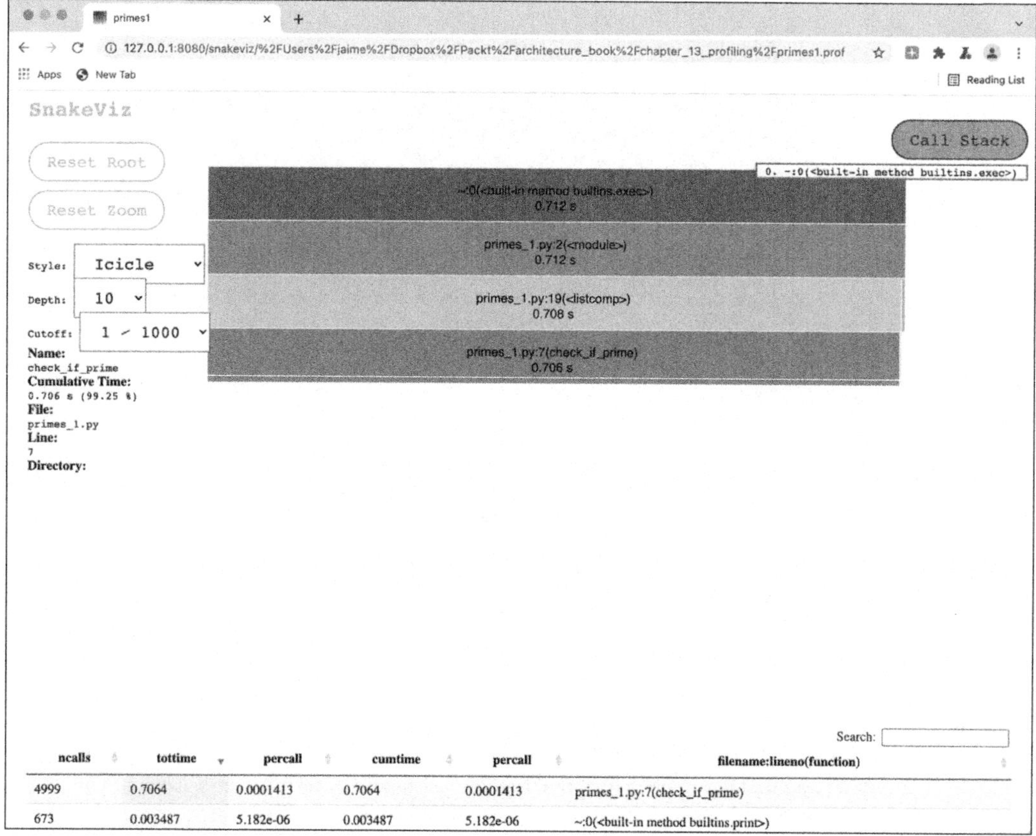

Figure 14.2: Checking the information about check_if_prime. The full page is too big to fit here and has been cropped purposefully to show some of the info.

We can confirm here that the bulk of the time is spent on `check_if_prime`, but we don't get information about what's inside it.

This is because `cProfile` only has function granularity. You'll see how long each function call takes, but not a lower resolution. For this specifically simple function, this may not be enough.

Do not underestimate this tool. The code example presented is purposefully simple to avoid spending too much time explaining its use. Most of the time, localizing the function that's taking most of the time is good enough to visually inspect it and discover what's taking too long. Keep in mind that, in most practical situations, the time spent will be on external calls like DB accesses, remote requests, etc.

We will see how to use a profiler that has a higher resolution, analyzing each line of code.

Line profiler

To analyze the `check_if_prime` function, we need to first install the module `line_profiler`

```
$ pip3 install line_profiler
```

After it's installed, we will make a small change in the code, and save it as `primes_2.py`. We will add the decorator `@profile` for the `check_if_prime` function, to indicate to the line profiler to look into it.

Keep in mind that you should only profile sections of the code where you want to know more in this way. If all the code was profiled in this way, it would take a lot of time to analyze.

The code will be like this (the rest will be unaffected). You can check the whole file on GitHub at `https://github.com/PacktPublishing/Python-Architecture-Patterns/blob/main/chapter_14_profiling/primes_2.py`.

```
@profile
def check_if_prime(number):
    result = True

    for i in range(2, number):
        if number % i == 0:
            result = False

    return result
```

Execute the code now with `kernprof`, which will be installed after the installation of `line_profiler`.

```
$ time kernprof -l primes_2.py
Primes
------
1
2
3
5
…
4987
4993
4999
------
Wrote profile results to primes_2.py.lprof

Real      0m12.139s
User      0m11.999s
sys 0m0.098s
```

Note the execution took noticeably longer – 12 seconds compared with subsecond execution without the profiler enabled. Now we can take a look at the results with this command:

```
$ python3 -m line_profiler primes_2.py.lprof
Timer unit: 1e-06 s

Total time: 6.91213 s
File: primes_2.py
Function: check_if_prime at line 7

Line #      Hits         Time  Per Hit   % Time  Line Contents
==============================================================
     7                                           @profile
     8                                           def check_if_
prime(number):
     9      4999       1504.0      0.3      0.0      result = True
    10
    11  12492502    3151770.0      0.3     45.6      for i in range(2,
number):
```

```
    12  12487503      3749127.0        0.3       54.2              if number % i
== 0:
    13     33359         8302.0        0.2        0.1                  result =
False
    14
    15      4999         1428.0        0.3        0.0          return result
```

Here, we can start analyzing the specifics of the algorithm used. The main problem seems to be that we are doing a lot of comparisons. Both lines 11 and 12 are being called too many times, though the time per hit is short. We need to find a way to reduce the number of times they're being called.

The first one is easy. Once we find a `False` result, we don't need to wait anymore; we can return directly, instead of continuing with the loop. The code will be like this (stored in `primes_3.py`, available at `https://github.com/PacktPublishing/Python-Architecture-Patterns/blob/main/chapter_14_profiling/primes_3.py`):

```
@profile
def check_if_prime(number):

    for i in range(2, number):
        if number % i == 0:
            return False

    return True
```

```
Let's take a look at the profiler result.

$ time kernprof -l primes_3.py
...
Real      0m2.117s
User      0m1.713s
sys       0m0.116s

$ python3 -m line_profiler primes_3.py.lprof
Timer unit: 1e-06 s

Total time: 0.863039 s
File: primes_3.py
Function: check_if_prime at line 7
```

```
Line #      Hits         Time  Per Hit   % Time  Line Contents
==============================================================
     7                                           @profile
     8                                           def check_if_
prime(number):
     9
    10   1564538     388011.0      0.2     45.0      for i in range(2,
number):
    11   1563868     473788.0      0.3     54.9          if number % i
== 0:
    12      4329       1078.0      0.2      0.1              return
False
    13
    14       670        162.0      0.2      0.0      return True
```

We see how time has gone down by a big factor (2 seconds compared with the 12 seconds before, as measured by `time`) and we see the great reduction in time spent on comparisons (3,749,127 microseconds before, and then 473,788 microseconds), mainly due to the fact there are 10 times fewer comparisons, 1,563,868 compared with 12,487,503.

We can also improve and further reduce the number of comparisons by limiting the size of the loop.

Right now, the loop will try to divide the source number between all the numbers up to itself. For example, for 19, we try these numbers (as 19 is a prime number, it's not divisible by any except for itself).

```
Divide 19 between
[2, 3, 4, 5, 6, 7, 8, 9, 10, 11, 12, 13, 14, 15, 16, 17, 18, 19]
```

Trying all these numbers is not necessary. At least, we can skip half of them, as no number will be divisible by a number higher than half itself. For example, 19 divided by 10 or higher is less than 2.

```
Divide 19 between
[2, 3, 4, 5, 6, 7, 8, 9, 10]
```

Furthermore, any factor of a number will be lower than its square root. This can be explained as follows: If a number is the factor of two or more numbers, the highest they may be is the square root of the whole number. So we check only the numbers up to the square root (rounded down):

```
Divide 19 between
[2, 3, 4]
```

But we can reduce it even further. We only need to check the odd numbers after 2, as any even number will be divisible by 2. So, in this case, we even reduce it further.

```
Divide 19 between
[2, 3]
```

To apply all of this, we need to tweak the code again and store it in `primes_4.py`, available on GitHub at `https://github.com/PacktPublishing/Python-Architecture-Patterns/blob/main/chapter_14_profiling/primes_4.py`:

```
def check_if_prime(number):

    if number % 2 == 0 and number != 2:
        return False

    for i in range(3, math.floor(math.sqrt(number)) + 1, 2):
        if number % i == 0:
            return False

    return True
```

The code always checks for divisibility by 2, unless the number is 2. This is to keep returning 2 correctly as a prime.

Then, we create a range of numbers that starts from 3 (we already tested 2) and continue until the square root of the number. We use the `math` module to perform the action and to floor the number to the nearest lower integer. The `range` function requires a `+1` of this number, as it doesn't include the defined number. Finally, the range step on 2 integers at time so that all the numbers are odd, since we started with 3.

For example, to test a number like 1,000, this is the equivalent code.

```
>>> import math
>>> math.sqrt(1000)
31.622776601683793
>>> math.floor(math.sqrt(1000))
31
>>> list(range(3, 31 + 1, 2))
[3, 5, 7, 9, 11, 13, 15, 17, 19, 21, 23, 25, 27, 29, 31]
```

Note that 31 is returned as we added the `+1`.

Let's profile the code again.

```
$ time kernprof -l primes_4.py
Primes
------
1
2
3
5
…
4973
4987
4993
4999
------
Wrote profile results to primes_4.py.lprof

Real      0m0.477s
User      0m0.353s
sys       0m0.094s
```

We see another big increase in performance. Let's see the line profile.

```
$ python3 -m line_profiler primes_4.py.lprof
Timer unit: 1e-06 s

Total time: 0.018276 s
File: primes_4.py
Function: check_if_prime at line 8
```

```
Line #      Hits         Time  Per Hit   % Time  Line Contents
==============================================================
     8                                           @profile
     9                                           def check_if_
prime(number):
    10
    11      4999       1924.0      0.4     10.5      if number % 2 == 0
and number != 2:
    12      2498        654.0      0.3      3.6          return False
    13
    14     22228       7558.0      0.3     41.4      for i in range(3,
math.floor(math.sqrt(number)) + 1, 2):
    15     21558       7476.0      0.3     40.9          if number % i
== 0:
    16      1831        506.0      0.3      2.8              return
False
    17
    18       670        158.0      0.2      0.9      return True
```

We've reduced the number of loop iterations drastically to 22,228, from 1.5 million in `primes_3.py` and over 12 million in `primes_2.py`, when we started the line profiling. That's some serious improvement!

You can try to do the test to increase `NUM_PRIMES_UP_TO` in `primes_2.py` and `primes_4.py` and compare them. The change will be clearly perceptible.

The line approach should be used only for small sections. In general, we've seen how `cProfile` can be more useful, as it's easier to run and gives information.

Previous sections have assumed that we are able to run the whole script and then receive the results, but that may not be correct. Let's take a look at how to profile in sections of the program, for example, when a request is received.

Partial profiling

In many scenarios, profilers will be useful in environments where the system is in operation and we cannot wait until the process finishes before obtaining profiling information. Typical scenarios are web requests.

If we want to analyze a particular web request, we may need to start a web server, produce a single request, and stop the process to obtain the result. This doesn't work as well as you may think due to some problems that we will see.

But first, let's create some code to explain this situation.

Example web server returning prime numbers

We will use the final version of the function `check_if_prime` and create a web service that returns all the primes up to the number specified in the path of the request. The code will be the following, and it's fully available in the `server.py` file on GitHub at `https://github.com/PacktPublishing/Python-Architecture-Patterns/blob/main/chapter_14_profiling/server.py`.

```
from http.server import BaseHTTPRequestHandler, HTTPServer
import math


def check_if_prime(number):

    if number % 2 == 0 and number != 2:
        return False

    for i in range(3, math.floor(math.sqrt(number)) + 1, 2):
        if number % i == 0:
            return False

    return True


def prime_numbers_up_to(up_to):
    primes = [number for number in range(1, up_to + 1)
              if check_if_prime(number)]

    return primes


def extract_param(path):
    '''
    Extract the parameter and transform into
    a positive integer. If the parameter is
```

```
    not valid, return None
    '''
    raw_param = path.replace('/', '')

    # Try to convert in number
    try:
        param = int(raw_param)
    except ValueError:
        return None

    # Check that it's positive
    if param < 0:
        return None

    return param


def get_result(path):
    param = extract_param(path)
    if param is None:
        return 'Invalid parameter, please add an integer'

    return prime_numbers_up_to(param)


class MyServer(BaseHTTPRequestHandler):

    def do_GET(self):

        result = get_result(self.path)

        self.send_response(200)
        self.send_header("Content-type", "text/html")
        self.end_headers()
        return_template = '''
            <html>
                <head><title>Example</title></head>
                <body>
                    <p>Add a positive integer number in the path to
display
                    all primes up to that number</p>
```

```
                <p>Result {result}</p>
            </body>
        </html>
        '''

        body = bytes(return_template.format(result=result), 'utf-8')
        self.wfile.write(body)


if __name__ == '__main__':

    HOST = 'localhost'
    PORT = 8000

    web_server = HTTPServer((HOST, PORT), MyServer)
    print(f'Server available at http://{HOST}:{PORT}')
    print('Use CTR+C to stop it')

    # Capture gracefully the end of the server by KeyboardInterrupt
    try:
        web_server.serve_forever()
    except KeyboardInterrupt:
        pass

    web_server.server_close()
    print("Server stopped.")
```

The code is better understood if you start from the end. The final block creates a web server using the base `HTTPServer` definition in the Python module `http.server`. Previously, we created the class `MyServer`, which defines what to do if there's a `GET` request in the `do_GET` method.

The `do_GET` method returns an HTML response with the result calculated by `get_result`. It adds all the required headers and formats the body in HTML.

The interesting bits of the process happen in the next functions.

`get_result` is the root one. It first calls `extract_param` to get a number, up to which to calculate the threshold number for us to calculate primes up to. If correct, then that's passed to `prime_numbers_up_to`.

```
def get_result(path):
    param = extract_param(path)
```

```
    if param is None:
        return 'Invalid parameter, please add an integer'

    return prime_numbers_up_to(param)
```

The function `extract_params` will extract a number from the URL path. It first removes any `/` character, and then tries to convert it into an integer and checks the integer is positive. For any errors, it returns `None`.

```
def extract_param(path):
    '''
    Extract the parameter and transform into
    a positive integer. If the parameter is
    not valid, return None
    '''
    raw_param = path.replace('/', '')

    # Try to convert in number
    try:
        param = int(raw_param)
    except ValueError:
        return None

    # Check that it's positive
    if param < 0:
        return None

    return param
```

The function `prime_numbers_up_to`, finally, calculates the prime numbers up to the number passed. This is similar to the code that we saw earlier in the chapter.

```
def prime_numbers_up_to(up_to):
    primes = [number for number in range(1, up_to + 1)
              if check_if_prime(number)]

    return primes
```

Finally, `check_if_prime`, which we covered extensively earlier in the chapter, is the same as it was at `primes_4.py`.

The process can be started with:

```
$ python3 server.py
Server available at http://localhost:8000
Use CTR+C to stop it
```

And then tested by going to `http://localhost:8000/500` to try to get prime numbers up to 500.

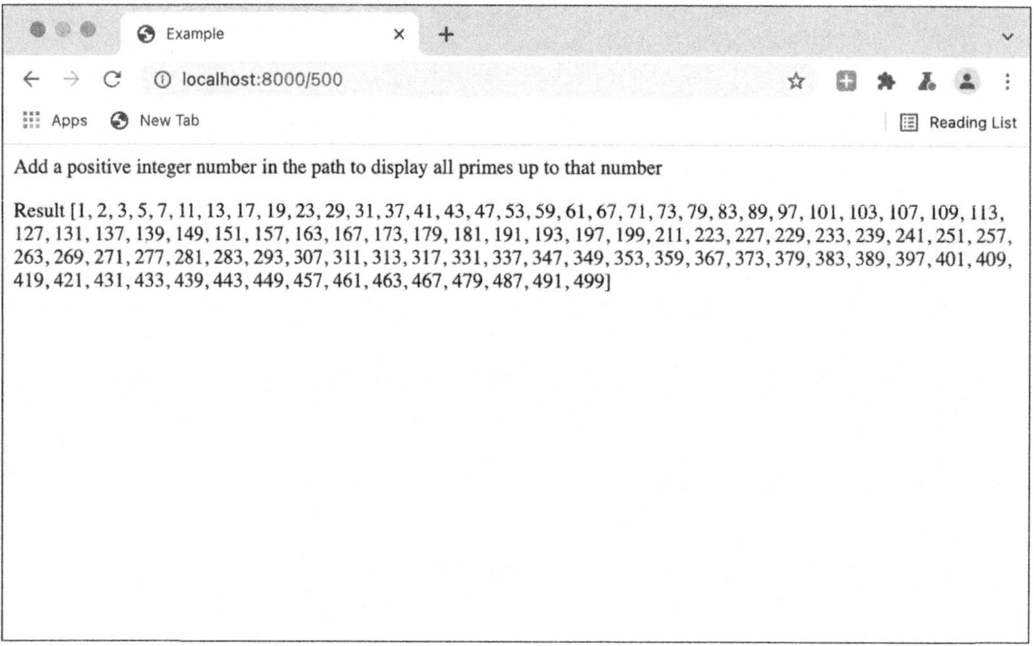

Figure 14.3: The interface displaying all primes up to 500

As you can see, we have an understandable output. Let's move on to profiling the process we used to get it.

Profiling the whole process

We can profile the whole process by starting it under `cProfile` and then capturing its output with. We start it like this, make a single request to `http://localhost:8000/500`, and check the results.

```
$ python3 -m cProfile -o server.prof server.py
Server available at http://localhost:8000
Use CTR+C to stop it
```

```
127.0.0.1 - - [10/Oct/2021 14:05:34] "GET /500 HTTP/1.1" 200 -
127.0.0.1 - - [10/Oct/2021 14:05:34] "GET /favicon.ico HTTP/1.1" 200 -
^CServer stopped.
```

We have stored the results in the file `server.prof`. This file can then be analyzed as before, using `snakeviz`.

```
$ snakeviz server.prof
snakeviz web server started on 127.0.0.1:8080; enter Ctrl-C to exit
```

Which displays the following diagram:

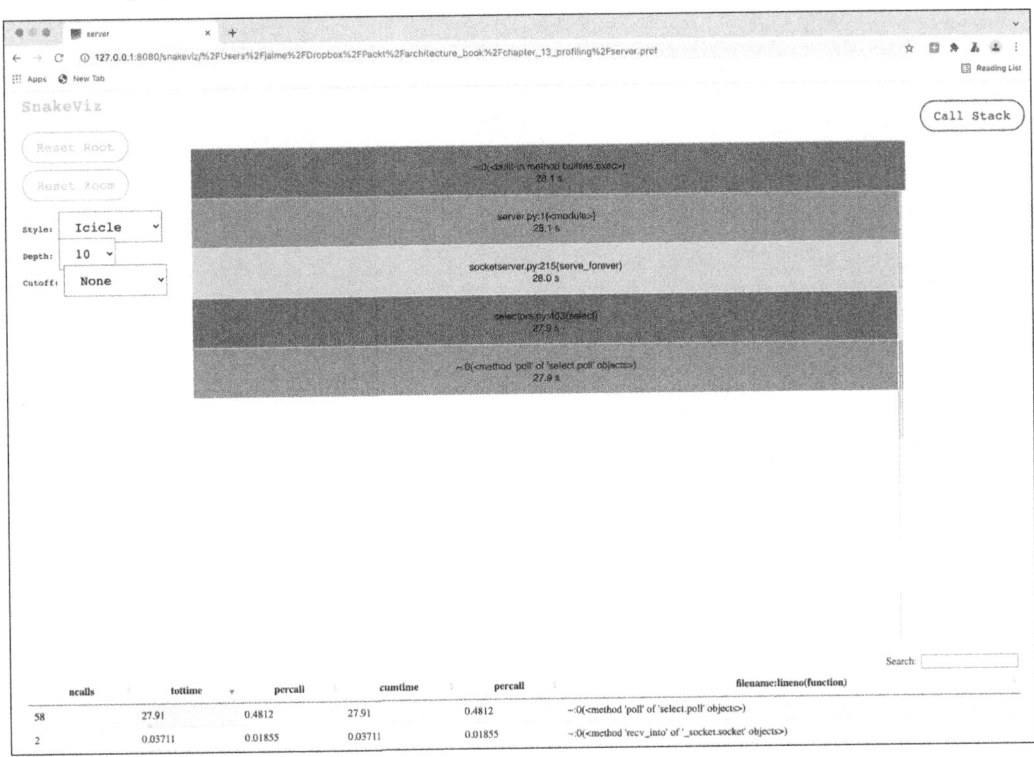

Figure 14.4: Diagram of the full profile. The full page is too big to fit here and has been cropped purposefully to show some of the info.

As you can see, the diagram shows that for the vast majority of the test duration, the code was waiting for a new request, and internally doing a poll action. This is part of the server code and not our code.

To find the code that we care about, we can manually search in the long list below for `get_result`, which is the root of the interesting bits of our code. Be sure to select `Cutoff: None` to display all the functions.

Once selected, the diagram will display from there onward. Be sure to scroll up to see the new diagram.

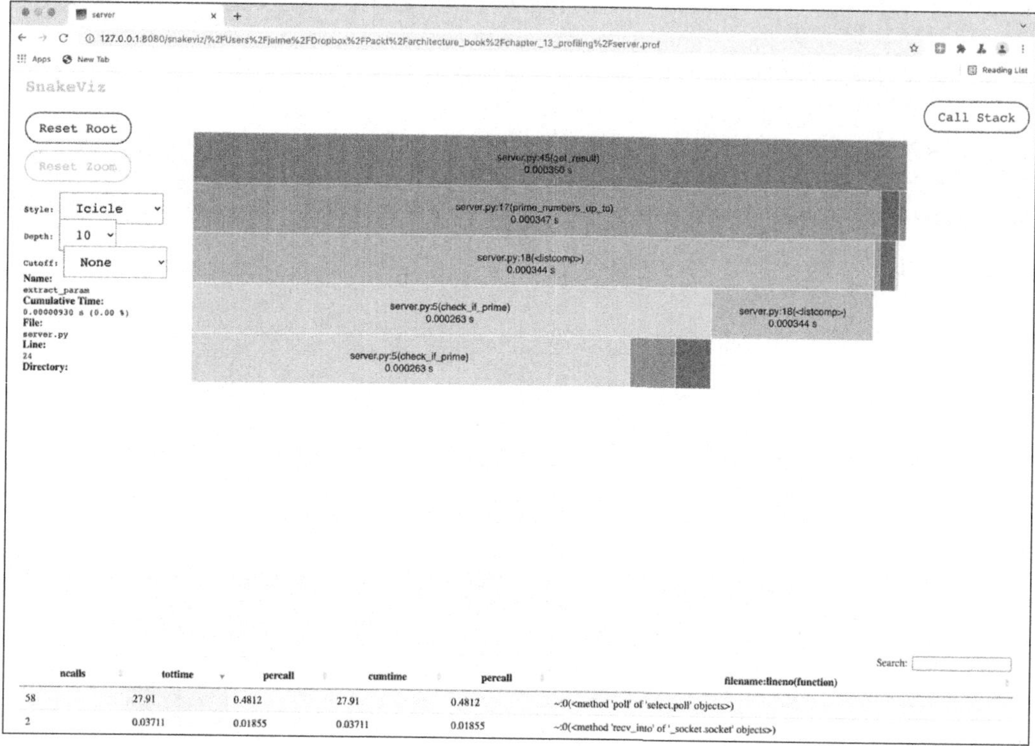

Figure 14.5: The diagram showing from get_result. The full page is too big to fit here and has been cropped purposefully to show some of the info.

Here, you can see more of the general structure of the code execution. You can see that most of the time is spent on the multiple `check_if_prime` calls, which comprise the bulk of `prime_numbers_up_to` and the list comprehension included in it, and very little time is spent on `extract_params`.

But this approach has some problems:

- First of all, we need to go a full cycle between starting and stopping a process. This is cumbersome to do for requests.
- Everything that happens in the cycle is included. That adds noise to the analysis. Fortunately, we knew that the interesting part was in `get_result`, but that may not be evident. This case also uses a minimal structure but adding that in the case of a complex framework like Django can lead to a lot of .

- If we process two different requests, they will be added into the same file, again mixing the results.

These problems can be solved by applying the profiler to only the part that is of interest and producing a new file for each request.

Generating a profile file per request

To be able to generate a different file with information per individual request, we need to create a decorator for easy access. This will profile and produce an independent file.

In the file `server_profile_by_request.py`, we get the same code as in `server.py`, but adding the following decorator.

```
from functools import wraps
import cProfile
from time import time


def profile_this(func):

    @wraps(func)
    def wrapper(*args, **kwargs):
        prof = cProfile.Profile()
        retval = prof.runcall(func, *args, **kwargs)
        filename = f'profile-{time()}.prof'
        prof.dump_stats(filename)
        return retval

    return wrapper
```

The decorator defines a `wrapper` function that replaces the original function. We use the `wraps` decorator to keep the original name and docstring.

This is just a standard decorator process. A decorator function in Python is one that returns a function that then replaces the original one. As you can see, the original function `func` is still called inside the wrapper that replaces it, but it adds extra functionality.

Inside, we start a profiler and run the function under it using the `runcall` function. This line is the core of it – using the profiler generated, we run the original function `func` with its parameters and store its returned value.

```
retval = prof.runcall(func, *args, **kwargs)
```

After that, we generate a new file that includes the current time and dump the stats in it with the `.dump_stats` call.

We also decorate the `get_result` function, so we start our profiling there.

```
@profile_this
def get_result(path):
    param = extract_param(path)
    if param is None:
        return 'Invalid parameter, please add an integer'

    return prime_numbers_up_to(param)
```

The full code is available in the file `server_profile_by_request.py`, available on GitHub at `https://github.com/PacktPublishing/Python-Architecture-Patterns/blob/main/chapter_14_profiling/server_profile_by_request.py`.

Let's start the server now and make some calls through the browser, one to `http://localhost:8000/500` and another to `http://localhost:8000/800`.

```
$ python3 server_profile_by_request.py
Server available at http://localhost:8000
Use CTR+C to stop it
127.0.0.1 - - [10/Oct/2021 17:09:57] "GET /500 HTTP/1.1" 200 -
127.0.0.1 - - [10/Oct/2021 17:10:00] "GET /800 HTTP/1.1" 200 -
```

We can see how new files are created:

```
$ ls profile-*
profile-1633882197.634005.prof
profile-1633882200.226291.prof
```

These files can be displayed using `snakeviz`:

```
$ snakeviz profile-1633882197.634005.prof
snakeviz web server started on 127.0.0.1:8080; enter Ctrl-C to exit
```

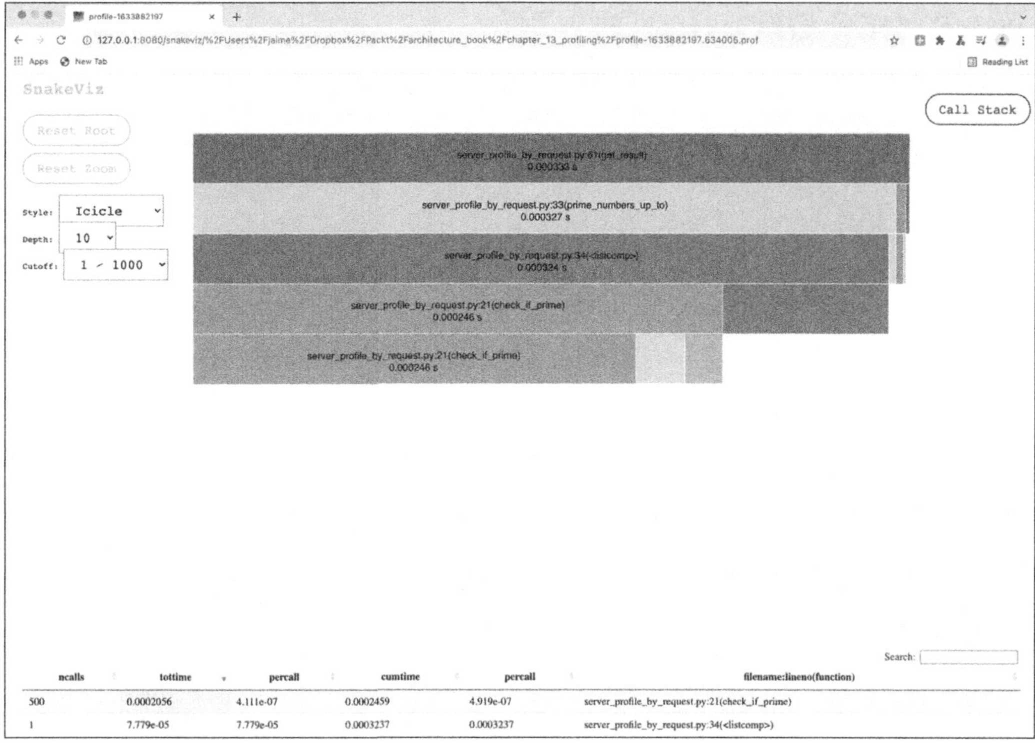

Figure 14.6: The profile information of a single request. The full page is too big to fit here and has been cropped purposefully to show some of the info.

Each file contains only the information from `get_result` onwards, which gets information only up to a point. Even more so, each file displays information only for a specific request, so it can be profiled individually, with a high level of detail.

The code can be adapted to adapt the filename more specifically to include details like call parameters, which can be useful. Another interesting possible adaptation is to create a random sample, so only 1 in X calls produces profiled code. This can help reduce the overhead of profiling and allow you to completely profile some requests.

This is different from a statistical profiler, as it will still completely profile some requests, instead of detecting what's going on at a particular time. This can help follow the flow of what happens for particular requests.

Next, we'll see how to perform memory profiling.

Memory profiling

Sometimes, applications use too much memory. The worst-case scenario is that they use more and more memory as time goes by, normally due to what's called a memory leak, maintaining memory that is no longer used, due to some mistake in the coding. Other problems can also include the fact that the usage of memory may be improved, as it's a limited resource.

To profile memory and analyze what the objects are that use the memory, we need first to create some example code. We will generate enough Leonardo numbers.

Leonardo numbers are numbers that follow a sequence defined as the following:

- The first Leonardo number is one
- The second Leonardo number is also one
- Any other Leonardo number is the two previous Leonardo numbers plus one

Leonardo numbers are similar to Fibonacci numbers. They are actually related to them. We use them instead of Fibonacci to show more variety. Numbers are fun!

We present the first 35 Leonardo numbers by creating a recursive function and store it in `leonardo_1.py`, available on GitHub at `https://github.com/PacktPublishing/Python-Architecture-Patterns/blob/main/chapter_14_profiling/leonardo_1.py`.

```
def leonardo(number):

    if number in (0, 1):
        return 1

    return leonardo(number - 1) + leonardo(number - 2) + 1


NUMBER = 35
for i in range(NUMBER + 1):
    print('leonardo[{}] = {}'.format(i, leonardo(i)))
```

You can run the code and see it takes progressively longer.

```
$ time python3 leonardo_1.py
leonardo[0] = 1
leonardo[1] = 1
leonardo[2] = 3
leonardo[3] = 5
leonardo[4] = 9
```

```
leonardo[5] = 15
...
leonardo[30] = 2692537
leonardo[31] = 4356617
leonardo[32] = 7049155
leonardo[33] = 11405773
leonardo[34] = 18454929
leonardo[35] = 29860703

real      0m9.454s
user      0m8.844s
sys 0m0.183s
```

To speed up the process, we see that it's possible to use memorization techniques, which means to store the results and use them instead of calculating them all the time.

We change the code like this, creating the `leonardo_2.py` file (available on GitHub at `https://github.com/PacktPublishing/Python-Architecture-Patterns/blob/main/chapter_14_profiling/leonardo_2.py`).

```
CACHE = {}


def leonardo(number):

    if number in (0, 1):
        return 1

    if number not in CACHE:
        result = leonardo(number - 1) + leonardo(number - 2) + 1
        CACHE[number] = result

    return CACHE[number]

NUMBER = 35000
for i in range(NUMBER + 1):
    print(f'leonardo[{i}] = {leonardo(i)}')
```

This uses a global dictionary, `CACHE`, to store all Leonardo numbers, speeding up the process. Note that we increased the number of numbers to calculate from `35` to `35000`, a thousand times more. The process runs quite quickly.

```
$ time python3 leonardo_2.py
leonardo[0] = 1
leonardo[1] = 1
leonardo[2] = 3
leonardo[3] = 5
leonardo[4] = 9
leonardo[5] = 15
...
leonardo[35000] = ...

real	0m15.973s
user	0m8.309s
sys	0m1.064s
```

Let's take a look now at memory usage.

Using memory_profiler

Now that we have our application storing information, let's use a profiler to show where the memory is stored.

We need to install the package `memory_profiler`. This package is similar to `line_profiler`.

```
$ pip install memory_profiler
```

We can now add a `@profile` decorator in the `leonardo` function (stored in `leonardo_2p.py`, on GitHub at `https://github.com/PacktPublishing/Python-Architecture-Patterns/blob/main/chapter_14_profiling/leonardo_2p.py`), and run it using the `memory_profiler` module. You'll notice that it runs slower this time, but after the usual result, it displays a table.

```
$ time python3 -m memory_profiler leonardo_2p.py
...
Filename: leonardo_2p.py
```

```
Line #    Mem usage    Increment  Occurences   Line Contents
============================================================
     5  104.277 MiB   97.082 MiB      104999   @profile
     6                                         def leonardo(number):
     7
     8  104.277 MiB    0.000 MiB      104999       if number in (0, 1):
     9   38.332 MiB    0.000 MiB           5           return 1
    10
    11  104.277 MiB    0.000 MiB      104994       if number not in
CACHE:
    12  104.277 MiB    5.281 MiB       34999           result =
leonardo(number - 1) + leonardo(number - 2) + 1
    13  104.277 MiB    1.914 MiB       34999           CACHE[number] =
result
    14
    15  104.277 MiB    0.000 MiB      104994       return CACHE[number]



Real      0m47.725s
User      0m25.188s
sys 0m10.372s
```

This table shows first the memory usage, and the increment or decrement, as well as how many times each line appears.

You can see the following:

- Line 9 gets executed only a few times. When it does, the amount of memory is around `38 MiB`, which will be the minimum memory used by the program.
- The total memory used is almost `105 MiB`.
- The whole memory increase is localized in lines 12 and 13, when we create a new Leonardo number and when we store it in the `CACHE` dictionary. Note how we are never releasing memory here.

We don't really need to keep all the previous Leonardo numbers in memory at all times, and we can try a different approach to keep only a few.

Memory optimization

We create the file `leonardo_3.py` with the following code, available on GitHub at `https://github.com/PacktPublishing/Python-Architecture-Patterns/blob/main/chapter_14_profiling/leonardo_3.py`:

```
CACHE = {}


@profile
def leonardo(number):

    if number in (0, 1):
        return 1

    if number not in CACHE:
        result = leonardo(number - 1) + leonardo(number - 2) + 1
        CACHE[number] = result

    ret_value = CACHE[number]

    MAX_SIZE = 5
    while len(CACHE) > MAX_SIZE:
        # Maximum size allowed,
        # delete the first value, which will be the oldest
        key = list(CACHE.keys())[0]
        del CACHE[key]

    return ret_value


NUMBER = 35000
for i in range(NUMBER + 1):
    print(f'leonardo[{i}] = {leonardo(i)}')
```

Note we keep the `@profile` decorator to run the memory profiler again. Most of the code is the same, but we added the following extra block:

```
    MAX_SIZE = 5
    while len(CACHE) > MAX_SIZE:
        # Maximum size allowed,
        # delete the first value, which will be the oldest
```

```
        key = list(CACHE.keys())[0]
        del CACHE[key]
```

This code will keep the number of elements in the `CACHE` dictionary within a limit. When the limit is reached, it will remove the first element returned by `CACHE.keys()`, which will be the oldest.

Since Python 3.6, all Python dictionaries are ordered, so they'll return their keys in the order they have been input previously. We take advantage of that for this. Note we need to convert the result from `CACHE.keys()` (a `dict_keys` object) to a list to allow getting the first element.

The dictionary won't be able to grow. Let's now try to run it and see the results of the profiling.

```
$ time python3 -m memory_profiler leonardo_3.py
...
Filename: leonardo_3.py

Line #    Mem usage    Increment  Occurences   Line Contents
=============================================================
     5   38.441 MiB   38.434 MiB      104999   @profile
     6                                         def leonardo(number):
     7
     8   38.441 MiB    0.000 MiB      104999       if number in (0, 1):
     9   38.367 MiB    0.000 MiB           5           return 1
    10
    11   38.441 MiB    0.000 MiB      104994       if number not in 
CACHE:
    12   38.441 MiB    0.008 MiB       34999           result = 
leonardo(number - 1) + leonardo(number - 2) + 1
    13   38.441 MiB    0.000 MiB       34999           CACHE[number] = 
result
    14
    15   38.441 MiB    0.000 MiB      104994       ret_value = 
CACHE[number]
    16
    17   38.441 MiB    0.000 MiB      104994       MAX_SIZE = 5
    18   38.441 MiB    0.000 MiB      139988       while len(CACHE) > 
MAX_SIZE:
```

```
    19                                               # Maximum size
allowed,
    20                                               # delete the
first value, which will be the oldest
    21   38.441 MiB     0.000 MiB        34994       key =
list(CACHE.keys())[0]
    22   38.441 MiB     0.000 MiB        34994       del CACHE[key]
    23
    24   38.441 MiB     0.000 MiB       104994    return ret_value
```

In this case, we see how the memory remains stable at around the `38 MiB`, that we see is the minimum. In this case, note how there are no increments or decrements. Really what happens here is that increments and decrements are too small to be noticed. Because they cancel each other, the report is close to zero.

The `memory-profiler` module is also able to perform more actions, including showing the usage of memory based on time and plotting it, so you can see memory increasing or decreasing over time. Take a look at its full documentation at `https://pypi.org/project/memory-profiler/`.

Summary

In this chapter, we described what profiling is and when it's useful to apply it. We described that profiling is a dynamic tool that allows you to understand how code runs. This information is useful in understanding the flow in a practice situation and being able to optimize the code with that information. Code can be optimized normally to execute faster, but other alternatives are open, like using fewer resources (normally memory), reducing external accesses, etc.

We described the main types of profilers: deterministic profilers, statistical profilers, and memory profilers. The first two are mostly oriented toward improving the performance of code and memory profilers analyze the memory used by the code in execution. Deterministic profilers instrument the code to detail the flow of the code as it's executed. Statistical profilers sample the code at periodic times to provide a general view of the parts of the code that are executed more often.

We then showed how to profile the code using deterministic profilers, presenting an example. We analyzed it first with the built-in module `cProfile`, which gives a function resolution. We saw how to use graphical tools to show the results. To dig deeper, we used the third-party module `line-profiler`, which goes through each of the code lines. Once the flow of the code is understood, it is optimized to greatly reduce its execution time.

The next step was to see how to profile a process intended to keep running, like a web server. We showed the problems with trying to profile the whole application in these cases and described how we can profile each individual request instead for clarity.

These techniques are also applicable to other situations like conditional profiling, profiling in only certain situations, like at certain times or one of each 100 requests.

Finally, we also presented an example to profile memory and see how it's used by using the module `memory-profiler`.

In the next chapter, we will learn more details about how to find and fix problems in code, including in complex situations, through debugging techniques.

Join our book's Discord space

Join the book's Discord workspace for a monthly *Ask me Anything* session with the author: `https://packt.link/PythonArchitechture`

15

Debugging

Generally speaking, the cycle for debugging problems has the following steps:

1. Detecting the problem. A new problem or defect is discovered
2. Analyzing and assigning priority to this problem, to be sure that we spend time on meaningful problems and focus on the most important ones
3. Investigating what exactly causes the problem. Ideally, this should end with a way of replicating the problem in a local environment
4. Replicating the problem locally, and getting into the specific details on why it happens
5. Fixing the problem

As you can see, the general strategy is to first locate and understand the problem, so we can then properly debug and fix it.

In this chapter, we'll cover the following topics to see effective techniques on how to work through all those phases:

- Detecting and processing defects
- Investigation in production
- Understanding the problem in production
- Local debugging
- Python introspection tools
- Debugging with logs
- Debugging with breakpoints

Let's take a look at the very first step when dealing with defects.

Detecting and processing defects

The first step is actually detecting the problem. This can sound a bit silly, but it's a quite crucial stage.

While we will mainly use the term "bug" to describe any defect, remember that it may include details like bad performance or unexpected behavior that may not be properly categorized as a "bug." The proper tool to fix the problem could be different, but the detection is normally done in a similar way.

Detecting problems can be done in different ways, and some may be more evident than others. Normally, once the code is in production, defects will be detected by a user, either internally (best case) or externally (worst case), or through monitoring.

Keep in mind that monitoring will only be able to capture obvious, and typically serious, errors.

Based on how problems are detected, we can categorize them into different severities, for example:

- **Catastrophic problems** that are completely stopping the operation. These bugs mean that nothing, not even non-related tasks in the same system, works
- **Critical problems** that stop the execution of some tasks, but not others
- **Serious problems** that will stop or cause problems with certain tasks, but only in some circumstances. For example, a parameter is not checked and produces an exception, or some combination produces a task so slow that it produces a timeout
- **Mild problems**, which include tasks containing errors or inaccuracies. For example, a task produces an empty result in certain circumstances, or a problem in the UI that doesn't allow calling a functionality
- **Cosmetic or minor problems** like typos and similar

Because every development team is limited, there will always be too many bugs and having the proper approach on what to pay attention to and what to fix first is critical. Normally bugs in the first group will obviously be quite pressing to fix and will require an immediate all-hands reaction. But categorization and prioritization are important.

Having a clear signal on what things to look for next will help developers have a clear view and be efficient by spending time on important problems and not whatever is the latest. Teams themselves can perform some triage of problems, but it's good to add some context.

Keep in mind that usually, you need to both correct bugs and implement new features, and each of these tasks can distract from the other.

Fixing bugs is important, not only for the resulting quality of the service, as any user will find working with a buggy service very frustrating. But it's also important for the development team, as working with a low-quality service is also frustrating for developers.

A proper balance needs to be struck between bug fixing and introducing new features. Also remember to allocate time for the corresponding new bugs introduced for new features. A feature is not ready when released, it's ready when its bugs are fixed.

Any detected problem, except the catastrophic ones, where context is irrelevant, should capture the context surrounding the steps that were required to produce the error. The objective of this is to be able to *reproduce* the error.

Reproducing the error is a critical element of fixing it. The worst-case scenario is that a bug is intermittent or appears to happen at random times. More digging will be required in order to understand why it is happening when it's happening.

When a problem can be replicated, you're halfway to the solution. The problem can be ideally replicated into a test, so it can be tested over and over until the problem is understood and fixed. In the best situations, this test can be a unit test, if the problem affects a single system and all the conditions are understood and can be replicated. If the problem affects more than one system, it may be necessary to create integration tests.

A common problem during an investigation is to find out what the specific circumstances are that are provoking the problem, for example, data that's set up in a particular way in production and that triggers some issue. Finding exactly what is causing the problem can be complicated in this environment. We will talk later in the chapter about finding a problem in production.

Once a problem is categorized and replicable, the investigation can proceed to understand *why*.

Visually inspecting the code and trying to reason where problems and bugs are is normally not good enough. Even very simple code will surprise you in terms of how it's executed. Being able to analyze how, in a particular case, the code is executing with precision is critical for analyzing and fixing problems that are found.

Investigation in production

Once we are aware that we have a problem in production, we need to understand what is happening and what the key elements that produce it are.

It's very important to remark on the importance of being able to replicate a problem. If that's the case, tests can be done to produce the error and follow the consequences.

The most important tools when analyzing why a particular problem is produced are the observability tools. That's why it is important to do preparation work in advance to be sure to be able to find problems when required.

We talked in previous chapters about logs and metrics. When debugging, metrics are normally not relevant, except to show the relative importance of a bug. Checking an increase in returned errors can be important to detect that there's an error, but detecting what error will require more precise information.

Do not underestimate metrics, though. They can help quickly determine what specific component is failing or if there's any relationship with other elements, for example, if there's a single server that's producing errors, or if it has run out of memory or hard drive space.

For example, a problematic server can produce apparently random errors, if the external requests are directed to different servers, and the failure is related to a combination of a specific request addressed to a specific server.

But in any case, logs will generally be more useful in determining which part of the code is behaving badly. As we saw in *Chapter 12, Logging*, we can describe error logs as detecting two kinds of problems:

- **Expected errors**. In this case, we did the work of debugging the error beforehand and knowing what happened should be easy. Examples of this can be an external request that returns an error, a database that cannot be connected to, etc.

  Most of these errors will be related to external services (from the point of view of the one raising the error) that are misbehaving. This could indicate a network problem, misconfiguration, or problems in other services. It is not rare that errors propagate through the system as an error may provoke a cascading failure. Typically, though, the origin will be an unexpected error and the rest will be expected ones, as they'll receive the error from an external source.
- **Unexpected errors**. The sign of these errors are logs indicating that something has gone wrong, and in most modern programming languages, a stack trace of some sort in the logs detailing the line of code when the error was produced.

By default, any kind of framework that executes tasks, like a web framework or task management system, will produce an error, but keep the system stable. This means that only the task producing the error will be interrupted and any new task will be handled from scratch.

The system should provide the proper handling for the task. For example, a web server will return a 500 error, and a task management system may retry the task after some delay. This may lead to the error being propagated, as we saw before.

In any of the two cases, the main tool to detect what the problem was will be logs. Either the logs show a known problem that is captured and properly labeled, or the logs show a stack trace that should indicate what specific part of the code is showing the error.

Finding the element and part of the code that is the source of the error is important for understanding the problem and for debugging the specific problem. This is particularly important in microservices architectures, as they'll have multiple independent elements.

We talked about microservices and monolithic architectures in *Chapter 9, Microservices vs Monolith*. Monoliths are easier to deal with in terms of bugs, as all the code is handled on the same site, but anyway they'll become more and more complex as they grow.

Keep in mind that sometimes it is not possible to totally avoid errors. For example, if there's an external dependency calling an external API and it has a problem, this may trigger internal errors. These can be mitigated, failing gracefully, or generating a state of "service not available." But the root of the error may not be possible to fix totally.

Mitigating external dependencies may require creating redundancy, even using different suppliers so as not to be dependent on a single point of failure, though this may not be realistic, as it can be extremely costly.

We can have these cases be notified to us, but they won't require further short-term action.

In other cases, when the error is not immediately obvious and further investigation needs to be done, it will require some debugging.

Understanding the problem in production

The challenge in complex systems is the fact that detecting problems becomes exponentially more complicated. As multiple layers and modules are added and interact with each other, bugs become potentially more subtle and more complex.

As we saw before, microservice architectures can be especially difficult to debug. The interaction between different microservices can produce complex interactions that can produce subtle problems in the integration of its different parts. This integration can be difficult to test in integration tests, or perhaps the source of the problem is in a blind spot of the integration tests.

But monoliths can also have problems as their parts grow more complex. Difficult bugs may be produced due to the interaction of specific production data that interacts in an unexpected way. A big advantage of monolithic systems is that the tests will cover the whole system, making it easier to replicate with unit or integration tests.

The objective in this step, though, should be to analyze enough of the problem in production to be able to replicate it in a local environment, where the smaller scale of the environment will make it easier and less invasive to probe and make changes. Once enough information has been collected, it's better to leave any production environment alone and focus on the specifics of the problem.

Remember that having a replicable bug is more than half the battle! Once the problem can be categorized as a replicable set of steps locally, a test can be created to produce it over and over and debug in a controlled environment.

Sometimes, general logging enabled is enough to determine exactly what the bug is or how to replicate it locally. In those cases, it may be necessary to research the circumstances that trigger the problem.

Logging a request ID

One of the problems when analyzing a large number of logs is correlating them. To properly group logs that are related to each other, we could filter by the host that generates them and select a short window of time, but even that may not be good enough as two or more different tasks can be running at the same time. We need a unique identifier per task or request that can trace all logs coming from the same source. We will call this identifier a request ID, as they are added automatically in many frameworks. This sometimes is called a task ID in task managers.

In cases where multiple services are involved, like in microservice architectures, it is very important to keep a common request ID that can work to trace the different requests between different services. That allows you to follow and correlate different logs in the system from different services that have the same origin.

The following diagram shows the flow between a frontend and two backend services that are called internally. Note that the `X-Request-ID` header is set by the frontend and it's forwarded to service A, which then forwards it toward service B.

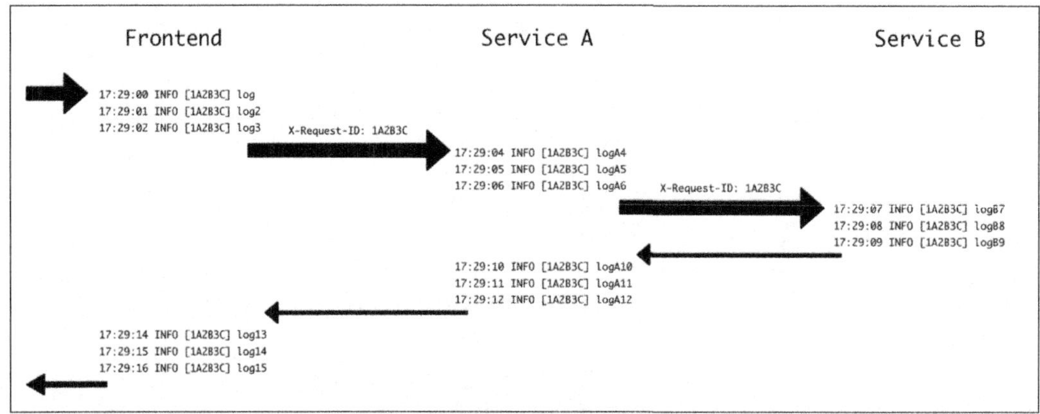

Figure 15.1: Request ID across multiple services

Because all of them share the same request ID, logs can be filtered by that information to obtain all the information about a single task.

To achieve this, we can use the module `django_log_request_id` to create a request ID in Django applications.

You can see the whole documentation here: `https://github.com/dabapps/django-log-request-id/`.

We show some code in GitHub at `https://github.com/PacktPublishing/Python-Architecture-Patterns/tree/main/chapter_15_debug` following the example across the book. This requires creating a virtual environment and installing the package, alongside the rest of the requirements.

```
$ python3 -m venv ./venv
$ source ./venv/bin/activate
(venv) $ pip install -r requirements.txt
```

The code has been changed to include some extra logs in the `microposts/api/views.py` file (as seen at `https://github.com/PacktPublishing/Python-Architecture-Patterns/blob/main/chapter_15_debug/microposts/api/views.py`):

```
from rest_framework.generics import ListCreateAPIView
from rest_framework.generics import RetrieveUpdateDestroyAPIView
from .models import Micropost, Usr
from .serializers import MicropostSerializer
import logging

logger = logging.getLogger(__name__)


class MicropostsListView(ListCreateAPIView):
    serializer_class = MicropostSerializer

    def get_queryset(self):
        logger.info('Getting queryset')
        result = Micropost.objects.filter(user__username=self.
kwargs['username'])
        logger.info(f'Querysert ready {result}')
        return result

    def perform_create(self, serializer):
        user = Usr.objects.get(username=self.kwargs['username'])
        serializer.save(user=user)


class MicropostView(RetrieveUpdateDestroyAPIView):
    serializer_class = MicropostSerializer

    def get_queryset(self):
        logger.info('Getting queryset for single element')
        result = Micropost.objects.filter(user__username=self.
kwargs['username'])
        logger.info(f'Queryset ready {result}')
        return result
```

Note how this is now adding some logs when accessing the list collections page and the individual micropost page. We will use the example URL `/api/users/jaime/collection/5`.

To enable the usage of the request ID, we need to properly set up the configuration in `microposts/settings.py` (https://github.com/PacktPublishing/Python-Architecture-Patterns/blob/main/chapter_15_debug/microposts/microposts/settings.py):

```
LOG_REQUEST_ID_HEADER = "HTTP_X_REQUEST_ID"
GENERATE_REQUEST_ID_IF_NOT_IN_HEADER = True

LOGGING = {
    'version': 1,
    'disable_existing_loggers': False,
    'filters': {
        'request_id': {
            '()': 'log_request_id.filters.RequestIDFilter'
        }
    },
    'formatters': {
        'standard': {
            'format': '%(levelname)-8s [%(asctime)s] [%(request_id)s]
%(name)s: %(message)s'
        },
    },
    'handlers': {
        'console': {
            'level': 'INFO',
            'class': 'logging.StreamHandler',
            'filters': ['request_id'],
            'formatter': 'standard',
        },
    },
    'root': {
        'handlers': ['console'],
        'level': 'INFO',
    },
}
```

The `LOGGING` dictionary is a characteristic in Django that describes how to log. `filters` adds extra information, in this case, our `request_id`, `formatter` describes the specific format to use (note that we add `request_id` as a parameter, which will be presented in brackets).

`handlers` describes what happens to each message, joining `filters` and `formatter` with information about levels to display and where to send the info. In this case, `StreamHandler` will send the log to `stdout`. We set all the logs on the `root` level to use this `handler`.

Check the Django documentation for more information: `https://docs.djangoproject.com/en/3.2/topics/logging/`. Logging in Django may take a bit of experience in setting all the parameters correctly. Take your time when configuring it.

The lines,

```
LOG_REQUEST_ID_HEADER = "HTTP_X_REQUEST_ID"
GENERATE_REQUEST_ID_IF_NOT_IN_HEADER = True
```

state that a new `Request ID` parameter should be created if not found as a header in the input and that the name of the header will be `X-Request-ID`.

Once all of this is configured, we can run a test starting the server with:

```
(venv) $ python3 manage.py runserver
Watching for file changes with StatReloader
2021-10-23 16:11:16,694 INFO     [none] django.utils.autoreload:
Watching for file changes with StatReloader
Performing system checks...

System check identified no issues (0 silenced).
October 23, 2021 - 16:11:16
Django version 3.2.8, using settings 'microposts.settings'
Starting development server at http://127.0.0.1:8000/
Quit the server with CONTROL-C
```

On another screen, make a call to the test URL with `curl`:

```
(venv) $ curl http://localhost:8000/api/users/jaime/collection/5
{"href":"http://localhost:8000/api/users/jaime/
collection/5","id":5,"text":"A referenced micropost","referenced":"dana
","timestamp":"2021-06-10T21:15:27.511837Z","user":"jaime"}
```

At the same time, you'll see the logs on the server screen:

```
2021-10-23 16:12:47,969 INFO     [66e9f8f1b43140338ddc3ef569b8e845]
api.views: Getting queryset for single element
2021-10-23 16:12:47,971 INFO     [66e9f8f1b43140338ddc3ef569b8e845]
api.views: Queryset ready <QuerySet [<Micropost: Micropost object (1)>,
<Micropost: Micropost object (2)>, <Micropost: Micropost object (5)>]>
[23/Oct/2021 16:12:47] "GET /api/users/jaime/collection/5 HTTP/1.1" 200
177
```

Which, as you can see, added a new request ID element, `66e9f8f1b43140338ddc3ef569b8e845` in this case.

But the request ID can also be created by calling with the proper header. Let's try again, making another `curl` request and the `-H` parameter to add a header.

```
$ curl -H "X-Request-ID:1A2B3C" http://localhost:8000/api/users/jaime/
collection/5
{"href":"http://localhost:8000/api/users/jaime/
collection/5","id":5,"text":"A referenced micropost","referenced":"dana
","timestamp":"2021-06-10T21:15:27.511837Z","user":"jaime"}
```

You can check the logs in the server again:

```
2021-10-23 16:14:41,122 INFO     [1A2B3C] api.views: Getting queryset
for single element
2021-10-23 16:14:41,124 INFO     [1A2B3C] api.views: Queryset ready
<QuerySet [<Micropost: Micropost object (1)>, <Micropost: Micropost
object (2)>, <Micropost: Micropost object (5)>]>
[23/Oct/2021 16:14:41] "GET /api/users/jaime/collection/5 HTTP/1.1" 200
177
```

This shows that the request ID has been set by the value in the header.

The request ID can be passed over other services by using the `Session` included in the same module, which acts as a `Session` in the `requests` module.

```
from log_request_id.session import Session
session = Session()
session.get('http://nextservice/url')
```

This will set the proper header in the request, passing through it to the next step of the chain, like service A or service B.

Be sure to check the `django-log-request-id` documentation.

Analyzing data

If the default logs are not enough to understand the problem, the next stage in those cases is understanding the data related to the problem. Typically, the data storage may be inspected to follow up on the related data for the task, to see if there's any indication about that.

This step may be complicated by either missing data or data restrictions that make it difficult or impossible to obtain the data. Sometimes only a few people in the organization can access the required data, which may delay the investigation. Another possibility is that the data is impossible to retrieve. For example, data policies may not store the data, or the data may be encrypted. This is a regular occurrence in cases involving **Personally Identifiable Information** (**PII**), passwords, or similar data.

Analyzing the stored data may require performing ad hoc manual queries to databases or other kinds of data storage to find out if the related data is consistent or if there is any combination of parameters that's not expected.

Remember that the objective is to capture information from production to be able to understand and replicate the problem independently.

In some cases, when investigating a problem in production, it is possible that changing the data manually will fix the issue. This could be necessary in some emergency situations, but the objective still needs to be to understand why this inconsistent situation of the data has been possible or how the service should be changed to allow you to deal with this data situation. Then the code can be changed accordingly to ensure that the problem doesn't happen in the future.

If investigating the data is not enough to be able to understand the problem, it may be necessary to increase the information on the logs.

Increasing logging

If the regular logs and an investigation of the data don't bear fruit, it may be necessary to increase the level of logging with special logs, following the problem.

This is a last-resort method, because it has two main problems:

- Any change in the logs needs to be deployed, which makes it costly and expensive to run.
- The number of logs in the system will be incremented, which will require more space to store them. Depending on the number of requests in the system, this can create pressure on the logging system.

These extra logs should always be short term, and should be reverted as soon as possible.

While enabling an extra level of logging, like setting logs to `DEBUG` level, is technically possible, this will probably increase the logs too much, and will make it difficult to know what the key ones are in the massive amount of logs. With some `DEBUG` logs, specifics of the area under investigation can be temporally promoted to `INFO` or higher to make sure that they are properly logged.

Be extra careful with information that's logged temporally. Confidential information like PII should not be logged. Instead, try to log surrounding information that can help find out the problem.

For example, if there's a suspicion that some unexpected character may be producing a problem with the algorithm to check the password, instead of logging the password, some code can be added to detect whether there's an invalid character.

For example, assuming there's a problem with a password or secret that has an emoji, we could extract only non-ASCII characters to find out if this is the problem, like this:

```
>>> password = 'secret password 🤪'

>>> bad_characters = [c for c in password if not c.isascii()]
>>> bad_characters
['🤪']
```

The value in `bad_characters` can be then logged, as it won't contain the full password.

Note that this assumption is probably easier to test quickly and without any secret data with a unit test. This is just an example.

Adding temporal logs is cumbersome, as it typically will involve several deployments until finding out the problem. It's always important to keep the number of logs to a minimum, cleaning up the useless ones as quickly as possible, and remember to remove them completely after the work is done.

Remember that the work is just to be able to reproduce the problem locally, so you can more efficiently investigate and fix the problem locally. Sometimes the problem may be deemed obvious after some temporal log, but, good TDD practice, as we saw in *Chapter 10, Testing and TDD*, tests displaying and then fixing the bug.

Once we can detect the problem locally, it is time to go to the next step.

Local debugging

Debugging locally means exposing and fixing a problem once we have a local reproduction.

The basic steps of debugging are reproducing the problem, knowing what the current, incorrect result is, and knowing what the correct result should be. With that information, we can start debugging.

A great way of creating the reproduction of the problem is with a test, if that's possible. As we saw in *Chapter 10, Testing and TDD*, this is the basis of TDD. Create a test that fails and then change the code to make it pass. This approach is very usable when fixing bugs.

Taking a step back, any debugging process follows the following process:

1. You realize there's a problem
2. You understand what the correct behavior should be
3. You investigate and discover why the current system behaves incorrectly
4. You fix the problem

Keeping this process in mind is also useful from a local debugging perspective, though at this point, it is likely that *steps 1* and *2* are already sorted out. In the vast majority of cases, the difficult step is *3*, as we've been seeing throughout the chapter.

To understand, once presented with the code, *why* the code is behaving as it is, a method similar to the scientific method can be used to systematize the approach:

1. Measure and observe the code
2. Produce a hypothesis on why a certain result is being produced
3. Validate or disprove the hypothesis by either analyzing the produced state, if possible, or creating a specific "experiment" (some specific code, like a test) to force it to be produced
4. Use the resulting information to iterate the process until the source of the problem is totally understood

Note that this process doesn't necessarily need to be applied to the whole problem. It can be focused on the specific parts of the code that can influence the problem. For example, is this setting activated in this case? Is this loop in the code being accessed? Is the value calculated lower than a threshold, which will later send us down a different code path?

All those answers will increase the knowledge of why the code is behaving in the way that it's behaving.

Debugging is a skill. Some people may say it's an art. In any case, it can be improved over time, as more time gets invested in it. Practice plays an important role in developing the kind of intuition that involves knowing when to take a deeper look into some areas over others to identify the promising areas where the code may be failing.

There are some general ideas that can be very helpful when approaching debugging:

- **Divide and conquer**. Take small steps and isolate areas of the code so it's possible to simplify the code and make it digestible. As important as understanding when there's a problem in the code is detecting when there isn't so we can set our focus on the relevant bits.

Edward J. Gauss described this method in what he called the "**wolf fence algorithm**" in a 1982 article:

There's one wolf in Alaska; how do you find it? First build a fence down the middle of the state, wait for the wolf to howl, determine which side of the fence it is on. Repeat process on that side only, until you get to the point where you can see the wolf.

- **Move backward from the visible error**. It's quite common that the source of a problem is not where an error is raised or obvious, but instead the error was produced earlier. A good approach is to move backward from the position where the problem is obvious and then validate the flow. This allows you to ignore all code that comes *after* the problem, and have a clear path of analysis.
- **You can make an assumption, as long as you can then prove that this assumption is correct.** Code is complex, and you won't be able to keep the whole codebase in your head. Instead, focus needs to be carefully moved across different parts, making assumptions about what the rest is returning.

As Sherlock Holmes once said:

When you have eliminated the impossible, whatever remains, however improbable, must be the truth.

Properly eliminating everything can be arduous, but removing proven assumptions from the mind will reduce the amount of code to analyze and verify.

But those assumptions need to be validated to really prove that they are correct, or we risk the chance of making a wrong assumption. It's very easy to fall into bad assumptions and think that the problem is in a particular part of the code when it really is in another.

Though the whole range of techniques and possibilities of debugging is there, and certainly sometimes bugs can be convoluted and difficult to detect and fix, most bugs are typically easy to understand and fix. Perhaps they are a typo, an off-by-one error, or a type error that needs to be checked.

Keeping the code simple helps a lot in later debugging problems. Simple code is easy to understand and debug.

Before we move on to specific techniques, we need to understand the tools in Python help in our investigation.

Python introspection tools

As Python is a dynamic language, it's very flexible and allows you to perform actions on its objects to discover their properties or types.

This is called *introspection*, and allows you to inspect elements without having too much context about the objects to be inspected. This can be performed at runtime, so it can be used while debugging to discover the attributes and methods of any object.

The main starting point is the `type` function. The `type` function simply returns the class of an object. For example:

```
>>> my_object = {'example': True}
>>> type(my_object)
<class 'dict'>
>>> another_object = {'example'}
>>> type(another_object)
<class 'set'>
```

This can be used to double-check that an object is of the expected `type`.

A typical example error is to have a problem because a variable can be either an object or `None`. In that case, it's possible that a mistake handling the variable makes it necessary to double-check that the type is the expected one.

While `type` is useful in debugging environments, avoid using it directly in your code.

For example, avoid comparing defaults of `None`, `True`, and `False` with their types, as they are created as singletons. That means there's a single instance of each of these objects, so every time that we need to verify if an object is `None`, it's better to make an identity comparison, like this:

```
>>> object = None
>>> object is None
True
```

Identity comparisons can prevent the kind of problem where the usage of `None` or `False` can't be distinguished in an `if` block.

```
>>> object = False
>>> if not object:
...     print('Check valid')
...
Check valid
>>> object = None
>>> if not object:
...     print('Check valid')
...
Check valid
```

Instead, only checking against the identity comparison will allow you to detect only the value of `None` properly.

```
>>> object = False
>>> if object is None:
...     print('object is None')
...
>>> object = None
>>> if object is None:
...     print('object is None')
...
object is None
```

The same can be used for Boolean values.

```
>>> bool('Testing') is True
True
```

For other cases, there's the `isinstance` function, which can be used to find if a particular object is an instance of a particular class:

```
>>> class A:
...     pass
...
>>> a = A()
>>> isinstance(a, A)
True
```

This is better than making comparisons with `type`, because it is aware of any inheritance that may have been produced. For example, in the following code we see how an object from a class that inherits from another will return that it's an instance of either, while the `type` function will only return one.

```
>>> class A:
...     pass
...
>>> class B(A):
...     pass
...
>>> b = B()
>>> isinstance(b, B)
True
>>> isinstance(b, A)
True
>>> type(b)
<class '__main__.B'>
```

The most useful function for introspection, though, is `dir`. `dir` allows you to see all the methods and attributes in an object, and it's particularly useful when analyzing objects from a not-clear origin, or where the interface is not clear.

```
>>> d = {}
>>> dir(d)
['__class__', '__class_getitem__', '__contains__', '__delattr__', '__
delitem__', '__dir__', '__doc__', '__eq__', '__format__', '__ge__', '__
getattribute__', '__getitem__', '__gt__', '__hash__', '__init__', '__
init_subclass__', '__ior__', '__iter__', '__le__', '__len__', '__lt__',
'__ne__', '__new__', '__or__', '__reduce__', '__reduce_ex__', '__
repr__', '__reversed__', '__ror__', '__setattr__', '__setitem__', '__
sizeof__', '__str__', '__subclasshook__', 'clear', 'copy', 'fromkeys',
'get', 'items', 'keys', 'pop', 'popitem', 'setdefault', 'update',
'values']
```

Obtaining the whole attributes can be a bit too much in certain situations, so the returned values can filter out the double-underscore ones to reduce the amount of noise and be able to detect attributes that can give some clue about the object usage more easily.

```
>>> [attr for attr in dir(d) if not attr.startswith('__')]
['clear', 'copy', 'fromkeys', 'get', 'items', 'keys', 'pop', 'popitem',
'setdefault', 'update', 'values']
```

Another interesting function is `help`, which displays the help from objects. This is particularly helpful for methods:

```
>>> help(d.pop)
Help on built-in function pop:

pop(...) method of builtins.dict instance
    D.pop(k[,d]) -> v, remove specified key and return the
corresponding value.

    If key is not found, default is returned if given, otherwise
KeyError is raised
```

This function displays the defined `docstring` from the object.

```
>>> class C:
...     '''
...     This is an example docstring
...     '''
...     pass
...
>>> c = C()
>>> help(c)
Help on C in module __main__ object:

class C(builtins.object)
 |  This is an example docstring
 |
 |  Data descriptors defined here:
 |
 |  __dict__
 |      dictionary for instance variables (if defined)
 |
 |  __weakref__
 |      list of weak references to the object (if defined)
```

All these methods can help you navigate code that's new or under analysis without being an expert, and avoid many checks with code that can be hard to search through.

Adding sensible `docstrings` is a great help not only for keeping the code well commented and adding context for developers working in the code, but also in case of debugging in parts where the function or object is used. You can learn more about `docstrings` in the PEP 257 document: `https://www.python.org/dev/peps/pep-0257/`.

Using these tools is good, but let's see how we can understand the behavior of the code.

Debugging with logs

A simple yet effective way of detecting what's going on and how the code is being executed is adding comments that are displayed either containing statements like `starting the loop here` or including values of variables like `Value of A = X`. By strategically locating these kinds of outputs, the developer can understand the flow of the program.

We touched on this earlier in this chapter as well as in *Chapter 10, Testing and TDD*.

The simplest form of this approach is **print debugging**. It consists of adding `print` statements to be able to watch the output from them, normally while executing the code locally in a test or similar.

Print debugging can be considered a bit controversial to some people. It has been around for a long time, and it's considered a crude way of debugging. In any case, it can be very quick and flexible and can fit some debug cases very well, as we will see.

Obviously, these `print` statements need to be removed after the process has been finished. One of the main complaints about this technique is precisely this, that there's a chance that some `print` statements intended for debugging are not removed, and it's a common mistake.

This can be refined, though, by instead of directly using `print` statements, using logs instead, as we introduced in *Chapter 12, Logging*.

Ideally, these logs will be `DEBUG` logs, which will only be displayed when running tests, but won't be produced in a production environment.

While logs can be added and not produced later, it's good practice anyway to remove any spurious logs after fixing the bug. Logs can accumulate and there will be an excessive amount of them unless they are periodically taken care of. It can be difficult to find information in a big wall of text.

The advantage of this method is that it can be done quickly and it can also be used to explore logs that can then be promoted to permanent ones, once adapted.

Another important advantage is that tests can be run very quickly, as adding more logs is a simple operation, and logs won't interfere with the execution of code. This makes it a good combination to use with TDD practices.

The fact that the logs won't interfere with the code and code can be running unaffected can make some difficult bugs based on concurrency easier to debug, as interrupting the flow of the operation in those cases will affect the behavior of the bug.

Concurrent bugs can be quite complicated. They are produced when two independent threads interact in an unexpected way. Because of the uncertain nature of what one thread will start and stop or when an action from one thread will affect the other, they normally require extensive logs to try to capture the specifics of that problem.

While debugging through logs can be quite convenient, it requires certain knowledge of where and what logs to set to obtain the relevant information. Anything not logged won't be visible in the next run. This knowledge can come through a discovery process and take time to pinpoint the relevant information that will lead to fixing the bug.

Another problem is that new logs are new code, and they can create problems if there are errors introduced like bad assumptions or typos. This will normally be easy to fix, but can be an annoyance and require a new run.

Remember that all introspection tools that we talked about before in the chapter are available.

Debugging with breakpoints

In other situations, it's better to stop the execution of the code and take a look at the current status. Given that Python is a dynamic language, it means that, if we stop the execution of the script and enter the interpreter, we can run any kind of code and see its results.

This is exactly what is done through the usage of the `breakpoint` function.

`breakpoint` is a relatively new addition to Python, available since Python 3.7. Previously, it was necessary to import the module `pdb`, typically in this way in a single line:

```
import pdb; pdb.set_trace()
```

Other than the ease of usage, `breakpoint` has some other advantages that we will see.

When the interpreter finds a `breakpoint` call, it stops and opens an interactive interpreter. From this interactive interpreter, the current status of the code can be examined and any investigation can take place, simply executing the code. This makes it possible to understand interactively what the code is doing.

Let's take a look at some code and analyze how it runs. The code can be found on GitHub at `https://github.com/PacktPublishing/Python-Architecture-Patterns/blob/main/chapter_15_debug/debug.py` and it's the following:

```
def valid(candidate):

    if candidate <= 1:
        return False

    lower = candidate - 1


    while lower > 1:
        if candidate / lower == candidate // lower:
            return False

    return True


assert not valid(1)
```

```
assert valid(3)
assert not valid(15)
assert not valid(18)
assert not valid(50)
assert valid(53)
```

Perhaps you are able to understand what the code does, but let's take a look at it interactively. You can check first that all the `assert` statements at the end are correct.

```
$ python3 debug.py
```

But we now introduce a `breakpoint` call before line 9, right at the start of the `while` loop.

```
    while lower > 1:
        breakpoint()
        if candidate / lower == candidate // lower:
            return False
```

Execute the program again and it now stops at that line and presents an interactive prompt:

```
$ python3 debug.py
> ./debug.py(10)valid()
-> if candidate / lower == candidate // lower:
(Pdb)
```

Check the value of `candidate` and both operations.

```
(Pdb) candidate
3
(Pdb) candidate / lower
1.5
(Pdb) candidate // lower
1
```

This line is checking whether dividing `candidate` by `lower` produces an exact integer, as in that case both operations will return the same. Execute the next line by hitting `n`, from the command `n(ext)`, and check that the loop ends and it returns `True`:

```
(Pdb) n
> ./debug.py(13)valid()
-> lower -= 1
(Pdb) n
```

```
> ./debug.py(8)valid()
-> while lower > 1:
(Pdb) n
> ./debug.py(15)valid()
-> return True
(Pdb) n
--Return--
> ./debug.py(15)valid()->True
-> return True
```

Continue the execution until a new `breakpoint` is found using the command `c`, from `c(ontinue)`. Note this happens on the next call to `valid`, which has an input of 15.

```
(Pdb) c
> ./debug.py(10)valid()
-> if candidate / lower == candidate // lower:
(Pdb) candidate
15
```

You can also use the command `l(ist)` to display the surrounding code.

```
(Pdb) l
  5
  6             lower = candidate - 1
  7
  8             while lower > 1:
  9                 breakpoint()
 10  ->             if candidate / lower == candidate // lower:
 11                     return False
 12
 13                 lower -= 1
 14
 15             return True
```

Continue freely investigating the code. When you are finished, run `q(uit)` to exit.

```
(Pdb) q
bdb.BdbQuit
```

After analyzing the code carefully, you probably know what it does. It checks whether a number is prime or not by checking if it's divisible by any number lower than the number itself.

We investigated similar code and improvements in *Chapter 14, Profiling*. This is, needless to say, not the most efficient way of setting code to check this, but it has been added as an example and for teaching purposes.

Another two useful debug commands are `s(tep)`, to get into a function call, and `r(eturn)`, to execute the code until the current function returns its execution.

`breakpoint` can also be customized to call other debuggers, not only `pdb`. There are other debuggers for Python that include more contextual information or with more advanced usages, like `ipdb` (`https://pypi.org/project/ipdb/`). To use them, you need to set the `PYTHONBREAKPOINT` environment variable with the endpoint for the debugger, after installing the debugger.

```
$ pip3 install ipdb
…
$ PYTHONBREAKPOINT=IPython.core.debugger.set_trace python3 debug.py
> ./debug.py(10)valid()
      8     while lower > 1:
      9         breakpoint()
---> 10         if candidate / lower == candidate // lower:
     11             return False
     12

ipdb>
```

This environment variable can be set to 0 to skip any breakpoint, effectively deactivating the debug process: `PYTHONBREAKPOINT=0`. This can be used as a failsafe to avoid being interrupted by breakpoint statements that haven't been properly removed, or to quickly run the code without interruptions.

There are multiple debuggers that can be used, including support from IDEs like Visual Studio or PyCharm. Here are examples of two other debuggers:

- `pudb` (`https://github.com/inducer/pudb`): Has a console-based graphical interface and more context around the code and variables
- `remote-pdb` (`https://github.com/ionelmc/python-remote-pdb`): Allows you to debug remotely, connecting to a TCP socket. This allows you to debug a program running in a different machine or trigger the debugger in a situation where there's no good access to the `stdout` of the process, for example, because it's running in the background

Using a debugger properly is a skill that requires time to learn. Be sure to try different options and get comfortable with them. Debugging will also be used while running tests, as we described in *Chapter 10, Testing and TDD*.

Summary

In this chapter, we described the general process of detecting and fixing problems. When working in complex systems, there's the challenge of properly detecting and categorizing the different reports to be sure that they are prioritized. It's very important to be able to reliably reproduce the problem in order to show all the conditions and context that are producing the issue.

Once a problem is deemed important, there needs to be an investigation into why this problem is happening. This can be on the running code, and use the available tools in production to see if it can be understood why the problem occurs. The objective of this investigation is to be able to replicate the problem locally.

Most issues will be easy to reproduce locally and move forward, but we also described some tools in case it remains a mystery why the issue is being produced. As the main tool to understand the behavior of the code in production is logs, we talked about creating a request ID that can help us to trace the different calls and relate logs from different systems. We also described how the data in the environment may have the key to why the problem is occurring there. If it is necessary, the number of logs may need to be increased to extract information from production, though this should be reserved for very elusive bugs.

We then moved on to how to debug locally, after replicating the problem, ideally, as we saw in *Chapter 10, Testing and TDD*, in the form of a unit test. We gave some general ideas to help with debugging, though it must be said that debugging is a skill that needs to be practiced.

Debugging can be learned and improved, so it's an area where more experienced developers can help their junior counterparts. Be sure to create a team where it is encouraged to help with debugging when required in difficult cases. Two pairs of eyes see more than one!

We introduced some of the tools that help with debugging in Python, which make use of the possibilities that Python presents for introspection. As Python is a dynamic language, there are a lot of possibilities, as it's able to execute any code, including all the introspection capabilities.

We then talked about how to create logs to debug, which is an improved version of using `print` statements, and, when done in a systematic way, can help to create better logs in the long run. Finally, we moved on to debugging using the `breakpoint` function call, which stops the execution of the program and allows you to inspect and understand the status at that point, as well as continuing with the flow.

In the next chapter, we will talk about the challenges of working in the architecture of a system when it's running and needs to be evolved.

Join our book's Discord space

Join the book's Discord workspace for a monthly *Ask me Anything* session with the author: `https://packt.link/PythonArchitechture`

16

Ongoing Architecture

Just as software itself is never truly complete, software architecture is never a finished piece of work. There are always changes, adjustments, and tweaks that need to be performed in order to improve the system: adding new features; improving performance; fixing security problems. While good architecture requires us to understand deeply how to design a system, the reality of the ongoing process is more about making changes and improvements.

We will talk in this chapter about some of those aspects, as well as dealing with some of the techniques and ideas around making changes in a real working system, keeping in mind that the process can always be improved further by reflecting on how the process is performed and following some guidelines to ensure that the system can be changed continuously while at the same time maintaining service to customers.

In this chapter, we'll cover the following topics:

- Adjusting the architecture
- Scheduled downtime
- Incidents
- Load testing
- Versioning
- Backward compatibility
- Feature flags
- Teamwork aspects of changes

Let's start by taking a look at why to make changes in the architecture of a system.

Adjusting the architecture

While for most of this book we've been talking about system design, which is the basic function of an architect, it is most likely that the bulk of their day-to-day job will be more focused on redesigns.

This is always an endless task, as working software systems are always under revision and expansion. Some of the reasons why it may be necessary to adjust the architecture of a system are as follows:

- To provide certain features or characteristics previously not available - for example, adding an event-driven system to run asynchronous tasks, allowing us to avoid the request-response pattern that was previously all that was available.
- Because there are bottlenecks or limitations with the current architecture. For example, only a single database is present in the system and there's a limit on the number of queries that can run.
- As systems grow, it may be necessary to divide parts to allow better control over them - for example, dividing a monolith into microservices, as we saw in *Chapter 8, Advanced Event-Driven Structures*.
- To increase the security of the system - for example, removing or encoding stored information that might be sensitive, like emails addresses and other **personally identifiable information** (**PII**).
- Big API changes, like introducing a new version of an API either internally or externally. For example, adding a new endpoint that works better for other internal systems to perform some action, where the calling services should be migrated.
- Changes in the storage system, including all the different ideas that we discussed in *Chapter 3, Data Modeling* when talking about distributed databases. This could also include adding or replacing existing storage systems.
- To adapt technologies that are obsolete. This can happen in legacy systems that have a critical component that is no longer supported, or a fundamental security problem. For example, replacing an old module with another that is capable of using new security processes because the old one is not maintained anymore and relies on old encryption methods.

- Rewrites using new languages or technology. This can be done to consolidate technologies if at some point a system was created using a different language, and, after a while, it is decided to bring it in line with the most used language to allow better maintenance. This scenario is typical in organizations that experienced growth, and at some point, a team decided to use their favorite language to create a service. After some time, this may cause problems by complicating maintenance as expertise in this language may be lacking. This can be even worse if the original developer has left the organization. It could be better to adjust or rewrite the service by integrating it into an existing one or replace it with an equivalent one in the preferred language.
- Other kinds of technical debt – for example, refactors that can clean the code and make it more readable, or to allow for changing names of components to be more precise, among other things.

These are just some examples, but the truth is that all systems require constant updating and adjusting, as software is rarely a finished task.

The challenge is not only to design these changes to achieve the expected results, but also to move from the starting point to the destination with minimal interruption to the system. These days the expectation is that online systems are only very rarely interrupted, setting a high bar for any change.

To achieve this, changes need to be taken in small steps, taking extra care to ensure that the system is available at all points.

Scheduled downtime

While ideally there should be no interruption in the system as a result of the changes made, sometimes it's simply not possible to perform big changes without interrupting the system.

When and whether it's sensible to have downtime may depend greatly depending on the system. For example, in its first years of operation, the popular website Stack Overflow (`https://stackoverflow.com/`) had frequent downtime, initially even every day, where the webpage returned a "*down for maintenance*" page during the morning hours in Europe. That changed eventually, and now it's rare to see that kind of message.

But that was acceptable in the early stages of the project as the bulk of their users used the site in line with North American hours and it was (and still is) a free website.

Scheduling downtime is always an option, but it's a costly one, so it needs to be designed in a way that minimizes the impact on the operations. If the system is an established 24x7 service that's critical for customers, or produces income for the business while up (like a store, for example), any downtime will have a pretty hefty price tag.

In other cases, like a small new service with very little traffic, customers will either be more understanding or there'll even be a good chance that they will be unaffected.

Scheduled downtime should be communicated beforehand to affected customers. This communication can take multiple forms, and will greatly depend on the kind of service. For example, a public web store may announce downtime with a banner on their page during the week informing that it won't be available on Sunday morning, but scheduling downtime for a banking operation may require months of advance notice and negotiation over when is the best time.

If possible, is a good practice to define maintenance windows to properly set clear expectations about times when the service will or might have a high risk of some sort of interruption.

Maintenance window

Maintenance windows are periods where it is communicated beforehand that maintenance might happen. The idea is to guarantee the stability of the system outside of maintenance windows while allocating clear times where maintenance might happen.

A maintenance window could perhaps be at weekends or nights in the most active timezone for the system. During the busiest hours of activity the service remains uninterrupted, and maintenance is only carried over when it can't wait, like when preventing or fixing a critical incident.

Maintenance windows are different than scheduled downtime. While in some cases it will happen, not every maintenance window needs to involve downtime - there is simply the possibility that it might happen.

Not every maintenance window needs to be defined equally - some may be safer than others and capable of doing more extensive maintenance. For example, weekends may be reserved for scheduled downtime, but nights during the working week may see regular deployments.

It's important to communicate maintenance windows in advance, for example designing a table like the following:

Days	Time	Type of maintenance window	Risk	Comments
Monday to Thursday	08:00 – 12:00 UTC	Regular maintenance	Low risk	Regular deployments considered low risk. No impact to service.
Saturday	08:00 – 18:00 UTC	Serious maintenance	High risk	Adjustments considered risky. While the expectation is that the service will be fully available, there is a chance that it will be interrupted at some point during the window.
Saturday	08:00 – 18:00 UTC	Notified Scheduled downtime	Service unavailable	One month's notice given. Essential maintenance that requires the service to be unavailable.

An important detail about maintenance windows is that they should be big enough to allow ample time for the maintenance to be done. Be sure to be generous with time, as it's better to set expectations with a large maintenance window that can be used safely for any eventuality, rather than a short one that often needs to be extended.

While scheduled downtime and maintenance windows will help frame the times where the service is active and what times are riskier for the user, it's still possible that some problem arises and causes a problem in the system.

Incidents

Unfortunately, at some point in its life, the system won't behave as it should. It will produce an error so important that it needs to be taken care of immediately.

An incident is defined as a problem that disrupts the service so much that it requires an emergency response.

This doesn't necessarily mean that the full service is totally interrupted - it could be a noticeable degradation of the external service, or even a problem in one internal service that reduces the quality of service overall. For example, if an asynchronous task handler is failing 50% of the time, external customers may only see that their tasks take longer, but that is probably important enough to take corrective action.

During incidents, using all monitoring tools available is critical to find the problem as soon as possible and be able to correct it. Reaction times should be as fast as possible while keeping the risk of corrective actions as low as possible. A balance needs to be struck here, and depending on the nature of the incident, riskier actions can be taken, for example when the system is completely down, as recovering the system will be more important.

Recovery during incidents will normally be limited by two factors:

- How good the monitoring tools are at detecting and understanding problems
- How fast a change can be introduced in the system, related to how quick it is to change a parameter or to deploy new code

The first of the above points is the *understand* part and the second is the *solve* part (though it may be necessary to make changes to get a better understanding of the problem, as we saw in *Chapter 14, Profiling*).

We cover both of these aspects in the book, with the observability tools examined in *Chapter 11, Package Management*, and *Chapter 12, Logging*. We also may need to use the techniques described in *Chapter 14, Profiling*.

Introducing changes to the system is tightly related to the **Continuous Integration** (**CI**) techniques that we discussed in *Chapter 4, The Data Layer*. A fast CI pipeline can make a big difference in how long it takes new code to be ready to deploy.

This is why these two elements, the observability and the time required to make a change, are so important. In normal situations, taking a long time to deploy or to make a change is normally just a minor annoyance, but in a critical situation, it could hinder the fixes that can help the health of the system to recover.

The reaction to an incident is a complicated process that requires flexibility and improvisation, which improve with experience. But there needs to be as well a continuous process of improving the uptime of the system and understanding the weakest part of the system, to avoid the problems or minimize them.

Postmortem analysis

Postmortem analysis, also called a post-incident review, is an analysis done after a problem has impacted the service. Its objective is to understand what failed, why, and take corrective measures to ensure that the problem doesn't happen again, or at least that it has a reduced impact.

Typically, a postmortem starts with the people involved in the correction of the problem filling in a template form. Having a template predefined helps to shape the discussion and focus on the remediation to carry out.

There are plenty of postmortem templates available online that you can search through to see if there's a particular one that you like, or just to get ideas. As with any other part of the process, it should be improved and refined as it goes along. Remember to create and tweak your own template.

The basic template should start with all the main details of **what** happened, followed by **why** it happened, and finally, the most important part: what are the **next actions** to correct the problem?

Remember that a postmortem analysis happens after the incident is over. While it could be good to take some notes while is happening, the focus during an incident is to fix it first. Focus on the most important thing first.

For example, a simple template could be the following:

Incident report

1. **Summary**. A brief description of what happened.

   Example: The service went down between 08:30 and 9:45 UTC on the 5th of November.
2. **Impact**. Describe the impact of the problem. What was the external problem? How external users were affected?

   Example: All user requests were returning 500 errors.

3. **Detection**. A description of how it was detected initially. Could it have been detected earlier?

   Example: The monitoring system alerted about the problem at 8:35 UTC, after 5 minutes of 100% error requests.

4. **Response**. Actions taken to correct the problem.

   Example: John cleaned the disk space in the database server and restarted the database.

5. **Timeline**. A timeline of events to understand how the incident developed and how long each phase took.

   Example:

   8:30 Start of the problem.

   8:35 An alert in the monitoring system was triggered. John started looking into the problem.

   8:37 It is detected that the database is unresponsive and cannot be restarted.

   9:05 After investigation, John discovered that the database disk was full.

   9:30 The logs in the database server had filled up the server disk space, causing the database server to crash.

   9:40 Old logs are removed from the server, freeing disk space. The database is restarted.

   9:45 Service is restored.

6. **Root cause**. A description of the identified root cause of the problem that, if fixed, will completely remove this problem.

Detecting the root cause is not necessarily easy, as sometimes a chain of events will be involved. To help find the root cause, you can use the *five whys* technique. Start describing the impact and ask why it happened. Then ask why this happened, and so on. Keep iterating until you have asked "why?" five times, and the resulting one will be the root cause. Don't take this to mean that you *must* ask "why?" exactly five times, but keep going until you can get a solid answer.

Take into account that the investigation can go further than the steps taken to recover the service during the incident, where a quick fix may have been enough to get out of the woods.

Example:

The server returned errors. *Why?*

Because the database had crashed. *Why?*

Because the database server ran out of space. *Why?*

Because the space was fully filled with logs. *Why?*

Because the log space on the disk was not limited and could grow indefinitely.

7. **Lessons learned**. Things that could be improved in the process, as well as any other element that went well and could be useful to know, like the usage of a certain tool or metric that was useful when analyzing the problem.

   Example:

   The amount of disk space that logs use should be limited in all cases.

   The disk space itself is not being monitored or alerted before it completely runs out.

   The alerting system is too slow and requires a high level of errors before alerting.

8. **Next actions**. The most important part of the process. Describe what actions should be performed to eliminate or, if that's not possible, mitigate the problem. Be sure that these actions have clear owners and are followed up.

If there's a ticketing system, these actions should be transformed into tickets and be prioritized accordingly to be sure that the proper team implements them.

Not only should the root cause be addressed, but also any possible improvements detected in the lessons learned part.

Example:

Action: Enable log rotation to limit the amount of space that logs can take up in all servers, starting with the database. Assigned to the operations team.

Action: Monitor and alert on the disk space to raise an alert if the disk space has less than 20% of the total available space, to allow faster reactions. Assigned to the operations team.

Action: Tweak the error alert to change it to alert when there's only one minute of 30% or more requests returning errors. Assigned to the operations team.

Note that the template doesn't have to be filled out in one go. Typically, the template will be filled in as much as possible, and a postmortem meeting will be held, when the incident can be analyzed and the template totally filled in, including the *Next action* part, which, again, is the most important part of the analysis.

Keep in mind that it's crucial that postmortem processes are focused on improving the system and not on assigning blame for the problem. The objective of the process is to detect weak spots and to try to make sure that problems are not repeated.

In recent years, an equivalent process to try to foresee problems has been put in place, especially before an important event.

Premortem analysis

The *premortem analysis* is an exercise to try to analyze what could go wrong before an important event. The event could be some milestone, launch event, or something similar that is expected to significantly change the conditions of the system.

The word "*premortem*" is quite a funny neologism that comes from the usage of "*postmortem*" as a way to refer to an analysis done after the fact, making an analogy with an autopsy. Though hopefully, nothing is dead yet!.

It can also be called a *preparation analysis*.

For example, there could be a marketing campaign launch that is expected to double or triple the amount of traffic that had previously been normal.

The premortem analysis is the reverse of a postmortem. You set your mindset in the future and ask: *What went wrong? What is the worst-case scenario?* From there, you verify your assumptions about your system and prepare for them.

Consider an analysis for the above example of tripling the amount of traffic on the system. Can we simulate the conditions to verify that our system is ready for it? Which elements of the system do we think are less robust?

All that can lead to planning for the different scenarios and running tests to ensure that the system will be ready for the event.

When doing any premortem analysis, be sure to have enough time to perform the necessary actions and tests to prepare the system. As usual, actions will have to be prioritised to be sure that time is well spent. But keep in mind that this preparation can be an endless task, and as time will be limited, it needs to be focused on the most important or sensitive parts of the system. Be sure to use as many data-driven actions as possible and focus the analysis on real data and not hunches.

Load testing

A key element of preparation in these cases is *load testing*.

Load testing is creating a simulated load that goes to an increased level of traffic. It can be done in an explorative way, i.e., let's find out what the limits of our system are; or in a confirmative way, i.e., let's double-check that we can reach this level of traffic.

Load testing is typically done not in production environments, but in staging ones, replicating the configuration and hardware in production, though it is normal to create a final load test verifying that the configuration in the production environment is the correct one.

An interesting part of load testing analysis in cloud environments is to ensure that any autoscaling in the system works correctly, so it provisions more hardware automatically when receiving greater load, and deletes it when it's not necessary. Caution is required here, as a full load test to the maximum capacity of the cluster can be expensive each time it's run.

The basic element of a load test is to simulate a typical user performing actions on the system. For example, a typical user can log in, check a few pages, add some information, and then log out. We can replicate this behavior using automated tools that work on our external interface.

A good way of using these tools is reusing any kind of automated testing that can be created, and using it as well as the basis for the simulation. This makes the integration or system test framework the unit to enable load testing.

Then, we can multiply that unit simulating the behavior for a single user multiple times to simulate the effect of `N` users, producing enough load to test our system.

For simplicity, it's better to use a single simulation that works as a combination of typical behaviors of users instead of trying to generate multiple smaller simulations trying to replicate different users.

As we said before, the usage of some system test that exercises the main parts of the system works very well in these cases, once you double-check that the behavior is compatible with the typical case in the system.

If necessary, or to perform tweaks, logs can be analyzed to generate an adequate profile of the typical interfaces exercised by the users. Remember to relay in data when possible. Load tests, though, are sometimes needed when there is no solid data, as they are done typically when new features are introduced, so estimations have to be used.

Remember to monitor the results of each simulation, and errors in particular. This will help detect possible problems. Load tests also exercise the monitoring of the system, so it's a good exercise in detecting weak points and improving on them.

The more intensive load tests are, the more problems they'll be able to capture. Then we can avoid those problems once real traffic is in play.

Keep in mind that creating the load can also suffer from its own bottlenecks. To multiply the simulations, it may be necessary to use multiple servers and ensure that the network is capable of supporting the traffic.

Multiplying the simulation can be done directly by starting the process multiple times. This procedure, though simple, is quite effective and can be controlled with simple scripts. It also has the flexibility that the simulation can be any kind of process, including readjusted system tests using any existing software. This speeds up the preparation of the load test and builds trust that the simulation is accurate, as it reuses existing software that has been tested previously.

It is also possible to use specific tools aimed at common use cases like HTTP interfaces, for example, Locust (`https://locust.io/`). This tool allows us to create a web session, simulating a user accessing the system. The great advantages of Locust are that it already has a reporting system embedded and can be scaled with minimal preparation. However, it requires the creation of a new session explicitly for the load test and is only capable of working with web interfaces.

Load tests should also be aimed at creating some headroom in the production cluster so they verify that the load is always under control, even in cases when it's growing, instead of finding bottlenecks during regular operations, which may produce incidents.

Versioning

When making changes to any service, a system needs to be in place to track the different changes. That way, we can understand what gets deployed when and what has changed from last week.

This information is really powerful when you're facing an incident. One of the riskiest moments in a system is when there's a new deployment, as new code can create new problems. It's not unusual that an incident is produced due to the release of a new version.

Versioning means assigning a unique code version to each service or system. It makes it easy to understand what software has been deployed and track down what has been changed from one version to another.

Version numbers are normally assigned in the source control system at specific points to precisely track the code at that particular point. The point of having a defined version is to have a precise definition of the code under that unique version number. A version number that is applicable to multiple iterations of the code is useless.

Version numbers are about communicating the differences in code when talking about different snapshots of the same project. Their main objective is to communicate and allow us to understand how software evolves, not only within the team, but externally as well.

Traditionally, versions were highly related to packaged software and different versions of the software that were sold in boxes, making them marketing versions. When the internal version was required, a *build number* was used, which was a consecutive number based on the number of times the software had been compiled.

Versions can not only be applied to whole software, but also to elements of it, as API version, library versions, etc. In the same way, different versions can be used effectively for the same software, such as for creating an internal version for the technical team but an external version for marketing purposes.

For example, some software could be sold as Awesome Software `v4`, have an API `v2`, and internally be described as build number `v4.356`.

In modern software, where the releases are frequent and the version needs to change often, this simple method is not adequate, and instead different version schemas are created. The most common is *semantic versioning*.

We talked about semantic versioning in *Chapter 2, API Design*, but the topic is important enough to be repeated. Note that the same concept can be used both for APIs and code releases.

Semantic versioning uses two or three numbers, separated by dots. An optional `v` prefix can be added to clarify that it refers to a version:

```
vX.Y.Z
```

The first number (`X`) is called the major version. The second (`Y`) is the minor version, and the last number (`Z`) is the patch version. These numbers are increased as new versions are generated:

- An increase in the major version indicates that the software is not compatible with previously existing software.
- An increase in the minor version means that this version contains new features, but they don't break compatibility with older versions.

- Finally, an increase of the patch version only covers bugfixes and other improvements like security patches. It fixes problems, but doesn't change the compatibility of the system.

Keep in mind that increasing a major version number can also mark changes that would ordinarily appear in minor version updates, too. A change in the major version number will likely bring new features as well as major overhauls.

A good example of this kind of versioning is the Python interpreter itself:

- Python 3 was an increase in the major version, and as such, code from Python 2 required changes to be run under Python 3
- Python 3.9 introduced new features compared with Python 3.8, for example, the new union operators for dictionaries
- Python 3.9.7 adds bugfixes and improvements over the previous patch version

Semantic versioning is very popular and it's particularly useful when dealing with APIs and with libraries that are going to be used externally. It provides a clear expectation, from just the version number, on what to expect from a new change, and allows clarity at the time of adding new features.

This kind of versioning, though, may be too restrictive for certain projects, and in particular, for internal interfaces. As it operates with small iterations that maintain compatibility along the way, only deprecating features after they are old, it works more like a window that is always evolving. Therefore, it's difficult to introduce a meaningful specific version.

For example, the Linux kernel decided to move away from semantic versioning for this reason, deciding that instead new major versions will be small and not change things, and won't carry any particular meaning: `http://lkml.iu.edu/hypermail/linux/kernel/1804.1/06654.html`.

When working with internal APIs, especially with microservices or internal libraries that change very often and are consumed by other parts of the organization, it is better to relax the rules and, while using something similar to semantic versioning, just using it as a general tool to increase version numbers in a consistent manner to provide an understanding of how the code changes, but without necessarily having to force changes in major or minor versions.

When communicating through external APIs, though, version numbers do not only carry a technical meaning, but also a marketing one. Using semantic versioning gives a strong assurance of the capacities of the API.

As versioning is so important, a good idea is to allow services to self-report their version number via a specific endpoint like `/api/version` or another easily accessed way to be sure that it's clear and can be checked by other dependant services.

Keep in mind that it can be possible to create a general version of a whole system, even if internally its different components have their own independent versions. In cases like online services, though, that can be tricky or pointless. Instead, the focus should be on maintaining backward compatibility.

Backward compatibility

The key aspect of changing architecture in a running system is the necessity of always keeping backward compatibility in its interfaces and APIs.

We also talked about backward compatibility in regard to databases changes in *Chapter 3, Data Modeling*. Here we will talk about interfaces, but it follows the same ideas.

Backward compatibility means that systems keep their old interfaces working as expected, so any calling system won't be affected by the change. This allows them to be upgraded at any point, without interrupting the service.

Keep in mind that backward compatibility needs to apply externally, as customers rely on a stable working interface, but also internally where multiple services interact with each other. If the system is complex and has multiple parts, the APIs connecting them should be backward compatible. This is particularly important in microservices architectures to allow the independent deployment of microservices.

This concept is quite simple, but it has implications on how changes need to be designed and implemented:

- Changes should always *be additive*. That means that they *add* options, and don't remove them. This makes any existing calls to the system keep using the existing features and options and doesn't disrupt them.
- Removing options should be done with extreme care, and only after verifying that they are not used anymore. To be able to detect that, we need to adjust the monitoring so we have real data that can clearly provide solid data to allow us to determine this.

> With external interfaces, it may be almost impossible to remove any option or endpoint, especially on APIs. Customers don't want to change their existing systems to adjust to any changes unless there's a good reason, and even in that case it will take a lot of work to adequately communicate it. We will talk later in this chapter about this situation.
>
> Web interfaces allow greater flexibility for changes as they are used manually by humans.

- Even additive changes in externally accessible APIs are difficult. External customers tend to remember the API as it is, so it can be difficult to change the format of existing calls, even if it's just adding a new field.

  This depends on the format used. Adding a new field in a JSON object is safer than changing a SOAP definition, which needs to be defined beforehand. This is one of the reasons why JSON is so popular – because it's flexible in the definition of the objects returned.

  Nonetheless, for external APIs it could be safer to add new endpoints if necessary. API changes are normally done in stages, creating a new version of the API and trying to encourage customers to change to the new and better API. These migrations can be long and arduous, as external users will require clear advantages to be persuaded to adopt the change on their end.

A good example of how painful a change in APIs can be is the migration from Python 2 to Python 3. Python 3 has been available since 2008, but took a long time to get any kind of traction, because programs written in Python 2 needed to be changed. The migration has been quite lengthy, even to the point that the last Python 2 interpreter (Python 2.7) was supported for ten years, from its first release in 2010 until 2020. Even with that long process, there's still code in legacy systems working with Python 2. This shows the difficulty of moving from one API to another if no backward compatibility is respected.

- Existing tests, both unit and integration tests, are the best way to ensure that the API is backward compatible. In essence, any new feature should pass the tests without a problem, as the old behavior won't change. Good test coverage of the API functionality is the best way to maintain compatibility.

Introducing changes in external interfaces is more complicated and normally requires the definition of stricter APIs and a slower pace of change. Internal interfaces allow greater flexibility, as their changes can be communicated across the organization in an incremental way that will allow adaptation without interrupting the service at any point.

Incremental changes

Incremental changes to the system, slowing mutating and adjusting the APIs, can be released in sequence with multiple services involved. But the changes need to be applied in sequence and keep backward compatibility in mind.

For example, let's say that we have two services: service A generates an interface displaying students taking exams, and calls service B to obtain the list of examinees. This is done by calling an internal endpoint:

```
GET /examinees (v1)
[
    {
          "examinee_id": <student id>,
          "name": <name of the examinee>
    }, …
]
```

There's a new feature that needs to be introduced in service A that requires extra information from the examinees, and requires us to know the number of times that each examinee has attempted a particular exam to sort them adequately by that parameter. With the current information, that's impossible, but service B can be tweaked to return that information.

To do so, the API needs to be *extended*, so it returns that information:

```
GET /examinees (v2)
[
    {
        "examinee_id": <student id>,
        "name": <name of the examinee>,
        "exam_tries", <num tries>
    }, ...
]
```

Only after this change is properly done and deployed can service A use it. This process happens in the following stages:

1. Initial stage.
2. Deployment of service B with `/examinees (v2)`. Note how service A will just ignore the extra field and keep working normally.
3. Deployment of service A reading and using the new parameter `exam_tries`.

All of the steps are stable. The service works without a problem throughout each one, so there's detachment between the different services.

This detachment is important because if there's a problem with a deployment, it can be reversed and only affects a single service, quickly reverting to the previous stable situation until the issue can be fixed. The worst situation is to have two changes in services that need to happen at the same time, as a failure in one will affect the other and reversing the situation may not be easy. Even worse, the problem could be in the interaction between them, and in that situation it won't be clear which one is responsible, because it could be both. It is important to keep to small individual steps where each step is solid and reliable.

This way of operating allows us to implement greater changes, for example, renaming a field. Let's say that we don't like the `examinee_id` field and want to change it for a more appropriate `student_id`. The process will go like this:

1. Update the returned object to include a new field called `student_id`, replicating the previous value in service B:

```
GET /examinees (v3)
[
    {
        "examinee_id": <student id>,
        "student_id": <student id>,
        "name": <name of the examinee>,
        "exam_tries", <num tries>
    }, ...
]
```

2. Update and deploy service A to use `student_id` instead of `examinee_id`.
3. Do the same in other services that possibly call service B.

Use monitoring tools and logs to verify this!

4. Remove the old field from service B and deploy the service:

```
GET /examinees (v3)
[
    {
        "examinee_id": <student id>,
        "student_id": <student id>,
        "name": <name of the examinee>,
        "exam_tries", <num tries>
    }, ...
]
```

5. Remove the old field from service B and deploy the service.

This step is technically optional, though it would be good for maintenance reasons to remove cruft from the API. But the reality of the day-to-day work means that it's likely that it will stay there, just not being accessed anymore. A good balance needs to be found between the convenience of leaving it be and maintaining a clean and updated API.

This illustrates how we can deploy changes without interrupting the service in terms of *what* is being deployed. But, how can we ensure that the services are always available while deploying a new version?

Deploying without interruption

To allow continuous releases without service interruption, we need to take the backward-compatible changes and deploy them while the service is still responding.

To do so, the best ally is the load balancer.

We talked about load balancers in *Chapter 5, The Twelve-Factor App Methodology*, and *Chapter 8, Advanced Event-Driven Structures*. They are really useful!

The process of a successful smooth deployment requires several instances of the service to be updated, as follows:

We are going to assume that we are using cloud instances or containers that can be created and destroyed easily. Keep in mind that you can treat them as workers under nginx or any other kind of web server acting as a load balancer inside a single server. This is how the `nginx reload` command works.

1. This is the initial stage, where all the instances have version 1 of the service to be updated:

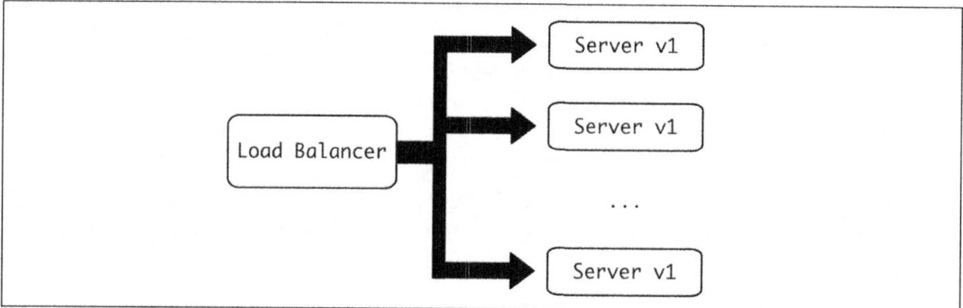

Figure 16.1: Starting point

2. A new instance with service 2 is created. Note that it's not yet been added to the load balancer.

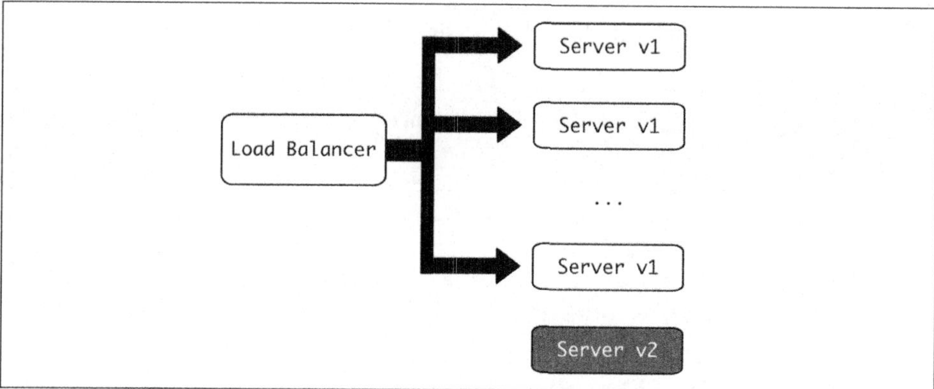

Figure 16.2: New server created

3. The new version is added to the load balancer. Right now, the requests can be directed to version 1 or version 2. If we followed the principles of backward compatibility, though, this should not cause any problems.

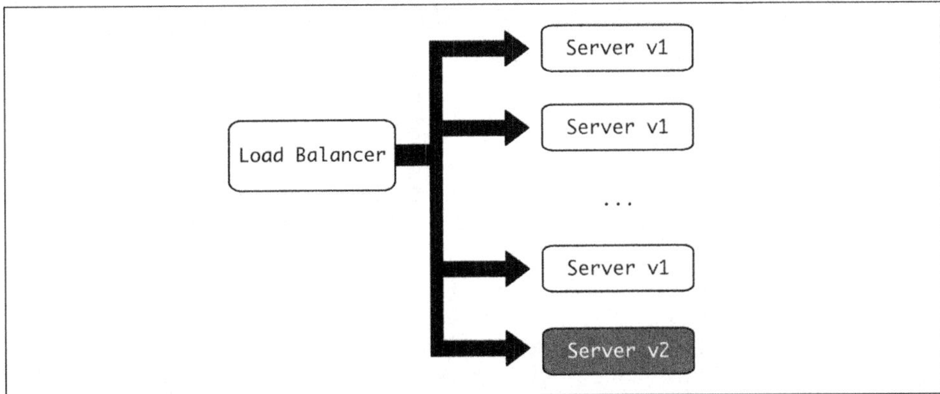

Figure 16.3: New server included in the load balancer

4. To keep the number of instances constant, an old instance needs to be removed. A careful approach here means starting by disabling the old instance in the load balancer, so no new requests will be addressed. After the service finishes all the already-ongoing requests (remember, no new requests will be sent to this instance), the instance is effectively disabled and can be removed totally from the load balancer.

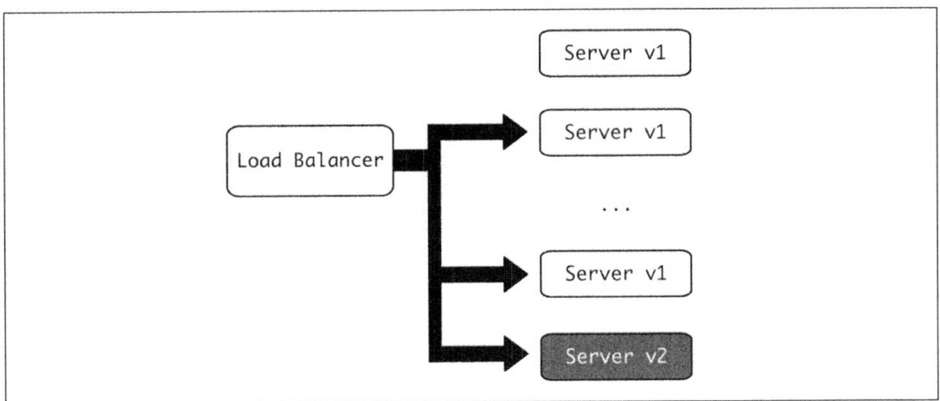

Figure 16.4: Removal of an old server from the load balancer

5. The old instance can be destroyed/recycled.

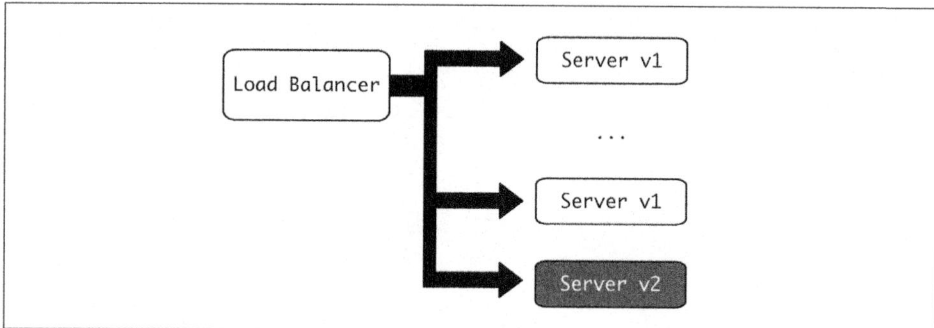

Figure 16.5: Old server has been totally removed

6. The process can be repeated until all instances are at version 2.

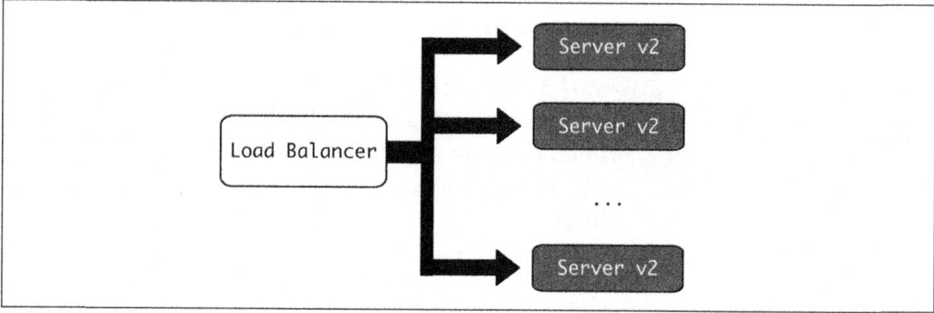

Figure 16.6: Final stage with all new servers

There are tools that allow us to do this process automatically. For example, Kubernetes will perform this automatically when rolling out changes to containers. We also saw that web services like nginx or Apache will do as well. But the same process can also be applied manually or through developing custom tools when an unusual use case demands it.

Feature flags

The idea of feature flags is to hide functionality that is still not ready to be released under a configuration change. Following the principles of small increments and quick iteration makes it impossible to create big changes, like a new user interface.

To complicate things further, these big changes will likely happen in parallel with others. There's no chance of delaying the whole release process for 6 months or more until the new user interface is working correctly.

Creating a separate branch that's long-lived is also not a great solution, as merging this branch becomes a nightmare. Long-living branches are complex to manage and always difficult to work with.

A better solution is to create a configuration parameter that activates or deactivates this feature. The feature can then be tested in a particular environment, while all the development continues at the same pace.

That means that other changes, like bug fixes or performance improvements, are still happening and being deployed. And the work done on the big new feature is merged into the main branch as often as usual. This means that the developed parts of the big new feature are also being released to the production environment, but they are not active yet.

Tests need to ensure that both options - the feature active and deactivated - work correctly, but working in small increments makes this relatively easy.

The feature will be then developed in small increments until it's ready for release. The final step is to simply enable it through a configuration change.

Note that the feature may be active for certain users or environments. This is how beta features are tested: they rely on some users being able to access the feature before it is fully released. The test users could be internal to the organization initially, like QA teams, managers, product owners, etc., so they can provide feedback on the feature, but using production data.

This technique allows us to grow in confidence and release big features without sacrificing small incremental approaches to it.

Teamwork aspects of changes

Software architecture is not only about technology, but a part of it is highly dependent on communication and human aspects.

The process of implementing changes in a system has some human elements affecting teamwork that need to be taken into consideration.

Some examples:

- Keep in mind that the work of a software architect typically lies in managing communication with multiple teams, which requires care and soft skills in both actively listening to teams and explaining or even negotiating design changes. Depending on the size of the organization, that could be challenging as different teams may have wildly different cultures.
- The pace and acceptance of technical changes in an organization are tightly related to the organization's culture (or subcultures). Changes in organizations' ways of working typically occur much more slowly, although organizations that can quickly change technologies tend to be faster in adjusting to organization-wide changes.
- In the same way, technology changes require support and training, even if it's purely within the organization. When requiring some big technology change, be sure to have a point of contact where the team can go to resolve doubts and questions.
  A lot of the questions can be solved by explaining *why* that change is required and working from there.
- Remember when we talked about Conway's Law of software architecture in *Chapter 1, Introduction to software architecture*, about how the communication structure and architectural structure are related. A change in one will likely affect the other, which means that big enough architectural changes will lead to organizational restructuring, which has its own challenges.
- At the same time, changes may have *winners* and *losers* in the affected teams. One engineer could feel threatened because they won't be able to use their favorite programming language. In the same way, their partner will be excited because now the opportunity to use their favorite piece of tech is amazing.

  This problem can be particularly poignant in team shuffling when people are moving around or when creating new teams. An important factor in the pace of development is to have an efficient team and making changes to teams has an impact on their communication and effectiveness. This impact needs to be analyzed and taken into consideration.
- Maintenance needs to be introduced routinely as part of the day-to-day operations of the organization. Regular maintenance should include all security updates, but also tasks like upgrading OS versions, dependencies, etc.

A general plan to deal with this kind of routine maintenance will provide clarity and clear expectations. For example: *the OS version will be upgraded within three to six months of a new LTS version being released*. This produces predictability, gives clear objectives to follow, and produces continuous improvement of the system.
In the same way, automatic tools that detect security vulnerabilities make it easy for the team to know when it's time to upgrade dependencies either in the code or in the underlying system.

- In the same way, the repayment of technical debt needs to be introduced as a habit to be sure that the system is healthy. Technical debt is typically detected by the teams themselves, as they'll have the best understanding of it, and is manifested with a progressively slower pace of code changes. If technical debt is not addressed, it will become more and more complicated to work with, making the development process more difficult and risking burnout by developers. Be sure to budget time to tackle it before it gets out of control.

As a general consideration, just keep in mind that changes in architecture need to be carried out by members of the team, and that information needs to be communicated and executed correctly. As with any other task where communication is an important component, this presents its own challenges and problems, as communicating with people, especially with several people, is arguably one of the most difficult tasks in software development. Any software architecture designer needs to be aware of this and allocate enough time to be sure to, on one hand, communicate the plan adequately, and on the other, receive feedback and adjust accordingly to get the best results.

Summary

In this chapter, we described the different aspects and challenges of keeping a system running while developing and changing it, including its architecture.

We started by describing different ways that architecture can require adjustments and changes. We then moved on to talk about how to manage changes, including the option of having some designated time where the system won't be available, and introduced the concept of maintenance windows to clearly communicate expectations of stability and change.

We next went over the different incidents that can happen when problems arise, and the system struggles. We went over the necessary continuous process of improvement and reflection after an incident of this kind happens, and also looked at preparation processes that can be used before a significant event where the risk increases, for example, because of a marketing push expected to increase the load of the system.

To deal with this, we next introduced load testing and how it can be used to verify the system's capacity for accepting a defined load, making sure that it's ready to support the expected traffic. We talked as well about the necessity of creating a versioning system that clearly communicates what version of the software is currently deployed.

Next, we talked about the critical aspect of backward compatibility and how is crucial in ensuring small, fast increments that are the key to continuous improvement and advancement. We also talked about how feature flags can help mix this process of releasing bigger features that need to be activated as a whole.

Finally, we described different aspects of how changes in a system and architecture can affect human collaboration and communication and how that needs to be taken into account while performing changes to the system, in particular changes that may affect the structure of the teams, which, as we've seen, will tend to replicate the structure of the software.

Join our book's Discord space

Join the book's Discord workspace for a monthly *Ask me Anything* session with the author: `https://packt.link/PythonArchitechture`

packt.com

Subscribe to our online digital library for full access to over 7,000 books and videos, as well as industry leading tools to help you plan your personal development and advance your career. For more information, please visit our website.

Why subscribe?

- Spend less time learning and more time coding with practical eBooks and Videos from over 4,000 industry professionals
- Improve your learning with Skill Plans built especially for you
- Get a free eBook or video every month
- Fully searchable for easy access to vital information
- Copy and paste, print, and bookmark content

At www.packt.com, you can also read a collection of free technical articles, sign up for a range of free newsletters, and receive exclusive discounts and offers on Packt books and eBooks.

Other Books You May Enjoy

If you enjoyed this book, you may be interested in these other books by Packt:

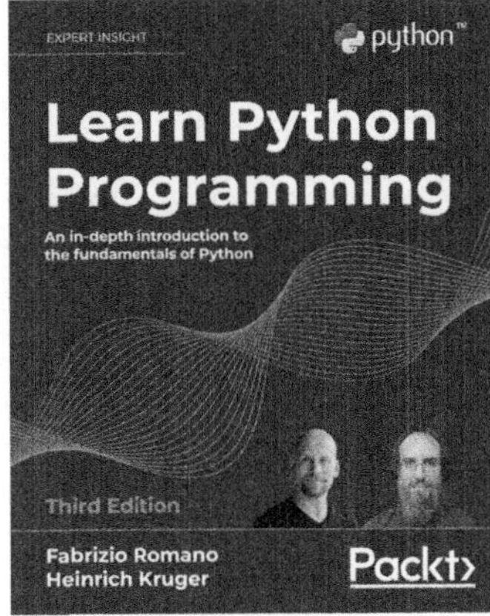

Learn Python Programming, Third Edition

Fabrizio Romano

Heinrich Kruger

ISBN: 9781801815093

- Get Python up and running on Windows, Mac, and Linux
- Write elegant, reusable, and efficient code in any situation
- Avoid common pitfalls like duplication, complicated design, and over-engineering
- Understand when to use the functional or object-oriented approach to programming

- Build a simple API with FastAPI and program GUI applications with Tkinter
- Get an initial overview of more complex topics such as data persistence and cryptography
- Fetch, clean, and manipulate data, making efficient use of Python's built-in data structures

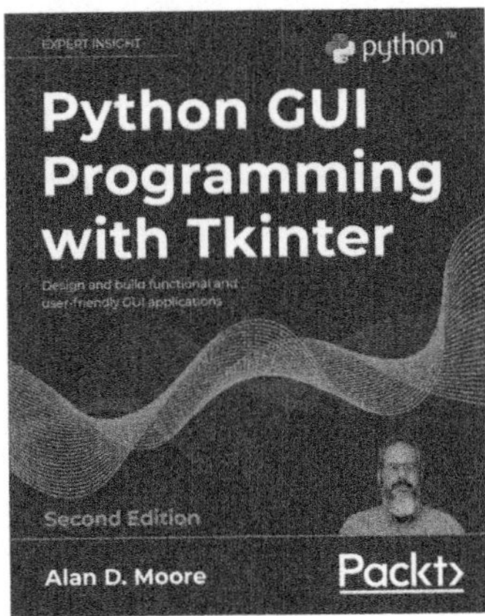

Python GUI Programming with Tkinter, Second Edition

Alan D. Moore

ISBN: 9781801815925

- Produce well-organized, functional, and responsive GUI applications
- Extend the functionality of existing widgets using classes and OOP
- Plan wisely for the expansion of your app using MVC and version control
- Make sure your app works as intended through widget validation and unit testing
- Use tools and processes to analyze and respond to user requests
- Become familiar with technologies used in workplace applications, including SQL, HTTP, Matplotlib, threading, and CSV
- Use PostgreSQL authentication to ensure data security for your application

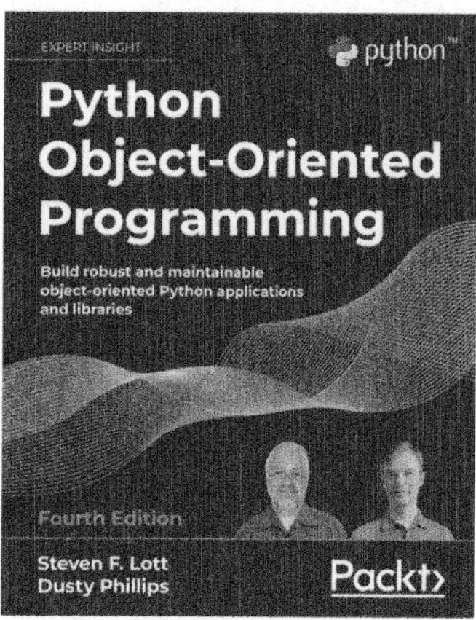

Python Object-Oriented Programming, Fourth Edition

Steven F. Lott

Dusty Phillips

ISBN: 9781801077262

- Implement objects in Python by creating classes and defining methods
- Extend class functionality using inheritance
- Use exceptions to handle unusual situations cleanly
- Understand when to use object-oriented features, and more importantly, when not to use them
- Discover several widely used design patterns and how they are implemented in Python
- Uncover the simplicity of unit and integration testing and understand why they are so important
- Learn to statically type check your dynamic code
- Understand concurrency with asyncio and how it speeds up programs

Packt is searching for authors like you

If you're interested in becoming an author for Packt, please visit `authors.packtpub.com` and apply today. We have worked with thousands of developers and tech professionals, just like you, to help them share their insight with the global tech community. You can make a general application, apply for a specific hot topic that we are recruiting an author for, or submit your own idea.

Share your thoughts

Now you've finished *Python Architecture Patterns*, we'd love to hear your thoughts! Scan the QR code below to go straight to the Amazon review page for this book and share your feedback or leave a review on the site that you purchased it from.

https://packt.link/r/1801819998

Your review is important to us and the tech community and will help us make sure we're delivering excellent quality content.

Index

D

E

F

G

H

I

N

O

P

Q

R

Printed in Great Britain
by Amazon